Managerial Communication
for
Modern Organizations

About the Authors

Prof. B.P. Mahesh Chandra Guru obtained Master's Degree in Mass Communication and Journalism (1980) and Ph.D. in Development Communication (1997). He has served as a journalist (*Panchama*, Kannada Fortnightly, Mysore), Research Associate (National Institute of Rural Development, Hyderabad), Assistant Director, Public Relations (Indian Standards Institution, Chandigarh), Assistant Professor (Bangalore University), Associate Professor (Mangalore University), Professor (University of Mysore) during 1980-2016. He has also served as Director of Students Welfare, Programme Co-ordinator of National Service Scheme, Examiner of Karnataka Public Service Commission/Union Public Service Commission, Member of Board of Appointment in various universities, Member of Karnataka Media Academy and Member of Peer Group of National Assessment and Accreditation during the last three decades. He has presented more than 200 papers in the national and international conferences and presided over several technical sessions. He has published widely in academic journals of repute. He has successfully guided 18 research scholars and adjudicated Ph.D. theses in Indian and foreign universities as a subject expert. He has been a Visiting Professor at prestigious universities and research institutions in India. He is the author of 12 books in Kannada and English. He is a media and research consultant to leading NGOs and media institutions in the country. He is the recipient of several awards for professional excellence and social service.
E-mail: bpmcguru@yahoo.com

Prof. B.K. Ravi obtained Master's Degree in Communication and Ph.D. in Communication. He has served as a journalist and Assistant Professor, Associate Professor and Professor in Bangalore University during the last 25 years. He has served the various universities across the country as a Visiting Professor, Member of Board of Studies and Board of Examiners. He has successfully guided 5 research scholars and adjudicated Ph.D. theses as a communication specialist. He has produced more than 100 programmes on current affairs and about 20 documentaries for television. He has delivered series of radio talks as a resource person. He has presented a good number of papers in the national and international conferences and presided over several technical sessions. He has published scholarly articles in reputed professional journals. He is actively involved as a media specialist in UNESCO, media organizations and NGOs. He has served as Member of Karnataka State Commission for Backward Classes, Karnataka Media Academy and other prestigious organizations. He has received several awards for academic excellence and social service. E-mail: bkravibu@gmail.com

Managerial Communication for Modern Organizations

B.P. Mahesh Chandra Guru
B.K. Ravi

CONCEPT PUBLISHING COMPANY PVT. LTD.
NEW DELHI-110059

ISBN-13: 978-93-5125-241-2 (HB)

First Published 2017

Published and Printed by

Concept Since 1974

Concept Publishing Company Pvt. Ltd.
Regd. Office:
A/15-16, Commercial Block, Mohan Garden,
New Delhi-110059 (INDIA)
Phones : 25351460, 25351794, *Fax* : 091-11-25357109
Email : publishing@conceptpub.com
Website: www.conceptpub.com

Editorial Office: H-13, Bali Nagar, New Delhi-110 015, India.

Cataloging in Publication Data—DK Courtesy: D.K. Agencies (P) Ltd. <docinfo@dkagencies.com>

Guru, B. P. Mahesh Chandra, 1957- **author.**
Managerial communication for modern organizations / B.P. Mahesh Chandra Guru, B.K. Ravi.
pages cm
Includes bibliographical references and index.
ISBN 9789351252412 (HB)
ISBN 9789351252429 (PB)

1. Business communication. 2. Communication in management. I. Ravi, B. K., author. II. Title.

HD30.3.G87 2016 DDC 658.45 23

Dedicated To

Prof. S.N. Hegde

Former Vice-Chancellor of University of Mysore:
Champion of Academic Excellence and Social Justice

Dr. H. Maheshappa, Ph.D.
Vice-Chancellor

Visvesvaraya Technological University
Jnana Sangama,
Belgaum-590018
Tele: 0831-2498224
Fax: 0831-2405467

Foreword

The subject of business management communication has been taught all over the world. Many scholars have studied the role of communication in the process of business management over a period of time. The business organizations have understood the role of communication in the process of business promotion especially in the age of globalization. Business management communication has been a subject of concern for the policy-makers, managers, scholars and other stakeholders in the present times. The ultimate goal of business management communication is to facilitate meaningful interaction between the business world and various stakeholders of business management. Business management communication plays a crucial role in modern organization, bringing all stakeholders of business together—management, investors, employees, suppliers, distributors, consumers, policy-makers, administrators, people and so on. Business management communication really matters in the age of competitive business management.

In the present age of competitive business management, the people constitute the supreme parliament. Effective customer relationship management is the need of the hour. Modern business houses cannot function effectively in the absence of image building, reputation management, sales promotion, community welfare, business promotion, media relations, customer relations, lobbying, persuasion and allied organizational communication activities. Empirical studies have revealed that systematic and scientific business communication activities have bridged the communication gap between modern business organizations and other stakeholders. A new generation of business communication scholars has emerged with a view to produce relevant theoretical and practical knowledge to the various stakeholders in the field of business communication.

The book primarily deals with the salient aspects of business communication such as basics of communication, fundamentals of management, foundations of business management communication, essentials of organizational communication, oral business management communication, written business management communication, electronic business management communication, business management communication approaches, case method of learning, presentation skills, negotiation skills, employment communication skills, group communication, social media application, inter-cultural communication, events management, ethical dimensions of business management communication and business research methods and techniques of business research report writing which assume profound academic and professional significance in the new millennium.

Dr. B.P. Mahesh Chandra Guru and Dr. B.K. Ravi have achieved commendable academic and professional excellence. They have served prestigious institutions in India and abroad as the prominent media and management specialists. The present book is the result of the authors' comprehensive understanding and analysis of the relevance of business management communication in modern society. I whole heartedly appreciate the scholarship and efforts of the authors who have provided a good deal of information, ideas and inputs on business communication management in this book. It is indeed a welcome addition to the body of knowledge in the field of business management communication. The book meets the objective of being a text book and reference book that provides useful details pertaining to business communication management to various stakeholders in India.

Jnanasangama
Date: 31-07-2015

Dr. H. Maheshappa
Vice-Chancellor

A Brief Synopsis of Managerial Communication for Business Organizations
(for MBA Course)

The subject of managerial communication has been taught all over the world. Many scholars have studied the role of communication in the process of business management over a period of time. The business organizations have understood the role of communication in the process of business promotion especially in the age of globalization. Business management communication has been a subject of concern for the policy-makers, managers, scholars and other stakeholders. The ultimate goal of business communication is to facilitate meaningful interaction between the business world and society. Managerial communication plays a crucial role in modern organization, bringing all stakeholders of business together—management, investors, employees, suppliers, distributors, consumers, policy-makers, administrators, people and so on. Communication support for business management really matters in the age of competitive business operations.

In the new millennium, the people constitute the supreme parliament. Effective customer relationship management is the need of the hour. Modern business houses cannot function effectively in the absence of image building, reputation management, sales promotion, community welfare, business promotion, media relations, customer relations, lobbying, persuasion and allied organizational communication activities. Empirical studies have revealed that systematic and scientific business management communication activities have bridged the communication gap between modern business organizations and other stakeholders. A new generation of business management communication scholars has emerged with a view to produce relevant theoretical and practical knowledge to the various stakeholders in the field of business management communication.

The book has 18 chapters. The 1st chapter deals with the basics of communication. The 2nd chapter contains the fundamentals of management. The 3rd chapter amplifies the foundations of business management communication. The 4th chapter provides the essentials of organizational communication. The 5th chapter presents the oral communication for business management. The 6th chapter focuses the attention of readers on written communication for business management. The 7th chapter emphasizes the electronic communication for business management. The 8th chapter highlights the business management communication approaches. The 9th chapter enumerates the case method of learning. The 10th chapter delineates the presentation skills for business management. The 11th chapter presents the negotiation skills for business management. The 12th chapter contains the details of employment communication skills for business management. The 13th chapter provides the group communication skills for business management. The 14th chapter consists of the essentials of social media for business management. The 15th chapter amplifies the events management for business promotion. The 16th chapter includes the inter-cultural communication for business management. The 17th chapter contains the significance of ethics of business management communication. The 18th chapter presents the salient features of business management research methods. The bibliography contains more than 300 references which are related to the subject of commerce and business management communication in India and abroad.

The book is the result of the author's comprehensive understanding and analysis of the need and importance of business management communication in modern society. The book provides a good deal of information on applied business management communication with special reference to India and other developing nations. The book meets the objective of being a text book and reference book that provides relevant details pertaining to managerial communication to various stakeholders in India including the faculty members of MBA course, researchers and students.

Preface

The subject of "Managerial Communication for Business Organizations" has been taught all over the world. Many scholars have studied the role of communication in the process of business promotion over a period of time. The business organizations have understood the role of communication in the process of business promotion especially in the age of globalization. Business management communication has been a subject of concern for the policy-makers, managers, scholars and other stakeholders. The ultimate goal of business management communication is to facilitate meaningful interaction between the business world and various stakeholders of business management. Managerial communication plays a crucial role in modern organization, bringing all stakeholders of business together–management, investors, employees, suppliers, distributors, consumers, policy-makers, administrators, people and so on. Managerial communication really matters in the age of competitive business management.

In the new millennium, the people constitute the supreme parliament. Effective customer relationship management is the need of the hour. Modern business houses cannot function effectively in the absence of image building, reputation management, sales promotion, community welfare, business promotion, media relations, customer relations, lobbying, persuasion and allied organizational communication activities. Empirical studies have revealed that systematic and scientific business communication activities have bridged the communication gap between modern business organizations and other stakeholders. A new generation of managerial communication scholars has emerged with a view to produce relevant theoretical and practical knowledge to the various stakeholders in the field of business communication.

The book has 18 chapters. The 1st chapter deals with the basics of communication. The 2nd chapter contains the fundamentals of management. The 3rd chapter reveals the foundations of managerial communication. The 4th chapter provides the essentials of organizational communication. The 5th chapter presents the oral business management communication. The 6th chapter focuses the attention of readers on written business management communication. The 7th chapter emphasizes the electronic business management communication. The 8th chapter highlights the business management communication approaches. The 9th chapter enumerates the salient features of case method of learning. The 10th chapter delineates the presentation skills for business management. The 11th chapter presents the foundations of negotiation skills for business management. The 12th chapter enumerates the various aspects of employment communication skills for business management. The 13th chapter invites the attention of readers on the salient features of group communication. The 14th chapter includes the need and importance of social media from business management point of view. The 15th chapter presents the salient features of events management for business promotion. The 16th chapter includes the various dimensions of inter-cultural communication for business management. The 17th chapter deals with the ethical dimensions of business management communication. The 18th chapter describes various business research methods and techniques of business research report writing. The bibliography contains more than 300 reference books which are related to the subject of business management communication in India and abroad.

The book is the result of the authors' comprehensive understanding and analysis of the need and importance of business management communication in modern society. The book provides a good deal of information, ideas and inputs on business communication management with special reference to India and other developing nations. The book meets the objective of being a text book and reference book that provides relevant details pertaining to business communication management to various stakeholders in India.

B.P. Mahesh Chandra Guru
B.K. Ravi

Contents

Foreword by ***Dr. H. Maheshappa****, Vice-Chancellor* vii

A Brief Synopsis of Managerial Communication for Business Organizations (for MBA Course) ix

Preface xi

Introduction xix

1. Basics of Communication **1**
- Introduction 1
- Concept of Communication 1
- Need for Communication 4
- Process of Communication 6
- Elements of Communication 8
- Types of Communication 9
- Barriers to Communication 11
- Mass Communication 11
- Guidelines for Successful Communication 12
- Media Convergence 14
- Ethics of Communication 17
- Conclusion 18

2. Fundamentals of Management **21**
- Introduction 21
- Concept of Management 21
- Nature of Management 22
- Scope of Management 24
- Functions of Management 25
- Art and Science of Management 29
- Schools of Management 29
- Scientific Study of Management 32
- Application of Managerial Skills 34
- Conclusion 35

3. Foundations of Managerial Communication **38**
- Introduction 38
- Concept of Business Communication 38
- Role of Communication in Management 40
- Communication System in Business Organizations 41
- Functions of Business Communication 42
- Process of Business Communication 45
- Basic Forms of Business Communication 48
- Conditions for Successful Business Communication 50
- Role of Communication in Crisis Management 51
- Conclusion 54

4. Essentials of Organizational Communication **56**
- Introduction 56
- Evolution of Organizational Communication 56
- Need for Organizational Communication 59
- Importance of Communication in Management 65
- Role of Communication in Business Organizations 68
- Communication Network of the Organization 71
- Communication Concerns of Managers 76
- Communication Training for Managers 80
- Characteristics of Successful Organizational Communication 81
- Conclusion 86

5. Oral Communication for Business Management **89**
- Introduction 89
- Concept of Oral Communication 89
- Importance of Oral Communication Skills 90
- Formal Oral Communication 91
- Public Speaking and Oral Reporting 94
- Guidelines of Successful Oral Communication 98
- Intercultural Oral Communication 104
- Conclusion 107

6. Written Communication for Business Management **109**
- Introduction 109
- Concept of Written Communication 109
- Significance of Business Writing 110
- Barriers to Written Communication 112
- Fundamentals of Effective Writing 114
- Types of Written Business Communication 120

- Process of Written Communication 123
- Conclusion 127

7. Electronic Communication for Business Management 129

- Introduction 129
- Evolution of Electronic Communication 129
- Nature and Scope of Electronic Business Communication 131
- Electronic Business Communication and Advertising 133
- Technology Enabled Electronic Communication 136
- Tools of Electronic Communication 138
- Effective Electronic Communication Skills 140
- Conclusion 142

8. Business Management Communication Approaches 144

- Introduction 144
- Fundamentals of Business Communication 144
- Role of Communication in Business Management 148
- The Business Communication Process 149
- Forms of Business Communication 151
- Basic Patterns of Business Messages 155
- Techniques of Business Report Writing 156
- Cross-Cultural Business Communication 159
- Technology-Oriented Business Communication 161
- Etiquette Advantages in Business Communication 163
- Conclusion 166

9. Case Method of Learning 168

- Introduction 168
- Concept of Case Method of Learning 168
- Nature of the Case Method of Learning 169
- Different Types of Cases 170
- Process of Case Method of Learning 171
- Case Analysis Approaches 174
- The Format and Contents of Written Case Analysis 175
- Conclusion 176

10. Presentation Skills for Business Management 178

- Introduction 178
- Concept of Presentation 178
- Essential Characteristics of Presentation 179
- Processes of Presentation 180
- Importance of Presentation in Business Organizations 186
- Conclusion 187

11. Negotiation Skills for Business Management **190**
- Introduction 190
- Concept of Negotiation 191
- Nature of Negotiation 191
- Significance of Negotiation 192
- Factors Affecting Negotiation in Business World 194
- Process of Business Negotiation Process 195
- Strategies for Successful Business Negotiation 196
- Conclusion 197

12. Employment Communication Skills for Business Management **200**
- Introduction 200
- Concept of Employment Communication 200
- Nature of Employment Communication 201
- Identification of the Needs of the Employers 202
- Essential Characteristics of CV 203
- Types of Interviews 207
- Attributes of Interviewees 209
- Strategies for Successful Interview 211
- Participation in Group Discussion 213
- Conclusion 215

13. Group Communication Skills for Business Management **218**
- Introduction 218
- Definitions of Group 218
- Characteristics of Group 219
- Group Decision Making 222
- Concept of Group Communication 223
- Theoretical Perspective of Group Communication 225
- Process of Group Communication 227
- Strategies for Successful Group Communication 230
- Effective Group Meeting Management 235
- Conclusion 236

14. Social Media for Business Management **239**
- Introduction 239
- Concept of Personal and Social Media 239
- Nature of Personal and Social Media 240
- Personal Media Messaging Systems 244
- Classification of Social Media 245
- Social Media for Dissemination of Creative Ideas 248

- Business Communication and Social Media 249
- Conclusion 254

15. Events Management for Business Promotion 257

- Introduction 257
- Concept of Events Management 257
- Need for Events Management 259
- Budgeting and Logistics of Events Management 261
- Career in Events Management 264
- Techniques of Events Management 267
- Organizing Media Event 272
- Conclusion 274

16. Inter-Cultural Communication for Business Management 277

- Introduction 277
- Concept of Intercultural Communication 277
- Intercultural Communication in the Age of Globalization 280
- Need for Developing Cultural Intelligence 283
- Guidelines for Effective Intercultural Communication 284
- Conclusion 289

17. Ethics of Business Management Communication 292

- Introduction 292
- Concept of Business Ethics 292
- Globalization of Economy and Business Ethics 295
- Academic Significance of Business Ethics 305
- Corporate Social Responsibility 307
- Ethical Foundations of Business Communication 308
- Conclusion 312

18. Business Management Research Methods 315

- Introduction 315
- Concept of Business Research 315
- Need and Importance of Business Research 317
- Nature and Scope of Business Research 318
- Types of Business Research 319
- Process of Business Research 321
- Business Research Report Writing Techniques 324
- Conclusion 329

Bibliography 331

Index 343

Introduction

Chapter 1: Basics of Communication

The basics of communication such as concept of communication, need for communication, process of communication, types of communication, barriers to communication, mass communication, media convergence and ethics of communication are discussed in this chapter. There is no substitute for quality-oriented and responsibility-centred communication in modern society in which rapid advances in communication science and technology tend to transform the mode and content of communication radically.

Chapter 2: Fundamentals of Management

The fundamentals of management such as concept of management, nature of management, scope of management, functions of management, significance of management and recent trends and developments of management are discussed in this chapter. Modern business environment demands application of scientific management principles and practices. In the new millennium, the managers are called upon to perform several tasks from organization development point of view.

Chapter 3: Foundations of Managerial Communication

The concept of business communication, foundations of business communication, functions of business communication, communication system in business organizations, process of business communication, basic forms of business communication and conditions for successful business communication are discussed in this chapter. Business communication enables the various stakeholders to work together and achieve the goals of business organizations. The principles and practices of business communication should be properly understood by the professionals who are required to play multi-faceted role in the competitive business environment.

Chapter 4: Essentials of Organizational Communication

The evolution of organizational communication, need for organizational communication, importance of communication in management, role of communication in business organizations, communication network of the organization, communication concerns of managers, communication training for managers and characteristics of successful organizational communication are enumerated in this chapter. The organizational environment should be properly understood by the various stakeholders in terms of policies, programmes, goods, services, duties, responsibilities, obligations and so on. Modern managers are required to develop a sense of empathy, communication skills, leadership qualities and corporate social responsibility in order to carry the internal and external stakeholders together at all times.

Chapter 5: Oral Communication for Business Management

The concept of oral communication, importance of oral communication skills, barriers to oral communication, principles of successful oral communication and intercultural oral communication are presented in this chapter. The most important oral communication skill is to come down to the level of participants, understand their feelings and enlist the active participation of people in the communicative exercise. The communicators should also know how to influence or motivate the participants. The entire oral communication exercise of give and take should facilitate a win-win end which is skilfully managed by the communicators.

Chapter 6: Written Communication for Business Management

The concept of written communication, purpose of business writing, importance of written communication skills, barriers to written communication, principles of effective writing, written communication skills and process of written business communication are presented in this chapter. The written business communication should convey the ideas and actions completely with minimal need for response. The business communicators are required to gain absolute mastery over the art and craft of written business communication in order to make it effective, creative and purposeful.

Chapter 7: Electronic Communication for Business Management

The concept of electronic communication, evolution of electronic media, purpose of electronic business communication, importance of electronic communication skills, effective electronic communication skills, process of electronic business communication and recent trends and developments in electronic business communication are presented in this chapter. The corporate communicators are required to make better connections with various stakeholders in a changing electronic business world. Business communication becomes more effective with the advancement of electronic media technologies and tools.

Chapter 8: Business Management Communication Approaches

The fundamentals of business management communication, role of communication in business management, the business communication process, forms of business communication, basic patterns of business messages, techniques of business report writing, cross-cultural business communication, technology-oriented business communication and etiquette advantages in business communication are discussed in this chapter. Modern business organizations have realized the role of communication in business management. New perspectives and practices have emerged over a period of time to facilitate meaningful interaction between the service providers and beneficiaries. The success of modern business organizations is depended on the practice of systematic business communication.

Chapter 9: Case Method of Learning

The concept of case method of learning, nature of case methods of learning, different types of cases, barriers to case methods of learning, process of case method of learning, case analysis approaches, strategies for successful case methods of learning and the structure of written case analysis are presented in this chapter. A case analysis should be a well planned, organized and systematic exercise which benefits the management and other stakeholders. A case analysis is an important component of the process of crisis management in modern organizations.

Chapter 10: Presentation Skills for Business Management

The concept of presentation, essential characteristics of presentation, process of presentation, importance of presentation in business organizations and other aspects are presented in this chapter. Presentation is a basic business management communication which is practiced across the world for the purpose of persuading various business stakeholders to accept the organizational policy, products and services. Presentation has become an important component of the process of business management in modern society.

Chapter 11: Negotiation Skills for Business Management

The concept of negotiation, nature of negotiation, significance of negotiation, factors affecting negotiation in business world, process of business negotiation process and strategies for successful business negotiation are presented in this section. Negotiation is a way of behaving that can develop mutual understanding and acceptance for achieving a shared purpose. A written negotiation is always safer under the normal circumstances since the terms and conditions are spelt out clearly in the agreement. The negotiators should know how to deal with deadlocks and establish a win-win situation.

Chapter 12: Employment Communication Skills for Business Management

The concept of employment communication, nature of employment communication, identification of the needs of the employers, factors affecting employment communication in business organizations, essential characteristics of curriculum vitae, salient features of application letter, strategies for success at interviews and techniques of participation in group discussion are presented in this chapter. The job seekers should identify the needs of the employers and fulfil them in order to obtain gainful employment opportunities in modern organizations. There is no substitute for quality oriented, skill oriented and capacity oriented employment communication which matters most in the business environment.

Chapter 13: Group Communication Skills for Business Management

The concept of group communication, nature and scope of group communication, factors affecting group communication in business organizations, essential characteristics of group communication, identification of the needs of the participants, strategies for successful group communication and advanced techniques and technologies of group communication are presented in this chapter. Adequate preparation, ground work, team building, agenda setting, open communication, freedom of expression, meaningful facilitation, consensus building and democratic environment are the prerequisites to effective group communication in business environment. Most of the work in business organizations is accomplished in small groups which demand competent team members and unified action.

Chapter 14: Social Media for Business Management

The concept of personal and social media, nature of personal and social media, personal media messaging systems, classification of social media, social media for dissemination of creative ideas and business communication and social media are presented in this chapter. The order and nature of communication through social media mainly depends on the extent of both parties' desire to establish a human relationship. Harmony is the hallmark of personal and business communication exchanged by the systematic use of social media. It is absolutely essential to develop skills of mutual understanding by creating rapport with the other person.

Chapter 15: Events Management for Business Promotion

The concept of event management, need for event management, budgeting and logistics of event management, career in event management, techniques of event management and organizing a media event are presented in this chapter. Event management has become an all pervasive activity in the world. Modern organizations primarily depend upon event management invariably to boost their image, reputation and credibility. The empirical evidence points to a higher level of organizational sophistication and a broader range of services offered among those organizations that are larger and complex by nature.

Chapter 16: Inter-Cultural Communication for Business Management

The concept of inter-cultural communication, nature and significance of inter-cultural communication, globalization and intercultural communication, need for developing cultural intelligence, guidelines for effective intercultural communication, media of intercultural communication in business organizations and recent trends and developments in intercultural communication for business promotion are presented in this chapter. The business executives and communicators need to be aware of cultural differences and adapt their style of communication when meeting people from different cultural backgrounds which vary in their concern for space and business relationships within it. Intercultural communication basically deals with people from other cultures in a way that minimizes conflict of interest and maximizes rewarding business relationships.

Chapter 17: Ethics of Business Management Communication

The concept of business ethics, globalization and business ethics, academic significance of business ethics, nature and scope of corporate social responsibility, ethical foundations of business communication and practice of virtue based business communication are enumerated in this chapter. The business organizations have certain obligations towards the stakeholders. Business ethics should be upheld in order to bring about meaningful structural and operational changes from business management point of view. The goal of business communication is to bring about mutually trustworthy and beneficial relationship between the business organizations and various stakeholders.

Chapter 18: Business Management Research Methods

The concept of business research, need and importance of business research, nature and scope of business research, types of business research, process of business research and business research report writing techniques are discussed in this chapter. There are various stakeholders of business management including the customers in the modern society. The management should be always willing to understand the changing business environment and cope with the hopes and aspirations of various stakeholders who matter most. The business research reports are submitted to the top management in order to facilitate suitable changes and modifications in the process of business management. The business research report is designed to solve certain business problems or answer business questions.

In the last of the book are Bibliography and Index.

Chapter 1
Basics of Communication

Introduction

Communication is the most fundamental requirement of every human being in the society. Communication is commonly defined as the process of sharing information, experience and expertise between the source of communication and users of communication services. Communication is also viewed as the exchange of information, education, entertainment, guidance, counselling and other services which benefit the mankind intellectually and otherwise. Scholars have considered communication as a relatively linear process of information transmission, causing or contributing to change in knowledge, attitudes and behaviours. Others view communication as a complex process which is closely associated with social, economic, political and cultural structures and processes. Communication basically involves better human relationship building through social and cultural 'togetherness' according to several experts. It has several characteristics of an inter-disciplinary and multi-disciplinary social science. Communication studies are largely influenced by several institutional and social needs and rapid growth of the modern media of communication like press, film, radio, television, computer, satellites and telecommunication channels. The discipline of communication had its roots in literary and linguistic studies carried out in Europe and American continents. The basics of communication such as concept of communication, need for communication, process of communication, types of communication, barriers to communication, mass communication, media convergence and ethics of communication are discussed in this chapter.

Concept of Communication

The word *communication* is derived from the Latin noun '*communis*' and the Latin verb '*communicare'*, meaning sharing of meaning and understanding based on friendship, mutual respect, equality and feeling of oneness. The closest Indian language equivalent to the original concept of communication is '*Sadharanikarana*', which means human relationship building through meaningful dialogue or communication. The basis of human communication is nothing but the sharing of love and understandings which enrich the human life and culture. It rests on the fundamental principle that all human beings are essentially the same, fed by the same nature and nurtured by the same creator. But a mere sending of messages from the source to the receivers does not constitute the real communication. There should be sharing of ideas, meanings, thoughts, feelings and other sentiments which lead to certain actions.

George Vardman (1973: 28) observes that effective communication is purposive symbolic interchange resulting in workable understanding and agreement between the sender and receiver. Practically, the exchange of information, ideas, experience and other inputs occur through different channels of communication across the globe. Communication is a never ending exercise which sustains the development of mankind in several ways.

Denis McQuail (1975: 21) defines: "Communication is a process which increases commonality, but also requires elements of commonality for it to occur at all. The act of communication becomes a futile exercise if the commonality is not established between the sender and receiver. A common language and tools of communication facilitate a sense of commonality and community". The scholar sees human communication in linear terms as the sending of meaningful messages from one person to another. Communication is not an act of sending discreet messages back and forth, but a process of mutual participation in a society which consists of members who share a common culture.

Trenholm Sarah (1990: 27) defines: "The transmission of information, ideas, emotions, skills, etc., by use of symbols—words, pictures, figures, graphs, etc. This act or process of transmission of useful information, education and entertainment basically constitutes communication". Human beings cannot expand their horizon of understanding, experience and expertise in the absence of planned communication flow between the resource persons and beneficiaries of knowledge and service.

Peter F. Drucker (1991: 11) states that for communication to be effective there has to be both information and meaning. The meaning requires communication. The art and craft of communication is developed by the people over a period of time. If the communication fails, it is very difficult to get the things done in society. Communication is an important element of the process of management and communication gap mars the progress of modern organizations.

Keith Davis and John Newstrom (1993: 08) opine that communication is the transfer of information and understanding from one person to another person. It is a way of reaching out to various people with facts and figures as and when required. Communication serves as a bridge between the source and receiver and facilitates better understanding and cooperation. There is no scope for the expansion of human mind and development of human personalities in the absence of constant communication flow.

Vilanilam (2005: 29) defines communication as the exchange of information between and among human beings for the promotion of mutual and common understanding and desirable social action. Communication takes place in society at various levels ranging from individual to mass society. The pyramid of communication has its base at the intrapersonal segment. Mass communication occupies only the apex of the pyramid. The world 'mass' means common people who are countless in number. The phrase "mass communication indicates the flow of information and communication to the large number of the people in which one's individuality is lost. The scholar has noted that communication bridges the gap between people and mainstream of knowledge and development."

Montagu and Matson (2008: 22) describe the fact of communication thus: "Communication is a fact in the world of human beings, animals and plants, and is an ever continuing process going on all the time. It is as necessary to human, animal and vegetable existence as life itself. The need for communication is as basic as the hunger for food and drink, perhaps even more so. Communication is the name we give to the countless ways that humans keep in touch-not just words and music, pictures and print, nods and becks, postures and plumages; to every move that catches someone's eye and every sound that resonates upon another's ear". The scholars have observed that communication is the basic necessity which fulfils all the requirements of human beings from knowledge expansion and development points of view.

Thus, communication can be perceived as the interchange of thoughts, experiences and ideas which benefits the sender and receiver. The effectiveness of communication is measured in terms of the degree of perception of the receiver. It is an important function which benefits both an individual and system. Generally speaking, communication is the process which includes telling, listening, understanding and responding activities. The receiver of communication cannot respond positively if the meaning is not properly and fully understood by him/her. Communication is indeed a fundamental activity that involves the use of words—whether it consists of speaking, listening, writing, reading and thinking. All these elements of communication constitute verbal communication. The non-verbal communication includes the use of sign language, action language or object language. It is present in all acts of speaking and writing under the normal circumstances.

Communication is a never ending task which facilitates commonality of understanding between the source and receiver. It is also interpreted as an inter-change of ideas between the two parties in order to bring about better understanding and rapport development which matter most in modern society. Communication is the process through which information, ideas, experiences and expertise are transmitted between the individuals and/or institutions in order to facilitate better understanding, cooperation and service.

Need for Communication

Communication etymologically implies sharing, a community of interests and social cohesion based on social needs and aspirations. The MacBride Commission (1980: 20) states: "Communication maintains and animates life. It is also the motor and expression of social activity and civilization. The task of communication has become ever more complicated and subtle to contribute to the liberation of mankind from want, oppression and fear and to unite it in community and communion, solidarity and understanding. However, unless some basic structural changes are introduced, the potential benefits of technological and communication development will hardly be put at the disposal of the majority of mankind". The Commission had called upon the stakeholders of communication and development to expand the services across the country and facilitate participatory communication opportunities in order to enlist the active participation of people in the mainstream of development.

Beltran (1978: 03) elaborates the need for communication thus: "A human being's need for communication is as strong and as basic as the need to eat, sleep and love. It is both an individual and a social need. It is both a natural individual demand and a requirement of social existence to use communication resources in order to engage in the sharing of experiences, through symbol-mediated interaction". The scholar has pointed out that no human being can ever grow as a complete man in the absence of constant communication support from various individuals and agencies.

Oral communication facilitates understanding between the source of communication and users of communication through the language while non-verbal communication conveys the message through signs, symbols and gestures. Oral communication reaches out to the limited number of users while non-verbal communication reaches out to plenty of users with a difference. It is highly significant because it conveys meaning to others without the help of words.

Baran and Davis (2000: 01) highlights the intricacies of non-verbal communication thus: "Just as a coding system must have semantic and syntactic rules, so must nonverbal signals as they are combined to form messages if they are to be treated as a coding system. This assumption delimits the non-verbal domain to the extent that it excludes behaviours that lack consistent meanings and behaviours that fail to be combined in systematic, grammatical ways with other nonverbal signals". The non-verbal communication also plays a major role in facilitating better understanding, cooperation and action which are the prerequisites to both individual and collective development.

The nature of communication is mainly dependent on the structure of a particular society. Communications in such a society will nagate the very meaning of communication. There are broadly five varieties of communication—intrapersonal communication (taking place within an individual), interpersonal communication (between individuals and groups), group communication (within members of a particular group), organizational communication (within employers and employees of an organization) and mass communication (within society or nation). However, mass communication has gained tremendous significations because of mass media which reach out to the millions of people all over the world.

In modern organizations, communication occurs between the organization and other stakeholders in order to inform certain things and persuade others to accept the policy, programme, product and service rendered by the business organizations. Scholars have identified the distinction between communication and mass communication. Communication really brings about mutual understanding while mass communication simply includes the dissemination of information or ideas without any mutual understanding between the two parties (source and receivers). The mass media like newspapers, magazines, film, radio and television have the capacity to provide the benefits of information, education and entertainment to countless number of people who are spread across the length and breadth of the society from local to global.

Communication basically involves active interaction with physical, biological and social environments. The people are required to adopt themselves to the changing environment by following right communication norms and channels. Verbal and non-verbal communications are required to enable the people to share experiences and expertise in the society. The human beings are required to communicate with others regardless of the languages and forms of communication. Montagu and Matson (2008: 22) distinguish between communication and information thus: "communication is not an act, but a process by which individuality enters into mental cooperation with individuality until they come to constitute a common conscience". The scholars have emphasized the role of communication in the human life. According to them communication flows always in order to facilitate sharing of information, ideas and other inputs to development.

Scholars have pointed out that communication is the life blood of all communities, organizations and societies. The growth and development of modern organizations has necessitated the two-way communication between the management and various stakeholders. The management cannot enter into the good books of various stakeholders and enlist their active participation in the process of management in the absence of effective communication.

Process of Communication

The earliest conceptualization of communication by Harold D. Laswell involved the five basic questions namely—Who? Says what? To whom? In which channel? With what effect? The scholar identified three prominent functions of communication namely—surveillance of the environment, correlation of components of society, and cultural transmission between generations. Communication was basically considered as a one-way process marked by the flow of information from a sender to a receiver. This was also known as linear model of communication which consisted of sender→message→media→message →receiver→action. According to this linear view, the receiver passively receives the message and acts as directed or desired by the sender.

The process of communication generally includes—five components namely—communicator, communicate, media, message and feedback. The communicator is supposed to understand the basic needs of the users and select the media which are accessible to the users. The messages should be easily understood by the users even though they involve complex ideas and terms. The communicators should also understand the feedback in order to make suitable changes and modifications in the art and craft of communication. In the process of communication, the various components discharge their functions according to their basic acculturation.

Most theorists agree that communication has three shades of meaning—exchange of information verbally, non-verbally and both for the purpose of establishing mutual understanding and cooperation. The source of communication should understand that receivers are not passive, but dynamic forces who can decide the fate of communications media.

According to Shannon–Weaver model, the process of communication basically contains information source (ideation), encoding (transmitter), channel (transmission), receiver (decoding) and acting (effect). Thus, the communication completes a full circle, bringing together the sender and receiver to become two components of the same mission. The source is the originator of the idea or message. The messages are composed of certain symbols which contain specific meaning to the source and receiver. The translation of an idea into a message appropriate for transmission by the source is called encoding. The channel is a means through which the message flows from the source to the receiver. Normally, the receiver is the person for whom the message is intended. The conversion of a particular message into a certain meaning by the receiver is called decoding. Ultimately, the receiver responds to the communication delivered by the source. It is known as feedback.

Davis and Newstorm (1993: 09) have pointed out that the only way the goal of management can be achieved in an organization is through the process of communication. The process of management becomes ineffective and dysfunctional in the absence of effective communication component. The communication runs through the entire process of management with the involvement of many players, channels, messages and reactions. Practically, communication is an indispensable component of the process of management. The efficient functioning of an organization primarily depends upon effective communication which builds sound human relations. Thus, effective communication matters most from the point of view of sound management of a system.

McQuail explains the concept of mass by using four important aspects namely—large aggregate, undifferentiated, mainly negative image and lacking order. Scholars have provided a new dimension to mass communication which basically involves sharing of information and communication between the mass media and people. Mass media are the means of communication which facilitate transmission of messages to large, heterogeneous, and anonymous masses of people living in different regions of a locality, nation or the world. Print media (newspapers, magazines, etc.), electronic media (radio, television, film, etc.) and new media (Internet, e-mail, etc.) are duly considered as mass media since they cater to the needs of millions of users.

Shanon and Weaver conceived of communication as a system composed of five essential parts plus noise namely—an information source, a transmitter, a channel, the receiver and the destination. Wilbur Shramm adapted Shannon and Weaver's model to human communication, but stressed on encoding and decoding aspects which are crucial in the process of communication. He defines: "communication is the sharing of information, ideas and attitudes". He endorsed the Aristotelian principle that communication always requires at least three elements—source, message and destination.

Scholars have noted that the process of communication is subjected to noise which distorts communication. The noise also hinders proper understanding between the sender and receiver. The communication distortions are caused by certain subjective factors such as the mindset of the sender or receiver. Sometimes the channel of communication may not be simple enough to convey the intended message to the receiver. The process of communication also includes certain filters which are psychological by nature. They include attitudes, beliefs, experiences, consciousness and ability to grasp the essentials of communication.

In reality, communication is basically a two-way process since the sender and receiver play a reciprocal and reversible roles. They considered communication essentially to be a reciprocal process and a mutual exchange of messages. The meaning of the message is usually perceived in the context of the receiver's understanding, experience, beliefs, feelings and so on. The two-way communication process is also known as transactional communication. Communication is a crucial factor associated with the process of management since it facilitates uninterrupted functioning of any organization in the present times. No individual or system would ever proceed towards progress without active communication in times of peace and crisis.

Elements of Communication

The process of communication basically involves certain elements such as message, sender, encoding, channel, receiver, decoding, acting and feedback. The message is the information disseminated by the source either written or spoken which is sent from source to receiver. The sender is the person who transmits, spreads, disseminates or communicates a message with the purpose of informing and persuading the receiver. Encoding is the process of changing the message from its psychological form into words, gestures, signs or pictorial forms. It means to put in ideas, facts, feelings and opinions into symbols. The channel of communication includes interpersonal, folk, modern and new media of communication which suits the convenience of the sender and receiver. The channel of communication could be audio and visual by nature. The receiver is the targeted audience of the message who understands, interprets and reacts according to the meaning of the message as transmitted by the sender. The decoding is the act of translating symbols into their ordinary meanings. But the total meaning lies in the meanings of the words (symbols) together with the tone and attitude of the sender.

The acting involves the response of the receiver which depends upon the proper understanding of the message. The receiver completes the chain of communication by responding to the message. The feedback is collected by the sender since it helps him/her to know as to whether the receiver received the message in the right spirit and responded as intended by the sender. The process of management also becomes complete if the decision makers understand the feedback from the beneficiaries of policies, programmes, products and services. The process of feedback assures the communicator or initiator of the action of its appropriateness and impact.

Types of Communication

The various types of communication include—Intra-personal communication takes place within an individual in the form of reflection, contemplation, meditation, introspection and so on. The people are bound to rely upon intra-personal communication from birth to death. It does not involve a separate sender and receiver, but enables accurate perception of one's self a[illegible]n understanding of the relationship between an individual and e[illegible]nt. Self-awareness is achieved through intra-personal communication which facilitates introspection among the individuals.

Inter-personal communication is direct face-to-face communication which takes place between two or more persons. It is more common, influential and persuasive form of communication that benefits both the parties. It facilitates meaningful interaction between an individual and other members of the family or group. All human beings require constant inter-personal communication throughout their lives in order to get the things done through proper interaction.

Group communication is an extension of inter-personal communication which is meant for interaction between the leader and others. Group communication takes place between the leader of the group and followers. It can be among small or large groups of people who retain their individual identities. It provides opportunities to seek information on any subject and facilitates participatory communication. The group communication facilitates better interaction between the leader and other members of the group through the collaboration of several individuals. Group communication takes place within a work team, committee or community which consists of a small group of people. Group communication provides an opportunity for better human understanding, interaction and cooperation.

Organizational communication occurs between the management and employees and organization and various stakeholder's namely, investors, suppliers, distributors, consumers, media professionals, government officials, members of the local community and so on. Organizational communication generally involves large groups working together in such a way as to accomplish the tasks of organizational management and development. Organizational communication provides adequate structure, communication flow, channels of communication and institutional messages.

Mass communication takes place between the modern mass media and society. It is also known as massive communication which involves big media and countless number of receivers. Hasan (2010: 14) states: "Any mechanical device that multiplies messages and takes it to a large number of people simultaneously is called mass communication". In this process, each receiver is a faceless individual with almost no opportunity for response or feedback. A large number of people who are not assembled at a single place receive the message disseminated through big media such as radio, television, film, etc. The audience tends to be heterogeneous rather than homogeneous in case of mass communication. Mass communication is intended to help the source of communication to reach out to various peoples and enlist their active participation in several nation building and problem solving exercises. National and international issues, events and developments are widely focused in mass communication.

Barriers to Communication

Scholars have also identified the barriers to communication which include—physical barriers, psychological barriers, and mechanical barriers. The physical barriers include—the competing stimulus, environmental stress, subjective stress and ignorance of the medium. The psychological barriers include self image, resistance to change, defensiveness, fear, linguistic barrier, cultural barriers, language and meaning. The mechanical barriers include the barriers which are raised by the communication channels employed for various types of communication.

Usually, the barriers to communication can be attributed to be sender and receiver. The sender oriented barriers include—absence of planning, thoughtless communication, wrong media selection, wrongful symbols, incorrect assumptions, selective perception, information overload, conflict of interest and so on. The receiver oriented barriers include—psychological barriers, social barriers, emotional barriers, poor listening, poor retention, mistrust, lack of interest, bias, semantic difficulties, perceptional error, slanting, inferring and so on.

These barriers to communication would affect the effectiveness of communication and create communication gaps and conflict of interest. Generally speaking, the absence of common frame of reference in the sender and receiver creates communication barriers. The physical noise and other constraints in the communicative environment also distort the overall meaning of the total message. The barriers to communication should be bridged in order to facilitate better understanding and cooperation between the individuals and institutions in modern society. Communication gap creates lot of confusions and contradictions. Hence, the various stakeholders of public education, welfare and development should facilitate active communication support.

Mass Communication

Scholars have also identified the functions and dysfunctions of mass communication since the consequences of communication are both manifest and latent in reality. In fact, every function can also become a dysfunction in certain situation. According to Wright (1959: 30), the consumer of predigested ideas, opinions and views becomes an ineffectual citizen, less capable of functioning as a rational man. The process of mass communication becomes effective if the means of communication enable the large groups of people in different locations to receive the same information in the same language. In this context, 'large' means immensely large, to be counted in the millions rather than in the thousands in various communicative circumstances. In reality, communication is the basic input to individual and collective development in all respects. Communication plays a vital role in the organization of people, thoughts and actions.

The role of communications media is well appreciated and documented by various scholars at different times. Walter Lippmann (1922: 19) once said: "Every newspaper when it reaches the reader is the result of a series of selections as to what items shall be printed, in what position they will be printed, how much space each shall occupy, what emphasis each shall have. There are no objective standards here. There are conventions". The observations made by Lippmann primarily deals with the media services which are delivered on the basis of established conventions and practices rather than professional ethics and considerations.

Melvin DeFleur (1970: 10) highlights the impact of media on society which reads: "The communication process is utterly fundamental to all of our psychological and social processes. Without repetitively in acts of communication with our fellows, none of us could possibly develop the human mental processes and human social nature that distinguishes us from other forms of life". The media are important institutions which make society more active. In the absence of media support, no system can ever progress in the age of competitiveness.

George Gerbner (1985: 13) refers to the process of mass communication which discharges massive symbol systems into the mainstream of common consciousness thus: "Mass communication is carried on through messages that the largely mass produced and/or distributed by complex industrial structures. The members of a public born in a particular cultural context select and interpret messages in a certain way. Their selection and interpretation depends on the system of messages that regulate social relationships. Such cultivation and public acculturation is carried on through the massively mediated messages which over a long period of time provide a functional perspective of *existence* (what is), *priority* (what is important), *values* (what is right and wrong) and *relationships* (what is related to what)".

Guidelines for Successful Communication

Communication is a planned, deliberate and systematic exercise which is carried out by the sender in consultation with the experts. As far as possible, the source of communication should not take the receivers for granted in this age of competitiveness. The perceptions of the sender and receiver are based on the mental images of the external world which are stored in their brains. In reality, the communicator and receiver do not have the same or similar education, experience, emotional make up and expectations. Hence, the source of communication should make an assessment of the requirements of the receivers and communicate accordingly.

The communicator should also select the media which are accessible to the beneficiaries. The medium is the message. The media which are simple, credible and popular should be used for the purpose of communication in order to facilitate better understanding of the messages among the beneficiaries. The messages should also be formulated by taking into account the culture, environment, education, social status, economic status and other factors. The message should be both known and understood by others whether it is verbal or non-verbal. Simplicity is the hallmark of communication. Communication becomes ineffective if the message is not fully and properly understood by the receiver in a given context.

Effective communication demands seven C's of communication according to Beebe and Masterson (1997: 02). They include—candidness, clarity, completeness, conciseness, concreteness, correctness and courtesy. The act of communication should be known for fairness to self and to others involved in the situation. Candid, open-hearted and sincere communication serves the purpose of communication. The source of the communication should also provide clear ideas and guidelines through simple words, sentences and language. The thoughts should be clear and well organized in order to facilitate commonality of understanding between the sender and receiver. The completeness of communication also matters most. The receivers should not miss important points or ideas in the form of public speaking, oral presentation, written presentation, audio-visual presentation and online presentation.

The source of communication should provide answers to all possible questions that could be raised by the receivers. The contents of communication should be very clear, crisp and concise. The communicators should also be very specific and definite in explaining issues and events to the receivers of communication. A more vivid way of expression is required to put across the ideas and views in a very convincing manner. The communicator is also required to provide correct information, ideas, opinions, views and other inputs in the form of communication. Correctness of facts matters most in the process of communication. In every act of communication courtesy also matters.

The source cannot boss over the receivers of communication. Insulting, wrongful and offensive words and phrases should not be used since they would belittle the communication. It is necessary to understand these guidelines of communication and facilitate better understanding between the source and receivers. The universal elements of communication should be grasped by the communicator in order to avoid communication barriers and enhance the status of communication.

Chaturvedi and Chaturvedi (2012: 06) observe: "Communication has a symbolic nature and is an act of sharing one's ideas, emotions, attitudes or perceptions with another person or group of persons through words, gestures, signals, signs or other modes of transmitting images. Communication is a living act, performed in specific contexts, in particular situations and with a definite goal. Human beings are poor communicators, but their communicative competence can be improved by learning and practicing effective communication skills". The individuals are always at the receiving end. The institutions are equipped with media resources, technologies and opportunities. Modern institutions are required to reach out to various people in order to bridge the communication gap and facilitate better rapport development.

Media Convergence

In the age of media convergence, the media professionals discharge their duties in the virtual environment which is part of the world of global communication. All communications media are interrelated sociologically, technologically and professionally. The contemporary generation of media professionals in print media, electronic media, new media, advertising, corporate communication, book publishing and other sectors are working with the help of electronic devices. Electronic processing and dissemination of data have become the essential features of media convergence.

Vilanilam (2005: 29) explains the interrelationship among the media in the age of media convergence thus: "Film and video editing is done electronically. Advertising agencies and PR firms make use of electronic processing of data; and book publishers use electronic processing, editing and printing, including desktop publishing (DTP) systems. Every medium is related to every other medium. Electronics is part of the print media as reports are processed on computers and transferred electronically to a main information bank from where they can be recalled and edited, processed again, photo-composed and made part of the page to be electronically prepared for offset printing. The phenomenon of compunication (computerized communication) is part of every medium's operation on the practical plane. Most pieces of equipment in the modern media world are electronically operated. The 'global village' which Marshall McLuhan spoke of in the 1960s has become a reality, at least in the technical sense, in the richer parts of the world. In a sociological sense too, there is interdependence in the media".

In the new age of information revolution, the ownership of mass media pattern is subjected to several changes. At present, chain ownership (means the same media company owns numerous outlets in a single medium), cross media ownership (means the same company own several media outlets), conglomerate ownership (means the ownership of several businesses, one of which is a media business) and vertical integration (means a media company monopolizes the production of the ingredients that go into the making of media products) are prominently found all over the world. In the present age of cross media, conglomerate and vertical integration ownership continues while media monopolization ultimately leads to the phenomenon of suppression of media freedom. Conglomeration and corporate mergers are witnessed in the present times especially in the US. Scholars have noted that mere diversification of ownership will not ensure diversity of news, views, programmes and services.

In the age of commercialization of media, competitive communication has become the order of the day. The media institutions are bound to ignore the cause of truth and public interest and distort the truth for commercial advantages. The present trend of media ownership concentration in fewer hands is not conducive to the principles of welfare state, good governance, positive media management and protection of public interest. The communication system in India is not conducive for meaningful social communication since it caters to the needs of the creamy layer of the total population. The mass media in India and elsewhere have also become 'class media' and promote the social myth of caste superiority through various outputs. The media professionals also represent the privileged sections of society since they are required to perform the duty of 'media executives' and 'sellers of products'.

Media critic Noam Chomsky (1989: 07) comments: "The media serve the interest of State and corporate power, which are clearly linked. The mainstream media not only allow the agenda of news to be bent in accordance with State demands and criteria of utility; they also accept the presuppositions of the State without question".

The observation made by Chomsky and other media critics is also true of most Indian and foreign media which are owned by the economic powers which rule the State. Media contents are primarily governed by the market forces, political pressures, business interests, casteist forces, government censorship, media regulations and other considerations which have deprived the people their right to free, fair and fearless communication. Development communication has become the biggest casualty in the age of media imperialism.

Vilanilam (2005: 29) comments on the media output thus: "The sociological view of all media output is that all of it, despite claims of truthfulness and a realistic reflection of society, is more a construction than an exact reflection of reality. And this constructed reality has the stamp of the intellect, technology, economics, politics, culture and history of the environment where it is constructed. Despite their claim to the contrary, journalists and other communicators in society are not entirely 'free agents' as they cannot be totally free from their professional and social environment".

The whole world has been converted into a single global village because of the revolutionary changes and developments in the field of communication, science and technology. In the new millennium, the people enjoy the benefits of all-time connectivity and all round interaction. The advent of modern electronic media has made communication instantaneous and immediate across the globe. The new media technologies have connected the sender and receiver in a timeless and spaceless web of communication. In business, both traditional and modern media of communication are used in order to facilitate better image building, reputation management, events management, sales promotion, marketing management, crisis management and so on.

The present generation mankind is also blessed with social media which involves a natural, genuine conversation between people about something of mutual interest, a conversation built on the thoughts and experience of the participants according to Dave Evans (2008: 12). The social media of communication are popular in modern society because they facilitate creativity and collaboration between the two parties. The social message assumes greatest credibility because it is based on natural and genuine conversation between communicator and receiver.

Ethics of Communication

Communication is indeed a value based profession which is the fourth estate of democracy. The social responsibility theory of communication demands that mass media should function in the society as the voice of the people and angel guardians of public interest. The issue of communication ethics assumes significance since there is increasing conflict of interest between corporate social responsibility and dynamics of free market economy. The media professionals are required to adhere to the ethical norms and demonstrate commitment to public service and respect for human values in modern society. The professionals should take stock of the ethical issues and social responsibility considerations while discharging their duties.

Tom Bethell (1977: 04) observes: "The US theory of a free press is based on the assumption that it is best achieved by not vesting any public body with the power to impose standards of 'responsibility' upon the press and that in the 'market place of ideas' truth will win out over falsity and that good newspapers would drive out bad ones". The Royal Commission (1949: 24) noted that journalism differs from other professions in that the direct responsibility which the individual practitioner normally bears to his clients is in journalism indirect and diffused. The direct relationship is between the newspaper and the reader and the responsibility is shared among all those who serve and shape the newspaper's personality, whether they are individual proprietors, directors, managers, or working journalists.

The First Amendment to the Constitution of USA guarantees to the US citizenry of the freedom of expression to participate actively in political and social affairs without fear of government interference. But the American Constitutions place certain legal restrictions on freedom of speech such as those relating to libel, obscenity and the regulation of electronic mass communication in order to ensure strict adherence to professional ethics and constitutional norms.

The Constitution of India also places series of reasonable restrictions on the freedom of speech and expression in order to facilitate professionally responsible actions on the part of media professionals. Several countries have constituted press councils and framed codes of ethics in order to uphold normative dimension of communication ethics which motivates the one who exercises the rights of expression to do so on the basis of a sense of moral obligation in the public interest. There is express recognition by professional organizations of the relationship of duty to the public. Schwarz (1966: 26) states: "The rule on care or the duty to check the truth, content and source of all news before publication is specified in all the State press laws. Besides, the press is also subject to laws which apply to everyone".

The Indian Press Council has identified certain norms and guidelines which precisely deal with code of ethics. They include—accuracy and fairness, verification before publication, respect for privacy, recognition of the right of reply, restraint in the coverage of communal disputes or clashes, avoidance of plagiarism, principles regarding recording of interviews and phone conversations, avoidance of obscenity and vulgarity and caution in criticizing judicial actions, writes Sanjay (1997: 25).

Several media critics have observed that the existing codes of ethics are ineffective in raising ethical standards of the media institutions. They have commonly suggested that the existing press councils should be replaced by media councils in order to cover all media operations. There is consensus among the scholars that media councils should act as genuinely independence bodies in order to promote adherence to media practitioners and a great sense of social responsibility among the media institutions.

Conclusion

Communication is indeed the life blood of human society. The failure of communication results in several disadvantages to the mankind and organizations. The source of communication cannot achieve the intended results if the communication fails due to certain reasons. The focus of communication should be on the receivers who share different demographic features. Essentially, every act of communication should be planned, deliberate and systematic in order to achieve the goals of modern organizations. The source of communication should understand the essentials of successful communication in modern society. The process of communication should have the universal elements of communication in order to produce the intended results.

Communications media have a social responsibility of promoting healthy discussions and debates in modern society on vital issues concerning public interest. In the age of globalization, communications media should not function as the instruments of profit making. The ethical norms require that media services should be accurate, fair and balanced. There is no substitute for quality-oriented and responsibility-centred communication in modern society in which rapid advances in communication science and technology tend to transform the mode and content of communication radically. The role of State in ensuring adherence to communication ethics and responsibility becomes crucial in the age of globalization of communication.

References

Baran, S.J. and Davis, D.K. (2000) *Mass Communication Theory*, Belmont, CA: Wadsworth.

Beebe, Steven, A. and John T. Masterson (1997) *Communicating in Small Groups: Principles and Practices*, New York: Longman, p. 6.

Beltran, Luis Ramiro (1978) Rural Communities in Developing Countries: The Prospects of Communication, *Issues in Communication*. No. 2, International Institute of Communications, London, UK.

Bethell, Tom (1977) Freedom of Speech and Expression' *Freedom Means*, International Communication Agency, USA, p. 41.

Bhusan, Uma (2012) *Introduction to Business Communication*, Jaico Publishing House, Mumbai.

Chaturvedi, P.D. and Mukesh Chaturvedi (2012) *Business Communication*, Chennai: Pearson, pp. 22-23.

Chomsky, Noam (1989) *Necessary Illusions*, Pluto Press, London, p. 5.

Davis, Keith and John Newstrom (1993) *Organizational Behaviour: Human Behaviour at Work*, New Delhi: Tata McGraw Hill, p. 399.

Ibid.

DeFleur, Melvin (1970) *Theories of Mass Communication*, David McKay, New York, p. 76.

Drucker, Peter F. (1991) *The New Realities*, New Delhi: Asian Books Private Ltd., p. 210.

Evans, Dave (2008) *Social Media Marketing*, New Delhi: Times Business Services, p. 31.

Gerbner, George (1985) *Mass Media Discourse: Message System Analysis* as a Component of Cultural Indicators. In T.A. Van Dijk (Ed.) *Discourse and Mass Communication: New Approaches* to the Analysis of Mass Media Discourse and Communication, Walterde Gruyter & Co., Berlin, p. 76.

Hasan, Seema (2010) *Mass Communication: Principles and Concepts*, CBS Publishers and Distributors Pvt. Ltd., New Delhi.

Karoli, Veera and Naghma Ahmed (2013) *Business Communication*, Thakur Publishers, Bengaluru, India.

Kaul, Asha (2009) *Business Communication*, PHI Learning Private Limited, New Delhi.

Lehman, Carol, M., Devvie D., DuFrene, Mala Sinha and Robin C. Walker (2012) BCOM, *An Innovative Approach to Learning and Teaching, Business Communication: A South Asian Perspective*, Cengage Learning, New Delhi.
Lesikar, Raymond, V., Marie E. Flatley., Kathryn Rentz and Neerja Pande (2012) *Business Communication, Making Connections in a Digital World*, New Delhi, India.
Lippmann, Walter (1922) *Public Opinion*, Harcourt Brace, New York, p. 268.
MacBride International Commission for the *Study of Communication Problems* (1980) Many Voices, One World, Report of the UNESCO, Paris.
McQuail, Denis (1975) *Toward Sociology of Communication*, Collier McMillan, London, UK.
Montagu, Ashley and Floyd Matson (2008) *The Human Connection*, McGraw Hill, New York.
Mukerjee, Hory Sankar (2013) *Business Communication: Connecting at Work*, Oxford University Press, New Delhi.
Royal Commission (1949) *Report on the Role of the Press*, London.
Sanjay, B.P. (1997) *Ethical Dilemmas: Emerging Trends and Issues, Communication Ethics: A South Asian Perspective*, Asian Media Information and Communication Centre, pp. 33-43.
Schwarz, Urs (1966) *Press Law for Our Times—The Example of the German Legislation*, The International Press Institute, Zurich, pp. 77-78.
Trenholm, Sarah (1990) *Human Communication Theory*, Englewood Cliffs, N.J: Prentice Hall.
Vardman, George (1973) *Effective Communication of Ideas*, New York: Van Nostrand Reinhold Company, p. 3.
Vilanilam, J.V. (2005) *Mass Communication in India: A Sociological Perspective*, Sage Publications Ltd., New Delhi, India, p. 17.
Wright, C.R. (1959) *Mass Communication: A Sociological Perspective*, Random House, New York, p. 21.

Chapter 2
Fundamentals of Management

Introduction

The word 'management' is widely discussed by the community of scholars all over the world. Management is a fundamental activity which forms the basis for successful conduction of the activities of modern organizations. Managers play a significant role in getting the things done by various persons associated with an organization. Management is universally defined as a set of organizational activities directed at organizations' resources with a view to achieve the goals of organization in an efficient manner. Management experts have dealt with the salient features of management in their studies. The management studies are greatly influenced by several factors including the growth and development of modern tools and strategies. Management is an applied discipline which is practiced all over the world on the basis of systematic principles and approaches. Scholars have also advocated that the combination of managerial, institutional, technological and inter-personal skills is extremely essential for a manager. The foundations of management such as the concept of management, nature of management, scope of management, functions of management, significance of management, recent trends and developments of management, scientific study of management and application of managerial skills are presented in this Chapter.

Concept of Management

The term 'management' is used since ancient times since management is primarily associated with the successful conduction of the activities of organizations. The various kinds of organizations are engaged in delivering goods and services to the mankind across the world. These organizations are found in all spheres of human life. The concept of management is best understood from a resource-based perspective. The term 'management' actually originated in the sixteenth century, but it is practiced vigorously since, the last two centuries. The art of management has been practiced since, the dawn of human civilization while the science of management began after post-industrial revolution. The discipline of management has been enriched by scholars, scientists, technocrats and philosophers over a period of time. The literature on management is growing very fast on account of the development of management of education and the betterment of management practice.

The American Management Association defines: "Management is the process of getting work done through people". In the modern times, modern organizations need a greater level of coordination and integration of all organizational activities to attain their goals through systematic application of management principles and practices. Management basically involves work efficiency which refers to doing things right by following the right methods. Managerial effectiveness is the key to an organization's success.

Ricky W. Griffin (2012: 09) defines: "Management involves a set of activities (including planning and decision making, organizing, leading and controlling) directed at an organization's resources (human, financial, physical and information) with the aim of achieving organizational goals in an efficient and effective manner".

Nature of Management

Management is a conscious, continuous and constant process which involves several functions such as policy making, planning, organizing, supervising, controlling, implementing, communicating, leading, guiding, evaluating and so on. The functions of management are performed regularly in modern organizations. There are several phases in the management process which demand planned, deliberate, systematic, coordinated and integrated decisions and actions. There are certain levels of management which include the differentiation of managers into three basic categories such as top, middle and first line.

There are few top managers who include office bearers, divisional heads and top managers who are primarily involved in decision making process. They also represent the organization to the external environment by meeting various stakeholders of organizational development. The middle level managers are more in number in most modern organizations. The middle managers are mainly responsible for implementing the policies and programmes developed by top managers. They also supervise, control and coordinate the activities of lower level managers. The middle managers also bridge the top and lower levels of management in the organizations. Large organizations normally require a good number of middle managers who play an important role in the effective implementation of organizational programmes. The first line or lower level managers usually supervise and coordinate the activities of the workforce in the organizations. They are commonly called as coordinator, supervisor, office manager and so on. They also oversee the day to day activities of the organization on the basis of meaningful supervision of the work of subordinates.

Empirical evidence states that good managers can propel an organization into unprecedented realms of success; whereas poor managers can devastate even the strongest of organizations. John Casesa (2009: 06) observes: "The speed with which Mulally has transformed Ford into a more nimble and healthy operation has been one of the most impressive jobs I have seen. It probably would have been gain over for Ford, but for the changes he has brought". The Chief Executive Officer plays a significant role in the process of management in all organizations. According to Lafley (2009: 12), the CEO's real and unique work draws on a uniquely external perspective that is inaccessible to the rest of the organizations unless the CEO's makes it accessible through choices and actions everyday.

There are also different areas of management in modern organizations such as personnel management, financial management, materials management, operations management, marketing management, information management, advertising management, publicity management, and promotion management. The managers are required to cultivate conceptual skills, technical skills, operational skills, managerial skills, inter-personal skills, communication skills, diagnostic skills, time management skills, crisis management skills, disaster management skills and so on. These skills basically contribute to the successful conduction of organizational activities in a competitive environment, observe Atwater *et al.* (2008: 01).

The nature of management differs from time to time, situation to situation and context to context in modern society. The nature of management also continues to change in large and complex organizations. The managers also perform various tasks in modern organizations. The pace of the modern manager's job is relentless due to work related pressures and compulsions. The characteristics of managerial work also vary in the present times, comment Davis *et al.* (1997: 07). Ritz-Carlton (2000: 14) has noted that contemporary managers spend most of their time now dealing with strategic and management issues. Education, experience, specialization, creativity, dynamism, environment, culture, politics, business, science, technology and other factors are closely associated with the management of modern organizations. Modern managers learn the art and craft of management through a combination of these factors which provide a foundation for the practice of management. The nature of managerial work continues to change in complex and often unpredictable ways, opines Hitt (2000: 11).

Scope of Management

Management is indeed an all pervasive activity. It is also a never ending organizational function. Management is essential in both profit-centred and service-centred organizations all over the world. In the present times, corporate houses primarily rely upon management to enhance the status, efficiency and success of organizational activities. Small, medium and large organizations require effective management which plays an important role in the process of organizational development. The small and medium organizations compete with the large organizations which are equipped well with capital resources, human resources and state of the art facilities. The large organizations can recover from any loss or crisis immediately as compared to small organizations. Effective management becomes inevitable in all types of modern organizations which are primarily profit-seeking organizations.

The non-profit organizations also need effective managerial support since they have to get into the good books of various stakeholders of social service and enlist their active participation in the implementation of socially beneficial activities. Application of sound management practices also enables the non-profit organizations to achieve their goals in a competitive environment. The non-government organizations primarily depend upon several stakeholders like government agencies, educational institutions, media organizations, philanthropic institutions, community organizations for the successful implementation of their social welfare programmes. Effective management matters most for the efficient delivery of goods and services in these organizations. The environment is always changing due to several factors. Especially, the economic and political climates also affect the process of organizational management.

The management of diversity has become an important challenge for modern organizations. The demographic features of the workforce in profit and service oriented organizations also matter most in the present time. The present generation of managers is required to cope with several changes and modifications in the systems and operations. Modern organizations need dynamic managers who are prepared to accept the changes and cope with the changing times and circumstances. Adoption of innovative technologies and practices is also very essential for the successful management of modern organizations.

Functions of Management

Management scholars have identified the generic functions of management such as planning, organizing, leading, motivating, coordinating, controlling and so on.

Planning

Planning is the foremost management function which involves identification of organizational objectives, policy formulation, identification of procedures and designing of methods for accomplishing the goals. The planning activities generally include—goals, objectives, policies, procedures, rules, strategies, tasks, resources, programme, budget and methods of operation. Planning sets the direction for the accomplishment of the goals of an organization. The basic steps involved in the planning process include—situational analysis, formulating desired goals, objectives and results, goal and plan evaluation, establishing goals and plans, chalking out strategies to achieve the goals and acknowledging the completion of organizational tasks. There are short term, mid-term and long term plans according to the duration. There are strategic plan, tactical plan and operational plan according to the levels of planning. Effective planning is required to achieve success in any organization. In a developing country like India systematic planning provides the means for the best utilization of resources and opportunities.

Organizing

Organizing is also an important function of management. An effective organizational structure involves primary level organizing, intermediate level organizing and ultimate level organizing. There is also a chain of command which involves the flow of authority originating from the top executive and reaching down to the worker. The modern organizations have to improve their effectiveness in competitive business environment. Organizations should be encouraged to achieve continuous improvement of the process, system, operations and inputs. Leadership qualities, entrepreneurship development, performance measurement, sound work culture and scientific evaluation are the common features of successful organization. Modern organizations are also required to adapt themselves to the changing environment and fulfil the needs of the people efficiently.

Leading

Leading is an important function of management which involves the process of influencing people to work for the achievement of the goals of the organizations. Certain leadership theories are also developed over a period of time by the management scholars. There are well established leadership styles which are used by modern managers over a period of time. Empirical studies have been conducted all over the world on various aspects of leadership development. Scholars have also emphasized the democratic-humanitarian leadership values which facilitate participatory management and development in modern organizations. The competitive business environment also demands the managers to lead their organizations on the basis of qualification, experience, leadership quality, problem solving ability, crisis management capacity and other traits. In a developing country like India participative or consultative approach facilitate better leadership development.

Motivating

Motivation is also a prominent management function which benefits modern organizations. There are certain theories of motivation which are formulated by the management experts. The personnel constantly need inspirational and emotional stimulation provided by motivation which is ranked as one of the most significant management functions. There are several approaches to motivation which are based on practical experience of the leaders. The scientific management approach to motivating people within the organizations was developed by Taylor. There are certain internal and external factors which motivate the individuals to work effectively in modern organizations. The material gains, professional gains, organizational gains and societal gains are the prominent situational factors which motivate the individuals to work well and contribute well for the progress of the modern organizations. Studies have revealed that the personnel should be motivated properly on the basis of developing affinity with the organization and commitment to organizational development.

Coordinating

Coordination is a management function which is indispensable for achieving unity in diversity among the personnel in modern organizations. Differences in beliefs, attitudes, behaviours, performance and other aspects of organizational management are bound to exist in modern organizations. Management experts have rightly pointed out that differentiation in management actually needs effective coordination which provides harmony out of differences. A true coordination must be based on a real commonality of interest in the attainment of the goals of modern organizations. The theory of coordination demands that every organization must grow out of a common interest and a common effort. There are several elements of cooperation which include balancing, timing and integrating. The goal of coordination can be achieved on the basis of sound policies, systematic procedures, united efforts and meaningful motivation factors. Coordination is also dependent on orderly synchronization of institutional efforts made by several personnel associated with different branches of modern organizations. Coordination is a never ending exercise which demands team spirit and collective actions.

Controlling

Controlling is a highly essential management function which prevents waste of time, resources, energies and opportunities in modern organizations. Appropriate preventive, corrective and promotional measures are required to achieve the goals of modern organizations. Effective checks and balances are required in modern organizations to prevent certain managerial errors and operational drawbacks. Controlling is an all pervasive organizational management function which embraces people, resources and actions. The organizational leaders are responsible for the development of suitable control mechanisms which safeguard the interest of organizations. Effective control has become an imperative for sound management of modern organizations. The changing environment and various situational factors justify the need for effective controlling mechanisms in organization. Practically, control has an ultimate connection with the development of system, management of people and delivery of goods and services. Management experts have also developed inter-disciplinary approaches to meaningful control of modern organizations. New technologies and strategies are also applied to the process of organizational control in modern times. Effective control is a prerequisite to standardize the organizational management, performance and services in modern competitive environment. Controlling mechanisms also motivate the individuals of an organization to contribute their best efforts under the challenging circumstances.

Communicating

Communication is an important management function since it is vital for the success of an organization. Communication is rightly viewed as the foundation of modern organizations by the scholars. The communication process includes source, message, channel, receivers and effect. The policies, programmes, goods, services and other aspects of organizational management should be received by the various stakeholders of organizational development effective communication is necessary to eliminate the barriers to participate in the process of organization building. The managers, supervisors and workers are required to communicate effectively in order to facilitate smooth organizational operations across geographical areas. Organizational leaders also have the responsibility of creating an environment which is conducive for the development of organization. Communication plays an important role in enhancing inter-personal relations and interaction among various stakeholders of organizational development. Tom Peters (1997: 13) stated that communication is interwoven in all aspects of the organizational management that includes channels to all stakeholders and the external environment. The organizational leaders are also responsible for the improvement of organizational performance through effective communication at various levels. Empirical studies have also rightly pointed out that personal, group and organizational success primarily revolves around organizational communication. Systematic communication provides competencies to individuals and organizations to continuously improve their performance. The importance of communication has increased in the age of information science and technological revolution.

Art and Science of Management

Scholars have debated over the true nature of management over a period of time. There are management experts who have rightly pointed out that management is a blend of both science and art. Hamel and Prahlad (1994: 10) have observed that successful executives recognize the importance of combining both the science and the art of management as they practice their craft.

Management is also viewed by the scholars as an art since creativity is the hallmark of management. Modern managers are required to provide an artistic touch to the managerial exercises. The managers also need vision, experience, expertise, creativity and other artistic inputs in order to take right decisions in the right time and do the right things by following the right methods. The present generation of managers must blend an element of intuition and personal insight with hard data and objective facts, argue Waldroop and Butler (1996: 15).

Managerial issues and problems need to be addressed in an objective, logical, scientific, systematic and rational way in order to enhance the status of management. Modern managers are required to generate a body of authentic data either through quantitative approaches or through qualitative approaches. Application of scientific principles and practices enriches the process of management in modern society. Hence, modern managers need scientific approach to solving the problems and building the institutions in this age of science and technology. Appropriate decisions and actions become a byproduct of systematic and scientific analysis of practical issues which have a bearing on the process of management.

In reality, most successful managers learn their skills and improve their capacity through a combination of artistic and scientific approaches to management. Effective management is also a byproduct of creative and systematic combination of the principles and practices of management. In recent years, the importance of integrated management has been widely recognized by the scholars. Good management is always required in traditional and non-traditional settings to meet the established goals on the basis of artistic and scientific management strategies and functions. Art and science have a profound influence on the practice of management regardless of space and time.

Schools of Management

Management scholars have examined the various aspects of management and formulated certain principles of management. They have also contributed various management theories which primarily deal with the improvement of the practice of management. The prominent schools of management include—the empirical school, the human behaviour school, the social systems school, the decision theory school and the mathematical school, according to Mrithyunjoy Banerjee (1986: 02).

The empirical school believes that management process, system and operations should be examined on the basis of scientific analysis of cases which generate a body of authentic data about management decisions and actions. The human behaviour school primarily deals with the inter-personal relations or human relations which matter most from the point of view of getting the things done by various stakeholders of management on the basis of effective persuasion. The social system school lays emphasis on the process of management which is a byproduct of social system based on cultural relationships. The decision theory school concentrates on rational approach to decision which is based on possible alternatives of a course of action. The mathematical school views management as a system of mathematical models and processes. The operations researchers or operations analysts perceive management as a logical process involving mathematical symbols and relationships. These five different schools of management have developed over a period of time starting with scientific management.

There are major schools of management theory which include—classical, behavioural, quantitative, systems, contingency and other approaches, according to Bhat and Kumar (2009: 05).

The classical school is viewed as the oldest formal school of management thought which came into existence in 1900 and onwards. It primarily dealt with increasing the capacity of the personnel and organizations based on systematic application of scientific management practices. It included bureaucratic, scientific and administrative management. The bureaucratic management relies on guidelines for structuring with formalization of rules, procedures and a clear division of labour. The scientific lays emphasis on the 'one best way' to deliver the goods. Administrative management focuses on the manager, basic managerial functions and professional obligations. Prominent among the scholars who developed classical school include—Frederic W. Taylor (author of *Principles of Scientific Management*), Henry Gantt (designer of *Charts for Planning and Controlling*), Frank Gilbreath (promoter of *Scientific Methods of Management*), Lillian Gilbreth (author of *Psychology of Management)*, Henri Fayol (father of *Modern*

Management), Peter Drucker (promoter of *Scientific Management*), Max Weber (major contributor to *Bureaucratic Management*) and so on.

The behavioural school of management was developed on the basis of advances in psychological theories and approaches. The scholars focused on understanding the factors associated with the evaluation of human behaviour at work in organizations. Prominent among the scholars who developed behavioural school include—Mary Parker (Proponent of Universal Goal of Organizational), Chester Burnard (author of *Functions of Executive*), Douglas McGregor (proponent of *Human Resources Management*, Frederic Herzberg (promoter of *Organizational Behaviour*) and so on. These scholars developed behavioural school of management on the basis of personality, attitudes, values, motivation, group behaviour, leadership, communication and other managerial issues.

The quantitative school of management focused the attention of scholars on improving the decision making power of modern organizations on the basis of application of mathematical and statistical models in management. This was developed during the Second World War since the military strategists tried to apply scientific knowledge and methods to solve the complex problems of war. George Danzig developed linear programming, an algebraic method of determining the optimal allocation of scarce resources. Computer application made lot of difference in the process of operations research. The management science was developed systematically on the basis of management information system. W. Edwards Deming also added certain dimensions to the operations management which emphasized productivity and quality of both manufacturing and servicing organizations.

The systems school of management was developed after Second World War on the basis of certain concepts and quantitative approaches from mathematics, statistics, engineering and other disciplines to solve the problems of organizations. The managers were called upon to use scientific analysis for understanding certain environmental conditions which affected the process of management. It is composed of certain inputs from the environment, outputs into the environment and feedback from the environment. The scholars concentrated on understanding the organization as an open system that transforms inputs into outputs. Ludwig von Bertalanffy believed that a general systems model could be used to unite science. The proponents of the school also emphasized the interaction between organization and environment in order to achieve equilibrium. These salient features of the school practically formed the basis for the development of contingency school of management subsequently.

The contingency school of management emerged in 1960s on the basis of situational approach to management. The scholars basically objected to the use of universal management practices and noted that managerial behaviour was dependent on various situational factors such as external environment, technological innovations, organizational characteristics, human behaviours and so on. Scholars like Joan Woodward, Paul Lawrence, Jay Lorsch, Fiedler and others theorized the organizational structure which was based on a variety of internal and external factors.

The contemporary management experts have added new approaches to management such as Total Quality Management, learning organizations, organizational excellence approach, chaos theory approach, eastern management approach, Western management approach and so on. The Total Quality Management approach emerged during the latter part of the twentieth century and emphasized the importance of improving the quality of management on the basis of certain strategies. The learning organizations approach highlighted the need for organizational efficiency. The excellence approach emerged on the basis of certain success stories and role models in the field of management. The Chaos theory emphasized that modern corporations should operate in a dynamic and efficient way in the midst of chaos. The eastern management school borrowed its principles and practices from historical events. The Western management school emerged on the basis of certain success stories of management in the west. The present managerial views are based on constant improvement of work efficiency and product quality.

Management scholars have also provided certain altèrnative theories of management based on traditional model, human relations model and human resources model. The traditional model reveals that the basic role of the manager is essentially controlling the system, people and operations. The human relations model includes the responsibility for maintenance of the human system which matters most from organizational management point of view. The human resources model identifies the role of manager as developer and facilitator of the organizational system. The scholars have also aired their serious criticism against the human relations school of management. They believe that it sans scientific validity and practical authenticity.

Scientific Study of Management

The process of management is as old as the mankind is but the science of management is of quite recent origin. In 1776 Adam Smith contributed the theory of division of labour which led to specialization of organizational activities. In the nineteenth century, Robert Owen emphasized the need for human resources and material resources management in industry. In 1830s, Charles Babbage called upon the leaders of organization to make use of scientific investigations and manage the organizations on the basis of authentic data. In the 1850s David C. McCallum propounded the principles of management.

The scientific principles and methods of management were developed in the twentieth century especially after the Second World War. The democratic forces defeated the fascists in this war and paved the way for the institutionalization of democracy as a new way of life all over the world. The independent nations adopted their own constitutions and created several organizations in all spheres of human life. The government, non-government and other modern organizations were systematically managed on the basis of sound principles and practices of management.

Several economic institutions and activities were also managed on the strength of skilful and efficient management. New schools of management also cropped up over a period of time. A new generation of scholars also emerged in the field of management who contributed several theories of management. Peter Drucker observed that the science of management was essentially a product of twentieth century. The science of management originated in two mainstreams namely scientific management and general administrative theory according to Banerjee (1986: 03).

Taylor and Fayol argued that there was no generally accepted theory of management emanating from general discussion. They pointed out that the fundamental principles of scientific management were applicable to all kinds of human activities ranging from simple individual acts to the work of great corporations. The concepts and methods of Taylor were subjected to improvement by a host of management researchers. Scholars also strongly urged that scientific management consisted of tested and tried methods of managing organizations on the basis of authentic data and ground realities. Ralph Currier Davis (1951: 07) identified the fundamentals of top management.

Banerjee (1986: 04) observes: "The science of management, which tells what is efficient, decides exactly how efficient it is and explains the why, includes much more than what is included in the term Scientific Management. Increased efficiency must begin with those higher up. This is the essence of scientific management". Scholars also identified the various factors associated with scientific management. The Taylor Society propounded 13th objectives of scientific management which were widely discussed by the scholars. Taylor is well-known as the father of scientific management which involved much deeper philosophy of administering human and physical resources in a technologically advanced world where man had gained greater control over his environment than ever before. Several institutions also applied the management principles of Taylor who achieved resounding success. Some scholars also criticized that Taylor's management philosophy was a *Utopian ideal* which was not practically relevant.

Chester Barnard provided a synthesis of functions of the executives. Scholars also developed quantitative approaches to management since numerical data were used to the management of organizations. The management process school, empirical school, human behaviour school, social system school, decision theory school and mathematical school were also developed. The scholars also propounded certain manager's theories of development. The traditional, human relations and human resources theories also emphasized the basic role of managers and functions of workers. Several institutions of management studies were also established all over the world to train new generation of qualified, experienced and competent managers. New trends in management were also analyzed by the scholars. Scholars also identified the major functions of management, levels of management and operations of management on the basis of extensive investigations.

Application of Managerial Skills

Management is an art and science of getting the things done by various stakeholders of management of modern organizations. In modern organizations, there are three levels of management namely—top level management, middle level management and lower management. The top level management consists of board of management, office bearers and divisional heads who are primarily responsible for agenda setting, policy making, directing and controlling all the activities of an organization. The top level management is primarily responsible for strategic decisions and long term policies which are executive in nature. The top level management should consist of visionaries, torch bearers and builders of modern organizations. The top level managers are required to gain an extensive knowledge of management roles and responsibilities in order to lead the organization in the right direction. They must be aware of both internal and external dynamics of organizational management in order to lead the organization towards success.

The middle level management usually consists of divisional heads, managers, section officers and other officials who are responsible for the implementation of the decisions made by the top level management. They are required to understand the standardized management strategies and take appropriate tactical decisions in order to boost the progress of modern organizations. They must make a comparative analysis of modern and traditional management approaches and make use of locally relevant management principles and practices. The middle level managers should have a specialized understanding of specific managerial tasks, skills and responsibilities. They are mainly responsible for supervising, controlling and guiding the activities of the personnel who constitute the lower management and functionaries.

The lower level management ensures that the decisions taken by the top level management and the plans designed by the middle level management are effectively carried out by the supervisors and other functionaries associated with the different branches of a modern organization. The lower level managers are responsible for taking short term decisions on the basis of ground realities. They must carry out their duties properly with a view to ensure the successful conduction of organizational works. The lower level managers are required to master certain basic skills in management and leadership skills which are essential for the effective implementation of organizational activities.

In the new millennium, standardized management principles and practices have cropped up on the basis of series of experiments that have enriched the process of management across the globe. The present generation of managers should also fulfil the requirements of modern organizations and rise to the occasion as effective institution builders. Advanced technologies and strategies should be adopted properly by the modern managers in order to cope with the challenges of business management in the present times. The globalization of economy has transformed all aspects of human life and society. The numbers of modern organizations continued to rise. There is need for unification of all sections of modern organizations to facilitate greater production and productivity on the basis of tested and tried management strategies and resources.

Conclusion

Scientific management is a wider subject which covers policy making, planning, programming, implementation, supervision, controlling, communicating, direction and other diversified institutional activities. There is increasing competition between different modern organizations in all walks of life in the age of globalization. A number of management schools and institutions have cropped up over a period of time in India and other countries. There is a drastic need for application of managerial skills and strategies in modern organizations. The globalization of economy has posed new challenges to the modern managers regardless of the nature and scope of operations across the world. The process of management should be strengthened on the basis of systematic study of dynamics of management. Modern managers are required to assume multi-faceted roles and shoulder different responsibilities in the new millennium. The present generation of managers are scientifically educated, organized, motivated and persuaded to accept different roles and responsibilities in order to boost the progress of the modern organizations under the most challenging circumstances.

References

Atwater, J. Brian, Vijay R. Kannan and Alan. A Stephens (2008) Cultivating Systematic Thinking in the Next Generation of Business Leaders, *Academy of Management Learning and Education,* 7 (1): 9-25.

Banerjee, Mrithyunjoy (1986) *Gems of Management*, Jaico Publishing House, Bombay, pp. 46-48.

Ibid., p. 4.

Ibid., p. 21.

Bhat, Anil and Arya Kumar (2009) *Management Principles, Processes and Practices*, Oxford University Press, New Delhi, p. 22.

Casesa, John (2009) Highly Respected Automobile Industry Consultant, *Business Week*, March 16: 31-32.

Davis, James, H., F. David Schooman and Lex Donaldson (1997) Toward a Stewardship Theory of Management, *Academy of Management Review,* January: 20-47.

Davis, Ralph Currier (1951) *The Fundamentals of the Top Management*, Harper and Brothers, New York, pp. 60-61.

Griffin, Ricky W. (2012) *Management Principles and Applications,* Cengage Learning, New Delhi, p. 28.

Hamel, Gary and C.K. Prahlad (1994) Competing for the Future, *Harvard Business Review,* July-August: 122-128.

Hitt, Michael, A. (2000) Transformation of Management for the New Millennium, *Organizational Dynamics,* Winter: 7-17.

Lafley, A.G. (2009) Role of CEO in Modern Organizations, *Harvard Business Review,* May: 62-63.

Peters, Tom (1997) The Search for Excellence Continuous, *Forbes,* 2 (12): 238-240.

Ritz-Carlton (2000) Training Tradition, *USA Today*, June 29: 3B.

Waldroop, James and Timothy, Butler (1996) The Executive as Coach, *Harvard Business Review,* November-December: 111-117.

Chapter 3
Foundations of Managerial Communication

Introduction

The success of every business organization is based on value based and effective business communication. Business communication takes place within and outside the business organization. Business communication is an important aspect of modern business management. The business communication plays a crucial role in the process of business promotion. Business communication is the force that binds the internal and external publics of an organization together and facilitates mutual cooperation in order to accomplish the business objectives. Effective business communication can be achieved by planned, deliberate and systematic two-way communication between the business organizations and various publics. In the age of globalization, business communication has become an instrument of successful running of business. The concept of business communication, foundations of business communication, functions of business communication, communication system in business organizations, process of business communication, basic forms of business communication and conditions for successful business communication are discussed in this Chapter.

Concept of Business Communication

In the new millennium, the business world is more interconnected than ever before. Business communication has become critical for the survival and development of modern business organizations. The need for business organizations to communicate with both internal and external stakeholders has become vital in the present times. Communication in a business environment is different from other environments. Communication is a binding force which unites the business organizations regardless of their size and area of operations. Business communication is an important component of business management in modern society. Every business organization has to establish and maintain cordial human relationship with the internal and external publics who matter most in the age of competitive business management. The modern business organizations have to enter into the good books of various stakeholders who are the patrons of business organizations. Business communication is necessary to realize the goals of business organizations on the basis of mutual understanding, cooperation and support.

Brown defines: "Business communication is a process of messages and persons which are associated with business. It consists of channels of communication". Business communication is a multi-dimensional process which involves several stakeholders and multi-directional flow of business communication. It basically includes the transfer of ideas, experiences and guidelines for the fulfilment of business objectives.

McFarland states: "Business communication may be broadly defined as the process of meaningful interaction between the business organization and other stakeholders. It facilitates meaningful interaction between the business organization and other sections in order to facilitate smooth running of the business organizations". Communication is an integral part of business organization. The importance of communication in business organizations has been recognized all over the world. It is a meaningful interaction among the people which facilitates the integration of various stakeholders and business communication involves a systematic process of telling, listening and understanding.

Harold Yasvin notes: "In our operation of business, communication system is playing an important and growing role. It is necessary that communication system should be such that everyone concerned should be able to understand the goals of business organizations and respond positively. Undoubtedly, business communication is the basis of modern business management. Its importance is being accepted by one and all". Business communication is an act of sharing of information, ideas and experiences in order to create better and harmonious understanding and relations between the business organizations and other stakeholders.

Singhal *et al.* (2006: 18) observe: "Business communication is necessary in order to realize the objectives of business organizations. It is the part of communication which is related to the business activities and helps to make the business dynamic and successful. Actually, the term business communication is used for the transfer of ideas, facts and information for the fulfilment of business objectives".

Bovee *et al.* (2009: 03) state: "In modern organizations, the communicators are required to develop communication skill and competence in order to facilitate better rapport development between the modern organizations and various constituent publics. Communicating in today's business environment requires some level of technical competence as well. Poorly designed and inappropriately used technology can hinder communication more than it helps".

The various stakeholders of business organization are held together by business communication. It is both interaction and transaction. Business communication is formally defined as the process whereby the decisional premises are transmitted from the business organization to various stakeholders. The business communication is required on regular basis in order to achieve the unity of command facilitate social interaction of people. Scholars have noted that communication is the most critical problem of business management in modern society.

Role of Communication in Management

Business communication is a multi-faceted communication between the business organization and other publics. It takes place on round the clock basis on the systematic application of business communication tools and technologies. It has both internal and external dimensions. The internal communication takes place between the management and employees on a regular basis. The management is responsible for educating, organizing, motivating and persuading the employees. The management has to communicate certain things to the employees in order to secure their active and willing participation in the process of institution building. The management should also create harmonious business environment by developing better relations between management and employees. The corporate communicators are also responsible for creating awareness among the leaders of the organization about various business trends and developments. Business communication is also responsible for creating coordination among different groups of business organization on the basis of mutual trust and cooperation. The management should also communicate the policies and programmes to the employees in order to improve their morale and enlist the active participation of employees in the process of business promotion.

Business communication also bridges the communication gap between the organization and various external publics. Effective customer relationship management is primarily dependent on business communication strategies, tools and techniques. Corporate advertising and communication activities are organized with a view to win over the customers who are the pillars of business organizations. The suppliers of materials should also be educated about the kind of raw materials, quantity, quality, time of supply, conditions of supply, payment and other facts. Business organizations have to establish good rapport with various government agencies which play a major role in providing license, permission and allied support. Business organizations should also make use of various communications media in order to build image and enrich their reputation in a competitive business environment. The local community should also be won over by the business organizations through meaningful philanthropic activities. The business organizations should also establish better coordination with other stakeholders of business promotion.

Communication System in Business Organizations

Business communication is the life blood of modern business organizations. It has to be practiced on the basis of sound principles and approaches. Business communication is something more than mere exchange of information and ideas between the organization and others. Sound business communication is necessary to realize the goals of business organization on the basis of tested and tried practices. Truthful, reliable and constructive business communication creates harmonious business environment. The art and craft of business communication should be perfected on the basis of ideological foundations. The business communicators should create a good business climate on the basis of meaningful communication exercises. Sound business communication is based upon mutual confidence and understanding between the business organization and stakeholders.

The success in business organizations primarily depends upon the effectiveness of communication between the organizations and other stakeholders. Mukerjee (2013: 14) notes: "The need for communication in business organizations arises because of the necessity of informing the various stakeholders about the organizational goals and services, convincing the customers to accept the goods and services and requesting other stakeholders to respond to the developmental needs".

Business communication is the basis of modern business management. In business, communication system can be successful only when it is effective and creative. Haneyager and Heinemann opine:

"Business communication is fundamental to the practice of management in modern business organizations. Business communication depends not only on transmitting the information, but it is also necessary to see their effect on the receiver. All the persons handling business communication should be competent enough to work effectively. Business communication is the basis of all business activities. It is a well established fact that effective business communication is necessary to make a business organization successful".

A well developed communication system is necessary for successful and smooth working of a business organization. Communication plays a significant role in any business enterprise regardless of its size and operations. Communication is an important management function. Communication can make or mar a business organization, according to Redfield. Merry Cooshing pointed out that effective communication is necessary ingredient for perfect management of business organizations. Business communication is needed to successfully implement the programmes of business organizations.

Modern business organizations remain active and dynamic with the help of effective business communication. The managerial decisions are put into practice with the effective business communication. A well designed and developed communication system is necessary for successful and smooth progress of business organizations. Effective business communication prevents conflict of interest between the management and various stakeholders. Hobs and Johnson also highlighted the need for effective business communication which is the lifeblood of modern business organizations. Harold Yasvin highlights the role of communication in the business organizations thus: "In our operation of business, communication system, communication is playing an important and growing role. We have to inform more persons, we have to listen from a wide section so as to understand their grievances well. We have to seek their cooperation in removing the problems so as to create atmosphere of mutual understanding and trust in the business organization".

Functions of Business Communication

Business communication has several elements in an organization. It also carries innumerable kinds of works in modern organizations. Following are the major functions of business communication.

Policy Oriented Communication

Modern business organizations formulate certain policies which need to be understood by various stakeholders of organizational management and development. Communication is required to clearly spell out the various policies and educate the stakeholders about the need, importance and relevance of policies which are formulated in an organization from time to time.

Plan Oriented Communication

Modern organizations design short-term, mid-term and long-term plans in order to achieve success in the implementation of various programmes. Plans have to be designed in consultation with the experts and subordinates within an organization. The employees should be educated about their roles and responsibilities in the successful implementation of plans.

Programme Oriented Communication

Modern organizations design several programmes for various stakeholders ranging from investors to customers. Communication is required to enlist active participation of various stakeholders in the process of implementation. Active and intelligent people's participation is required in all the programmes of an organization.

Implementation Oriented Communication

An organization should also develop a structure by involving various resources, people, tasks, responsibilities and delegation of authority. Meaningful implementation of various organizational programmes depends upon right kind of education and motivation at various levels. The management should also get into the good books of various stakeholders and succeed in enlisting their active participation in the implementation of various programmes.

Supervision Oriented Communication

The management of an organization has to effectively supervise the activities of various subordinates constantly and consistently. Supervision basically involves on the job training, orientation and motivation by several heads of the departments and managers. Communication is required in supervising the day-to-day activities of modern organizations.

Controlling Oriented Communication

The heads of the departments and managers are also required to control the people effectively while they are in action. Communication is required to issue orders, instructions and advice which facilitate meaningful controlling. Wasteful expenditure should be avoided as far as possible. Controlling also involves prevention of unhealthy practices and adoption of progressive measures. Thus, communication is required to control the people and their activities in the right direction.

Directing Oriented Communication

Communication is also required to efficient directing of various subordinates in modern organizations. Without active communication, meaningful direction, delivery of goods and achievement of the goals of organization cannot be achieved under normal circumstances. The higher authorities require communication skills in order to direct the activities of the organizations and get the things done from the subordinates.

Motivating Oriented Communication

Modern organizations are required to motivate the various stakeholders and involve them actively in the affairs of the organization. Team work is not possible without proper motivation. Motivation is required to build sound human relations, carry the people together, integrate actions and facilitate the development of organizations. Efficient functioning of modern organizations requires sound motivation which demands active communication.

Coordinating Oriented Communication

Large and complex organizations demand coordination within and outside the organization. Coordination can be brought about if communication unites superior and subordinate officials and brings about mutual understanding among them. Coordination can be achieved when the members of a working group are united, integrated and motivated to work together and produce better results.

Rapport Development Oriented Communication

Effective communication is indispensable for building up sound human relations in modern organizations. Communication plays an important role in building and sustaining human relations in a competitive business environment. Good working conditions and environment should be created in order to enter into the good books of various stakeholders of organizational development. Communication is also required to avoid illusions and misunderstanding which create barriers to participation and progress.

Work Environment Oriented Communication

The management should boost the morale of the workers, foster team spirit and motivate the employees for better performance and progress. Creation of a highly conducive working environment is crucial for the successful conduction of the business in modern organizations. Hence, communication is required to increase the morale of the workers, enhance job satisfaction and enrich organizational status.

Efficient Functioning Oriented Communication

The management is also primarily responsible for the efficient functioning of an organization. The effectiveness of management depends upon its ability to understand the various stakeholders and make them understand their roles and responsibilities. Communication is a link that unites management and stakeholders for effective functioning in different capacities. In the absence of effective communication, the work efficiency cannot be increased. Thus, communication is an indispensable component of the process of management.

Process of Business Communication

Business communication takes place between the organization and internal and external stakeholders in a business environment. Constant communication flow occurs between the organization and others in order to achieve the objectives of business in a competitive environment. The function of business communication is to bring the management and employees together and enable them to develop partnership and deliver mutually beneficial services. Business communication helps in creating meaningful coordination among different groups of people operating the business in large and complex business organizations. It creates mutual understanding, confidence and cooperation among different groups in a business organization. The management is also responsible for improving the morale of the employees who are responsible for the delivery of goods and services.

The business communication is also required to convey to the management changing business environment and allied facts pertaining to business promotion. Business communication also creates harmonious business environment through better human relationship development between the management and others. Business communication is required to motivate the suppliers of raw materials and other goods for speedy and efficient production and distribution of goods and services. It is required to convince the distributors to come forward and deliver the goods and services across the region or nation with confidence. It is basically oriented to enhancing customer relationship through image building and reputation management exercises.

The business communication also plays a vital role in building mutually beneficial relationship between the media and business organization. The policy makers and other government officials should also be persuaded to extend necessary political support for the smooth conduction of business affairs. The local community should also be persuaded by the corporate communicators to extend necessary moral and material support toward achieving the goals of business organizations. The business firm has to establish good rapport with various Government and non-government agencies in order to facilitate smooth conduction of business affairs. Hence, business communication takes place on round the clock basis between the management and others to facilitate smooth functioning of business.

The process of business communication primarily includes certain major components such as source, encoding, receiver, channel, interpretation and reaction. The business organizations are the primary sources of business communication. The corporate communicators are indeed the spokespersons of business organizations who are authorized to communicate with various stakeholders on behalf of the business organization. They are professionally competent communicators who are well versed with the art and craft of business communication.

The business communication occurs through different forms in modern society. The business messages are usually invisible or in abstract form. Therefore, encoding is necessary to convert ideas into symbols.

The language becomes the main instrument of business communication while encoding any business message. Several factors namely communication skill, knowledge, experience, environment, social and cultural elements influence the encoders, state Singhal *et al.* (2006: 19).

The various stakeholders of modern business namely—employees, investors, distributors, customers, media professionals, government officials, local citizens and others are the receivers of business communication. Modern business organizations are required to establish and maintain mutually beneficial relationship with various stakeholders who matter most from business promotion point of view. Hence, corporate communicators have to remain constantly in touch with various stakeholders and enlist their active participation in the process of business promotion.

The business communication takes place through several channels, tools and technologies in modern society. Oral communication, written communication, electronic communication, outdoor communication, indoor communication and other forms of business communication are utilized to reach out to various stakeholders including the customers in business environment. Several channels of communication are used by the corporate communicators for variety of purposes. Multi-media are also envisaged as a holistic communication from business promotion point of view.

The business communication also primarily depends upon proper understanding of the messages by the receivers. Therefore, decoding is necessary to make people understand the messages. The words, symbols, charts, technologies and other elements of business communication are used by the receivers to translate the message which is complex. The receivers should be enabled to understand the context of communication, purpose of communication, essence of communication and other aspects of business communication without any difficulty or constraint.

The purpose of business communication is duly served if the receivers grasp the correct meaning and respond to the message favourably the organizational communicators are responsible for educating and persuading various stakeholders to accept the points of view of business organizations and respond positively. The success of business communication primarily depends upon the establishment of mutual confidence, goodwill and cooperation between the sender and receiver. The business communication services should be designed in accordance with the needs and demands of the receivers who matter most in modern business environment. Thus, the process of business communication includes several components which are equally important.

There are several factors which make business communication unique in the present times. Modern business organizations are required to conduct business across borders by involving heterogeneous groups of people. They have to make use of modern communication tools and technologies in order to cater to the needs of various stakeholders constantly. The importance of business communication is realized by modern corpòrate houses which have invested sizeable chunk of their resources on business communication management. Thus, business communication is very crucial for the success in the world of competitive business since communication matters.

Basic Forms of Business Communication

Business communication takes place through a wide range of communications media in modern society. Traditional, modern and advanced channels, tools and techniques of business communication are used in the present times. The basic forms of business communication include—non-verbal communication, verbal communication, written communication and electronic communication. In the rural and tribal areas, the business organizations have to depend upon traditional or folk media and inter-personal communication channels which are effective means of communication. In the rural and urban areas non-verbal communication primarily serves as an effective form of business communication. The business communicators primarily make use of non-verbal communication which is dependent on body language and other symbols.

The business organizations also make use of spoken form which is known as verbal communication. The exchange of ideas, experiences and opinions is done with the help of spoken words through group discussion, exhibition, demonstration, training, orientation, broadcasting, Internet and other channels. The exchange of ideas and opinions takes place between the sender and receiver through direct and indirect communication situations. Verbal communication occurs most of the times in business organizations because of reliability simplicity and other factors. Verbal communication becomes relevant because exchange of ideas and opinions is more effective by nature.

The business organizations rely upon written communication such as circular, memo, letter, newspaper, magazine, newsletter, house journal and so on. The communicators make use of simple and effective language symbols in order to convey a specific meaning through written communication which is formal in nature. The institutional publications and other print media carry the messages which serve as written proof. The written messages also communicate the ideas and opinions clearly to the receivers. Modern business organizations make use of verbal and written communication forms in order to establish rapport with various stakeholders.

The audio-visual communication is also known as electronic communication which is increasing very fast in modern business organizations. The electronic media facilitate earliest communication between the business organizations and others because of the technological advancements. In the age of information revolution, electronic media are most effective form of business communication since they provide instantaneous, interactive and participatory communication services across the globe. Thus, modern business communication takes place through multi-media of communication. Several communication experts have contributed different models of communication over a period of time. The transactional process model of organizational communication presented by John Benberg and Millian Willmont is widely quoted by the scholars of business communication. They have stated that organizational communication process becomes effective if it is based on mutual cooperation of sender and receiver for its success.

Harold Yasvin observes: "Undoubtedly, effective communication is the basis of modern business and management. In our operation of business, communication system is playing an important and growing role. Modern business organizations have to deal with several stakeholders, listen to different sections of business, resolve conflicts of interest, integrate all stakeholders and enlist the active support of one and all for business promotion".

Constant communication is required for continuous productivity and sustainability of modern organizations. The management can carry the various stakeholders in the right direction and achieve the goals on the basis of effective communication. Effective decision making and implementation require sound system of communication in modern organization. The process of managing communication in organizations has a number of elements which need to be integrated under the banners of 'fraternity', 'commonality', 'continuity' and 'sustainability'. Effective business communication is highly essential for successful working of any organization in the present age of competitiveness.

Conditions for Successful Business Communication

The business communication takes place in the world of reality that surrounds management and various stakeholders. The absence of a common frame of reference usually affects the smooth interpretation of ideas, opinions and thoughts between the sender and receiver who share different environments. The business communicators should basically understand the social and business context in which communication takes place between the business organizations and other stakeholders. The business communication is practiced under certain assumptions which are not necessarily communicated to the other parties. The perceptional error also creates certain barriers to business communication. The business communicators and receivers are not supposed to have same ways of thinking under the normal circumstances.

The business communicators should understand the ground realities and cater to the needs of the receivers to the best of their abilities. They must ensure that the receivers fully understand their points of view and respond to their needs favourably. Keith Davis has identified the five elements in the process of business communication namely—receive, understand, accept, use and give feedback. Without these elements, the process of business communication becomes incomplete and ineffective. The success of business communication mainly depends upon the communication of accurate messages by using the accessible channels of communication. The business communication should be based on candidness which facilitates the dissemination of accurate messages.

The business communicators should use simple, relevant and familiar words which enhances the clarity of business communication. The principle of completeness requires that corporate communicators communicate the essentials of business communication. The success of business communication is also dependent on conciseness of communication. The business communicators should also understand the need for concreteness which means communication of specific and definite points of view. The business communication becomes fruitful if it is known for correctness of ideas, channels and meanings. In business communication courtesy also matters because it is necessary to respect the points of view of others equally. Hence, business communication becomes effective if the corporate communicators understand the universal elements in business communication.

Shirley Taylor offers the following ten tips for successful business communication:

1. Extend your knowledge of language by reading.
2. Listening is just as important as speaking.
3. Think well and plan all your communications carefully.
4. Use clear, simple and appropriate language.
5. Consider other people's view points and be open minded.
6. Select appropriate media for business communication.
7. Consider the best time for the communication.
8. Use words and language which are relevant to the topic concerned.
9. Obtain feedback to ensure that management brings about suitable changes and modifications in the delivery system.
10. Maintain high standards in all your methods of business communication.

Business communication should be practiced on the basis of sound principles, tools, technologies and strategies. The relationship between the organization and receivers of business communication should be properly understood. The context of business communication and the circumstances under which business communication takes place should also be evaluated before delivering business communication services. The implications of new communication technologies and advanced methods of business communication should be understood by the corporate communicators in order to enrich the process of business communication. The system of communication in business organizations, role of corporate communicators, selection of media, formulation of messages, diffusion of information, collection of feedback and other aspects of business communication should be properly understood by the corporate communicators.

Role of Communication in Crisis Management

Business communication plays a vital role in the current business world. It is also required to manage the crisis in modern society. Crisis occurs accidentally in the modern society. There is no individual, system and society without crisis. It is the byproduct of certain misunderstandings between the management and various stakeholders. Some vested interest also create crisis which needs to be managed on the basis of clarity, confidence and competence. Practically, it is not possible to procrastinate about the crisis which arises on account of ego clash or split personality among the people associated with an organization. Certain conflicts, crises and disasters also arise in modern organizations due to several factors such as hostility, negative thinking, negligence, rivalry, misunderstanding and so on. A conflict is defined as a disagreement between two or more individuals or groups who intend to gain acceptance of certain views over others. It can be resolved on the basis of proper understanding and sincere dialogue. A crisis is defined as an unfavourable situation which creates barriers to understanding, cooperation and unity. It can also be resolved through proper management approaches. A disaster is a manmade tragedy which occurs when the mankind antagonizes the nature due to greed and negative approaches. Disaster management demands lot of preventive measures, preparation and mobilization of timely actions. During all these three occasions, communication plays an important role.

The role of communication in crisis management is widely discussed by the scholars and others concerned. Communication occupies an important role in times of crisis. Communication in crisis situations requires a high degree of agility in order to respond to demands of individuals who are affected by the situation. The management is also answerable to the media and society in times of crisis. Communication should be tailor made in order to firmly deal with the crisis and provide complete information to various stakeholders about the nature, causes, magnitude, preventive measures and so on in times of crisis. Adequate care should be taken to avoid speculations on the basis of undocumented hypotheses and circumstances.

Steven Fink states: "A crisis is an unstable time or state of affairs in which a decisive change is impending—either one with the distinct possibility of a highly undesirable outcome or one with the distinct possibility of a highly desirable and extremely positive outcome". The mindset of the management matters most from the point of view of effective and successful crisis management which has four stages namely hidden crisis, pre-crisis, the crisis and post-crisis. The management should do serious introspection in times of crisis and manage the crisis on the basis of ground realities and feasible strategies. The organizational leaders should make use of the media to diffuse the crisis and gain the public confidence and support.

Bhushan (2012: 02) observes: "A crisis is a significant, unpredictable, disruptive event that has potentially negative results. The event stimulates news media coverage. The public scrutiny may impact the organization's normal operations, and its aftermath may significantly damage an organization and its employees, products, services, financial condition and reputation". Modern business organizations are bound to experience crisis which is a byproduct of conflict of interest between the management and other stakeholders. In times of crisis, organization should rise to the occasion and manage the crisis through effective media campaigns and persuasive efforts.

Karoli and Ahmad (2013: 08) observe: "Although in the initial stages of the crisis situation there is little information or quantifiable data available, information should always be provided about what is known and decisions made with a view to solve the problem. People expect answers and solutions, and the situation can become socially stressful if there is a perception that not enough is being done in the face of a crisis situation. Anticipation and preparation are also essential in the management of crisis".

A crisis is bound to have certain psychological, sociological, cultural, ecological, political and other factors. Cognitive functions are significant in crisis response and coping. Sociological factors should also be understood by the crisis managers for the purpose of providing convincing and persuasive communication services cultural factors and differences should also be ironed out by the crisis managers and communicators. Ecological factors should be addressed with utmost care and responsibility. All these factors should be borne in mind and adequate grounds are also required for effective crisis management in the organization. The head of the organization, spokespersons, cultural ambassadors and organizational communicators need proper orientation, negotiation skills and crisis management capacity. Negotiation plays an important role in the process of crisis management.

Communication is undoubtedly an important factor which strengthens the process of negotiation. In fact, negotiation is governed by shared formal and informal rules negotiated by the bargainers. Communication is required to facilitate tacit bargaining through effective verbal and non-verbal communications which constitute the fabric of negotiations. Communication is central to the bargaining process which involves agreements, settlements, contracts and other factors. An effective communication is directly proportional to an effective negotiation. The organizational leaders, negotiators and communicators should be able to achieve success even under the most difficult and challenging crisis situations. Highly constructive, organized and creative arguments and justifications also matter most from the point of view of crisis oriented communication.

Conclusion

Communication is a major component of modern business management. The significance of communication in the process of business management is widely discussed by several scholars. Studies have also revealed that business communication is vital to the success of business management in modern society. Business communication is required to persuade the various stakeholders to take appropriate actions which benefit the business organization concerned. Business communication is essential to build trust and team work among the employees. Organizational communicators are required to persuade the external stakeholders constantly and enlist their active participation in the process of business promotion. Business communication is managed through verbal, written, electronic and multi-media forms in modern society. Business communication enables the various stakeholders to work together and achieve the goals of business organizations. Communication also plays a vital role in crisis management. The principles and practices of business communication should be properly understood by the professionals who are required to play multi-faceted role in the competitive business environment.

References

Beebe, Steven A. and John T. Masterson (1997), *Communicating in Small Groups: Principles and Practices*, New York: Longman.

Bhusan, Uma (2012), *Introduction to Business Communication*, Jaico Publishing House, Mumbai.

Bovee, Courtland, John V. Thill and Mukesh Chaturvedi (2009), *Business Communication Today*, Delhi: Pearson, pp. 16-18.

Bursk, Edward C. and Stephen A. Greyser (1968), *Advanced Cases in Marketing Management*, London: Prentice Hall, International Inc.

Chaturvedi, P.D. and Mukesh Chaturvedi (2012), *Business Communication*, Chennai: Pearson, pp. 22-23.

Hartley, Peter (2004), *Group Communication*, London: Routledge.

Hasan, Seema (2010), *Mass Communication: Principles and Concepts*, CBS Publishers and Distributors Pvt. Ltd., New Delhi.

Karoli, Veera and Naghma Ahmed (2013), *Business Communication*, Thakur Publishers, Bengaluru, India.

Kaul, Asha (2009), *Business Communication*, PHI Learning Private Limited, New Delhi.

Lehman, Carol, M., Devvie D., DuFrene, Mala Sinha and Robin C. Walker (2012) BCOM, *An Innovative Approach to Learning and Teaching, Business Communication, A South Asian Perspective*, Cengage Learning, New Delhi.

Lesikar, Raymond V., Marie E. Flatley, Kathryn Rentz and Neerja Pande (2011), *Business Communication—Making Connections in a Digital World*, Tata McGraw Hill Education Private Limited, New Delhi, pp. 6-9.

Mary, Ellen Guffey (2002), *Business Communication: Process and Product*, Cengage Learning, London, UK.

Mathew, M.J. (2002), *Business Communication: Theory and Practice*, Jaipur: RBSA Publishers, India.

Mukerjee, Hory Sankar (2013), *Business Communication: Connecting at Work*, Oxford University Press, New Delhi.

Pal, Rajendra J.S. and Korlahalli (1996), *Essentials of Business Communication*, Sultan Chand & Sons, New Delhi.

Raghavan, K.S. and K.N. Prasad (2009), *Library and Information Systems: From Alexandrian Heritage to Social Networking*, Bangalore: Ess Ess Publications, India.

Rai, Urmila and S.M. Rai (1992), *Business Communication*, Bombay: Himalaya Publishing House, p. 3.

Singhal, D.D., V.K. Mittal, N.C. Gara and V.S. Vyas (2006), *Business Communication and Management*, Jaipur: Indus Valley Publications, p. 3.

Ibid., pp. 22-23.

Chapter 4
Essentials of Organizational Communication

Introduction

After the Second World War many countries in the world became politically independent and established several educational, political, economic, social and cultural organizations. Public and private sectors came into existence in order to produce and distribute the goods and services for the consumption of people. In the new millennium several corporate houses are established in order to cater to the needs of people who matter most in a democratic society and business environment. Business is a socio-economic activity flourishing in a specific cultural ethos. Modern organizations cannot function effectively in the absence of multi-faceted communication strategies, resources and services in the age of competitive business. There are various stakeholders who are held in high esteem in modern business world. Practically, it is not possible for the business organizations to achieve their goals in the absence of mutually beneficial relationship between the organization and various stakeholders. Hence, organizational communication assumes great significance in modern society. The evolution of organizational communication, need for organizational communication, importance of communication in management, role of communication in business organizations, communication network of the organization, communication concerns of managers, communication training for managers and characteristics of successful organizational communication are enumerated in this Chapter.

Evolution of Organizational Communication

An organization is indeed 'a human community' that needs the contributions of everyone to function and be successful according to management guru Peter Drucker (1991: 11). Yates (1989: 32) documents the evolution of internal communications thus: "The period from 1850 to 1920 was one of great change in the size and structure of American firms. Before 1850, the economy was dominated by small firms owned and managed by a single individual or a partnership and operating in a local or regional market. In the early years of the twentieth century, it became clear that reliance on impersonal systems contributed to morale problems among workers and managers. The need to transcend reliance on the individual in favour of dependence on system became a central tenet of systematic management. The principles of systematic management entered public discourse early in the twentieth century. One of the tools that they used in humanizing the workplace was a new form of internal communications, the in-house magazine or shop paper. By the second decade of the twentieth century, committee meetings or 'shop conferences' of managers gained currency as a way to elicit necessary cooperation at the lower levels of management. Internal communications also played a role in reactions to the depersonalization of systematic management".

The spread of the telegraph and of railroads around the middle of the century encouraged firms to serve larger, regional and national markets in Europe and American continents. *Ad hoc* managerial methods worked well for small, owner-managed firms in a less competitive environment. The philosophy of modern management had not evolved in the early period. During the period from 1850 to 1920, formal internal communications emerged as a major tool of management, exerted toward the goal of achieving system and, thus, efficiency. By the end of that period, control through communication was a fact of life in the workplace all over the world.

The transformation in the nature, extent and role of economy was substantially complete by the end of First World War. The major elements of the modern economic, management and communication systems and the role of communication in management had been established by 1920. The managerial revolution in America and Europe occurred in the post-First World War. New concepts of development, management and communication also emerged. Several experiments took place in the art and craft of management in general and communication in particular. The industrial houses and business organizations were generally managed by *ad hoc* methods that require little formal internal communications until late nineteenth century.

In the beginning, internal communications were essentially the principal tools for managerial control. Richard Edwards, for example, defines it narrowly as "the ability of capitalists and/or managers to obtain desired work behaviour from workers." For him, control is exercised only in relation to low-level workers and is essentially coercive in nature. Beniger, another scholar uses control in a very broad sense, as "purposive influence towards a predetermined goal." In the middle of the twentieth century, there was emergence of systematic management to replace *ad hoc* management which was a major force driving the developing of formal internal communications. In the 1980s, corporate management and Corporate Communication emerged as new and advanced disciplines all over the world.

In the past, there were small business enterprises which were controlled and coordinated through informal internal communications principally by inter-personal communication channels such as word of mouth, letters, group meetings and so on. Today, massive corporations have come into being all over the world which are held together by networks of communication up, down and horizontal. The informal and primarily oral mode of interaction gave way to a complex and extensive formal communication system depending heavily on print, electronic and inter-personal modes of communication. Advanced communication technologies are also extensively used for the purpose of internal communications.

Organizational communications has become a challenging task of our times especially in organizations with a global presence where corporate headquarters is responsible for organizing intercommunications in geographically dispersed locations. A new bandwagon of corporate communicators has emerged over the years across the globe. They should be aware of the message and media which are appropriate in a given context. Today, employees are processing more information than ever before in respect of their organizations, projects, goals, objectives, challenges, opportunities and so on. Hence, multi-media are required to handle effectively organizational communication activities. Corporate communicators need to be aware of their receivers' habits and idiosyncrasies before deciding on message and media for organizational communication. A proper understanding of the attitudes, behaviours, needs and demands of the receivers will determine the best media to use in order to get the messages across the community of employees.

The evolution of Corporate Communication also received the attention of the historians and researchers across the globe. The revolutionary changes in communication, science and technology also had an impact on the processes of management and communication. These technological developments supported the growth of organizational communications. Thus, developments in managerial methods, communication technologies and communication genres brought about the evolution of organizational communications. Formal communication infrastructural facilities were built in modern organizations. Impersonal policies, procedures, processes, and orders flowed down the hierarchy. Internal communication also played a crucial role in the process of systematic organizational management and development.

Need for Organizational Communication

Communication was perceived as a bottleneck since certain technical issues were involved primarily in the process of organizational communication. Modern organizations are required to share good human relationship and social and economic rapport with various organizations in modern society. Any conflict of interest or discord with the stakeholders would be detrimental to the progress of the business organizations. The intervention of various stakeholders in the working of the business organizations is significant.

Most experts on organizations, management and leadership assert that effective communications is the foundation for sound organizational management. Internal Communication is required to unite all employees and motivate them to put forth integrated efforts toward the accomplishment of the goals of an organization. Internal Communications may be oral, written, face to face, virtual, one-to-one or in a small group. It is usually intended to facilitate harmonious relationship between the management and workers. In reality, internal communications is an instrument of employee relations which includes all communications within an organization.

Effective organizational communication consists of downward, upward and horizontal communication patterns which are vital means of addressing organizational concerns. Meaningful organizational communications helps to establish formal roles and responsibilities for the employees in particular. It also enables the management to identify strengths, weaknesses, opportunities and threats which help in the process of decision making and fosters the spirit of being together, working together and growing together in modern organizations.

In every organization, there are several stakeholders who play a major role in the process of organizational development. They include—employees, investors, suppliers, distributors, consumers, media professionals, government policy makers and officials, local publics and so on. The management is required to get into the good books of employees who are indeed the backbone of modern organizations. Employees should be taken into confidence by the management. Without their support and participation, modern organizations cannot communicate convincingly with the outside world. It is well-known that the root cause of most internal problems being faced by an organization often stems from ineffective communication. Internal communications has become a hot ticket in Corporate Communication. Experience reveals that employees who are better informed are more satisfied, feel more involved in the affairs of the organizations and ultimately contribute more to the success of the organization.

Redfield (1996: 24) puts it: "An organization consists of individuals and groups of people who have to interact with each other and who are required to work for a common organizational purpose. Communication is an important tool in sharing of ideas and purposes. Hence, an organization is required to have a healthy communications policy to facilitate the processes for achievement of its objectives".

An ideal management realizes that a satisfied and enthusiastic employee is an extremely effective and credible public relations advertisement. The employee relations assume great significance in the present times. The corporate leaders and communicators are required to identify the employee audiences for effective internal communication. Employee relations programmes should be designed on the basis of the organization's internal communications. Candid communications between management and employees is critical in this age of competitiveness. Internal communications must be targeted to reach out to specific sub-groups who broadly constitute 'Internal Publics or Employees'.

Modern organizational communication is also branded as 'corporate communication' regardless of the nature and activities of organizations—public and private. An organization has to enter into the good books of various publics and enlist their active participation in the process of institution building. Verma (2005: 30) comments: "Corporate Communication in most Indian organizations suffered from a clear imbalance. While there is a clear cut emphasis on external communication, which is aided by professional agencies, internal communication is always given the back seat, with very little planning, precision and professionalism. Hence, an organization is required to have a healthy internal communications policy to develop suitable internal communications system and deliver goods".

The employees play a crucial role in the production, distribution and other activities of modern organizations. The employees cannot be taken for a ride by the management in this age of people's participation. The employees should be taken into confidence by the management and persuaded to produce maximum goods and services under the challenging business environment. Seitel (1987: 25) observes: "The goal of any employee communications must be credibility. The task for management is to convince employees that it not only wants to communicate with them, but that it wishes to do so in a truthful, frank, and direct manner. The employee public is a savvy one. Employees cannot be conned because they live with the organization every day. They generally know what's going on whether management is honest with them or not. That's why management must be truthful". Internal communications assumes great significance since employees are important segment of modern organizations. The management cannot get the things done and achieve maximum success in the absence of effective internal communications which facilitates meaningful employee relations.

Turner (2004: 27) comments: "Employees are no different from any other public relations audience. The most important principle is that communications should be candid and complete. They should cover topics of primary concern to employees and use media which employees find most credible and desirable. Finally, a system of two-way communication should be used so that employees can express their sentiments. An effective communications programme can raise employee morale immensely. An employee who feels fully informed and who understands the strategies and circumstances of the organization is far more likely to be supportive of the organization's goals". Internal communications bridge the gap between the management and employees. It facilitates sustainable understanding and co-operation between the management and employees. Poor internal communications would bring down employee morale and participation in the affairs of the organization.

Hendrix (2001: 14) states: "Effective research on employee relations is built on an understanding of the client's personnel, the opportunity or problem that serves as a reason for communication with the work force, and the specific identification of the employee audiences to be targeted for communication. The principles of effective communications are virtually the same for employee relations as for most other forms of public relations, although two-way communication and audience participation should be stressed. Special events are an excellent way to employ these elements in employee relations. Evaluation of employee communication should refer back to each stated objective".

Organizational communications is an important component of organizational management in public and private sectors. The management should strive its best to increase employee knowledge of significant organizational policies, activities and developments, enhance favourable employee attitudes toward the organization, accomplish greater employee adoption of behaviours, make the employee force organizational spokespersons in the community and receive employee feedback from organizational communications according to Hendrix (2001: 14).

Dev (2005: 10) highlights the importance of internal communications thus: "Internal communication is essential for every organization. Internal communications is a vital tool for binding on organization, enhancing employee morale, promoting transparency and reducing attrition. Ironically, while everybody understands and talks about the significance of internal communications, very few are able to manage efficiently. Both the long-term and short-term fallout of ineffective internal communication can be damaging for an organization. It can start from the spread of rumours to disillusionment among employees to a gradual destruction of the company's brand image. Worse, it may also lead to the slow death of the organization".

McNamara (2007: 20) enumerates the key principles to effective organizational communication thus: The organization will remain stilted if the management does not comprehend and fully support organizational communication, effective internal communications start with effective skills and communication (basic skills in listening, speaking, questioning and sharing feedback), sound meeting management skills enhance the effectiveness of communication and organizational leaders, managers and supervisors should develop effective communication skill and responsibility.

Rockwell International, an internationally reputed organization identifies the goals of organizational communications which include: to keep all communications understandable and to avoid ambiguity or lack of clarity, to communicate regularly and not just in crisis situations, to provide completely reliable information and to present all the facts needed to arrive at a reasonable judgement, to disseminate information—particularly about changes—in advance of, not after, the fact when possible, to communicate on the basis of what employees want to know about their company and their jobs; and to provide information helpful to employees in understanding and performing their job responsibilities, to recognize the accomplishments and contributions of employees, to clarify the reasons for policies and procedures; and to build an understanding of the economic 'facts of business life' required for a successful operation, to stimulate awareness on the part of employees that the company has a sincere interest in their security and well-being, to help develop a sense of employee pride in association with a progressive company, to encourage employee aid in the company's support of worthwhile community projects and civic affairs, to encourage employees to express attitudes and opinions; and to provide the interest for a free flow of information both upward and downward; and to present a continuing overview of company products and operations so employees are knowledgeable about their company.

Turner (2004: 27) further elaborates the role of top management in organizational communications. It reads: "Top management must be involved in employee communications at least to the extent of giving their full support to the communications process and to the release of important information that employees need to know. If management is even more involved in employee communications, the communicator should use that participation intelligently. The communicator should honestly assess the strengths and weaknesses of individual top managers and design and implement appropriate communications activities to use the top managers' time and energy most effectively". Top management is indeed the driving force of organizational development in general and boosting the morale and performance of employees in particular. Hence, their full-fledged participation in developing appropriate internal communications would go a long way in boosting the progress of the organization and promoting the welfare of the employees.

Center and Jackson (2003: 06) reveal the benefits of employee participation thus: "The benefits of mutually satisfactory employee-employer relations are significant. There are fewer work stoppages, less absenteeism, higher productivity, and fewer errors. Practitioners are called on to participate more or less continuously in four phases of an employee's work experience, namely, the start (recruiting programmes or help-wanted advertising, orientation sessions, tours, or kits of information), on-the-job working conditions (employee publications, bulletin boards, feedback systems, training meetings, morale boosters, surveys of attitudes, complaint sessions and teleconferencing), rewards and recognition (award programmes, implementation of employee participation in civic affairs, staging of political science or economic education events, old-timers' parties, open houses, wage increases or bonuses, promotions, annual reports to employees, and so on) and work stoppage or termination (communications in a strike, lay off, boycott problems, news about benefits for retirees, a retiree publication, projects to help laid-off employees relocate, or exit interviews). It is apparent that the most important people are those at the bottom—the front liners. They make the product, deliver the service, sell the goods, and provide essential support mechanisms. In short, they more than anyone are the organization".

Vita (2007: 31) observes: "Internal communications measurement is critical to understanding the attitudes and opinions of the employees who are the most important assets of an organization". Modern organizations are required to develop appropriate internal communications measurement tools in consultation with the experts in Corporate Communication. Constant evaluation of internal communications brings about qualitative improvement of the tools, techniques and resources of internal communications.

Bacal (2007: 02) identifies the advantages of internal communications thus: "It permits employees to make more decisions online since they have the tools and knowledge needed to make the "right" decisions, encourages a sense of identification, on the part of staff, with the goals, mission and procedures of the organization, which can result in a sense of "making a difference", has the potential for reducing day-to-day conflict and helps staff feel a part of the organization". Identification of the common culture needed, available communication tools, determination of suitable communication tools, description of how to use the communication tools, planning for remediation, planning for implementation, actual implementation and continuous monitoring and revision of internal communications tools and techniques constitute the outline of ICP steps according to Bacal.

Kallan (2006: 15) states: "The multi-disciplinary and multi-level perspective to organizational communications is generally termed as integrated internal communications. A multi-disciplinary perspective refers to incorporation of different communication internal disciplines (organizational, corporate, management and business communication) and also the inclusion of communication external disciplines (management and international business). A multi-level perspective refers to the incorporation of all formal and informal communication taking place internally at all levels of an organization".

An educated employee is a valuable team member. The positive corporate culture starts at the top and the generosity of management extends beyond employees to customers. The employees who genuinely care about each other and the organization take extra steps to ensure customer satisfaction. The top management is fully responsible for developing constructive internal communications system in the organization. The more employees know about their corporations, the better equipped they are to provide valuable input for the overall progress of the organization.

Meaningful organizational communication strategies and activities encourage effective communication and real team work which are the prerequisites to the progress of the organization. The employees and other stakeholders should be properly informed, educated, counselled and guided at various stages of their service in the organization through appropriate organizational communications tools, media, strategies and activities. This would bring the stakeholder always closer to the management and enhance their active participation in the process of organizational development. Successful corporations create a work force that understands the mission, goals, values and procedures of the organization. The ultimate goal of organizational communications is to aim the employees and other stakeholders at a set of common goals on which they can act effectively every day. This brings coherence to the work place and allows better coordinated action for sustainable organizational development.

Importance of Communication in Management

Effective communication is a very important factor in every aspect of life in general and organizational management in particular. Most of the time in modern organizations is spent on communication either verbally, listening, reading and writing. Besides this, communication is given secondary importance and most of the managements do not properly handle communication with the employees and other stakeholders. With the rapidly changing global economy, advanced organizational communication has become a necessity for all the stakeholders including employees in modern organizations.

Bartlett and Ghoshal (2002: 03) highlight the organizational communication right thus: "In today's organization, most managers understand the strategic implications of the information-based, knowledge-driven and service-intensive economy. They know what the new game requires: speed, flexibility and continuous self-renewal. They even are recognizing that skilled and motivated people are central to the operations of any company that wishes to flourish in the new age".

Turner (2004: 27) emphasizes the role of communication in modern organizations thus: "The return on investment in communication can be significant and lead to a contribution to success. It is now recognized as a dynamic two-way flow rather than a unidirectional passing on of information. This means giving a voice as well as ears to employees. It means satisfying the media and the city about the efficacy of the organization's people strategy and practice. And it means satisfying the board as to the wisdom of its investment in the organization's human capital. Yet we still have divergent views about what we mean by communication and the value of dealing with communication issues in a strategic way. We have to understand the contribution of organizational communication in the process of human resources management. Effective communication for the HR professional will require a refinement of the knowledge, skills, attitudes and behaviours that have been necessary to date".

Venkataraman (1995: 29) identifies the purposes of communication in modern organizations as follows:

1. Communication acts as a basic foundation of management since it provides the key to facilitate the exchange of ideas, information as well as meeting of minds.
2. Communication plays a vital role in planning the organizational activities. The making of a plan requires facts and figures which can only be made available through effective communication.
3. The formal organizational structure hinges on an effective communication system. Informal communication within the organization is responsible for holding together the members of a primary social group.
4. Communication also plays a pivotal role in rational decision making, organizational control, as well as building and maintenance of employees' morale.

Smythe (2002: 26) recalls the importance of the internal communications thus: "Internal communications becomes harder, though, because of changes in the world of work over the past few years. This means that employees are no longer locked-in lifers subject to command and control management. They are mobile, informed and less likely to put up with superficial communications claptrap. They will demand to know what's going on, where the organization is heading and what role they have in it. The internal communicator now has to play a major part in providing this information, not as a photocopier of information but as an adviser with teeth".

Constant communication between the employer and employees actually minimize the usual conflicts between these two parties in modern organizations. The employees must be motivated to work for organizational goals rather than personal goals. They must also have adequate opportunities to influence and determine organizational goals and be motivated to work for them. The top management should lay emphasis on collaboration and team building which would change the potential courses of conflicts into positive forces for better organizational management. Appropriate internal communication patterns and practices are very essential to achieve corporate goals and objectives.

In a changing business environment, the employees are more mobile than ever before. Modern organizations are also more competitive in a global market-place. There is an increasing need to stay in touch with people and exchange information, ideas and expertise. With the rapidly changing world economy, organizational communication has become a necessity for the employers and employees. In particular, the internal communications within the organizations is primarily responsible for holding the employees together and get the things done in a congenial atmosphere. The usual 'chain of command' is 'line of communication' is not completely successful in carrying forward the employees toward progress either individually or organizationally. Systematic internal communications which is downward, upward and horizontal is a vital means of achieving organizational integration, harmony, coordination, control and progress.

Organizational communication is practiced all over the world as an effective instrument of establishing mutually beneficial rapport between the organizations and constituent publics. Internal communications has become an important component of organizational communication. The managements have realized that the practice of internal communications needs constant experimentation and enrichment. The professionals are aware that they must shape up or ship out especially in this age of competitiveness. Organizational communication research is a total endeavour which calls for systematic evaluation of organizational communication in terms of set-up, infrastructural facilities, human resources, technologies, agenda setting, strategy making, planning, programming, and implementation. Organizational communicators have agreed that research is an integral part of the organizational communication.

Internal communications is an important component of organizational communication which enables the employees to understand the organization's culture, obligations, responsibilities and challenges. It also brings the management and employees nearer and dearer. It provides the employees unique opportunities to express their point of view besides understanding their role in the process of organizational development. Several tools, media and resources are utilized for the purpose of internal communications. Professionals who are well versed in the art and craft of organizational communication including internal communications are recruited to handle the internal communications which creates suitable opportunities for interactions between the management and employees.

Globalization of Indian economy has resulted in the entry of multinational corporations who found abundant market scope in India. Corporate management and communication scenario have undergone revolutionary changes in India. Indian corporate sector has realized the importance of organizational communication in general and internal communications in particular. The emerging trends and development in the global economic environment and the corresponding transition in the management and communication policies in India have made the managements realize the importance of organizational communication in age of competitive business.

Communication scenario in Indian corporate sector is quite encouraging in the present times. Internal communications continue to be an area of concern both to the employers and employees. The practice of organizational communication continues to confront the Indian corporate sector every moment. These factors bear eloquent testimony to establish the important role internal communications is likely to play on the survival and development of public and private undertakings in the new millennium in a developing country like India.

Role of Communication in Business Organizations

An era of globalization of economy began in the last quarter of the twentieth century. Globalization of economy also became a full-fledged activity in the 1990s. Globalization of Indian economy has resulted in the entry of multinational corporations which enjoyed abundant market scope in India. Rapid expansion of Indian economy in general and public and private undertakings in particular took place with the entry of multinational corporations. These undertakings evolved and introduced new concepts of management of which Corporate Communication is an important dimension.

Following Fayol and Taylor's principles of scientific management, the emphasis shifted to maximizing productivity and competitiveness by optimizing the utilization of capital resources and human resources. Effective Human Resources Management (HRM) started with Elton Mayo's Human Relations thought which put a greater emphasis on organizational communication. A new discipline called Corporate Communication emerged on account of rapid strides in economy, management and information technology which necessitated greater research in this area. In this context, organizational management and Corporate Communication forms an inevitable link among the corporate body and constituent publics.

The need for self-expression is inevitable in the present times in all modern organizations in the age of globalization. Corporate Communication helps establish a mutually beneficial relationship between the management and employees on the one hand and between the organization and stakeholders on the other hand. In a world that constantly grows complex, sophisticated and even bigger, the need for two-way persuasive Corporate Communication becomes more inevitable in the modern society. In a democratic society, the constituent publics have a right to information, right to participation, right to agitation and right to empowerment. Hence, Corporate Communication provides opportunities for meaningful dialogue between the government and people in general and between modern organizations and various stakeholders in particular. The harmonious functioning of government and corporate houses demands organized Corporate Communication.

Corporate Communication serves a variety of organizations in modern times. It is an approach to problems by itself. Any modern organization that deals with various publics has a need for Corporate Communication. Today, political parties, religious institutions, cultural organizations, voluntary organizations, education institutions, business organizations, industrial organizations, trade unions, government organizations, NGOs—all need systematic and sustainable Public Relations activities which are now broadly practiced as Corporate Communication. The tools of Corporate Communication include—publicity, propaganda, lobbying, advertising, persuasion, etc.

Corporate Communication plays an important role in modern organizations. It is necessary to understand the stakeholders in modern society. Prominent among them include—employees, shareholders, suppliers, distributors, consumers, media professionals, government servants, local citizens and so on. Corporate Communication has emerged over the years as a prominent management function that brings modern organizations closer to various stakeholders who matter most in this age of competitiveness. It enables modern organizations and constituent publics to maintain mutually beneficial relationships.

The British Institute of Public Relations defined the function of Public Relations which is now vigorously practiced as Corporate Communication as an effort to establish and maintain mutual understanding between an organization and its publics. Modern organizations cannot achieve their goals in the absence of active and willing participation of various stakeholders in their affairs.

Cutlip *et al.* (2004: 08) have emphasized the need and importance of Corporate Communication thus: "Organizational adjustment as the outcome of Public Relations suggests a management level, policy influencing role and calls for corrective action in addition to communication". Corporate Communication is not merely confined to that of presenting the points of view of the organization but to prevail upon the leaders of the organization to reconcile or adjust in the public interest those aspects of corporate behaviour which have a social significance.

Baskin *et al.* (1977: 04) emphasize the role of Corporate Communication thus: "In a complex global society, business, government, non-profit and other organizations must have people who can communicate the needs of the organization to its various constituents and, at the same time, communicate the concerns of those publics back to the organization. In this environment of rapid social change, every organization must evolve or die. Corporate Communicators must possess the communications expertise and social sensitivity necessary to help organizations adopt to their changing environments". Corporate Communication is required to establish, maintain and sustain mutually acceptable and rewarding relationships between the organization and its various publics. Without effective people-friendly, cause-oriented, mission-oriented and progress-oriented Corporate Communication it is not possible to achieve progress in this age of competitiveness.

Corporate Communication is an art and science of developing a reciprocal understand, goodwill, co-operation and support between modern organizations and stakeholders. It facilitates image building, institution building, nation building, problem solving, crisis management and other challenging tasks of modern times. Corporate Communicators are required to gain absolute knowledge, experience, expertise and competence in order to cope with various needs, challenges and demands.

Hence, modern organizations require specialists in various aspects Corporate Communication in the age of competitiveness.

Communication Network of the Organization

Communication occupies an enviable status in the process of organizational management. Organization primarily depends upon the communication skills and competence which constitute an important aspect of effective management. Organizational communication is the system by which production and distribution operations are effectively communicated and carried out. Organizational relationships are developed and maintained through interpersonal communication which forms the basis for effective management of modern organizations.

Communication forms the basis of mutual understanding and cooperation between the management and members of the organization. In every organization, effective communication is fundamental to its existence and sustainable development. The process of coordination becomes ineffective in the absence of communication planning and execution. Communication and control are mutually dependent factors in modern organizations. The top management cannot control the middle management, lower management and employees in the absence of effective communication. The goals and targets should be meaningfully communicated to the lower layers of the organization.

Peter Drucker highlights the importance of communication in business thus: “Colleges teach the one thing that is perhaps most valuable for the future employees to know. But very few students bother to learn it. This one basic skill is the ability to organize and express ideas in writing and speaking. As soon as you move one step from the bottom, your effectiveness depends on your ability to reach others through the spoken or the written word. And the further away your job is from manual work, the larger the organization of which you are an employee, the more important it will be that you know how to convey your thoughts in writing or speaking. In the very large organization, this ability to express oneself is perhaps the most important of all the skills a person can possess”.

Several scholars and professionals have rightly stated that good communication is necessary in order to continually apply research findings and improve business operations. Organizational communication categories of a business organization consist of—internal-operational communication, external-operational communication and personal communication according to Lesikar *et al.* (2011: 19). All the communication that occurs in conducting work within a business is internal operation. This is the communication among the business's workers that is done to create, implement and track the success of the business's operating plan. The work related communicating that a business does with people and groups outside the business is external operational communication. This is the business's communication with its publics—suppliers, service companies, customers, government agencies, the general public and others. Personal communication is mainly concerned with the management of day to day business operations. Although not an obvious part of the business's plan of operation, personal communication can have a significant effect on the success of that plan. When wisely undertaken, it makes business more successful, pleasant and fulfilling according to the scholars.

Communication in the organization is the heart and soul of management. Two-way communication is essential for the flow of information from the top to the bottom and from the bottom to the top of the organization. It is also essential to facilitate horizontal flow of information in order to prevent delay in communication and performance of duties and responsibilities within the organization. The top management and others associated with the supervisory structure of the organization cannot motivate the employees without effective internal communication to deliver the goods and services in a competitive environment. The employees should be educated about the competitive business environment in order to prepare grounds, implement the programmes and deliver the goods with utmost efficiency. Sound organizational communication also helps to project good image in the eyes of the public.

Modern organizations depend on communication in order to reach out to various publics and enlist their active cooperation support for business promotion and organizational development activities. Perry (2002: 23) highlights the importance of communication thus: "To stand out from the competition, you must demonstrate the unwritten requirements that are now most in demand—leadership and communication skills". Undoubtedly, modern competitive business environment demands competent leaders and creative communicators who can race against the time and achieve the goal of business promotion under the challenging circumstances.

There is a high correlation between organizational development and effective communication according to the empirical evidence. Professional communicators are called upon to assume the multi-faceted role in modern organizations since image building and reputation management activities have to be carried out on round the clock basis in modern society. Effective coordination of the activities of many groups of people ranging from employees to media professionals demands good communication skills.

Don Zatyko states: "Communication is the most used skill in almost every job. How you communicate your accomplishments to others is a reflection of the quality of your work. Sure, you must know how to do your tasks to accomplish great results, but that is only a portion of professional success. Good communication skills are required to report your results to others, persuade colleagues to take action and (most importantly at review time) sell your successes to management". In the present times, organizational communication matters most from the point of view of successful management of issues, events and results. Effective communication produces rich dividends from organizational development point of view.

Mark Federighi observes: "Communication is essential to building trust and teamwork among employees. To become a successful leader, you must have a great team. Just look at Michelangelo. He didn't paint the Sistine Chapel by himself, but with the help of his team. It is considered one of the best works in history. It is all about the team". The success of any organization primarily depends upon team work, coordination and integration of efforts. All these activities precisely call for creative communication and leadership development which go hand in hand in modern business world.

The organizational communication can be classified into upward communication, downward communication and horizontal communication according to the principle of direction. Upward communication denotes the flow of information from the lower level to the higher level. Downward communication is the flow of information through the organizational structure level by level, i.e., from higher level to the lower level. Horizontal communication denotes the flow of information horizontally between personnel in one division and personnel of equal, lower or superior status in other divisions.

In modern organization, several channels of communication are used for the purpose of establishing meaningful rapport between the management and employees regardless of their status. They include—oral communication, written communication, audio-visual communication, and new media of communication. The organizational communicators are also required to practice external communication which is very vital to the existence and sustenance of the organization concerned. External communication is the transmission of information to the people outside the organization and its receipt from outsiders. The shareholders, suppliers, distributors, consumers, government officials, media professionals, local public and others constitute the external publics. Modern organizations should keep in constant touch with the external publics who also matter most from the point of view of organizational development.

In every organization, formal and informal communication systems have to be built over a period of time in order to enlist the active participation of the employees in the decision making, institution building, image building, reputation management, sales promotion, events management, crisis management and other processes. Formal communication is the transmission of direction of information in the formal organizational structure namely top to bottom. Every business organization is a well established formal network of communication. Lesikar *et al.* (2011: 19) state that the bulk of the communication flows through formal channels which include—upward, lateral and downward movement of information in the form of reports, memos, e-mail and such within the organization. It also includes the downward movement of orders, instruction, advisories and announcements. It further involves the broad dissemination of company information through the organizations newsletter, bulletin boards, e-mail, intranet or portal; and the channelling of company information out to its various publics in forms of external operational communication. These officially sanctioned lines of communication cause certain forms of communication, or *genres,* to exist within the organization.

Informal communication is the transmission of messages between members of a group on the basis of informal relations and understanding among people in a flexible and friendly working environment. According to Lesikar *et al.* (2011: 19) the informal communication network comprises the thousands upon thousands of personal communication that may or may not support the formal communication network of a business. Such communications follow no set pattern; they form an ever-changing and infinitely complex structure linking the members of the organization. Typically, it is really not a single network but a complex relationship of smaller networks consisting of certain groups of people.

Lesikar *et al.* (2011: 19) enumerate the three context for organizational communication namely—organizational context, professional context and personal context. According to them, the larger context includes the general business—economic climate, the language, the values and customs in the surrounding culture: and the historical moment in which the communication is taking place. The relationship of the communicators also forms an important context for organizational communication. The type and culture of the organization have a bearing on the organizational context and shape the communication choices in many ways. The professional roles assumed by the organizational communicators also impact the content and language of organizational communication from the professional context point of view. The family, education, religion, culture and other factors are associated with the personal context of organizational communication.

The process of communication in a business organization normally consist of ten basic stages namely: (a) sensing a need for communication, (b) defining the situation, (c) considering possible communication strategies, (d) selecting a course of action, (e) composing the message, (f) sending the message, (g) receiving the message, (h) interpreting the message, (i) deciding on a response and (j) replying to the message according to Lesikar *et al.* (2011: 19).

The organizational communicators are required to develop absolute clarity of thought and deed from communication point of view. They should primarily develop a perspective of organizational communication on the basis of the assessment of the communication needs of various stakeholders. The communicators should also develop a well informed sense of communication situation in order to deliver the message through proper media, format and contents. They should also develop appropriate communication strategies which suit the organizational context and beneficiaries' context. Selection of an appropriate course of action also assumes great significance in order to facilitate optimum utilization of resources and elicit favourable response from the internal and external publics. Message formulation also plays a major role in the process of communication since the quality and creativity of the message makes lot of difference from the point of view of facilitating mutual understanding between the source and receivers. Dissemination of the messages through proper media selection strategy should be undertaken by the organizational communicators in order to solicit the cooperation and support of various stakeholders. The receivers should be enabled to receive the right message in right time through right channel.

The receivers should also be motivated to interpret the messages in the right spirit in order to avoid any communication barrier between these two parties. The receiver should also be adequately persuaded to respond positively to the message through proper understanding, goodwill and confidence. The receivers should also be enabled to provide proper feedback in order to facilitate the delivery of goods or modification of the approaches to business transactions. Thus, organizational communication should be practiced with utmost care, concern and responsibility in order to avoid communication gap, conflict of interest and other setbacks. The process of organizational communication should invariably be subjected to scientific evaluation of the impact of communication and improvement of business transactions.

In the new millennium, corporate social responsibility is widely discussed and debated. The process of globalization brings in its wake global norms of business behaviour in general and protection of public interest in particular. Business communicators should develop a positive approach by taking into account the ethical dimension of organizational communication. The organizational communication activities need to be justified professionally and ethically since marketing and sales are related to truth, honesty and social responsibility. Modern organizations are required to develop specific forms of organizational communication that enable them to get their work done and safeguard public interest. In reality, organizational communication in business organizations involves ethics.

Communication Concerns of Managers

Management is generally defined as a unified, organized and coordinated system of conduction of organizational affairs in order to achieve the common goals. Communication cements all kinds of gaps between the management and other internal publics. Chaturvedi and Chaturvedi (2012: 07) state: "Communication is the system by which production and distribution operations are controlled and coordinated and the results correlated to the objectives. The unity of purpose and commitment to a single organizational goal can be developed only through the persuasive power of communication".

The size of the organization also matters from communication management point of view. The large size of organizations poses problems in communication on account of greater production, distribution, collaboration and other activities. New communication technologies are also developed in order to facilitate instantaneous and interactive communication in modern organizations. The employees are also duly considered as the human components of business and the need for live channel of communication between the management and employees has increased over a period of time regardless of the size and operations in modern organizations.

Experts have stated that good organizational communication system is vital for the sustainable development of modern organizations. The management can also create a healthy working atmosphere if the decision making is transparent, delivery system is accountable and a sense of belonging is created among the employees. Pratt and Whitney observe: "The most important audience for a company's communications is not the customer, as is commonly believed, but the employee". The management should also enable the employees to understand the realities of the business and develop the sense of accountability. The conflict of interest between the management and employees should also be resolved through participatory communication and management programmes.

In the changing business environment of economic liberalization, privatization and globalization, communication has become an important component of organizational management. Communication has also emerged as equally important organizational function like production, distribution, personnel management, resource mobilization, finance management, marketing and so on. All organizational activities are brought under the single umbrella of corporate communication which is known for multi-directional and multi-faceted activities. In this integrated form, corporate communication is directed at image building, reputation management, events management, crisis management, marketing management, sales promotion, employee relations, supplier relations, investor relations, distributor relations, consumer relations, government relations, media relations, community relations, cultural relations and allied organizational functions. Communication has emerged as an important too in the successful management of various organizational activities.

Modern organizations can function without conflicts and crises if there is a democratic, friendly, flexible and working atmosphere. Besides this, the success of an organization primarily depends on the free flow of information—upward, downward and horizontal. The top management is responsible for the organization and implementation of effective communication system across the organization on round the clock basis. The managers should also the enabled to cultivate better communication skills and leadership qualities. A sound system of communication should be established within the organization by the management.

Mintzberg (1973: 21) has pointed out those managers need effective communication skills to perform interpersonal role, informational role and decisional role. The interpersonal role refers to situations in which the manager acts as a figurehead, leader and liaison officer. Interpersonal role is necessary to ensure effective operation of the organization's systems and to maintain proper relationships within the organizations and with clients, suppliers and other functionaries. The informational role refers to situations in which the manager acts as a monitor, disseminator and spokesperson. Proper maintenance of product and service standards can be ensured through timely monitoring and structuring activities through interactive communication and feedback mechanism. The decisional role refers to situations in which the manager acts as an entrepreneur, troubleshooter, resource allocator and negotiator. The managers should acquire relevant information, upgrade their information and apply the information inputs in day to day situations for the purpose of smooth functioning of the system.

Communication needs to be practiced in every organization in order to fulfil the human needs of the people who constitute the workforce. The employees should be enabled to fulfil their physiological needs such as food, shelter, protection, harmony and so on. The security and safety needs of the employees should also be fulfilled by the management. The social needs of the employees such as love, respect, recognition, participation and belongingness should also be considered as primary needs by the management. The ego needs of the employees are related to the right of the employees for promotion, progress and betterment of professional standards should be fulfilled by the management. The self actualizing needs of the employees to reach highest status in the profession, organization and society should also be fulfilled by the management. The role of communication in the fulfilment of the human needs of the employees should be appreciated by the management and the managers should be encouraged to identify these needs of the employees through close interaction and fruitful human relations.

Drucker (1991: 11) had discussed the human side of enterprise with reference to traditional view of human capital and modern view of satisfying the needs of the employees. The traditional approach to management focused mainly on getting the things done by the employees rather than caring for job satisfaction, job security and job promotion aspects of the employees. The modern approach to management considers the employees as human capital and addresses the fulfilment of their higher level needs. The communication focus in this context shifts from the language of control and information to that of motivation and persuasion. In every organization, communication matters since it brings the management and employees together and facilitates smooth functioning of the organization.

The managers are required to learn the art and craft of communication since it is rightly considered as a means of empowerment of people. The managers should also develop necessary skills of using traditional and modern tools and technologies of communication. The managers should be aware of conducting meetings, seminars, conferences, group discussions, presentations, negotiations, exhibitions, demonstrations and other communicative exercises inside and outside the organizations. Managers can deliver the goods and services if they are aware of their communicative duties, obligations and approaches. The managers are called upon to create the desired human relationship with the employees in order to elicit favourable response.

The communication concerns of the manager are widely discussed in the age of corporate communication. The manager spends most of his time in speaking, writing, supervising, controlling, coordinating and integrating functions which fundamentally involve communication skills and competence. The success of a manager primarily depends on how actively he/she interacts with the subordinates and persuades them to deliver the goods and services in a congenial atmosphere. The manager also functions as a bridge between the top management and employees in general and between his branch and other branches of organizational activities.

Communication basically involves human relations which matters considerably in the management of modern organizations. Practically, communication primarily deals with human relationships that exist between the management and employees. The establishment and maintenance of positive human relations is essential to successful organizational management. The managers should be enabled to adapt their messages to the intended recipients. The managers should learn the technique of adopting the language of communication to the employees. Modern organizations develop specific communication forms, contents and strategies that enable them to get the things done in a congenial work atmosphere.

Modern organizations cannot achieve commendable progress in the absence of sustainable communication with various stakeholders who are at the giving end socially, culturally, politically and economically. The subject of organizational communication is of paramount importance because the outlook of the organizations and other stakeholders has significantly changed in the age of globalization. Modern organizations face several challenges in the age of economic transformation and technological revolution they have to keep communication as a key performance indicator for all their managers and workers. They have to understand the need to connect with the various stakeholders, understand key issues and address these issues at the earliest, observe Mukerjee (2013: 22).

Communication Training for Managers

Managers are called upon to understand the elements that form the structure of an organizational communication network and operations at different levels. It is not possible to facilitate the healthy growth and smooth functioning of modern organizations without a well organized internal communication network and motivated team of organizational communicators. In a complex organization which has too many levels of operations and hierarchy, managers practically find it very difficult to facilitate interactive communication between the management and employees. Drucker (1991: 11) notes: "Large organizations have more recently moved towards a 'flatter structure' of information based management and executives 'walk down' the jobs. This is obviously to facilitate information flow downwards and to prevent employees from getting frustrated by their sense of isolation".

Nobody is born as a communicator. Communicators are indeed made in modern organization. They need proper education, training and orientation in the development of the art and craft of communication. There are more complexities in large organizations which have the internal and external publics who share heterogeneous groups. New communication technologies have emerged over a period of time and gained an upper hand over the traditional oral and written forms of organizational communication. In the world of competitive business, managerial success primarily depends upon the development of leadership qualities and communication skills.

Modern organizations have accorded importance to human resources management which includes communication skill and capacity development. Advanced institutions have realized the importance of communication skill development in the process of personality development. There are formal and informal courses in communication skill development regardless of the nature of organizational size, system and operations. Modern universities and educational institutions have designed training courses and workshops for the development of communication skill of modern managers. Specialists are involved as resource persons in order to develop the communication skills which are essential for smooth coordination, control and supervision of organizational activities. These communication courses and programmes are based on simulating real work and life situations in the workplace and elsewhere. The young generation of students is also taught the art and craft of communication in the colleges and universities in order to improve their personality, leadership quality and managerial competence.

Characteristics of Successful Organizational Communication

In Communist countries agriculture, industry, health, education, transportation, communication and other spheres of national economy are organized under public sector. In those countries, there is absolutely no scope for privatization of economy. In a democracy, there is mixed economy. Both public and private sectors are encouraged to grow in a democratic society. In India, there is mixture of public and private sectors as far as national economy are concerned. The Constitution of India too has duly paved the way for the advancement of public and private sectors in the post-Independence era. The State and Central Governments own, manage and control the public sector undertakings while the independent persons or agencies own, manage and control the private sector undertakings in India and other democratic societies.

In any organization, there is a need for congenial internal working atmosphere. The management and employees are required to share meaningful and cordial human relations. The management cannot take the employees for granted. The employees should also remain loyal and extend whole hearted support to the management in order to ensure healthy growth and development of the organization. The management is primarily responsible for creating a congenial and competitive working atmosphere by cementing all communication gaps between the organization and employees. The management cannot function always in an ivory tower. The employer cannot also always remain in the cabin. The management and employees are required to cultivate better human relations and work together for the achievement of the goals of the organization. This kind of harmonious blending of organizational interest and employees interest naturally constitute 'internal relations' which is a must for the attainment of organizational development in a competitive environment.

Effective communication is a very important factor in every aspect of life in general and organizational management in particular. Communication is given secondary importance and most of the managements do not properly handle communication with the employees.

With the rapidly changing global economy, advanced organizational communication has become a necessity for all the stakeholders including employees in modern organizations.

Empirical evidence suggests that informed and updated employees and stakeholders are the pillars of modern organizations which cannot do away with their communication obligations and functions. It is important to communicate regularly with people in order to enlist their active participation in the institution building and business management processes. The modern business environment has become multi-cultural by nature and people from different regions and cultures are called upon to work together for the prosperity of the organization concerned. Hence, organizational communication is required to sustain the development of modern corporate houses on the basis of participative approaches.

Bartlett and Ghoshal (2002: 03) highlight the organizational communication right thus: "In today's organization, most managers understand the strategic implications of the information-based, knowledge-driven and service-intensive economy. They know what the new game requires: speed, flexibility and continuous self-renewal. They even are recognizing that skilled and motivated people are central to the operations of any company that wishes to flourish in the new age".

Turner (2004: 27) emphasizes the role of communication in modern organizations thus: "The return on investment in communication can be significant and lead to a contribution to success. It is now recognized as a dynamic two-way flow rather than a unidirectional passing on of information. This means giving a voice as well as ears to employees. It means satisfying the media and the city about the efficacy of the organization's people strategy and practice. And it means satisfying the board as to the wisdom of its investment in the organization's human capital. Yet we still have divergent views about what we mean by communication and the value of dealing with communication issues in a strategic way. We have to understand the contribution of organizational communication in the process of human resources management. Effective communication for the HR professional will require a refinement of the knowledge, skills, attitudes and behaviours that have been necessary to date".

Venkataraman (1995: 29) identifies the purposes of communication in modern organizations as follows.

1. Communication acts as a basic foundation of management since it provides the key to facilitate the exchange of ideas, information as well as meeting of minds.

2. Communication plays a vital role in planning the organizational activities. The making of a plan requires facts and figures which can only be made available through effective communication.
3. The formal organizational structure hinges on an effective communication system. Informal communication within the organization is responsible for holding together the members of a primary social group.
4. Communication also plays a pivotal role in rational decision making, organizational control, as well as building and maintenance of employees' morale.

Smythe (2002: 26) recalls the importance of the internal communications thus: "Internal communications becomes harder, though, because of changes in the world of work over the past few years. This means that employees are no longer locked-in lifers subject to command and control management. They are mobile, informed and less likely to put up with superficial communications claptrap. They will demand to know what's going on, where the organization is heading and what role they have in it. The internal communicator now has to play a major part in providing this information, not as a photocopier of information but as an adviser with teeth".

Constant communication between the employer and employees actually minimize the usual conflicts between these two parties in modern organizations. The employees must be motivated to work for organizational goals rather than personal goals. They must also have adequate opportunities to influence and determine organizational goals and be motivated to work for them. The top management should lay emphasis on collaboration and team building which would change the potential courses of conflicts into positive forces for better organizational management. Appropriate internal communication patterns and practices are very essential to achieve corporate goals and objectives.

The salient features of organizational communications include: transparency, openness, independence, clarity, timeliness, honestly and two-way communication. In the beginning, organizational communications were handled by the personnel management section. Today, organizational communications are handled by the Corporate Communication division. It is technically practiced under the banner of 'employee relations'. This division is indeed a moderator of interaction between the employer and employees. This division is also responsible for developing and maintaining various channels of organizational communications which include—inter-personal communication, institutional communication, new communication technologies and so on.

Karoli and Ahmad (2013: 16) identify three approaches to organizational communications which are as follows:

Arrow Approach: Communications are carefully constructed and aimed at a target audience. It assumes the more accurate the message, the clearer the understanding of the recipient. Problems arise when it is taken for granted that information is mostly transmitted by words and that recipients are passive receptors.

Circuit Approach: Communications are achieved with positive relationships and job satisfaction of employees through understanding and discussions. It assumes that communicating is grounded in mutual understanding. Problems arise because of the myopic view that understanding will lead to agreement and that this understanding should be the sole goal of organizational communications.

Dance Approach: Communications are achieved through an intricate combination of the practice, understanding and intuition. It believes that the communication involves the coordination of meanings, the understanding of common rules and the recognition of patterns between two or more people.

In this age of competitiveness, organizational communications should be managed scientifically since modern organizations require the active contribution of everyone to function and be successful. An overwhelming majority of the business organizations today are employees even though they function with different designations such as administrators, managers, supervisors and workers. Effective organizational communications is required to encourage everyone to think about the organization and his or her work. In a highly competitive economy, successful organizations are those that consider an organization as a human community and deliver goods and services in accordance with the felt needs and aspirations of the employees. Organizational communications is required to provide the communication channel between employers and employee groups since, it is important on both sides of the relationship. Organizational communication is required to facilitate two-way relationship building and communication system.

The foundations of management of organizational communication are enumerated by Center and Jackson (2002: 06) thus: 1. Employees must be told first, 2. Tell the bad news along with the group, 3. Ensure timeliness, 4. Employees must be informed on subjects they consider important and 5. Use the media that employees trust.

Organizational communications should be managed by the organizations according to tested and tried methods of management. Prioritization, planning, execution and evaluation are the foundations of internal communications management. Think tank, idea bank, scientific planning, systematic execution and monitoring and evaluation of internal communications would enrich the process and impact. The success of internal communications mainly depends on informational, attitudinal, behavioural and practical aspects of organizational communications management.

The tools of organizational communications can be classified into inter-personal, print, electronic and news media. On the job training, face-to-face meetings, group discussion, guidance, counselling, team briefing, seminar, open house, get-together, audio-visual presentations, speaker's bureaus and other interaction-*cum*-participation oriented exercises constitute inter-personal tools of organizational communications. House journal, brochure, leaflets, pamphlets, annual reports, training manuals, booklets, employee handbooks, bulletins and briefing notes, newsletters, special supplementary and other printed means constitute print media and tools of organizational communications. Inter-com, closed circuit TV, Internal television, newsreels, documentaries, video cassettes, teleconferences, telephone and other electronic means constitute electronic media and tools of organizational communications. Telephone, Fax, E-mail, Internet, video conferencing and other multi-media constitute news media and tools of organizational communications.

Organizational communications is part and parcel of corporate administration. It is an important branch of corporate management in the present times. The foundations and practices of organizational communications should be thoroughly grasped by the management and corporate communicators. Emerging trends and developments in the field of organizational communications should also be taken note of by both the parties. New experiments are also very essential to improve the quality of organizational communications. Tested and tried methods should also be adopted by the modern organizations. Quality-oriented organizational communications programmes mainly rely upon talented corporate communicators. Therefore, attracting excellent leaders who are good communicators should be a top priority for on organization. The tools of organizational communication should be consciously chosen. It is also important for the modern public and private undertakings to develop communication infrastructural facilities including employees-oriented website in order to make organizational communications an effective instrument of building modern organizations on the basis of meaningful human relations.

Conclusion

Modern organizations have become very large, complex and competitive over a period of time. Communication is indeed the life blood of modern organizations. Communication failures and break downs bring about conflict of interest between the management and stakeholders. There are several types of organizational communication. Participatory communication and management assume great significance in this age of competitive business. The most important aspect of organizational communication is the fact that it takes place in the world of reality that surrounds us. The organizational environment should be properly understood by the various stakeholders in terms of policies, programmes, goods, services, duties, responsibilities, obligations and so on. Modern managers are required to develop a sense of empathy, communication skills, leadership qualities and corporate social responsibility in order to carry the internal and external stakeholders together at all times.

References

Allen, R.K. (1977) *Organization Management through Communication*, Harper & Row, New York, U.S.A.

Bacal, Robert (2007) *Internal Communication Strategies—The Neglected Strategic Element*, Bacal & Associates, Ontario, Canada.

Bartlett, C.A. and Ghoshal, S. (2002) Building Competitive Advantage Through People, *MIT Sloan Review,* Vol. 43 (2), Winter, 2002.

Baskin, Otis, Craig Aronoff and Dan Lattimore (1997) *Preface to Public Relations: The Profession and the Practice*, Brown Benchmark Publishers, Madison, p. xiii.

Bhusan, Uma (2012) *Introduction to Business Communication*, Jaico Publishing House, Mumbai.

Center, Allen H. and Patrick Jackson (2002) *Public Relations Practices: Managerial Case Studies and Problems*, Sixth Edition, Prentice Hall of India Private Limited, New Delhi, India, p. 38.

Chaturvedi, P.D. and Mukesh Chaturvedi (2012) *Business Communication*, Chennai: Pearson, pp. 22-23.

Cutlip, Scott M., Allen H. Center and Glen M. Broom (2004), *Effective Public Relations*, Pearson Education Private Limited, Singapore, p. 6.

Davis, Keith and John Newstrom (1993) *Organizational Behaviour: Human Behaviour at Work*, New Delhi: Tata McGraw Hill, p. 399.

Dev, Sudipta (2005) The Importance of Internal Communication, *Weekly Insight for Technology Professionals*, www.expresscomputeronline.com, February 07, 2005.

Drucker, Peter F. (1991) *The New Realities*, New Delhi: Asian Books Private Ltd., p. 210.

Evans, Dave (2008) *Social Media Marketing*, New Delhi: Times Business Services, p. 31.

Hasan, Seema (2010) *Mass Communication: Principles and Concepts*, CBS Publishers and Distributors Pvt. Ltd., New Delhi.

Hendrix, Jerry A. (2001) *Public Relations Cases*, Fifth Edition, Wadsworth, U.S.A., pp. 108-113.

Kallan, Hanna (2006) *Integrated Internal Communications in the Multi-national Corporation*, Ph.D. Thesis, Robert Gordon University, Iso-Britannia, U.K.

Karoli, Veera and Naghma Ahmed (2013) *Business Communication*, Thakur Publishers, Bengaluru, India.

Kaul, Asha (2009) *Business Communication*, PHI Learning Private Limited, New Delhi.

Lehman, Carol, M., Devvie D., DuFrene, Mala Sinha and Robin C. Walker (2012) BCOM, *An Innovative Approach to Learning and Teaching, Business Communication, A South Asian Perspective*, Cengage Learning, New Delhi.

Lesikar, Raymond V., Marie E. Flatley, Kathryn Rentz and Neerja Pande (2011) *Business Communication—Making Connections in a Digital World*, Tata McGraw Hill Education Private Limited, New Delhi, pp. 6-9.

McNamara, Carter (2007) *Basics in Internal Organizational Communications*, In Field Guide to Leadership and Supervision, Authenticity Consulting, LLC.

Mintzberg, Henry (1973) *The Nature of Managerial Work*, New York: Harper Collins College Division.

Mukerjee, Hory Sankar (2013) *Business Communication: Connecting at Work*, Oxford University Press, New Delhi.

Perry, David (2002) Do you have the skills most in demand today? *The Wall Street Journal*, May 20, www.careerjournal.com

Redfield (1996) *Communication in Management*, Prentice-Hall, New Jersey, U.S.A., p. 17.

Seitel, Fraser P. (1987) *The Practice of Public Relations*, Third Edition, Merrill Publishing Company, Columbus, pp. 363-366.

Smythe, J. (2002) The Rise of the Internal Communicator, *Profile IPR Magazine*, May, 2002, pp. 41-48.

Turner, Paul (2004) *Organizational Communication: The Role of the HR Professional*, Jaico Publishing House, Mumbai, India, pp. 6-12.

Venkataraman, N. and Prescott, J.E. (1990) Environment-Strategy Coalignment: An Empirical Test of its Performance Implications, *Strategic Management Journal,* Vol. No. 11 (1), pp. 1-23.

Venkataraman, T.S. (1995) Communication in Management, *The Hindu,* September 23rd, 1995.

Verma, Pawan K. (2005) Effective Internal Communication, In Kushal, K.B., S. Ravishankar, H.L. Kaila and R.K. Mishra (Eds.) *Perspectives for Effective Management*, Himalaya Publishing House, Mumbai, India, pp. 114-119.

Vita, Emma De (2007) *Internal Communications Measurement*, J:/effective com. htm May 12, 2007. p. 1.

Yates, JoAnne (1989) *Control Through Communication: The Rise of System in American Management*, The Johns Hopkins Press Ltd., London, U.K., pp. 1-20.

Chapter 5
Oral Communication for Business Management

Introduction

Oral communication is also one of the types of business communication in modern organizations. The managers, supervisors, employees and corporate communicators depend on oral communication when they interact with the internal publics and external publics. Oral communication is also the oldest form of communication which preceded the written and electronic communication. In business organizations, oral communication is used more than written, electronic and other forms of business communication. Effective oral communication has the power to build good human interactions which make the fortunes of modern business organizations. The intercultural business communication situations also require thoughtful oral communication. The organizational leaders and communicators spend more time talking than writing in business world. The concept of oral communication, importance of oral communication skills, barriers to oral communication, principles of successful oral communication and intercultural oral communication are presented in this Chapter.

Concept of Oral Communication

Oral communication is the interchange of verbal messages between the communicator and receiver. It is also known as verbal communication which is known for immediacy, informality and naturality. The people gain oral communication skills over a period of time in their lives. Oral communication is also an intrinsic part of human development. The business executives and communicators spend most of their time on oral communication under normal circumstances. In business organizations talking, listening, committee meetings, group discussions, conferences, speeches, lectures, telephonic conversations and other kinds of oral communication occur on a regular basis. Oral communication is both formal and informal exercise which benefits both the parties in business organizations. Oral communication is primarily dependent on words which convey several ideas. The oral communication is a vital part of business communication.

Importance of Oral Communication Skills

The organizational leaders and communicators should understand the nature and importance of oral communication in business transactions. They must know when to choose oral communication instead of other forms of business communication. They should also learn the art and craft of oral communication and apply oral communication skills to new communication technologies also. The organizational leaders are basically the voice of the business organizations and they spend most of their times on oral communication in their day to day situations. These communicators should be able to rise to the occasion and build sound image for the organizational services and products in a competitive business environment.

Experience reveals that it does not matter what the organizational communicators say but rather, how effectively they put across things, convince people and persuade the stakeholders to accept the products and services of business organization. The business communication basically involves more oral communication which is face to face interaction between individuals or groups of individuals. The business communicator should be able to introduce, emphasize, elaborate, convince, negotiate and persuade the people who matter most from business promotion point of view.

Oral communication has two dimensions namely: (a) communication between the organizational leaders and employees, and (b) communication between the organizational communicators and constituent publics. The corporate leaders need effective oral communication skills in order to persuade the employees and get the things done. The employees also have a right to information, participation and progress in the modern democratic environment. The management also has the responsibility to ensure job security, job satisfaction and job promotion to the community of employees despite certain limitations. Constant dialogue and interaction between the management and employees are required to cement the communication gaps and foster better cooperation between these two parties.

The need for constant interaction between modern business organizations and constituent publics is ever increasing in the age of globalization. In the new millennium, people matter most. Modern business organizations should know how to develop mutually beneficial relationship between the organization and various publics. Conscious efforts are required to bring the various external publics closer to the mainstream of organizational life and enlist their active participation in the process of business promotion. Series of oral communication in different forms should be organized in order to facilitate rapport development between the organization and investors, suppliers, distributors, consumers, local community, government bodies, media institutions and other important segments of the society. Series of dialogues, conferences and other oral communicative opportunities have to be created in order to build a treasure house of goodwill which is greater than capital resource.

Formal Oral Communication

In modern business organizations, formal oral communications such as talking, listening, participating in meetings, talking by phone and dictating are carried out on day to day basis. The leaders and communicators spend most of their time in talking to various publics. Talking is defined as the oral expression of knowledge, view points and emotions through appropriate words which fit into the different contexts, observe Lesikar *et al.* (2011: 07). Talking replaces many of the body movements which facilitate better grasping of ideas and views. The elements of good talking include—voice quality, style, word choice and adaptation.

Oral communication becomes effective if the voice quality is good. The voice quality primarily includes the vocal sounds one hears when another speaks. The primary voice quality refers to the pitch and resonance of the sounds made by the speaker. Good voice quality facilitates better communication since it involves pitch, delivery speed and volume. The talking style also matters most especially in oral communication. It refers to how the three parts of voice quality—pitch, speed and volume blend together. These parts practically constitute the personality of the speaker and talking style refers to a set of voice behaviours that give uniqueness to a person.

The choice of words also matters most in oral communication. It is related to the vocabulary of the speaker. As far as possible, the communicator should make use of the words which are found in the vocabulary of the listeners. The communicators should select the words which appropriately convey the intended meaning in a given oral communication context. The effectiveness of oral communication also depends on the adaptation which means fitting the message to the needs of the intended listeners. Thus, oral communication is depended on voice quality, talking style, choice of words and adaptation of the speakers.

The business leaders and communicators also participate in formal and informal meetings and get together. The group discussions, committee meetings, conferences, feedback sessions and other formal occasions involve disciplined, deliberate and systematic oral communication. The leaders are assertive, but they treat others in a very formal way during the business discussions and transactions. The business leaders and communicators should be aware of the procedures and formalities of conducting business meetings. They should also adopt useful techniques of conducting meetings in the business organizations. They include—agenda setting, item by item discussion, complete discussion, coordinating discussion, active participation of the parties, control of time, summarizing the meeting and so on. The organizers and participants should understand each other's needs and demands and put across their views in the meetings without giving any scope for communication gap and conflict of interest.

The process of oral communication becomes ineffective in the absence of proper listening. The impatient, poor and inadequate listening hampers the oral communication and cause miscommunication. Listening is primarily an act of sensing sounds of the spoken words. The active listening basically involves sensing, filtering and remembering the points of view expressed by the organizers of formal meetings. The participants should listen to the communicators very carefully and remain attentive to their observations. The filtering is the process of giving symbols meanings through the unique contents of each person's mind. The listeners' minds serve as a sort of filter through which they derive meanings to the incoming messages. Filtering is also formed by certain contents of mind such as knowledge, emotions, beliefs, biases, experiences, expectations and so on. Remembering what the participants hear is the third activity involved in the process of listening. The participants should improve their listening ability in order to grasp the essentials of oral communication fully and properly. Listening also basically involves focusing the attention on the contents of the oral communication and reserving judgement.

Lesikar *et al.* (2011: 07) have referred to the ten commandments of listening which include—stop talking, put the talker at ease, so the talker you want to listen, remove distractions, empathize with the talker, be patient, hold your temper, go easy on argument and criticism, ask questions and grasp the essentials. The ultimate success of listening primarily depends on stop talking while listening. In every act of talking, the non-verbal communication also accounts for more of a total message than words do. The non-verbal communication includes communication without words. The body positions, movements and other factors constitute the non-verbal symbols which have several meanings. Practically, the non-verbal communication includes four major types such as body language, space, time and paralanguage.

The physical movements of the communicators while addressing the participants basically constitute the body language. In particular, the face, eyes, gestures, posture, physical appearance and other movements represent the body language. The human bodies send non-word messages through arms, fingers, expression, posture and so on. The appearance of human bodies during group meetings and public speeches also matters in the process of oral communication. The space is another type of non-verbal language. The space language is crafted by the culture of the group. There are four types of space which exists in an oral communication situation namely—intimate, personal, social and public. In each of these spaces, the communication behaviour differs and conveys different meanings. The time is a third type of non-verbal communication. In non-verbal communication, the time orientations also communicate several things. The organizers of meetings should be aware of the value of time and ensure that the events happen at scheduled times. The paralanguage is the fourth type of non-verbal communication which involves how the organizers communicate certain things with word symbols. It is the communication effect of the speed, pitch, volume and connectivity of spoken words. The paralanguage meanings are also conveyed by consistencies and inconsistencies which affect oral communication. As a matter of fact, consistency between the words the communicators choose and how they deliver them to the participants matters a lot from the point of view of better understanding. The active listeners always wish to listen between the lines of a spoken message to determine the true meaning a communicator is sending. The colour and physical context also communicate different meanings.

Public Speaking and Oral Reporting

Bhusan (2012) studied the elements and benefits of public speaking which enable the organizational leaders and communicators to make effective public presentations, convince the audience and obtain their support for the cause or mission. The scholar also identified certain personal, organizational, social and cultural benefits of public speaking in modern business environment. Determining the purpose, assessing the environment, identifying the needs of audience, gathering supportive information, organizing the presentation, utilizing appropriate presentation tools and aids, responding to the questions, convincing the audience and persuading the target group enhance the status of public speaking.

The corporate leaders and communicators are required to address various gatherings during different occasions in order to educate and persuade the stakeholders regarding the policies, programmes, products and services of the organizations. The art of public speaking cannot be acquired over night by the speakers. They have to constantly improve their public speaking skills and capacity on the basis of proper reading, understanding and interacting exercises. There are several techniques of cultivating better public speaking skills. They include—selection of appropriate topic, academic preparation, organization of the information, assessment of the needs of the participants, attention compelling introductory remarks, identification of salient features, presentation of key elements, interpretation of prominent points, utilization of quotable quotes, emphasizing the transitions between parts, summarizing the major aspects, presenting a fitting conclusion, receiving questions, clarifying important things, thanking the audience and so on.

Selection of Appropriate Topic

The business leaders and communicators should select appropriate topic which suits the time, context, environment and participants. The purpose of organizing the public function should be properly understood by the communicators who are the chief spokespersons of the business organizations. The context of the public function is the basis for the selection of topic for public speaking. The speakers should not waste their time and energy by choosing the wrong topic and emphasizing the irrelevant things which do not fit into the context of public speech.

Academic Preparation

The success of public speaking primarily depends upon the academic preparation made by the speakers. They must do serious research and reference works in order to obtain specific, relevant and adequate information on the topic concerned from authentic sources. The reliability, validity and credibility of the contents matter most from effective public speaking point of view. The speakers should also consult the veterans, specialists and other authorities in the subject concerned in order to procure right ideas and inputs for successful presentation in the lecture session.

Organization of the Information

The speakers should also organize the body of the speech under different concepts and compartments. This would prevent confusion in the minds of the audience while receiving knowledge, experience and expertise during public speech. The salient features of the subject of public speech should be identified and relevant facts and figures should be brought under each and every item. Meaningful organization of the contents enhances the credibility of the speaker.

Assessment of the Needs of the Participants

The speakers should also have the right perception in their minds about the participants who represent different psychographic, sociographic and demographic features. In particular, the speakers should provide a tailor made speech which suits the time, context and convenience of the participants. Delivery of need based, target group specific and subject specific public speech makes the exercise very interesting and rewarding.

Attention Compelling Introductory Remarks

The opening part of the speech should be attention compelling in order to elicit the active and willing participation of the audience in the process of learning. The opening part should be thought provoking and prepare grounds for patient hearing of the speech and successful conduction of public meeting. The opening should setup the subject of coverage in a very appealing, creative and persuasive manner. Sound introduction leads to active participation of the participants in the public function and creates confidence in the minds of the audience.

Identification of Salient Features

The public speakers should identify the salient features of the topic concerned. A good background, historical context, present state of affairs, major problems, success stories, role models, good accomplishments, contemporary challenges and future course of action should be properly identified by the speaker. This would make the audience believe that the speakers have made sincere preparation and come prepared to share their perceptions on vital aspects of the subject concerned. They will participate in the function and grasp the salient features of the context, subject and significance.

Presentation of Key Elements

The public speech becomes relevant if the speakers present the key elements in a proper sequence along with facts, figures, examples, justifications and so on. The incorporation of key elements in the public speech enhances the status, credibility and utility of public speech. The participants should not be taken for granted by the speakers through presentation of insignificant and irrelevant matters. The success of public speech primarily depends on the presentation of most important points in the most appetizing manner.

Interpretation of Prominent Points

The public speech is most likely to contain certain technical, scientific, legal, operational and allied details. Such points may not be simply understood by the participants with formal presentation. The speakers are required to simplify, elaborate and justify those prominent points so that the participants would understand those ideas and retain them in their minds. The speeches should be built around major issues and pertinent questions which constitute the subtopics of the subject concerned.

Utilization of Quotable Quotes

The public speech would not become interesting on the basis of facts and figures. The utilization of quotable quotes would enrich the process of understanding. Such quotable quotes should be used sparingly, appropriately and contextually in order to enrich the quality of public speech. Absence of quotable quotes makes the public speech dull and boring. Hence, the speakers should collect useful quotable quotes which invite the attention of listeners and sustain their active involvement in the process of learning.

Emphasizing the Transitions between Parts

The speakers are required to emphasize the transitions between the divisions or compartments. This would enable the listeners to understand the emphasis laid by the public speakers on certain vital aspects of public speaking. The listeners are most likely to miss the major points if they are not stressed by the speakers adequately without clear transitions. The listeners should succeed in moving from ideas to ideas and sustaining the fruitful participation of the audience in the public functions.

Summarizing the Major Aspects

The public speakers should be aware of the time constraint and perform their duties to the best of their ability within the given time-frame. They should not take away the valuable time of other speakers and also participants. The concluding remarks should clearly highlight the future course of action and solicit the active participation of the audience in the process of institution building or problem solving. The speaker should conclude his observation in strong language and words that gain public attention.

Presenting a Fitting Conclusion

A fitting conclusion should bring the speech to a climatic end and create lasting impression in the minds of the participants. The speaker should make a strong appeal to the audience in the concluding part. Sincere attempt should also be made by the speaker to gain the confidence of the participants and enlist their active participation for the successful conduction of business in modern society. The concluding remarks matter most than other contents of public speech.

Receiving Questions

The public speakers should also anticipate certain questions which are likely to arise in the minds of the participants. The speakers should encourage the participants to air their questions and seek suitable clarifications. The speakers should understand that the audiences have a right to information and participation in a democratic environment. The speakers should never get annoyed if the participants express their difference of opinion on the subject of presentation. In a democracy the speakers should also agree or disagree in order to maintain a cordial understanding between the organization and stakeholders.

Clarifying Important Things

The public speakers may also include certain key concepts and deal with complex ideas, processes and actions. The ordinary participants may not be able to grasp all the complex ideas due to certain limitations. The participants have every right to seek clarification from the speaker on vital aspects which are beyond their understanding. The speakers are duty bound to clarify such things on the spot on the basis of sound facts, ideas, experiences and expert views. This would convince the participants and make them understand all important aspects of public speech.

Thanking the Audience

The speaker should have the courtesy which enhances their stature. In any public function, the speaker should be courteous to the audience and respect their rights and opinions. The speaker should also thank the organizers and audience for their patient hearing. This kind of demonstration of healthy mannerism would convince the participants and make them feel that their participation in the public function was a rewarding exercise.

Guidelines of Successful Oral Communication

Effective oral communication is the prerequisite to successful management of business in modern society. The organizational leaders and communicators should achieve the goals of business promotion through proper network development, employee relations management, customer relations management, distributor relations management, government relations management, media relations management, community relations management, investor relations management and allied activities. All these relationship building exercises primarily depend on effective business communication which also includes all time oral communication within and outside the business organizations.

Communication experts have identified the guidelines for effective oral communication which include—audience analysis, context of communication, personal appearance, posture, walking, facial expression, gestures, boy language, use of voice, pitch variation, vocal emphasis, use of visuals, adaptation, persuasive communication, sincerity of purpose, simple language, familiar words, specific points, presentation of full facts, clear articulation, presence of mind, polite tone, prevention of insulting remarks, prevention of repetition, flexible approach, audience orientation, cool temperament, participatory communication, persuasive communication and so on.

Audience Analysis

Oral communication primarily demands systematic analysis of the background, needs and demands of the audience. The communicator should assess the characteristics of the audience and present audience oriented oral communication which attracts greater attention.

Context of Communication

Oral communication should be highly contextual. The communicator should understand the context in which he/she is required to share ideas, experience and expertise on a given topic. Unnecessary and irrelevant presentation should be avoided by the communicator in order to make oral communication relevant.

Personal Appearance

The communicator should dress in a manner appropriate for the audience or occasion. He/she should look neat, clean and well groomed in order to attract the attention of the audience. The communicator should also present himself/herself in a very simple and dignified manner in order to suit the occasion.

Posture

The posture also matters most in times of oral communication. The posture is likely to be the most obvious of the things that audiences see in them. The facial expression, eye movement, body movement and other aspects are noticed by the audience seriously.

Walking

The audiences also observe the way the communicator walks before them. The manner of walking conveys an impression of confidence. It would be wise to avoid too much walking, awkward steps and unhealthy body movements while delivering oral communication.

Facial Expression

The facial expression includes smiles, frowns, eye contact and other communicative physical movements of the speaker. The communicator should consciously avoid unusually facial expressions that convey unintended meanings to the audience. The communicator should choose the facial expressions that aptly convey the intended meanings to the audience.

Gestures

The gestures have vague meanings but they communicate in times of oral communication. Like posture, the gestures also contribute decisively to the message communicated by the communicator. The physical movements of the communicator also convey certain things to the audience.

Use of Voice

Good voice is a prerequisite to good oral communication. Like physical movements, the voice should not hinder the concentration of listeners on the message. The voices usually cause difficulties on account of lack of pitch variation, lack of variation in speed, lack of vocal emphasis and unpleasant voice quality.

Pitch Variation

The communicator should not talk in monotones since it represents lack of variation in pitch. The communicator should not fail to vary pitch in accordance with the situational requirements. The voice of the communicator demands wide variations in pitch in order to sustain the interest of the audience.

Vocal Emphasis

The communicator should emphasize the words, meanings and messages by varying the manner of speaking. Lack of vocal emphasis by varying pitch, pace and volume mars oral communication. The communicator should be audible enough to make things clear. It is essential to understand that variety is the key to making the voice more effective in oral communication.

Use of Visuals

The spoken word may not be always audible and understandable due to in built constraints. Visuals can certainly help overcome the limitations of spoken words. The oral communication also demands strong visual support in terms of slides, charts, tables, films and the like.

Adaptation

The communicator should adapt himself/herself to the communicative environment in general and needs of the audience in particular. The communicator should also watch the audience and read their minds while making the speech or presentation. The facial expressions of the audience indicate their willingness, satisfaction and participation. Hence, the communicator should not take the audience for granted.

Sincerity of Purpose

The communicator should be sincere enough to deliver goods to the best of his/her ability. Sincere preparation, presentation and adaptation would make oral communication really effective. The communicator should be committed to the cause and cater to the needs of the audiences.

Simple Language

Simplicity is the hallmark of business communication. Oral communication should also be very simple, clear and understandable. The communicator should not use scholarly language of oral communication since it would create series of semantic barriers.

Familiar Words

The communicator should be aware of the culture of communication and use familiar words which make audiences understand things properly. Use of unfamiliar words irritates the audiences and creates several communication gaps. Hence, the success of oral communication precisely depends upon use of familiar words.

Specific Points

The communicator should not emphasize the general aspects of the subject concerned and waste time on unnecessary details. Instead, the communicator should focus the attention of the audiences on the specific aspects of the subject and do justice to the role as effectively as possible.

Presentation of Full Facts

The communicator should be aware of the salient features of the topic concerned and provide all the details and facts in an appetizing manner in order to satisfy the needs of the audiences. There should not be any uncertainties in the minds of the audience with respect to the coverage of the subject and presentation of the full facts.

Clear Articulation

The communicator should be good in articulation. The audiences should be satisfied with the application of communication skills and adoption of presentation skills while delivering oral communication. Each and every aspect of oral communication should be clearly spelt out and well articulated in order to avoid confusion and dissatisfaction in the minds of the audiences.

Presence of Mind

The communicator should have the presence of mind and consciously express his/her views before the audiences. The communicator should also read the minds of the audiences, understand their psychology, adapt to the communicative environment and deliver goods. This would make oral communication active and alive.

Polite Tone

The communicator should not use unparliamentarily, irritating, unpleasant and uncivilized words and body language. The tone and tenor should be pleasant, friendly and decent enough to win over the hearts of the audience. Hence, polite tone makes lot of difference in the oral communication endeavour.

Prevention of Insulting Remarks

The communicator is free to make observations about the policies, programmes and contributions of the organization concerned. But the communicator should not make any derogatory remarks which would irritate and belittle others. Insulting remarks should be totally avoided in order to maintain a friendly atmosphere during the course of oral communication.

Prevention of Repetition

The communicator should consciously avoid unnecessary repetition of certain ideas or points since they would create inconvenience to the listeners. The audiences look forward to hearing new and relevant ideas from the communicator. Repetition of ideas is a wasteful exercise which reduces the significance of the occasion.

Flexible Approach

The communicator should not demonstrate any authoritarian, rigid and unfriendly mannerisms while addressing the audiences. The communicator should be very informal, friendly and flexible in order to exhibit adaptation in the environment. Flexible approaches are always welcome by the audiences.

Audience Orientation

The communicator should basically understand the background, needs and expectations of the audience before delivering the goods. The communicator should also read the minds of the audience while making presentation and provide audience-friendly observations which would fit into a given context.

Cool Temperament

The communicator should remain very cool, calm and patient while making observations before the gathering. The audiences are free to differ with the communicator on certain aspects. The communicator should encourage the audiences to express their points of view and differences of opinion without any prejudice. The communicator should express his/her points of view with all humility and respect for the mission.

Participatory Communication

The public function and other forms of oral communication become effective if the participants are allowed to share their perceptions about the issues raised by the communicator. Horizontal communication provides equal opportunity for both the parties and the communicator can have the benefit of feedback and interaction. Participatory communication enhances the value of oral communication in all situations.

Persuasive Communication

The communicator should present the points of view and persuade the audience to accept the policies, programmes, goods and services of the organization concerned. The communicator should also convince the audiences on the basis of truthful, objective and reliable information, ideas and justifications. The oral communication becomes highly effective if the communicator persuades the audience to respond to the needs of the organization favourably.

Intercultural Oral Communication

Culture is the basis for all kinds of communication including oral communication the communicators are required to understand the cultural context of oral communication in order to avoid the problem of miscommunication. Culture is the way of life of a group of people and the communicators should fit into their oral communication into a given cultural context. The body positions and movements differ among cultures. The manners of walking also differ among cultures. Communication with body parts (hands, arms, head, eyes, etc.) varies from culture to culture. The different attitudes of different cultures towards various factors of human relationships are also the bi-products of culture which cause communication problems.

There are certain factors which are associated with intercultural oral communication namely—time, space, odours, frankness, intimacy of relationship, values and expression of emotions according to Lesikar *et al.* (2011: 07). The oral communication depends upon the time which needs to be efficiently used by the organizers and communicators. They strive to meet deadlines, to be punctual, to conduct business quickly and to work on a schedule. In some cultures, people view time in a more relaxed way. In business negotiations, the people in these cultures move at a deliberately slow pace and touch upon the main issue.

The space is also a prominent factor associated with intercultural oral communication which is viewed differently by different cultures. In some cultures, the participants maintain distance while in other cultures they remain close to each other. The people view personal space as a right and tend to respect this right of others.

The body odours are viewed differently by the people who represent different cultures. The body odour is perceived as an act of friendship to breathe the breath of the person with whom they converse and to feel their presence by smelling. Sometimes encounters between people with widely differing attitudes could lead to serious miscommunication in intercultural oral communication.

The frankness also matters from intercultural oral communication point of view. Some people tend to be relatively frank or explicit in their relationships with others while others tend to be far more reticent or implicit in their relationship. The people representing low-context culture are more frank and explicit as compared to the people who represent high-context cultures.

The intimacy of relationships among people also varies in different cultures. In some cultures, strict social classes/castes exist and class/caste determines how intimately people are addressed and treated in intercultural oral communication. This difference in attitude toward class/caste status matters most in oral communication. The superior-inferior relations also differ and affect the oral communication context.

Each culture has different human values and professional values which matter in intercultural oral communication. The view about the relationships of employers and employee also differ by culture. The expectations of the participants in intercultural oral communication also differ from context to context and from mission to mission with reference to business communication.

The expression of emotions is also a prominent factor associated with the intercultural oral communication. The social behaviours vary by culture. The emotional displays in times of joy and sorrow are also influenced by the culture. The communicators should recognize the emotional differences and participate carefully in intercultural oral communication.

The intercultural oral communication techniques are not universally acceptable mainly because of the cultural differences. The eastern and western cultural contexts are different and the intercultural oral communication practices should fit into these cultural differences. Hence, the communicators should learn the cultures of those with whom they communicate orally and otherwise.

Debra Fine (2010: 02) observes: "The ability to connect with others through small talk can lead to big things. The oral communication skills and networking techniques are interrelated in the business field. The communicators play a vital role in establishing fruitful business interactions between the business organizations and various sections of society".

The success of oral communication primarily depends upon conversing, listening and body language. The communicators should keep the listener's interest in mind and provide facts and figures which cater to their needs. The communicators should also carefully listen to the points of view of the audiences and provide necessary clarifications and justifications. The body language of the communicators also matters from the point of view of effective oral communication. In the age of globalization, intercultural oral communication has become highly inevitable in business organizations. The cultural differences should be properly understood by the communicators since business transactions are taking place in multi-cultural society. The communicators should gain absolute familiarity with conventions, social norms and business operations of the respective cultural groups. The intercultural situations demand thoughtful, planned and organized oral communication services to achieve the goal of business promotion.

Conclusion

In reality, the communication style has more to do with whom the communicators talk to than what they are. Studies suggest that intercultural oral communication is based on the cultural intelligence developed by the communicators. Effective oral communication helps in getting friendly cooperation in social and business situations. The communicators should know the meaning and business purpose of oral communication. They should also learn how to break the ice and initiate effective oral communication during different communicative situations. Their ability to connect with others through meaningful dialogues, discussions and conversations can lead to big success in business world. The communicators should also comprehend oral communication skills and techniques in order to enlist the active participation of various stakeholders in the process of business promotion in modern competitive business world. The most important oral communication skill is to come down to the level of participants, understand their feelings and enlist the active participation of people in the communicative exercise. The communicators should also know how to influence or motivate the participants. The entire oral communication exercise of give and take should facilitate a win-win end which is skilfully managed by the communicators.

References

Bhusan, Uma (2012) *Introduction to Business Communication*, Jaico Publishing House, Mumbai, pp. 130-176.

Fine, Debra (2010) *The Fine Art of Small Talk*, www.DebraFine.com

Hasan, Seema (2010) *Mass Communication: Principles and Concepts*, CBS Publishers and Distributors Pvt. Ltd., New Delhi.

Karoli, Veera and Naghma Ahmed (2013) *Business Communication*, Thakur Publishers, Bengaluru, India.

Kaul, Asha (2009) *Business Communication*, PHI Learning Private Limited, New Delhi.

Lehman, Carol, M., Devvie D, DuFrene, Mala Sinha and Robin C. Walker (2012) BCOM, *An Innovative Approach to Learning and Teaching, Business Communication, A South Asian Perspective*, Cengage Learning, New Delhi.

Lesikar, Raymond V., Marie E. Flatley, Kathryn Rentz and Neerja Pande (2011) *Business Communication—Making Connections in a Digital World,* Tata McGraw Hill Education Private Limited, New Delhi, pp. 504-505.

Mehrabian, Albert (1968) Communication Without Words, *Psychology Today,* September: 53-55.

Mukerjee, Hory Sankar (2013) *Business Communication: Connecting at Work,* Oxford University Press, New Delhi.

Rankin, P.T. (1928) The Importance of Listening Ability, *English Journal,* 17 (1): 623-630.

Chapter 6
Written Communication for Business Management

Introduction

Business communication has several types, namely, oral communication, written communication, electronic communication, interpersonal communication, intercultural communication and so on. The communication should command attention, facilitate easy understanding and bring about mutual cooperation between the organization and other stakeholders. Written communication is a creative, intellectual and organized communication which remains in black and white. The source of communication should be aware of the needs and expectations of prospective readers or users. The producers of written business communication should also be aware of the essential principles and techniques of effective written communication. They must be very choosy and selective while making use of words, phrases and language for the purpose of written communication. Broadly speaking, written communication is an art of communicating the messages which facilitate better understanding between the organization and various stakeholders. The concept of written communication, purpose of business writing, importance of written communication skills, barriers to written communication, principles of effective writing, written communication skills and process of written business communication are presented in this Chapter.

Concept of Written Communication

Communication is an important component of business management in modern society. The success of business enterprise mainly depends upon good communicators who can function as effective spokespersons of business organizations. Empirical studies have emphasized the importance of communication in business management. Especially, the written communication assumes profound significance in the business world. Effective business communication between the management and employees in general and between the organization and various stakeholders in particular is essential. Writing is indeed a specific mode of communicating the messages to different receivers during different occasions and with specific purposes.

Corporate communicators produce different forms of written business communication which convey information, ideas, instructions, decisions and actions of the business organizations in written form. The purpose of written communication is duly served if the target groups understand the intended messages, meanings and contexts and respond positively and favourably. Hence, written communication basically involves drafting, re-reading, revising and polishing the contents and language of written form of communication. Written communication becomes alive, active and useful if the source of communication makes use of appropriate words, language, contents and format. In the modern corporate houses and other institutions written communication needs to be planned, organized, edited and finalized in accordance with the well established principles and practices. Communication that commands attention and can be understood easily by the receivers is essential for successful conduction of business affairs.

Significance of Business Writing

Business writing is an art and craft which is cultivated by the communicators over a period of time. Effective business writing does not happen overnight. The basic communication skills are essentially the same as those required for effective business writing. Business writing has twin objectives namely—writing to inform and writing to persuade. The informative writing presents the information to the receivers or users who are required to develop necessary awareness about the aims, objectives, goods, services and contributions of business organizations in modern society. The corporate communicators provide necessary information to the various stakeholders about the day to day activities of the business organizations concerned.

The investors require information about the business status and income generating opportunities. The employees need information about job security, job satisfaction, job promotion, employee welfare and other aspects. The distributors need information about the mode of distribution of goods and services, incentives for distributors and advantages of distributing the goods and services. The customers need information about the products, salient features of the products, advantages of the products, pricing of the products, availability of the products and other facilities. The media representatives need information about the organizational profile, features, products, services and social benefits. The government agencies need information about the norms, guidelines, specifications, fulfilment of statutory norms and other obligations. The community needs information about the philanthropic activities of the organization. All these stakeholders need information on day to day basis in order to understand the organization and respond to the requirements of the organization. Hence, corporate communicators are required to present written communication services which are highly informative and useful to various sections of society.

The business organizations are also required to provide persuasive written communication which aims at convincing the other parties and enlisting their active participation in the process of business promotion. The organizational communicators are responsible for providing creative, argumentative, justifiable and persuasive communication services to various stakeholders. The employees should be persuaded by the organization to extend the best possible cooperation on the basis of pro-employee policies and actions. The investors should be persuaded to contribute more funds in view of the secured financial status of the business organization. The distributors should be persuaded to distribute the goods and services across the country or region in view of distributor friendly policies and programmes. The consumers should be persuaded to continue their loyalty and patronage in view of the delivery of consumer friendly goods and services. The government organizations should also be persuaded to extend timely and necessary cooperation in view of the corporate social responsibility of the business organizations. The local community should also be persuaded to extend the benefit of patronage to the business organization in view of their socially beneficial goods and services. The media professionals should also be persuaded to portray the business organizations positively on the basis of their sound policies and programmes. Hence, all these stakeholders should be constantly persuaded by the corporate communicators to strengthen the foundations of business organizations.

"Informative and persuasive business written communication should be constantly made available to various stakeholders. The communicators should effectively change the mindset of various stakeholders and project the business organizations in a positive manner", observes Perry (2003: 10). The written communication should be enriched on the basis of sound ideas, facts, figures, arguments, justifications and persuasive inputs. The written communication should be able to evoke intended response from the various stakeholders in times of need. The communicators' point of view should be well organized and presented in order to remain in the good books of people who matter most in the present times. The written business communication continues to enjoy greater significance even in the age of electronic revolution. It has the power to attract the attention of many people and provide useful evidence as and when required. The written communication also remains for quite a long time as very useful reference material.

Barriers to Written Communication

Basically, the people across the world inhabit different perceptual and verbal worlds. The meaning extracted from a message can differ from the intended meaning due to perceptual differences. The meanings are naturally found in the minds of the people on the basis of their culture, environment, experience and other factors. The communicator and user have two minds which are not alike. The meaning extracted from a message can differ from the intended meaning under normal circumstances. The meanings are also unstable and imperfectly represented by the symbols. There is no intrinsic relationship between the communication symbols including the words because of the different environmental factors and social conventions. The social and professional influences also cause the meaning to change during the communicative context. The cultural differences also cause drastic variations in terminology and the assumed meanings of words. The source and target group can use certain words which mean entirely different things. Usually, bypassing occurs when communicators are unaware of that they are using the same word in different ways.

Lesikar *et al.* (2011: 08) state: "Conveying information is not the only important goal of business communication. Cultivating positive relationships is also critical to successful communication. Getting important information from one place to another is critical to the success of any business organization. Every act of communication carries with it an implied view of the communicators' relationship". Written business communication has the power to achieve positive or negative effects. The communicator should be aware of the human element of communication which matters most under normal circumstances. Communication gaps occur if the source of communication fails to understand the significance of adaptation which means fitting every facet of communication solution to the intended recipients. The communicators should put the receivers at the heart of communication efforts in order to elicit favourable response. This does not happen most of the times in case of written business communication since the source is not aware of the needs and demands of the receivers.

In reality, the flow of written communication in a business organization forms a complex and ever changing network. Chaturvedi and Chaturvedi (2011: 02) note: "Communication gaps also occur if the writers fail to follow the principles of unity and coherence that bind words into sentences, sentences into units or paragraphs and paragraphs into essays (the full composition). When this transformation of thought into language is not effected under the guiding principles of language, the muddy clutter hides the meaning and makes it difficult to understand the writer's thoughts. The message may be buried under a mountain of unnecessary words, or an unnatural style may conceal the writer's true intentions. Instead of letting business letters be friendly, interest and persuasive, such writing makes them overly formal and dull".

Written communication is a time consuming process. It involves proper collection of ideas, planning of writing, drafting of contents, editing of contents and so on. It involves more formalities and the communicator should stick to the format and contents. The communicator also remains away from the target group physically and otherwise. It may not be possible for the communication to enlist immediate feedback about the contents and correctness of communication. The communicator is also required to gain absolute command over the art and craft of written communication in business organizations. Absence of the prerequisites to written communication would also pose serious threats and disadvantages.

The written communication becomes complex if the communicator fails to ensure clarity of thought and expression. The source of communication is required to understand the background, status, needs, expectations and attitudes of the receivers of communication. The purpose of business writing is defeated if the appropriate and specific words and symbols are not used by the writers. The use of scientific, technical and complex ideas would also create confusion in the minds of the readers in the absence of simplification of written communication. Each and every written communication should be purposeful, specific and contextual in order to convince the other parties and persuade them to respond favourably. Otherwise, written communication would be wrongful, futile and unrewarding.

Fundamentals of Effective Writing

The success of business management primarily depends upon effective communication. The corporate communicators should be aware of their role and responsibility with reference to written business communication. Lehman *et al.* (2012: 07) identify the process of written communication thus—determining the purpose of communication, identification of the needs of target group, understanding the context of communication, choosing appropriate channels of communication, adapting message to the needs of the target group, organizing the contents of communication, editing the messages and preparation of the final draft.

The source of communication should have adequate understanding of the process of written communication which involves several elements such as—(1) purpose of communication, (2) needs of the target group, (3) clarity of thought, (4) accuracy of facts, 5) concrete language, (6) effective tone, (7) brevity in presentation, (8) appropriate words, (9) active verbs, (10) designing of messages, (11) short sentences, (12) meaningful paragraph, (13) conversational style, (14) positive approach, and (15) meaningful editing and design.

Purpose of Communication

The communicators should be aware of the purpose of written communication in business organizations. They must understand the background of communication, objective of communication, format of communication, contents of communication and techniques of writing precisely and perfectly. Clarity of thought is the hallmark of business writing. The business writing is duly guided by a purpose. The business communicator is required to understand the context properly and deliver the goods which are absolutely tailor made and need based. Active business communication is based on successful persuasion of the target group on the basis of credible, creative, authentic and adequate facts.

Needs of the Target Group

The target group of written communication should be properly understood by the communicator in terms of demographics, sociographics and psychographics. Nothing should be imposed on the target group in the name of business communication. The background, culture, status, attitudes, needs and demands of the target group should be properly understood by the communicator in order to provide area specific, subject specific and target group specific written business communication. The source of communication should develop clear perceptions of the requirements of the audience in order to enhance the impact of written communication and business relations.

Clarity of Thought

The corporate communicators should perceive their mission in a proper way and identify the salient features of written business communication. The format, contents, facts, arguments, justifications and other aspects of written communication should be clearly understood by the communicators. In particular, the communicators should pay special attention to the attitudes and demands of the prospective readers and cater to their needs properly. The communicators should also understand the context of messages and any environmental factors which would affect understanding between the source and target groups. Written communication should be based on expertise and competence which enhance the credibility. The communicators should demonstrate excellent persuasive communication skills. Effective business writing skills have become crucial for both effective communication and organizational productivity. The communicators should ensure that all the relevant ideas are presented in the text in order to elicit desired response from the target group. This would ensure the success of written communication in letter and spirit.

Accuracy of Facts

The corporate communicators should present very accurate facts, figures, explanations and justifications which stand the test of reasoning. The messages should be communicated correctly in terms of facts, figures, grammar, spelling, punctuation and other elements of written communication. It is necessary to examine the context of words and phrases used in written communication in order to avoid ambiguity and confusion. The communicators should also have a better control over the message. They must apply proper writing techniques for adapting messages to the target group. The communicators should choose the words that have a precise meaning and arrange the facts in a way that the main idea and subordinate ideas are presented in a proper manner. Accuracy is the hallmark of business communication and enhances the validity and reliability of communication.

Concrete Language

The corporate communicators are required to use words and phrases which are grammatically and contextually correct and appropriate. The communicators should select the right level of language for communication. They should also understand the importance of organizing a message to achieve the desired response. The purpose of business communication should be served on the basis of proper understanding of the central idea of message. As far as possible, standard language of written communication which is commonly acceptable and understandable should be used. Practically speaking, concrete is the diametrically opposite to the word abstract. The communicators should use concrete words which stand for things that exist in the real world. The use of concrete language enhances the status of written business communication.

Effective Tone

The corporate communicators are required to choose the appropriate tone in terms of formality. The tone basically refers to the feelings created by words used to communicate a message in the written communication. The communicator and receiver should enjoy the benefit of good human relationship through the reflection of healthy feelings in the written communication. Muriel Harris states: "The level of formality is the tone in writing and reflects the attitude of the writer towards the subject and audience. The tone can be informal, semi-formal and strictly formal. The communicators should use the informal tone for social or personal communication. But, formal tone should be used while communicating to the superiors in the organizations concerned". The written business communication should have informal tone and contain colloquialisms which are casual words or phrases used in informal business writing. The communicators should be aware of the tone in order to promote positive business relationship.

Brevity in Presentation

Written communication should not be very lengthy since it takes more time for reading and understanding the things. The writers should not include unnecessary words and details in the written communication. Brevity lies in using minimum words avoiding unnecessary and irrelevant details which confuse the readers. The communicators should avoid using too many words and sentences which take away the precious time of the readers. They should also use specific facts and figures by using vivid and image building words appropriately. They should not repeat certain things unless absolutely essential. Long clauses, phrases and sentences should also be avoided carefully. The over use of passive voice also hampers written communication. The communicators should follow the formula of brief, bright and brisk while writing different letters and other forms of written communication.

Appropriate Words

The business communicators should choose words that have a precise meaning and avoid pretentious words and phrases. The context of the message and fitness of the words should be properly examined before use in written communication. There are some words which do not fit into a given communicative context. Certain words also fail to convey specific ideas or information to the readers. The communicators should judge the appropriateness of words, phrases and clauses while communicating certain things in writing. As far as possible, most appropriate words which provide intended meanings should be used in the written communication. Unnecessary words and symbols should be avoided in order to prevent communication gaps. The regional words which fit into the geographical area and communicative context are more acceptable under normal circumstances.

Active Verbs

Actually verbs contribute a lot towards making the writing quite interesting and lively because they contain the action of the sentence. There are certain active verbs which communicate the actions and motivate the readers. The communicators can make the verbs more active by using active voice. The process of written communication becomes alive and meaningful if the writers use active verbs and avoid camouflaged verbs. The communicators are required to avoid camouflaged verbs by writing concretely and preferring active voice.

Designing of Messages

The communicators have to design the messages on the basis of salient features of the actions taken by the corporate houses. The messages should be simple, direct, specific and flexible enough to facilitate better understanding between the organization and various stakeholders. The messages have to convey precise meanings. The writers should be familiar with vocabulary, context and specificity of the written communication. The writers should possess adequate knowledge of language and use a set of messages which convey the intended meanings. The message should not contain any discriminatory words which do not treat people equally. The writers should also make use of correct idioms, phrases, words and sentences which bring about greatest understanding among the readers. The writers should use their knowledge and experience in order to adapt their messages to the readers.

Short Sentences

The communicators should use short words and sentences which communicate things in a better manner. The use of long words and sentences usually hinders written communication. Short sentences also communicate things with better clarity and convenience. The short sentences really matter in written communication. The communicators have to design short sentences that manage the information. The communicators should cultivate an awareness of the different sentence types and elements in order to communicate better messages. In reality, construction of short and efficient sentences saves the time and effort of the users. The short sentences also communicate better because of mind limitations. The users can also get the clear messages through short sentences. The contents have to be limited in a proper way in order to design short sentences which attract the attention of the readers. The basic technique of shortening the sentences is to use the words economically. The communicators should give the right emphasis to the contents since written business communication contains several items of information.

Meaningful Paragraph

The written communication should also have well planned, organized and presented paragraphs. The communicator should provide different paragraphs under different compartments of contents. Clear writing demands that the communicator presents different contents under different paragraphs in the order of descending importance. The communicator should understand the importance paragraphing in the process of written communication. Paragraphs also make ideas stand out independently and attract the attention of the readers on each and every element of communication. Paragraphing also involves logical thinking and presentation of several ideas. Normally, the contents of a paragraph should concern one topic or idea in order to maintain unity of thought and action. The unity means that a paragraph builds around a single topic or element or idea. Readability tests have revealed that short paragraphs, well organised, is better than long paragraphs. Most readers also prefer to read short paragraphs. The communicators should understand the importance of well made sentences and paragraphs which move the readers logically and smoothly from point to point.

Conversational Style

The written communication becomes alive and active if the facts are presented in the conversational style. The written communication should also enable the communicators to build goodwill. In reality, writing in conversational language creates favourable effects in the minds of the readers. The language of written communication which resembles conversation becomes quite natural and warm. The communicators should be aware of the fact that building goodwill through written messages is a good business practice. The users of written communication are influenced by their human contact with the business transactions. The adoption of conversational style in business written communication also persuades the receivers to accept the point of view of business organizations and respond positively to the needs of business organizations. "The conversational language also leaves an impression that readers like. The conversational style basically involves the you-viewpoint which produces goodwill and influences people favourably" according to Shelby and Reinsch (1995: 11).

Positive Approach

The written communication is primarily dependent on the you-viewpoint which produces better persuasion of the readers. Some scholars have advocated that use of you-viewpoint is courteous by nature. This approach produces better results when the business goals are ethical. The written communication demands positive words and approaches which are usually best for message goals especially when persuasion and goodwill are needed. The writers should adopt positive approach to written business communication since it stirs up the readers' desire for participation and progress. The positive approach also puts the readers in the write frame of mind and persuades them to respond positively. The communicators should demonstrate adequate courtesy which is a major contributor to goodwill in business documents. The adoption of positive approach in a written message communicates more than the message.

Meaningful Editing and Design

The written business communication should be subjected to meaningful editing and designing. Editing is a systematic exercise which is carried out by the editors who are known as surgeons of words. Editing is also a means of purification of written communication with due respect to vocabulary, knowledge, language, presentation and other aspects of communication. The editors should also have microscopic eyes in order to detect the mistakes and provide alternative words and phrases which enrich the process of communication. Editing also basically involves giving proper emphasis to the contents in the message. The contents should be examined in order to avoid glorification, exaggeration and other wasteful exercises which harm the written communication. The beginning, body and ending of the written communication carry emphasis. The rule of emphasis applies whether the unit is the message, a paragraph of the message or a sentence within the paragraph. The business communication format, contents and design vary from letter to letter and context to context. The use of negatives impede understanding and creates unfavourable situations. Each and every written businėss document deserves a separate identity and design. In reality, design is not mere decoration but it is a systematic art of presentation of facts.

Types of Written Business Communication

In modern business organizations several types of business communication are used for the purpose of establishing rapport between the organization and various stakeholders. Prominent among them include—letters, memos and e-mails.

Letters

The letters are the oldest form of business communication. The letters are addressed to various stakeholders. The format of a typical business letter includes—date, inside address, salutation, body and complementary remarks. Letters are brief pieces of business communication which attract the attention of the stakeholders. An ideal business letter is addressed to the person or organization by name. The early part of the letter contains the subject and relevant references. The introductory part of the letter primarily presents the idea. The body of the letter consists of major ideas, details and justifications. The last part of the letter contains closing messages or remarks. The techniques of writing business letters are developed by the seasoned business executives and communicators over a period of time. "The letters are primarily considered as an exchange between real people as a strategic means of accomplishing business goals. The business letters are written with a fond hope of generating favourable response from the parties concerned", comments Stevenson (1988: 13). The writers should use pleasant, attractive and persuasive words and phrases in order to get into the good books of the parties and seek their whole hearted cooperation and support for the business endeavour. The present emphasis is on strategy and humanness which enhance the status of written communication.

Circulars

A circular is a communication meant to convey information of a business firm to customers and other stakeholders of business management. The source of communication intends to convey certain messages to various receivers within the organization. It also carries communication to a number of persons who are directly associated with the business firm. The circulars are presented in the printed or cyclostyle formats which are less expensive. The circulars are essential tools of business publicity and propaganda. The circulars become effective if they are brief, bright and brisk in nature.

Notices

The notices are also issued by the corporate communicators to various business stakeholders. They convey certain messages which are read by a large number of people. The notices are communicated in the indirect speech and serve the purpose of communicating the organizational issues, trends and developments. The notices should be communicated in such a way that receivers understand the messages and respond to them immediately.

Memos

The memorandums or memos are a form of letter written inside the business organization. They are written messages which are exchanged by the employees in the conduct of their day to day works in different capacities. In the age of information revolution, they are processed electronically as faxes. The memos are usually addressed to the persons within the office or organization in order to communicate day to day decisions and actions. A memorandum is also often referred to as a memo which is commonly used by a person to appeal to the higher authorities in order to get the things done. The superior authorities also write memos to the subordinates and instruct them regarding their role and responsibility in the business organization. A memo is always written in a friendly, flexible, cooperative and respectful way. The memos which are not in good taste would hamper human relations in the organizations concerned. "A memo also remains as a permanent record of the official transaction which takes place between the superior and subordinate authorities and *vice versa*", state Winsor (2003: 15). Hence, the memo should be drafted with care, responsibility and creativity. The techniques of writing memos are much like those for written business communication formats and contents.

E-mails

In the present times, e-mail is the most commonly used mode of communication between the organization and other stakeholders. The stakeholders are also free to send e-mail to the business organizations in order to seek the delivery of goods and services. The e-mail is also known as the quickest channel of written communication which contains information, documents, and pictures. The messages can be sent instantaneously to multiple people or sources at the same time. This makes e-mail communication a crucial part of business management in the present times. The senders should be aware of the e-mail account of the receivers and communicate things in a proper way. The sender has the freedom to send a copy of the e-mail to several persons at the same time. An e-mail does not require any formal format and contains like salutation or closing remarks. Few words are enough to communicate the intended messages to the right persons in the right time. The principles of writing e-mail include clear, crisp and concise. The sender should be aware of the grammatical and punctuation aspects of e-mail communication. Today, the e-mail software has a signature feature which is automatically attached to the message. The e-mail communication becomes highly effective with the use of short sentences and paragraphs. The communicator should make sure that the message is accurate, brief and understandable to achieve the desired results, according to Bhusan (2012).

Instructions

Instruction is one of the important uses of business communication. Instructions, by nature, are simply steps which explain how to accomplish a particular task. The instructions should be clear, correct, appropriate, relevant and persuasive in order to achieve desired results. Usually, all instructions are directed at the subordinates in modern organizations. Instructions should also contain a proper background information, objectives, methodologies, formalities and procedures in order to facilitate better implementation of the suggested action. Instructions should be drafted on the basis of proper guidelines, warnings and implications. Bhusan (2012) states: "Logical sequences of actions, discriminations and judgements leading to successful outcomes, concise, understandable and direct instructions are appropriate for users".

Process of Written Communication

The process of written business communication has three stages namely—planning, organizing, format, selection of channels, drafting, revising and editing. These three stages are inter-related aspects which are practically chronological by nature. Each piece of business writing is entirely different from situation point of view. The business communicators are required to give equal importance and careful attention to all three stages which are recursive, not strictly linear.

Planning

The business communicator is required to prepare grounds for writing on the basis of systematic planning. The writer should understand the concept of writing, nature of writing, scope of writing, objective of writing, users of writing and effects of writing in a proper manner. The writer should develop a working definition of the problem which is addressed by him/her. The nature and scope of writing should also be clearly understood by the writer. The objective of writing should also be grasped in order to present target group specific and objective specific contents to the readers. The writer should also understand the attitude, needs and demands of the readers in order to provide tailor made communication. The communicator should recognize the importance of organizing the written communication for developing messages to achieve the desired response. The communicator should also develop clear perceptions of the receivers to enhance the impact of written communication from human relations development point of view. It is also necessary to consider the context of the message and any environmental influences that affects its content. The personal, professional and organizational contexts of the users should be fully understood by the writer. Besides this, the writer should also know the need and importance of written communication from the organizational business point of view. Hence, the writer should develop a proper perspective of written business communication.

Organizing

The communicator should recognize the importance of organizing a message before developing messages to achieve the desired response. The writer should also gather relevant and adequate information through various sources in order to provide a comprehensive written communication. The writer is also required to do some systematic research and collect primary and secondary sources of information about the mission of writing. The people who are directly associated with the phenomenon, system and process are competent enough to share their first hand experience about the subject concerned. The authorities who make comments and criticisms on the basis of their scholarship, experience and expertise also provide useful secondary sources of information on a given subject. The communicator should organize the message which would present sequence of ideas clearly and logically to achieve desired goals of business management. The central idea, attention compellers, effective outline, anticipated receiver reaction and value of communication should be assessed before delivering the written communication. In business organizations, the communicators should gather adequate data about the products, services and other business transactions from various sources which are reliable and valid. Formal and informal data collection techniques should also be used to gather adequate information.

Format Development

The communicator should understand the multiple issues which might affect the content of the messages. The organizational culture and flow of communication affect the format and content of written business communication. The business communicator should choose the right format which fits into a given written communication context. There are a wide range of established forms of business communication. Letters, reports, broachers, pamphlets, memorandum, agreement, house journal, press release and other forms of business communication are found in modern business organizations. The communicator should choose the appropriate format and fit the contents into it in a proper way. Right business communication format should be identified and developed in order to reach out to various readers within and outside the business organization.

Selection of Channels

The business communicator has several channels of business communication namely—oral communication, written communication, electronic communication, inter-personal communication, extension communication, multimedia communication, and so on. The communicator should choose the appropriate channel for communicating the business message. The user friendly and inexpensive channels of written communication should be used as far as possible. The written communication channel naturally provides readers the opportunity to take the time necessary to process the information according to their convenience. The communicator should choose the most appropriate channel of business communication and prepare the contents according to the requirements of the channel concerned. Each channel demands a different written form of communication and the writer should provide channel-specific written business communication in order to enhance the feasibility of communication.

Drafting

The business communicator should draft the contents in a systematic way after considering the purpose, type, audiences' needs, appropriate channel and other factors. The drafting exercise should be carried out in accordance with the mission, target group, channel, format and other aspects of written business communication. The drafting should be undertaken on the basis of proper presentation of facts, figures, arguments, justification and so on. Proper compartmentalization of facts or ideas should be ensured at the stage of drafting. A creative beginning, brief historical context, present state of affairs, challenges of business, future of business, nature of service and other aspects should be properly highlighted in the draft. The writer should present all relevant ideas in the proper order and include each and every important element of business communication without fail. The communicator should draft the messages on the basis of deductive and inductive sequences. In case of deductive sequence, the message begins with the major idea. But, in inductive sequence, the message withholds the major idea until accompanying details and explanations are presented. This would facilitate better presentation of facts and figures relating to business transactions between the organization and various stakeholders. Lehman *et al.* (2012: 07) identified the 7C's to effective business writing which include—completeness, conciseness, consideration, concreteness, courtesy, clarity, and correctness.

Revising

The business communicator should revise the contents and reorder them properly in consultation with the veterans and seasoned business writers. The writer should also discuss the contents with colleagues and superiors in order to find out certain missing elements and add better ideas and inputs on the basis of consultation. There is nothing wrong in the revision of the contents if they are not up to the mark in letter and spirit. The use of words, phrases, sentences, paragraphs and other elements should be checked again and again in order to prevent unnecessary details and unwanted contents in the draft. The business writing should be simple, direct, specific, reader friendly and flexible in order to enhance better understanding, rapport development and business prospects. The written communication should be revised properly in order to adapt the messages to fit the receiver's needs. The communicator should draft meaningful messages that would demand the attention of the receivers and build goodwill. The revised draft should contain the appropriate message outline in order to achieve the desired response. The written communication should be revised thoroughly in order to convey the messages effectively.

Editing

The business writers are capable of presenting the facts and figures, but the editors are capable of finding out the mistakes and making the writing fit for publication. The editors are also known as conscience keepers, surgeons of words and creative designers. Their services should be properly utilized in the business organizations in order to improve the quality and contents of business written communication. The editors can also examine the appropriateness of contents, presentation and design and provide quality oriented finished products. The process of editing also involves rewriting, proof reading, readability test and evaluation of contents. The editors can look at spelling errors, grammatical errors, presentation related errors, mechanical errors and other barriers to written communication. They are competent enough to provide the writings which are free from mistakes and disorders. Hence, editing of written communication facilitates purification of writing and improvement of presentation of written communication. The editors are responsible for making the important formatting decisions in the business organizations. Their services have to be utilized in a proper manner by the business communicators. The editors are required to convey the business messages in a positive and tactful tone by using positive, simple and appropriate words for effective business communication.

Conclusion

Written business communication demands the application of tested and tried parameters, principles and practices. Readability is the hallmark of written business communication. The communicators should disseminate clear, correct and complete information in order to facilitate better understanding, rapport development and business transaction between the source and receiver. The written business communication is widely used all over the world. Today written communication has become an important component of business communication in all business organizations. The formats are standardized and contents are designed on the basis of certain experiments. The written business communication should convey the ideas and actions completely with minimal need for response. The business communicators are required to gain absolute mastery over the art and craft of written business communication in order to make it effective, creative and purposeful.

References

Bhusan, Uma (2012) *Introduction to Business Communication*, Jaico Publishing House, Mumbai, pp. 212-240.

Ibid.

Chaturvedi, P.D. and Mukesh Chaturvedi (2011) *Business Communication—Concepts, Cases and Applications*, Delhi: Pearson, p. 116.

Hasan, Seema (2010) *Mass Communication: Principles and Concepts*, CBS Publishers and Distributors Pvt. Ltd., New Delhi.

Kameda, Naoki (1996) *Business Communication Toward Transnationalism: The Significance of Cross-Cultural Business English and its Role*, Tokyo: Kindiabungeisha, p. 34.

Karoli, Veera and Naghma Ahmed (2013) *Business Communication*, Thakur Publishers, Bengaluru, India.

Kaul, Asha (2009) *Business Communication*, PHI Learning Private Limited, New Delhi.

Lehman, Carol, M., Devvie D., DuFrene, Mala Sinha and Robin C. Walker (2012) BCOM, *An Innovative Approach to Learning and Teaching, Business Communication, A South Asian Perspective*, Cengage Learning, New Delhi, p. 72.

Lesikar, V., Raymond, Marie E. Flatley, Kathryin Rentz and Neerja Pande (2011) *Business Communication: Making Connections in a Digital World*, New Delhi: Tata McGraw Hill Education Private Limited, pp. 20-21.

Mukerjee, Hory Sankar (2013) *Business Communication: Connecting at Work*, Oxford University Press, New Delhi.

Perry, David (2003) Do you have the skills most in demand today?, *Career Journal*, www.careerjournal.com

Shelby, Annette N. and Lamar Reinsch, Jr. (1995) Positive Emphasis and You-Attitude: An Empirical Study, *Journal of Business Communication*.

Sterne, Jim and Anthony Priore (2000) E-mail marketing: Using E-mail to reach your *Target Audience and Build Customer Relationship*, New York: John Wiley & Sons, p. 141.

Stevenson, J. (1988) *Language, Thought and Representation*, Chichester: John Wiley.

Trompnaars, Fons and Peter Woolliams (2003) *Business Communication Across Cultures*, London: Capstone, p. 53.

Winsor, Dorothy A. (2003) *Writing Power: Communication in an Engineering Centre*, Albany: Suny Press.

Zikmund, William G. (2003) *Business Research Methods*, Mason, O.H: South Western, p. 279.

Chapter 7
Electronic Communication for Business Management

Introduction

In the present times, business communication is practiced with the help of advanced electronic means of communication which are known for greater access, credibility and popularity. The new information and communication technologies offer numerous advantages but the legal and ethical implications should be examined carefully by the communicators in modern business organizations. Electronic channels of business communication are known as barrierless channels which make people believe what they here and see are true. The contemporary universe of digital electronic media offers increasingly greater control over listening, viewing and electronic interaction. The electronic messages can reach out to the target group and increase the efficiency. Modern managers and organizational communicators should know about the latest technological advancements and understand how they will affect the future of business organizations. The concept of electronic communication, evolution of electronic media, purpose of electronic business communication, importance of electronic communication skills, effective electronic communication skills, process of electronic business communication and recent trends and developments in electronic business communication are presented in this Chapter.

Evolution of Electronic Communication

The process of communication has undergone series of changes and developments over a period of time. In the beginning, people developed the capacity to communicate using speech, signs and other modes. It was called as 'interpersonal communication'. Subsequently, folk media of communication were developed as the human civilization advanced. Folk songs, folk dance, folk theatre and folk traditions constituted the gamut of folk media. The advent of printing also paved the way for the growth of journalism. In 1920s, Guglielmo Marconi developed radio telegraphy as a means of communication. Radio was the only instantaneous electronic medium for over 30 years. In 1940s Baird invented television as an audio-visual means of communication. Television emerged as a media power house and became the most sought after medium for advertising. In the last quarter of twentieth century, computer, telecommunication and satellite communication channels were developed. Since then, the audience switched over to cable, satellite and the Internet. The new millennium is known as the information revolution age.

Medoff and Kaye (2011: 09) observe: "Television in its many forms—broadcast, cable, satellite, videocassette, DVD and now online and cell phones—has been the centre point of media for over 50 years. The Internet, the network of networks that connect computers to each other, allows users to find information, entertainment and personal communication and to do so easily for a low cost. Although everyday use of the Internet is still in its infancy (since the early 1990s), the Internet is a *paradigm breaker*—a medium that deface previous models of electronic media. It has grown more rapidly than any other medium in history".

The traditional media share characteristics such as audience, time, display, distribution, distance and storage but the electronic media are not constrained by time and distance factors. Modern organizations have increasingly used the electronic media for organizational communication and business communication purposes. The electronic media industry has changed dramatically over the past 20 years after the economic liberalization. The present age is also known as the age of media convergence. The Internet has emerged as a new mass medium at unprecedented speed especially for business communication. The Internet enables communication with a large audience for low cost and short period. The convergence is the combining of media and geographical boundaries have disappeared over a period of time. The modern organizations are using advanced methods of connecting with their stakeholders as well as different platforms such as television sets, telephones and computers. The advent of digital technology has enabled the organizations to use various electronic media at the same time over one device for corporate advertising and communication purposes. The study of electronic media is important not only as a field of intellectual pursuit but electronic media have become dynamic forces in the age of globalization.

Nature and Scope of Electronic Business Communication

In the early 1920s, radio stations were established for the purpose of commercial broadcasting. The age of chain broadcasting began in 1926 and the number of radio receivers grew dramatically all over the world. The manufacturers sold inexpensive radio sets to the masses. Radio exposed the audience to the concept of commercial broadcasting. The Second World War witnessed the commendable growth of radio as a means of commercial broadcasting. Radio broadcasting gained from the increased advertising. Railway stations also broadcast variety of commercial advertising programmes through amplitude modulation broadcasting. The frequency modulation broadcasting emerged in 1960s. High fidelity stereo systems became very popular and the radio's share of the total advertising market grew commendably in 1990s. The introduction of digital service in radio stations has enhanced the status of radio as a means of commercial broadcasting. The cable companies also started offering audio services during the same period and the Internet became the largest source of digital audio in the present times. It is much less expensive to enjoy the benefit of online connection in radio broadcasting. The online radio offers several benefits to modern customers than broadcast stations.

John Logie Baird developed a workable system to send live television images in 1926. Zworykin is also credited with developing a television receiver using *kinescope.* This was accomplished by pointing a film camera at a TV monitor while the shows were broadcast live. During 1930s, electronic television system was developed and introduced to the public by David Sarnoff. In 1941, commercial television broadcasting began in America. Colour television was introduced in 1950s. Digital television sets emerged in 1990s. Television became the most prominent medium of commercial broadcasting over a period of time. The public and private television channels gained adequate revenue from commercial broadcasting. The satellite to home television also became a reality and the networks maintained their superiority because of technological advancements and privatization of television broadcasting. The regrouping of networks also enhanced the status of commercial television broadcasting. The direct broadcast satellite became economically viable. In the age of digital television, the television stations have gained the capacity of transmitting multiple programmes across the globe.

The cable delivery system has enhanced the status of television broadcasting. The cable industry distributed programmes from different sources other than broadcast networks. The cable systems also provide local programming channels on the basis of satellite technology development. Satellites are used for the purpose of distributing radio and television programmes. The telephone has also provided one to one and point to point communication in modern society and organizations. The cell phones have also widened the horizon of business communication. The use of electronic point to point or one to one communication for business has increased commendably. The digital cell phones have become cheap, versatile and dependable in the new millennium. The delivery of radio and television services *via* the Internet has grown remarkably on account of faster connections and improved telecasting. The modern organizations are using Internet and Wi-Fi for the purpose of corporate advertising.

Internet is an electronically networked system which was actually envisioned in 1960s, but it became a possibility in 1990s. The Internet resources include—the web, e-mail, podcasting, YouTube, blogs, electronic news groups, instant messages, chat, social network sites and twitter. The Internet resources have evolved into multidimensional resources. The World Wide Web consists of billions of pages within hundreds of millions of websites which present information in text, graphic, audio and video formats. The web has altered the media use habits, lifestyles and consumption patterns of millions of people.

Sterne and Priore (2000: 14) observe: "The electronic mail has created online marketing and billing, business to business e-mail, and new systems for collecting and verifying online signatures in modern society. The podcasting is a mixture of Personal on Demand and broadcasting concepts. Podcasts are produced by radio and television stations and networks of individuals and institutions who share different aspirations. The YouTube is the widely used sites, with millions of users watching plenty of videos and short clips that range from music to advertisements".

The blogs also constitute a type of website that allows users to interact directly with the blog host. The blog readers are free to get the benefit of exchange of views on goods, services, problems and so on. The electronic mailing lists are similar to e-mail which are addressed to individual recipients who share commonality of interest. The newsgroups also bring people together with similar interest. The chat room is a two-way online communication channel which enables the participants exchange live and real time messages on all aspects of human life including business. The instant messaging also facilitates the conduction of real time conservations with people who share different interest. The social network sites also serve as a means of keeping in touch with friends, relatives and associates. The twitter is the newest social network range which allows open access to the senders and receivers of electronic message. The web browsers serve as tools of online communication. All these new tools and technologies are used by the people across the world for variety of purposes including business communication. The Internet users also connect to the web both instrumentally and ritualistically. The bloggers have facilitated redistribution of media power into the hands of many consumers and users. The blogs have assumed the role of watchdogs of public interest since the bloggers constitute an endless parade of experts. The traditional media are struggling for their existence in the age of new media.

Medoff and Kaye (2011: 09) observe: "Digitization, convergence and consolidation of media are the way of the future. Although media consumers will benefit from technological advances, individuals, consumer groups and the government are concerned about a small number of companies controlling too much of the industry. In the future, the audience will have more electronic media choices, with better technical quality and more portability, but it will also have to struggle with having a smaller number of competitors in the industry and the possible negative consequences that creates".

Electronic Business Communication and Advertising

Business houses used radio stations as important sources of business communication. Radio was cheaper mode of business communication. Organizational activities, goods and services were communicated to large number of people through local, regional and national broadcasting networks in India and other developing nations. Radio talks, group discussions, interviews, features and other formats were prominently used by the business houses in order to gain public attention and appreciation. Corporate advertising activities were also carried out in good number by using radio stations. The radio stations faced the problem of increasing cost of operating and started radio advertising in 1920s in order to boost the sale of goods and services manufactured by public and private organizations. In the beginning, the advertising agencies were enabled to produce radio commercials along with the sponsoring companies. The advertising agencies were paid by the sponsoring companies for their creative works while the sponsoring companies gained the benefits of brand recognition and sales promotion. The advertising agencies and advertisers had absolute control over the programme contents which revealed the social benefits of the goods and services. The emergence of network radio programmes paved the way for individual radio station programming. The business organizations used them to launch publicity campaigns actively. The advertisers paid for the broadcasting of products and services. Empirical studies have revealed certain advantages of radio oriented business communication and advertising such as flexibility, portability, ubiquitous, high reach, better exposure, low production cost, low advertising cost, and simplicity.

In 1950s, television became a very prominent medium of communication in general and business broadcasting in particular. Television talks, discussions, interviews, features, profiles and other programmes were broadcast by the business houses at various levels in order to build image for the products and services. Television also catered to the needs of business houses as prominent means of business communication across the globe. Television advertising became very popular and account of better economic growth and development all over the world. The television industry grew along with the economic sector and the advertisers turned towards the television for commercial broadcasting. A new trend of magazine style of television emerged and it was later known as spot or participation advertising. Television earned income through selling time within and between programmes to several sponsors. The advertisers came forward to promote television advertising which brought the consumers and products together. Television enabled the consumers to understand the salient features of the products and services in several places including their own living rooms.

The television advertising revenues increased remarkably in 1950s. During 1960s, the television commercials were sold in 60 second units known as spots. There was astonishing growth of television as a medium of commercial broadcasting during the decades of 1980s and 1990s. The duration of spots varied but advertisers were the primary gainers of television commercials which boosted the image advertising. The cable television also offered advertisers several advanced and specialized channels that attracted niche audiences and consumers. The advantages of television communication and advertising include—high reach, high exposure, audio-visual, mass appeal, iniquitous, diversity, persuasiveness, emotional, entertaining and so on. Television gained an upper hand over newspapers, magazines and radio as an instrument of commercial broadcasting. The commercials served educational, social and economic purposes.

In the new millennium, Internet has become an interactive medium of business communication all over the world. It has opened up new vistas for advanced business communication and advertising. The computer technologies and tools have enabled the modern organizations to achieve the goal of business management on the basis of systematic identification of tasks, allocation of resources, implementation of business projects and evaluation of the results. The personal information management tools have emerged has excellent planning tools for scheduling business communication tasks. The word processing programmes facilitate meaningful editing of electronic contents and dissemination of instantaneous information services. Modern consumers are enabled to interact with the manufacturers, distributors and other purchasers. The online business communication and advertising have enriched the process of online communication and marketing. The banner advertisement has become the prominent form of online advertisement in the new age. It has increased the interest of consumers and enabled the modern consumers to make fast purchasing since banners are found on all types of websites. Modern advertisers have intelligently used click—through banners which are known for exciting visual presents and creative contents. The online advertising has other features such as superstitials, extramercials, webmercials, pop-unders, skyscrapers, and other forms which constitute 'digital age hydras'. The Internet is earning adequate advertising revenue from video ads since digital video is the fastest growing online advertising segment of our times. Online communication and advertising basically includes—online product placement, advertorials, informercials and buzz marketing which have attracted the new generation of consumers. The editorials of websites primarily promote the products and services which are especially designed to persuade the web users.

Electronic communication and advertising have played a crucial role in promoting free enterprise and competition in the age of globalization. The electronic media such as radio, television and Internet have boosted the economy through sales promotion exercise despite certain disadvantages and limitations. Critics have also stated that a new phenomenon of guerilla advertising has affected the public interest due to its manipulative characteristics. Multimedia channels are used by the modern business houses for variety of purposes constantly and continuously. The organizational communicators are trained in the application of traditional and new media for business communication purposes.

Technology Enabled Electronic Communication

Broadcasting technologies, satellite communication technologies and computer communication technologies basically constitute the gamut of electronic communication in modern business environment. George Guilder has stated that new communication technologies affirm our intellectual power and creativity. Bill Gates, media icon has rightly predicted that communication technologies would help leverage the abilities of modern organizers and communicators to find, use and share information on all aspects of human life under one common umbrella. Paul Saffo, Director of the Institute for the Future has opined that electronic communication technologies have enabled the people move from mass media to personalized media.

The electronic communication technological tools have enhanced the human ability to communicate all over the world within and outside the organizations. The modern tools facilitate smooth gathering, sharing and using of information about various business activities. The computer tools enable the source of communication and users of communication to find a variety of information quickly and accurately because of the availability of electronic formats and contents. The data on various aspects of organizational management and business promotion can be gathered from internal or external computers. The electronic means have brought about amazing internal and external access to online catalogues and databases in modern business organizations. The modern electronic database tools also provide a convenient way to collect information on round the clock basis.

Lesikar *et al.* (2011: 08) comment on computers, human intellect and organizational nervous thus: "An executive provides vision and direction, makes decisions, diagnoses and solves problems, negotiates, convinces and coaches people. All these actions depend on the executive's ability to think creatively and communicate clearly; clear communication and creative thinking can be enhanced by the use of computers. Unfortunately, most people don't realize the computer's role as a valuable thinking tool seems to be a secret. Grammar and style checkers are definitely important for the business writer. A wide variety of reference books is available for easy access. Graphics and designing programmes assist in supplementing textual materials with visuals. Speech input is new technology that will free the writer from keying messages. Today's software gives the writer many options for presenting messages. The mobile technology expands the physical environment of the message sender. The voice messaging systems are gaining business use. Video conferencing combines oral and video media. Technology enables us to add audio and video to our written documents. Facsimile, e-mail, text messaging, instant messaging and blogs are widely used for transmitting written messages. Computer tools assist groups on a wide variety of tasks in modern business organizations".

The electronic media technologies and tools have revolutionized the process of business communication since they can be used at the same place or at different places. They provide ample opportunities for interactive communication between the source and receivers. The collaborative tools change the group process and improve its output quality in modern business environment. The modern electronic tools will continue to enhance the business communication process. Joseph Tucci, CEO of EMC Corporation forecasts that innovation will continue forever and that companies will continue to use it to help improve productivity.

In the new millennium, e-mail, instant messaging, web-communication and voice and wireless technologies have become prominent tools of electronic communication for modern organizations. The e-mail facilitates the fast, convenient, efficient, eco-friendly and economically viable business communication. Useful subject line, idea-based communication, sequence of ideas based communication, proper use of shortened terms, useful graphic treatment and other guidelines are usually followed for preparing e-mail messages for business communication. The instant messaging represents a blending of e-mail with conversation. The communicators should use a few easily recognized abbreviations, acronyms, short sentences and other techniques. The senders should be aware of the legal and ethical implications and strictly abide by certain laws like copyright laws, cyber laws and so on.

The communicators should also give familiar with various web plot forms in order to disseminate the marketing messages. Suitable web based software should be used on the basis of proper security clearance, checks and balances. The communicators should be very brief, use attention compelling devices and avoid placing critical information. They must also be aware of voice and wireless technologies in business communication and make use of suitable wireless communication systems. The mobile telephones have become standard accessory for modern organizations all over the world. The communicators should also adopt certain healthy practices while conducting teleconferences and video conferences which involve many-to-many communication. They should be aware of technological limitations of these devices and adapt appropriate communicating style to maximize effectiveness of business communication.

Tools of Electronic Communication

The e-mail, instant messaging, web communication and voice and wireless technologies are the major tools of electronic communication in the new millennium, according to Lehman *et al.* (2012: 07).

E-mail

The electronic mail has become the most widely used communication tool in modern organizations. It facilitates the fast, convenient and all round flow of information among the users at various locations and time zones. The e-mail increases the efficiency and reduces the cost of communication considerably. It basically represents a substantial savings to modern organizations by avoiding long-distance telephone costs and postal mail charges. The business organizations communicate 24 hours a day and 365 days a year by using electronic messages which can bridge the communication gap between the sender and receiver across the globe. The effectiveness and utility of electronic mail is also enhanced through careful use of jargon, technical words and shortened terms. The graphic highlighting also enhances the status of e-mail communication which is based on certain etiquette which is the buzzword for proper behaviour on the Internet. The business organizations should develop an effective system for handling e-mail.

Instant Messaging

Instant messaging (IM) basically represents a blending of e-mail with conversation. This real time e-mail technology allows the business leaders and executives to interact with the people of their choice. The business use of instant messaging has witnessed a phenomenal growth over a period of time. This tool does not involve any expenditure and hardware facilities. The users can ask few quick questions and make appropriate decisions during business meetings. The e-mail communicators should abide by the copyright laws and ethical norms. They must also exercise caution against e-mail viruses and hoaxes.

Web Communications

The World Wide Web is truly a universal communication medium regardless of organizations and objectives. It has the capacity to reach out to a broad audience in diverse locations. The business organizations can establish a public web presence to extend their area of operations and increase their business transactions. The Intranet distributes various types of information to the insiders of modern organizations at numerous locations. The extranet enables the various stakeholders to access necessary information from the business houses of their choice. But Intranets and extranets practically restrict the access to those visitors with authorization such as a password. Modern business organizations use the web communication to communicate with various stakeholders. The web based project software applications allowed information to be viewed from any computer with Internet access. The user is required to have proper security clearance and passwords. Modern business organizations can post online any amount of information to various users through web communication. The Hyperlinks on a page can link to web pages or other types of files such as sound, video or interactive programmes. The web blog formats are adapted for business communication uses since they can store knowledge in searchable archives for future use.

Voice and Wireless Communication

The voice and wireless communication extends to voice mail systems and cell phone usage. The voice and data can be transmitted by using wireless communication systems. The voice mail technology allows flexibility in staying in touch without the aid of a computer. A voice mail message can also be used as evidence in a legal proceeding. The mobile telephones are indeed a standard accessory for many organizations and individuals throughout the world. The radio frequencies that transmit the voice signals can be picked up by other equipment regardless of the distance. The text messaging also puts an even greater premium on conciseness. Each medium requires its own appropriate communication style in order to maximize the effectiveness of business communication. The wireless communication technologies have considerably affected the contemporary business across the globe. The impact of wireless communication is significant as voice to text and text to voice technology continues to develop in the new millennium. Modern teleconferencing and video conferencing tools also facilitates effective business communication. The video conferencing is used to achieve progress in business and other spheres of human life. It is also strengthening the bonds between modern organizations and various stakeholders. It provides modern business organizations with the ability to interact and work with others across the globe.

Effective Electronic Communication Skills

The electronic media have bridged all communication gaps in all spheres of human life including the business world. The managers, supervisors and employees are required to cultivate better electronic communication skills in order to facilitate optimum use of electronic media for business management. The modern organizations cannot function in a vacuum especially in the age of online business. They should develop skilled and competent communicative manpower in order to race against the time and reach out to various publics on round the clock basis. Every business organization needs an effective electronic communication system to enable the employees to develop a clear understanding of their roles, responsibilities and growth opportunities within the organization.

Trompnaars and Woolliams (2003: 16) comment: "In this age of competitive business environment, active electronic communication system is vital for the sustainable development of an organization. This system is required for continual sharing of ideas, experiences and interactive meetings between the management and employees. The management should also be enabled to cultivate good human relationship between the organization and various stakeholders since business communication matters. Electronic communication system is required to establish and maintain mutually beneficial relationship between the organization and other stakeholders".

In the changing business environment of multinational operation and competition, electronic communication system has become an important component of marketing management. Like policy making, planning, programming, implementing, controlling, supervising, directing and coordinating, business communication too has evolved into a distinct discipline in the form of organizational communication. Several technological changes and developments in the age of information revolution have taken place and policy makers have understood the role of electronic communication system as an important tool in the successful management of industrial and business organizations.

Electronic communication skills cannot be gained overnight by the leaders, managers and employees in modern organizations. These skills have to be acquired on the spot while communicating with various key players who play a crucial role in the management and development of modern organizations. The policy makers have to identify the new trends in electronic business communication due to technological advancements which have taken place over a period of time. Perry (2003: 11) states: "The large size of the modern organizations also poses serious challenge in the process of business communication. The successful utilization of electronic media for business communication and advertising purposes primarily depends upon the skills of the people who use them in modern organizations".

The globalization of business in the new millennium demands that organizational leaders and communicators develop better media literacy, gain familiarity with advanced electronic media and apply the media for the purpose of business communication with internal and external publics who are located in far-flung locations. Today, people across the world use electronic media as instant means of business communication regardless of time and space. Electronic media have also become most preferred mode of corporate communication and advertising in the world. The language and culture of electronic communication differ from place to place, culture to culture and organization to organization.

Lehman *et al.* (2012: 07) observe: "Business messages should reflect correct, standard English and contemporary language used in a professional business setting. Outdated expressions and dull clichés reduce the effectiveness of a message and the credibility of the source. Instead, substitute fresh, original expressions that reflect contemporary language patterns. The handy verbal shortcuts are convenient, quick, easy to use and often include simple metaphors and analogies that effectively communicate the most basic ideas or emotions or the most complex business concept. The business writers should use simple, informal words that are readily understood and less distracting than more difficult, formal words. Concise communication includes all relevant details in the fewest possible words. In particular, concise communication, application of visual enhancements and remaining sensitive to international audiences would boost electronic business communication".

The selection of media, formulation of messages, delivery of information, receipt of information and reaction of the target group should be firmly grasped by the organizational leaders and communicators. With increasing globalization, constant interaction between organizations and various stakeholders has become highly inevitable. This necessitates the electronic media orientation and cultivation of electronic media skills on the part of the organizational leaders and communicators. In the international business environment, electronic communication has become a prominent method of instantaneous communication in modern organizations.

Conclusion

Electronic media have grown commendably all over the world in the age of information explosion. The advent of electronic media has added a new dimension to corporate communication and advertising across the world. The policy-makers, managers, professionals and communicators should understand the nature and importance of electronic communication in business transactions. They should learn the key skills of electronic communication and apply electronic communication skills to new business challenges and opportunities. Today, organizational communicators spend maximum time for electronic communication which is next only to oral communication in modern business environment. The choice between using oral and electronic communication is guided by considering the suitability of the purpose and nature of the subject of business communication. Electronic media have more advantages rather than disadvantages from business communication point of view. The corporate communicators are required to make better connections with various stakeholders in a changing electronic business world. Business communication becomes more effective with the advancement of electronic media technologies and tools.

References

Bhusan, Uma (2012) *Introduction to Business Communication*, Jaico Publishing House, Mumbai.

Chaturvedi, P.D. and Mukesh Chaturvedi (2011) *Business Communication—Concepts, Cases and Applications*, Delhi: Pearson, p. 116.

Hasan, Seema (2010) *Mass Communication: Principles and Concepts*, CBS Publishers and Distributors Pvt. Ltd., New Delhi.

Kameda, Naoki (1996) *Business Communication Toward Transnationalism: The Significance of Cross-Cultural Business English and its Role*, Tokyo: Kindiabungeisha, p. 34.

Karoli, Veera and Naghma Ahmed (2013) *Business Communication*, Thakur Publishers, Bengaluru, India.

Kaul, Asha (2009) *Business Communication*, PHI Learning Private Limited, New Delhi.

Lehman, Carol, M., Devvie D., DuFrene, Mala Sinha and Robin C. Walker (2012) BCOM, *An Innovative Approach to Learning and Teaching, Business Communication, A South Asian Perspective*, Cengage Learning, New Delhi, pp. 208-216.

Lesikar V., Raymond, Marie E. Flatley, Kathryin Rentz and Neerja Pande (2011) *Business Communication: Making Connections in a Digital World*, New Delhi: Tata McGraw Hill Education Private Limited, pp. 20-21.

Medoff, Norman J. and Barbara K. Kaye (2011) *Electronic Media—Then, Now and Later*, Amsterdam: Elsevier, pp. 5-6.

Mukerjee, Hory Sankar (2013) *Business Communication: Connecting at Work*, Oxford University Press, New Delhi.

Perry, David (2003) Do you have the skills most in demand today?, *Career Journal*, www.careerjournal.com

Schultz, Heidi (2000) *The Elements of Electronic Communication*, Boston: Allyn and Bacon, pp. 43-47.

Shelby, Annette N. and Lamar Reinsch, Jr. (1995) Positive Emphasis and You-Attitude: An Empirical Study, *Journal of Business Communication.*

Sterne, Jim and Anthony Priore (2000) *E-mail Marketing: Using E-mail to reach your Target Audience and Build Customer Relationship*, New York: John Wiley & Sons, p. 141.

Stevenson, J. (1988) *Language, Thought and Representation*, Chichester: John Wiley.

Trompnaars, Fons and Peter Woolliams (2003) *Business Communication Across Cultures*, London: Capstone, p. 53.

Winsor, Dorothy A (2003) *Writing Power: Communication in an Engineering Centre*, Albany: Suny Press.

Zikmund, William G. (2003) *Business Research Methods*, Mason, O.H: South Western, p. 279.

Chapter 8
Business Management Communication Approaches

Introduction

Communication occupies an enviable place in the process of business communication. The need for business communication is seldom questioned in the age of globalization. Studies have also revealed that business needs good communicators, negotiators, cultural ambassadors and other facilitators of business promotion. Communication is vital to every aspect of business management. Experience reveals that by improving the communication skills and competence, the organizational leaders and officials can also improve the chances for successful conduction of business. Effective communicators are in high demand since there is a high correlation between communication skills and business promotion. In the new millennium, technology magnifies the participatory business communication which occurs on round the clock basis across the globe. Communication is absolutely essential in the business world since it promotes the mutual trust between the organization and various stakeholders. Effective business communication is necessary in the present age of competitiveness in order to improve business operations and achieved success. The fundamentals of business communication, forms of business communication, basic patterns of business messages, techniques of business report writing, cross-cultural business communication and technology oriented business communication are presented in this Chapter.

Fundamentals of Business Communication

Communication plays an important role in business organizations since they need good communicators. Evidence of the importance of communication in business organizations is found in several studies.

Scholars have noted that communication is important to business management. Communication is also the most important skill for the executives and functionaries in modern business organizations. Good communication skills are required to build mutual trust between the business organization and various stakeholders. Effective communication skills are vital for the successful business management in modern society.

The business communicators are required to understand the principles and practices of business communication. The business communicators are required to adapt themselves to the changing business environment in general and aspirations of various business stakeholders in particular. The business executives and functionaries should know that communication matters most in the modern business environment. They must choose the words, phrases and other language symbols which communicate intended messages effectively and efficiently. Simplicity is the hallmark of business communication. The communicators should also know how to fulfil the communication requirements of various stakeholders by adapting their media, messages and strategies.

Simple words, shorts sentences, specific contents, relevant examples, supportive facts and figures, concrete ideas, and other inputs are essential to make business communication appropriate and useful. Business communicators are required to understand the ground rules and prevent barriers to communication. Concrete words and sentences usually stand for things that exist in the real world. Concreteness also means specificity or exactness of messages which reach out to the target group without any delay or discrepancy. The use of active and strong verbs also makes business communication alive and purposeful. Active voice is more preferable than passive voice since it avoids any kind of accuse of the target group.

Bhusan (2012) pointed out that communication barriers act as circuit breaker in the process of business communication and have to be avoided for an effective business communication process. Modern organizations are required to expand their business operations beyond their own countries in the age of globalization. The corporate leaders, managers and communicators should provide business communication services which create sound corporate culture and facilitate successful business management.

It is better to communicate ideas in organized way and normal order. Selection of most precise and highly contextual words, sentences and dialogues also makes business communication quite meaningful. The business communicators should also consciously avoid certain contents that discriminate against religion, race, nationality, sex, age, disability and so on. The discriminatory and objectionable contents do not auger well for business communication. The contents should not displease the target groups. Unfair references should also be avoided in order to prevent negative reactions. The communicators should also avoid certain contents which displease the people.

Narayanamurthy (2001: 15) Founder Chairman of Infosys Technologies Limited observes: "Communication is most impactful and yields the best results when you use simple, direct and powerful statements or quotes to convey your ideas". Business communication should be practiced on the basis of powerful adages and aphorisms. The communicators should know how to adapt their business messages to different groups and contexts in a pluralistic society like India. The contents should be formulated with a view to give the right emphasis to most important ideas and actions the oral, written and electronic business communication should be carried out on the basis of use of readable or understandable contents which fit into various groups and situations.

Business communicators should also ensure great care in designing the communication contents which involve grouping and ordering of various ideas and actions. The communicators are required to cultivate an awareness of different communication types, formats and elements in order to do justice to their role as better communicators. Effective contents would also save the time, energy and efforts of the target groups. Brief, bright and brisk communication delivers the message in every effective way because of mind limitations of the receivers. The communicators should also be aware of the word economy since they must use shorter ways of communicating things.

Surplus words, ideas and contents should be eliminated since they add nothing to the process of understanding. The advent of communication technologies including computers has changed the business communication culture over a period of time. Unnecessary repetition of words or ideas should be avoided in order to give every idea its due emphasis and emphasize the contents which are most important from business communication point of view. The receivers of business communication are also wish to receive the messages which communicate easily and quickly. All parts of a message should concern one idea or thought in order to facilitate better understanding. The communicators should also avoid excessive ideas or details which cost the unity of thought and action. Illogical and unjustifiable contents and constructions would produce communication barriers. Hence, the contents of business communication should concern specific ideas and actions for better persuasion of the target group to accept ideas, products and services. The communicators should also succeed in making good use of topic sentences which can help make good compartments.

Lesikar *et al.* (2012: 09) note: "Increased globalization and integration with diverse audiences across borders is making people realize the value of simple unambiguous language, clearly worded direct sentences and cogently linked coherent paragraphs". Effective business communication yields better results in a competitive business environment. The communicators should communicate the ideas in a matter of fact way since it produces goodwill effect and clarity of thoughts. The communication skills should affect the human relationship to go far to determine the success of the business operations.

Rodman (2001: 16) comments: "Your attitude requires writers first to view a real-world situation from the reader's perspective and then to show in the text of the document a sensitivity to the reader's perspective. When simply using 'you' and 'yours' rather than 'I' or 'mine' will sometimes help to express a you-attitude, it would be both simple-minded and incorrect to equate you-attitude with the dominance of you in the text". Business communication in conversational language has a favourable effect. Getting the desired effects is a matter of communicating skill and of understanding the people who matter most in the business environment. In face-to-face communication, words, voice, facial expressions, gestures and such combine to determine the effect of the message. In case of written communication, the words should be chosen in such a manner that they combine all essential elements of communication which promote business.

The language of business communication also communicates more than the message. User-friendly language sounds well in building good will between the source of communication and target group. Unhealthy language destroys the goodwill development exercise. The communicators should be sincere enough to reach out to the target group on the basis of adoption of goodwill techniques. Exaggerations are obviously insincere since exaggerated statements or comments involve the use of superlatives which are devoid of objectivity. The contents of business communication should also get proper emphasis. Hence, most important ideas and actions should be emphasized on the basis of certain meaningful guidelines and healthy practices.

Role of Communication in Business Management

Business organizations primarily depend on communication in order to sell the goods and services across the globe in a competitive business environment. There are so many stakeholders who are responsible for the successful management of business organizations and activities. Business leaders have also realized that systematic business communication is necessary to persuade various stakeholders of business management on a regular basis and enlist their active participation. Drucker (1991: 04) has rightly pointed out that communication skill and competence are the prerequisites to business promotion in modern society.

Lesikar *et al.* (2012: 10) identify three categories of communication in business namely—internal operational, external operational and personal. All the communication that occurs in conducting work within a business is internal operational. The work related communication that a business does with people and groups outside the business is external operational communication. Personal communication is the exchange of information and feelings among people in the business organization. All these communications are vital to business success.

Modern business organizations have formal and informal communication networks. The formal network consists of the official, more stable lines of communication. The informal network consists of personal communications within the organization. The business organizations have felt the need for constant communication between the organization and rest of the publics who are directly associated with the organization in different capacities. But, each business organization is sustained by its own culture which affects all management functions including business communication, according to Schein (2004: 17).

Don Zatyko comments: "Communication is the most used skill in almost every job. How you communicate your accomplishments to others is a reflection of the quality of your work. Sure, you must know how to do your tasks to accomplish great results, but that is only a portion of professional success. Good communication skills are required to report your results to others, persuade colleagues to take action, and (most importantly at review time) sell your successes to management". Business organizations should develop a team of skilled, creative and competent business communicators who can build reputation for the organization concerned through efficient delivery of messages. Numerous communication—related activities occur in all business organizations. All these communication activities are carried out in business because communication is essential to the organized effort involved in contemporary business management.

Communication plays a crucial role in cultivating positive relationships between the organization and beneficiaries. Organizational communicators are called upon to create and maintain mutually beneficial relationship which is highly essential to successful business management. Every act of business communication should be decided in consultation with the specialists. Business organizations should be willing to adapt themselves to the changing business environment. The business communicators should develop appropriate communication strategies, enrich their communication skills, reach out to the target group, persuade the target group to accept the product and service and retain the goodwill of receivers constantly.

Communication really matters in modern business organizations. The organizational leaders, executives and other functionaries are required to improve their communication skill and competence which invariably improve the chances for success in business organizations. Business executives have also identified communication skill as the prerequisite to success in business field. The recent technological innovations and advancements have added a new dimension to business communication. Application of new technologies and strategies is essential for effective business communication management in the new millennium.

The Business Communication Process

In reality, the business communication is an interpersonal goal-directed process, observe Lesikar *et al.* (2012: 11). They have identified 10 basic elements of business communication process with respect to communicator-1 and communicator-2. They include—communicator-1 senses a communication need, defines the problem, searches for possible solutions, selects a course of action, composes the message and delivers the message. The communicator-2 receives the message, interprets the message, decides on a response and response to a message. Both parties in a communication event influence the outcome of that event in a business organization.

The source of communication understands the need for business communication in the first step. The source also defines the problem in order to plan a communication event. In the 3rd stage, the source develops a communication design and identifies appropriate communication strategies. In the 4th stage, the source examines the cost-benefit ratio and decides possible business communication strategies. In the 5th stage, the source composes the message which fits into the context of business and environment of receivers. In the 6th stage, the source delivers the message to the receivers with a fond hope of generating favourable response.

The receivers of communication receive the message in the 7th stage. In the 8th stage, the receivers interpret the message and forms judgements. In the 9th stage, the receiver decides on a particular response by taking into account the individual needs and gains. In the 10th stage the receiver responds to the message either positively or negatively on the basis of an analytical approach. Thus, business communication involves several stages and two important players namely source and receivers. Practically, business communication involves analytical ability, creative mindset and judgement capacity of the receivers.

The process of business communication also involves certain elements and stages, according to communication experts. It includes—understanding the context of business, target group, selection of media, formulation of messages, editing of messages, delivery of messages, collection of feedback and so on. All these elements of business communication should be properly understood by the communicators.

The context of business should be properly grasped by the communicators in terms of geography, sociology, economics, politics, culture, linguistics and other factors. Each and every business communication is different from other contexts and contents. The background, needs and demands of the target group should be properly understood in order to design and implement appropriate business communication messages and programmes. The media which are close to the hearts and souls of the target group should be chosen as far as possible.

The message formulation is a planned and deliberate exercise. The objectives of business communication should be properly understood in order to plan the business communication on the basis of individual, professional and organizational contexts. Authentic facts and figures should be organized in order to deliver the messages in the right spirit. The communicators should also make use of creative and authoritative script writers who can fit into the medium. The messages should be drafted on the basis of salient features of business communication. The format, structure and contents of business communication should be revised properly in order to facilitate greatest understanding among the greatest majority of receivers.

The messages should be delivered in a highly readable or understandable format, structure and contents. The language of business communication should be simple, informal and creative by nature. The communicators should use the techniques of clear communication since correctness is the hallmark of business communication. The communicators are responsible for designing the communication delivery system and carrying out the operations. Business communication should be based on democratic and user friendly approaches. The current emphasis is on strategy and humanness in business communication.

Business communication services should be delivered in accordance with the felt needs and demands of the users. The messages should convey ideas completely with minimal need for response. The fitness of business communication should be evaluated by the communicators. Hence, feedback collection on analysis assumes significance in business communication process. A positive reaction from the users calls for directness. The purpose of business communication is served very well if the receivers grasp the messages and respond to the senders positively. Negative impressions should be overcome through positive business communication which includes convincing ideas, suggestions and guidelines.

Forms of Business Communication

The major forms of business communication include—oral communication, written communication, electronic communication and extension communication. Oral communication is also one of the types of business communication in modern organizations. The managers, supervisors, employees and corporate communicators depend on oral communication when they interact with the internal publics and external publics. Oral communication is also the oldest form of communication which preceded the written and electronic communication. In business organizations, oral communication is used more than written, electronic and other forms of business communication. Effective oral communication has the power to build good human interactions which make the fortunes of modern business organizations.

In business organizations talking, listening, committee meetings, group discussions, conferences, speeches, lectures, telephonic conversations and other kinds of oral communication occur on a regular basis. Oral communication is both formal and informal exercise which benefits both the parties in business organizations. Oral communication is primarily dependent on words which convey several ideas. The oral communication is a vital part of business communication. The organizational leaders are basically the voice of the business organizations and they spend most of their times on oral communication in their day to day situations. These communicators should be able to rise to the occasion and build sound image for the organizational services and products in a competitive business environment.

Oral communication has two dimensions namely—(a) communication between the organizational leaders and employees, and (b) communication between the organizational communicators and constituent publics. The need for constant interaction between modern business organizations and constituent publics is ever increasing in the age of globalization. In the new millennium, people matter most. Modern business organizations should know how to develop mutually beneficial relationship between the organization and various publics. In modern business organizations, formal oral communications such as talking, listening, participating in meetings, talking by phone and dictating are carried out on day to day basis. The leaders and communicators spend most of their time in talking to various publics.

The choice of words also matters most in oral communication. It is related to the vocabulary of the speaker. As far as possible, the communicator should make use of the words which are found in the vocabulary of the listeners. The communicators should select the words which appropriately convey the intended meaning in a given oral communication context. The effectiveness of oral communication also depends on the adaptation which means fitting the message to the needs of the intended listeners. Thus, oral communication is depended on voice quality, talking style, choice of words and adaptation of the speakers. The business leaders and communicators also participate in formal and informal meetings and get together. The group discussions, committee meetings, conferences, feedback sessions and other formal occasions involve disciplined, deliberate and systematic oral communication.

The corporate leaders and communicators are required to address various gatherings during different occasions in order to educate and persuade the stakeholders regarding the policies, programmes, products and services of the organizations. The art of public speaking cannot be acquired overnight by the speakers. They have to constantly improve their public speaking skills and capacity on the basis of proper reading, understanding and interacting exercises. There are several techniques of cultivating better public speaking skills. They include—selection of appropriate topic, academic preparation, organization of the information, assessment of the needs of the participants, attention compelling introductory remarks, identification of salient features, presentation of key elements, interpretation of prominent points, utilization of quotable quotes, emphasizing the transitions between parts, summarizing the major aspects, presenting a fitting conclusion, receiving questions, clarifying important things, thanking the audience and so on.

Written communication is a creative, intellectual and organized communication which remains in black and white. The source of communication should be aware of the needs and expectations of prospective readers or users. The producers of written business communication should also be aware of the essential principles and techniques of effective written communication. They must be very choosy and selective while making use of words, phrases and language for the purpose of written communication. Broadly speaking, written communication is an art of communicating the messages which facilitate better understanding between the organization and various stakeholders.

Business writing is an art and craft which is cultivated by the communicators over a period of time. Effective business writing does not happen overnight. The basic communication skills are essentially the same as those required for effective business writing. Business writing has twin objectives namely—writing to inform and writing to persuade. The informative writing presents the information to the receivers or users who are required to develop necessary awareness about the aims, objectives, goods, services and contributions of business organizations in modern society. The corporate communicators provide necessary information to the various stakeholders about the day to day activities of the business organizations concerned.

The investors require information about the business status and income generating opportunities. The employees need information about job security, job satisfaction, job promotion, employee welfare and other aspects. The distributors need information about the mode of distribution of goods and services, incentives for distributors and advantages of distributing the goods and services. The customers need information about the products, salient features of the products, advantages of the products, pricing of the products, availability of the products and other facilities. The media representatives need information about the organizational profile, features, products, services and social benefits. The government agencies need information about the norms, guidelines, specifications, fulfilment of statutory norms and other obligations. The community needs information about the philanthropic activities of the organization.

Written communication is a time consuming process. It involves proper collection of ideas, planning of writing, drafting of contents, editing of contents and so on. It involves more formalities and the communicator should stick to the format and contents. The communicator also remains away from the target group physically and otherwise. It may not be possible for the communication to enlist immediate feedback about the contents and correctness of communication. The communicator is also required to gain absolute command over the art and craft of written communication in business organizations. Absence of the prerequisites to written communication would also pose serious threats and disadvantages. The source of communication should have adequate understanding of the process of written communication which involves several elements such as: (1) purpose of communication, (2) needs of the target group, (3) clarity of thought, (4) accuracy of facts, (5) concrete language, (6) effective tone, (7) brevity in presentation, (8) appropriate words, (9) active verbs, (10) designing of messages, (11) short sentences, (12) meaningful paragraph, (13) conversational style, (14) positive approach, and (15) meaningful editing and design.

Electronic channels of business communication are known as barrierless channels which make people believe what they here and see are true. The contemporary universe of digital electronic media offers increasingly greater control over listening, viewing and electronic interaction. Modern managers and organizational communicators should know about the latest technological advancements and understand how they will affect the future of business organizations. In the last quarter of twentieth century, computer, telecommunication and satellite communication channels were developed. Since then, the audience switched over to cable, satellite and the Internet. The new millennium is known as the electronic communication revolution age.

Electronic communication and advertising have played a crucial role in promoting free enterprise and competition in the age of globalization. The electronic media such as radio, television and Internet have boosted the economy through sales promotion exercise despite certain disadvantages and limitations. Critics have also stated that a new phenomenon of guerilla advertising has affected the public interest due to its manipulative characteristics. Multimedia channels are used by the modern business houses for variety of purposes constantly and continuously. The organizational communicators are trained in the application of traditional and new media for business communication purposes.

In the changing business environment of multinational operation and competition, electronic communication system has become an important component of marketing management. Like policy making, planning, programming, implementing, controlling, supervising, directing and coordinating, business communication too has evolved into a distinct discipline in the form of organizational communication. Several technological changes and developments in the age of information revolution have taken place and policy makers have understood the role of electronic communication system as an important tool in the successful management of industrial and business organizations.

Electronic media have grown commendably all over the world in the age of information revolution and explosion. The advent of electronic media has added a new dimension to corporate communication and advertising across the world. The policy-makers, managers, professionals and communicators should understand the nature and importance of electronic communication in business transactions. They should learn the key skills of electronic communication and apply electronic communication skills to new business challenges and opportunities. Today, organizational communicators spend maximum time for electronic communication which is next only to oral communication in modern business environment. The choice between using oral and electronic communication is guided by considering the suitability of the purpose and nature of the subject of business communication. Electronic media have more advantages rather than disadvantages from business communication point of view.

Basic Patterns of Business Messages

Effective business messages are required for attracting the attention of the target group regardless of the context of communication and media of communication. Business communication is practiced all over the world by using several media of communication. Writing business messages is a challenging task Lesikar *et al.* (2012: 12) have discussed the process of writing which includes planning, drafting and revising.

According to them, planning consists of three general activities such as gathering and collecting, analyzing and organizing and choosing a form. The communicators should gather relevant information from different sources with a focus on the goal of business communication and mission of the business promotion. Primary and secondary sources of information available through several individuals and forms should be gathered adequately. The source of communication should also verify the authenticity and credibility of the information resources. The appropriateness, adequacy and relevance of the information gathered by the source should be systematically analyzed.

Organization of the materials should be undertaken on the basis of the channels of communication and requirements of various communications media. The source should efficiently choose the form, channel and format for effective delivery of the messages. Specific decisions should be taken by the source about the delivery of messages in a highly persuasive manner in order to evoke favourable response from the receivers of business communication. The communicators are required to organize the materials, contents and other resources which would evoke positive response from the target group. The materials should be presented in a logical pattern which would persuade the target group to accept the product or service delivered by the business organization concerned.

The business communicators should decide the form, channel and format for the delivery of highly persuasive business messages. They should choose the form which will fit into a given communication context and cater to the needs of target group. The formatting is an integral part of business communication which demands flexibility, perfection, continuity and persuasion. The communicators should provide relevant ideas which would enhance productivity and profitability in the business environment. They should also make wise decisions about formatting in consultation with the experts.

The business messages should be disseminated on the basis of sound principles and practices of reporting, editing and designing. Creativity also matters in business communication. Lesikar *et al.* (2012: 13) suggest: "An attractive, readable format is critical to any message's success. In more recent times emphasis shifted to structure and strategy of content and humanness of wording. Effective business communication facilitates fast decisions and actions which would benefit the manufacturers and advertisers".

Techniques of Business Report Writing

The word 'report' is derived from the Latin word 'reportare' which means to carry back. A report is a description of an event carried back to someone who was not present on the scene. A report, by definition, is a "statement describing what had happened, what is happening and what is likely to happen". In business organizations, periodic reports should be submitted to the various stakeholders through different channels in order to invite their attention on the business issues, trends and developments.

According to Raymond V. Lesikar and John D. Pettit, "A business report is an orderly, objective communication of factual information that serves some business purpose". Reports are regularly disseminated to the target groups since they are vital tools to the communicative needs of the users. The business report serves a variety of purpose in modern society. Business reports are produced by the manufacturing agencies with a view to educate, motivate and persuade the target groups about the products and services made available to the mankind.

The business reports are classified into different categories on the basis of form, direction, functional use and content normally. The major types of report include—formal report, informal report, analytical report, upward-directed report, downward-directed report, internal report, external report, periodic report and functional report, according to Lehman *et al.* (2012: 07).

The formal report is a structured, organized and logically presented report which contains suitable facts, figures and contents. An informal report carries objective information from one area of an organization to another. An analytical report presents the existing business state of affairs along with necessary solutions and suggestions. An upward report is directed at the superior authorities with facts and appeal. The downward report is directed at the subordinates with suitable instructions and directions. The internal report travels within an organization from one section to another section on the basis of information and ideas for better coordination. The external report travels outside the organization from the management to various stakeholders on the basis of business performance and promotional initiatives. The periodic report contains the existing state of affairs, business transactions and future course of action. The functional report serves a specified purpose within an organization.

The nature, scope and magnitude of the business usually determine the diversity of reports. Lesikar *et al.* (2012: 13) defined: "A business report is an orderly and objective communication of factual information that serves a business purpose". The key words are orderly, objective, communication, factual information and serving a business purpose. This definition covers the wide spectrum of business reports which warrant the attention and action of various stakeholders of business management in modern economy.

The business report should introduce the main objective and focus the attention of leaders on the mission statement. The report should also present the salient features of the main topic with suitable facts, figures and examples. The factors associated with the main theme should be perfectly ordered and delineated in order to bring about better understanding among the receivers. The communicators are required to conduct systematic fact finding exercise in order to provide specific information to the readers. Suitable experiments and surveys are required to generate primary data from the field. The Internet and other print resources also provide adequate secondary data on the subject concerned. The report should also contain adequate interpretations that will guide the contents and meet the needs of users. Factual reporting, authentic facts, credible views, reliable data, simple comments, valid claims, proper verification and systematic authentication are the inputs for business reporting.

The contents of business report should have different compartments in order to ensure meaningful process of dividing the contents and better understanding among the readers. Lesikar *et al.* (2012: 13) provide specific guidelines for writing the business report thus: "In writing the report, communicate clearly and quickly. When drafting, get the right things in the right order. Do not strive for a perfect first draft. Your finished report should communicate clearly and adequately. Two critical ingredients are a reader-centred beginning and ending. Such characteristics as objectivity, consistency in time view point, transition and interest can also enhance the reception of your report". The specific guidelines include—determine the purpose, identify the factors, gather the information needed, interpret the information, organize the material, plan the writing, assign parts to be written, write parts assigned, revise collaboratively and edit the final draft.

Lehman *et al.* (2012: 08) enumerate the process of business report which contains several steps namely—recognizing and defining the problem, selecting a method of solution, collecting and organizing the data and arriving at an answer. In the first step, the source of business communication should make a clear statement of purpose, formulate hypotheses, define technical terms and identify documenting procedures. In the second step, the business communicator should select appropriate printed, electronic, new media and other sources of communication in order to identify suitable solutions to the business problems. In the third stage, the business communicator should collect relevant secondary data from various sources and means, organize the contents and place citations in the proper manner. In the fourth stage, the business communicator should ensure systematic analysis of data, present suitable findings and offer necessary suggestions for the improvement of business transactions.

The characteristics of a good business report include—accuracy, simplicity, completeness, brevity, readability, visibility, reliability, validity, creativity, economy, timeliness, fairness, logical presentation and so on. There are informational reports, interpretative reports, analytical reports, critical reports, special reports, technical reports, scientific reports, environmental reports, business reports, sport reports and so on. The process of reporting is not necessarily confined to only business sector. It practically encompasses all spheres of human life.

The business communicators should adopt well defined guidelines. They should ensure that the introductory part effectively introduces the subject. Objectivity in business reporting is highly essential. The facts, figures and other contents should be valid. Personal writing is more useful than impersonal writing. The report should content a consistent time view point throughout the exercise. The past time view point should furnish the historical perspective. The present time view point should provide the current perspective. Meaningful transitions are also required to connect the various compartments of business report. Suitable transition sentences should be used to render connectivity and provide integrated communication. The writers should be choosy well using transitional words which explain relationships. The business report should be perceived by the readers as highly interesting piece of writing. Appropriate attention compelling devices can also be used wherever necessary.

Cross-Cultural Business Communication

Business operations are always guided by the culture which is a way of life of a group of people. Barnouw (1963: 02) defines: "Culture is a way of life of a group of people... the stereotyped patterns of learning behaviour, which are handed down from one generation to the next through means of language and imitation". The culture is also defined as the shared ways in which groups of people understand and interpret the world, according to Trompenaars and Woolliams (2003: 18).

Cultural differences are found in all spheres of human life regardless of space and time. People living in different countries are bound to share different cultures which affect values, habits and other aspects of life of people. These differences are a major source of problems when people of different cultures try to communicate. The people also tend to view the ways of their culture as normal and the ways of other cultures as peculiar. This tendency is called as ethnocentrism which adversely affects the business transactions including communication across cultures. The food habits, lifestyles and other approaches also vary from culture to culture. The body language and communication patterns also differ from culture to culture, according to Axtell (1998: 01).

The attitudes and behavioural patterns are also the bi-products of culture. There are several factors which are associated with cross-cultural communication and human relationships development. People from different cultures often vary in their attitudes and approaches towards business. The human relationships also vary in different cultures. The social and economic status also affects the communication patterns and public relations. The human values are also created by the cultural ethos and norms. Each culture has different values concerning human relationship, business transaction and so on.

In the age of globalization, technological advances and communication exercises have brought the whole business environment under one common umbrella. Modern business houses are required to communicate across cultures effectively in order to enhance business transactions and prospects. The goods and services of business houses are distributed domestically and globally among the customers who share diverse cultural and linguistic backgrounds. Business houses should also cultivate the art of winning people from other cultures and nations in this age of competitive business.

Lesikar *et al.* (2012: 13) justified the need for cross-cultural business communication thus: "Communicating across cultures effectively improves your productivity and efficiency and promotes harmonious work environments". The present generation of customers is found throughout the length and breadth of the world which has multi-cultures. In this age of multi-culturalism, business houses should also expand their operations and cater to the needs of customers who represent different cultures across the globe. The business communicators should also understand the various features of cross-cultural communication which involves proper understanding of cultural differences in order to overcome certain barriers to interaction.

The communication principles and practices are not universally common due to cultural differences. The communication problems also arise due to the cultural and linguistic diversity. The communication barriers are bound to occur in international communication on account of such diversity. The differences among languages make equivalent translations difficult since languages are based on the cultural ethos, human values and other differences. The multiple meanings of words also create communication barriers. The business communicators should understand the concept, practice and techniques of cross-cultural communication in order to bring about better understanding, cooperation and transaction between the two parties. In the age of globalization and Internet revolution, English is the primary language of international business management and communication.

Scholars have examined the relationship between business communication and cross-cultural communication. The significance of cross-cultural business communication has been discussed at length by the communicators. The words which are derived from the culture also present certain practical communication problems. Experience reveals that business communicators should not use slang in cross-cultural communication. The words and phrases which are used in usual business communication should be avoided consciously in cross-cultural communication in order to prevent misunderstandings and inconveniences. Experts have also suggested the use of simple, basic English for communicating across cultures for the purpose of business management. It is also necessary to continuously check for meaning in different contexts in order to ensure the accuracy of business communication purpose.

Technology-Oriented Business Communication

Communication technologies have widened the scope of communication in different spheres of human life. The new technologies affirm the intellectual power and creativity in the new millennium. The new media have helped the mankind to move from mass media to personalized media. In particular, the social media have killed the distance, hierarchy, time and other impediments to participatory communication. The new communication technologies such as hardware, software and web-based tools have enhanced the process of communication remarkably. These tools and technologies have become all pervasive on account of their commendable communicative power. In the era of media convergence, computer tools are used effectively for the purpose of business communication.

The technology networks have placed the world at the fingertips. The emergence of new media for business communication has brought about remarkable changes and developments in the process of business management. The new communication technologies offer various advantages such as—collecting and analyzing data, shaping messages to be clearer and more effective and communicating quickly and efficiently with others over long distances. These media also reduce travel time and increase work efficiency in several ways. Business related information can be disseminated and shared between the source and receivers in the form of text, images, audio and video through Internet. The Intranets also allow modern business organizations to post-information and resources for various stakeholders including the employees. The protected information and resources on business management are made available to various stakeholders including the customers through Extranets. The electronic information resources and services also enhance the status of data organization, data integrity and data security.

The advanced computer tools are used for planning, gathering, writing and presenting business communication messages for different media. Lesikar *et al.* (2012: 13) enumerated the technology-enabled business communication thus: "Outlining or brainstorming programmes help in planning the content of a message. Outlining tools are included in most word processors. Today's large-screen monitors make this an effective use. By using *Personal Information Management* (PIM) tools, you can plan time for completing writing projects. Computer programs help you analyse and interpret data with statistics and graphics. The graphics programmes help you understand the data and create graphics. Word processing software is clearly the dominant writing tool of most writers. Today's word processors allow you to use other writing tools from within the word processor or that integrate seamlessly with it. Insert allows the writer to add characters at any point, while delete lets the writer delete characters. The use of advanced word processing features also saves time. Today's software gives the writer many options for presenting the messages. The mobile technology has expanded the physical environment of the message sender. Voice messaging systems are gaining business use. Video conferencing combines oral and video media. Technology enables us to add audio and video to the written documents".

The new technologies and tools are widely used in business for sending a variety of oral and visual messages to the various stakeholders of business management. The mobile phones have enabled the business people to ensure optimum productive use of their time and energy. The voice messaging systems are increasingly used for business communication. The video conferencing systems have facilitated interactive and participatory business communication. The facsimile, e-mail, text messaging, instant messaging, blogs and other devices have added new dimension to written business communication. The blogs have become effective tool for participatory communication. The computer tools have also assisted the traditional group for a variety of business tasks. The discussion tools have enabled the business parties to overcome the limitations of time and distance. The human resources play a vital role in the process of business communication since they control the message formulation activities. The need for oral and written business communication will never decrease even in the new age of technology-enabled communication.

Etiquette Advantages in Business Communication

The business executives and communicators are required to understand the business oriented etiquette and follow them in letter and spirit. Etiquette is a code of behaviour that delineates expectations for social behaviour which boost the status of business organization and credibility of various stakeholders. Etiquette is commonly defined as a set of manners, courtesies, social conventions and all those behaviours that make human interactions with others pleasant and considerate. The etiquette is a testimony of personality, bearing, demeanour; presence and style accepted by convention are authority. Etiquette also helps in leaving a good, clear and long-lasting impression on the recipients.

Radhika Shapoorjee observes: "Etiquette underscores consistency and continuity, is learned and acquired and thereby establishes credibility about a person's background. Through etiquette, we know about a person's philosophy of life that affects work behaviour". Etiquette concerns itself with the demonstration of good thoughts and deeds which represent the culture, legacy and civilization of the associates in the modern business environment. Clarence Thomas notes: "Good manner will open doors that the best education cannot". Thus, etiquette is a means of establishing the human personality and credibility in modern society.

Lehman *et al.* (2012: 08) list out certain business etiquette of executives as follows:

- Introduction, greeting and art of conversation,
- Dressing and grooming,
- Hosting, dining, wining and guest behaviour,
- Office etiquette,
- Travel norms,

- Business gifts, and
- Cross-cultural nuances.

Introduction, Greeting and Art of Conversation

In a business setting, certain activities such as greetings, handshakes, introductions, exchange of visiting cards and so on are carried out consciously. The participants should understand the need for expressing civilized body language, mannerisms and behavioural patterns. Usually, age, gender and hierarchy matter in introductions. The cultural values also affect business etiquette. A good conversation should also facilitate sound networking, human relationships and business promotion opportunities. Good topics for conversation should be identified. The introduction should prepare grounds for mutual understanding and cooperation between the organizers and participants.

Dressing and Grooming

The business executives and communicators should know how to be groomed and well dressed at work. Business norms and social conventions normally define dressing and grooming. The participants should dress consciously, consistently and responsibly for various occasions and weather conditions. They should also wear trousers, slacks, foot wear, necktie and other things which display neatness and dignified.

Hosting, Dining, Wining and Guest Behaviour

The organizers are required to invite the guests for breakfast, lunch, dinner and parties graciously and well in advance. The place, time, menu and other arrangements should fit into the culture and convenience of the participants. The seating and serving arrangements should also be friendly and supportive. The purpose is to network, negotiate and build sound business relationships. The host should enable the guests to enjoy the occasion in a free, comfortable and secured environment.

Office Etiquette

Modern organizations attract many stakeholders including the customers and general publics. The management is primarily responsible for creative, pleasant, convenient and harmonious working environment. The managers and other functionaries are required to understand the work space etiquette which matters most from business communication point of view. The civic amenities, infrastructural facilities, formal communication activities, decent attire, friendly approaches and other requirements make office etiquette meaningful. Hospitality management also assumes great significance. Seating and serving arrangements should be made properly in order to win over the hearts of various stakeholders who play a decisive role in the process of business management.

Travel Norms

Modern business Organizations are required to understand the differences in travel demand and the needs across specific population groups. They should assess the viability of programmes, and the impacts of projects and policy on system users. They should properly understand the differences in travel demand and the needs across specific population groups. The business executives are required to follow certain healthy travel norms in order to project the individual and institutional reputation. The executives should follow the instructions regarding permission to visiting foreign countries and other places for official and business related assignments. They should obtain timely official clearance from the Competent Authority or concerned head of the business organization. They should prevent the foul play which adversely affects business transactions and communication.

Business Gifts

Business-to-business gift giving is an incredibly powerful sector in the promotional products industry. Business gifting is an accepted practice in the corporate world. Modern business organizations have opted for business gift giving. However, organization size and industry matter from the point of view of business gifts which establish good relationships and high retention rates with clients and employees. Normally business gifts are made available with a view to build goodwill, thank customers, develop business, recognize the performance of the employees, influence purchasing decisions and develop mutually beneficial relationship. Business gifts are quite effective in achieving the business goals in modern times.

Cross-Cultural Nuances

Culture is the sum total of values and behavioural patterns which are developed over a period of time in modern organizations and societies. It is dynamic and change oriented for several reasons. The modern business is also known for competitive management. The business executives are required to understand the 'cross-cultural conflict' and cope with the changing cultural ethos since contemporary society is made up of various subcultures by virtue of members of any society are multicultural.

Conclusion

Business communication is practiced all over the world on the basis of certain norms, guidelines, tools, technologies and strategies. Modern business organizations have realized the role of communication in business management. The horizon of business management has been widened on the basis of systematic business communication. New perspectives and practices have emerged over a period of time to facilitate meaningful interaction between the service providers and beneficiaries. The success of modern business organizations is depends on the practice of systematic business communication. The organizational communicators should understand the correctness of communication and facilitate constant rapport development between the business organizations and various stakeholders. Modern business organizations primarily depend upon communication which is an invaluable resource for successful business management. The advent of new technologies has also considerably enhanced the utility of business communication in modern society.

References

Axtell, Roger, E. (1998) *Gestures: The Dos and Taboos of Body Language Around the World*, Wiley & Sons, New York, p. 43.

Barnouw, V. (1963) *Culture and Personality*, Dorsey Press, Chicago, p. 4.

Bhusan, Uma (2012) *Introduction to Business Communication*, Jaico Publishing House, Mumbai, pp. 1-20.

Drucker, Peter F. (1991) *The New Realities*, New Delhi: Asian Books Private Ltd., p. 210.

Hasan, Seema (2010) *Mass Communication: Principles and Concepts*, CBS Publishers and Distributors Pvt. Ltd., New Delhi.

Kaul, Asha (2009) *Business Communication*, PHI Learning Private Limited, New Delhi.

Lehman, Carol, M., Debbie D. DuFrene, Mala Sinha and Robyn C. Walker (2012) BCOM: *An Innovative Approach to Learning and Teaching Business Communication*, New Delhi, p. 224.

Ibid., p. 391.

Lesikar, Raymond, V., Marie E. Flatley, Kathryn Rentz and Neerja Pande (2012) *Business Communication, Making Connections in a Digital World*, New Delhi, India, p. 76.

Ibid., p. 338.

Ibid., p. 357.

Ibid., pp. 112-116.

Ibid., pp. 602-626.

Mukerjee, Hory Sankar (2013) *Business Communication: Connecting at Work*, Oxford University Press, New Delhi.

Murthy, Narayana, N.R. (2001) *A Better India, A Better World*, Penguin Allen Lane, pp. 159-160.

Rodman, Lilita (2001) You-Attitude: A Linguistic Perspective, *Business Communication Quarterly*, 64 (4): 11-12.

Schein, Edgar, H. (2004) *Organizational Culture and Leadership*, Jossey- Bass, San Francisco, p. 72.

Trompenaars, Fons and Peter Woolliams (2003) *Business Across Cultures*, Capstone, London, p. 53.

Chapter 9
Case Method of Learning

Introduction

A case is generally a written account of real or simulated managerial problems, dilemmas and situations which call for timely and appropriate solutions. The case study method of teaching relating to the management issues and solutions is a crucial component of the modern pedagogy of business schools across the globe. The scholars, professionals, researchers and students spend a good deal of time in understanding the concept, nature, scope, process and utility of case study method. A case analysis is a deliberate exercise in critical thinking and understanding of the concepts, causes and remedial measures concerning a particular event, issue and problem. In modern business organizations, the case analysis method enables the policy makers understand the basic problem and make use of the possible solutions offered by the experts concerned. The concept of case method of learning, nature of case methods of learning, different types of cases, barriers to case methods of learning, process of case method of learning, case analysis approaches, strategies for successful case methods of learning and the structure of written case analysis are presented in this section.

Concept of Case Method of Learning

A case analysis is a professional exercise in critical thinking and understanding of the nature of problem, magnitude of the problem, causes, consequences and solutions. Professionally seasoned, skilled and competent authorities in case analysis are entrusted with the task concerned in order to sensitize the policy makers and administrators in modern business organizations. Cooper and Schindler observe: "A single, well-designed case study can provide a major challenge to a theory and provide a source of new hypotheses and constructs simultaneously".

A case analyst is required to understand the concept of the case, nature of case analysis, problems involved in a case analysis, consequences of a case, alternative solutions to the case and other aspects in order to provide logical solutions and facilitate conflict resolution in modern business organizations. The analysts should demonstrate adequate concern, responsibility and authority for reaching a logically satisfying solution which benefits the business organization.

Nature of the Case Method of Learning

The case analysts should know that the case should have a problem for the readers to solve. The case should have enough information in it that readers can understand what the problem is and, after thinking about it and analyzing the information; the readers should be able to come up with a proposed solution. Writing an interesting case study is a bit like writing a detective story. A good case is more than just a description. It is information arranged in such a way that the reader is put in the same position as the case writer was at the beginning when he or she was faced with a new situation and asked to figure out what was going on. A description, on the other hand, arranges all the information, comes to conclusions, tells the reader everything, and the readers really do not have to work very hard.

The case analysis is a planned, deliberate and systematic exercise carried out by the experts in operations management, crisis management and case study management in modern society. A case analysis involves different dimensions, parameters and techniques. The case analysis usually varies from case to case, situation to situation and time to time. There are no universally acceptable principles and practices of case analysis. There are several factors which are associated with a particular crisis management. The organizational leaders should be sensitized about the nature of the case, causes of the case, consequences of the case and solutions to the case concerned on the basis of systematic evaluation. An ideal case study is primarily based on comprehensive understanding of the critical operations management issues faced by modern organizations which are large and complex by nature.

The group dynamics or organizational dynamics matter most from the point of view of scientific case analysis. The subject matter of a case can also focus on various issues, challenges, constraints, limitations and opportunities of organizational management. The analysts are required to understand the concept, process, magnitude, solutions and other aspects of crisis management in order to effectively analyze the case and offer suitable solution which benefits the organizers and other constituent publics. The basic characteristic of a case analysis is that it presents a problem / event / crisis in its entirety and offers practically viable solutions to the management for effective resolution of the crisis.

Different Types of Cases

Practically speaking, a case can be divided into theoretical and factual cases. The theoretical case studies are meant for understanding the theoretical concepts in various disciplines such as public administration, business management, marketing management, human resources management, and crisis management. The academic case studies are used as examples to concretize abstract concepts. The interplay of ideas is presented in the form of action, interaction and conflict among the persons involved in a life-like situation described by the case concerned. The theoretical case method uses the principles of oral, non-verbal and written communication to demonstrate the dynamics of effective organizational communication in modern society.

The factual case studies describe and illustrate an organization's experience and efforts to overcome different practical problems and critical situations. The factual cases are based on authentic facts and present critical management issues with complete facts and figures. The factual case analysis requires a systematic approach to identification of the main problem, causes and practically viable solutions. The experts suggest the best solution from amongst the alternative solutions in order to diffuse the crisis and enable the management to improve the delivery system. The factual case studies also deal with the corporate management issues and crises belonging to functional area of management or operations management in modern business organizations. The factual case analysis also follows the fundamental techniques of identification of causes and consequences and evaluation of possible alternatives and solutions which benefit the business organizations. The case analysis basically requires the application of analytical reasoning to the main problem and logical solution. The case analysis is carried out in modern business organizations to overcome the crises and offer practically viable solutions which benefit the management as well as the affected parties. The case analysis is also an important component of crisis management in modern organizations regardless of the nature of operations, space and time.

Process of Case Method of Learning

Systematic case analysis contains several stages namely: (a) understanding the process of case analysis, (b) identification of major factors for case analysis, (c) defining the problem, (d) grasping the causes of the problem, (e) developing alternative solutions, (f) evaluating the relevance of alternative solutions, (g) choosing the best alternative, and (h) developing a plan of action.

Understanding the Process of Case Analysis

The case analysis is carried out by an expert in the art and craft of case analysis especially in business organizations. An effective case analysis requires an indepth understanding of the case and its context. The analyst has to ensure a comprehensive study of all the factors and forces which are responsible for the occurrence of a crisis in a business organization. The business environment, organizational management, delivery system, working conditions, group dynamics and performance levels should be thoroughly examined by the analyst in order to understand the process of case analysis. Besides this, an analyst should also diagnose the nature of the crisis and understand the parameters and procedures for the successful conduction of case analysis on the basis of facts, issues and ideas.

Identification of Major Factors for Case Analysis

The case analyst has to grasp the major problems or issues in a case study. The analyst should also understand the basic relationship between the problem and the factors responsible for it. The analyst should also identify the factors which facilitate effective conduction of case analysis and establish the cause and effect relationships. The organizational climate, working conditions, attitude of the management, perception of the employees, inter-departmental coordination, delivery of the goods and services, satisfaction of various stakeholders, system of image building and reputation management, impact of the goods and services and other factors matter most in a modern business organization. Hence, the analyst should take note of the various factors responsible for the occurrence of a crisis or problem in a business organization.

Defining the Problem

The case analyst should carefully define the problem which needs to be formulated in precise words. This would also enable the analyst to develop a meaningful perspective about the case analysis. A proper understanding of the nature, scope, magnitude, impact, solution and future course of action would enable the analyst to deliver the goods on the basis of clarity of thought and deed.

Grasping the Causes of the Problem

The case analyst should understand the various causes of the case and establish clearly the cause and effect relationship. The analyst should also establish logical links between the problems and causes in order to conduct the case analysis efficiently. The analyst should collect the facts and figures which constitute the basic and authentic data through proper investigation. A systematic study of working atmosphere and operations management would also enable the analyst to identify the business-related factors affecting the problem to be resolved.

Primary Data Collection

The case analyst is required to conduct an extensive interview with the people who have first hand experience about the problem concerned. The people who are directly associated with the organization in different capacities should be approached with a set of specific questions for collection of primary data. This would also enrich the process of writing a case report on the basis of authentic primary data and systematic analysis of data.

Organized Presentation of Report

The analyst should also know how to organize the data (primary and secondary) under different components in order to present item-wise interpretation and discussion. The report should also present the factors in a chronological and systematic order. The analyst should also have different compartments such as introduction, background, organizational policy, working environment, various stakeholders, present state of affairs, system failure, causes, consequences, remedial measures and so on.

Developing Alternative Solutions

The analyst should also conduct participant observation, collect primary data, consult various stakeholders and identify the alternative solutions to a problem concerned. The analyst should also identify practically viable, professionally sound and operationally relevant solutions on the basis of systematic fact finding and consultation of various parties responsible for the resolution of a problem or conflict in the business organization. The general alternatives normally do not serve the purpose of conflict resolution. The analyst should identify the specific alternative ranging from most viable to least viable in a given context. The analyst should have adequate presence of mind, environmental surveillance and meaningful contemplation in order to arrive at the right alternative solutions to the questions raised in a crisis situation.

Evaluating the Relevance of Alternative Solutions

The analyst should examine the appropriateness of various solutions in a given crisis context and compare the various alternatives from the feasibility point of view. Practically, all alternative solutions are not equally useful to the leaders of the organization from the point of view of crisis management. The analyst should compare the various alternatives and decide on the best course of action which needs to be followed by the leaders of the organization.

Choosing the Best Alternative

The analyst should choose the best alternative which would diffuse the crisis and help both the parties to arrive at a win-win situation in business organization concerned. The best alternative identified by the analyst should be examined in terms of immediate term and long term utility in order to develop a future course of action that suits the business organization.

Developing a Plan of Action

The analyst should also suggest the most appropriate plan of action that would facilitate mutually beneficial conflict resolution in a business organization. The leaders of the organization should be enabled to follow the most relevant, feasible and appropriate plan of action on the basis of authoritative evaluation of the crisis and identification of plan of action for the resolution of the crisis. Ultimately, the analyst should examine as to whether the plan of action is based on a comprehensive evaluation of all the aspects of the problem which has been addressed in the business organization.

The process of case analysis is a time consuming exercise which warrants complete understanding of the problem, cause and effect relationship, examination of suitable alternatives, adoption of the best alternative and diffusion of crisis on the basis of a meaningful plan of action. The case analysis has to be carried out by the expert by taking into account several factors and alternatives in modern business environment.

Case Analysis Approaches

The case analysis demands several attributes and approaches on the part of an analyst. Chaturvedi and Chaturvedi (2011: 04) have identified the key approaches to case analysis such as thorough knowledge of the concerned subject, analytical ability, ability to think critically, ability to evaluate and ability to infer. The analyst should have a thorough knowledge of the subject concerned in order to authoritatively diagnose the case, identify the factors, analyze the causes and suggest appropriate remedial measures. A thorough knowledge of the attitudinal and behavioural patterns is a must to develop the right perspective and proceed in the right direction for an effective case analysis.

The case analysis is also primarily dependent on the analytical ability of the expert who carries out case analysis. The analyst has to go deeper into the situation described in the case. A case analysis involves more than casual understanding and description of the state of affairs. The analyst should be competent enough to identify the various components of a case analysis and establish new relationships and interactions effectively in a given crisis situation. The analyst should also meticulously examine the reliability and validity of the logic used to establish the cause and effect relationship.

The analyst should also have necessary ability to think critically which goes beyond the obvious understanding and the hidden truth underlying the conflict concerned. A systematic case analysis also demands looking beyond what meets the eye and developing a questioning approach in which the analyst accepts an idea only after proper verification of truth. The analyst should also have the ability to evaluate the set of viable solutions, identify the most appropriate solution and suggest the best plan of action which facilitates successful resolution of conflict. The analyst should also understand the strong reasons for a particular judgement.

The case analysis also demands the ability to infer on the part of the analyst. The analyst should be able to comprehend the whole problem from a realistic perspective. The analyst should be able to draw the inferences which are valid and useful in a given crisis situation. A case analysis normally does not illustrate the dilemmas of an individual but it represents the problems encountered by a business organization because of system failure. A case analysis should be undertaken on the basis of systematic fact finding and examination of alternatives in a crisis situation. An analyst's answer or solution should stand the test of reasoning, fit into a given context and facilitate conflict resolution.

The Format and Contents of Written Case Analysis

A case analysis should be a well organized piece of scientific analysis and critical thinking on the part of the analyst. The writing of a case analysis represents a well organized structure, format and contents. It also follows a sequence of steps which are involved in the presentation of an investigative report. A case analysis contains certain basic elements such as—(a) the title of the case, (b) historical context of the case, (c) nature of the case, (d) scope of analysis, (e) significance of the case, (f) statement of the problem, (g) formulation of hypotheses, (i) factors of analysis, (h) design of the analysis, (j) tools of data collection, (k) analysis of the case, (l) drawing of inferences, (m) identification of alternative solutions, (n) justification of the best solution and (o) recommendations of the plan of action, according to Peter Drucker.

The title of the case represents the central problem of the case. The historical context presents an overview of past events and present issues. The nature of the case deals with the seriousness and magnitude of the case. The scope of analysis deals with the limits of the case analysis. The significance of the case provides a sound justification for the conduction of case analysis. The statement of the problem identifies the goals of the case and enumerates what needs to be achieved by the case analysis concerned. The design of the analysis presents the methodological details such as instruments of the study, tools of data collection and methods of analysis. The tools of data collection usually include—personal observation, interview schedule and collection of primary data through interview. The analysis component enumerates the aspects of analysis, discussion of cause and effect relationship and testing of hypothesis. The analyst also draws certain inferences on the basis of systematic discussion of cause and effect relationship. The analyst also identifies certain solutions which may not be equally good from crisis management point of view. The analyst also provides the best solution which will fit into a given context. The analyst also recommends for the most appropriate plan of action which would diffuse the crisis. Thus, a written case analysis contains several elements which make the process of writing complete and meaningful.

Conclusion

Case analysis is carried out by an expert in order to enable the policy makers to understand the problem, identify the factors, analyze the consequences and adopt the best course of action for the diffusion of the crisis. There are several steps involve in a case analysis. The case analyst should also possess adequate qualification, experience and expertise in order to absolute justice to his/her role. There are no right or wrong solutions to a crisis situation. But the analyst should suggest the most appropriate solution and plan of action in order to facilitate meaningful crisis management in business organizations. A case analysis should be a well planned, organized and systematic exercise which benefits the management and other stakeholders. A case analysis is an important component of the process of crisis management in modern organizations.

References

Baran, S.J. and Davis, D.K. (2000) *Mass Communication Theory*, Belmont, CA: Wadsworth.

Barnes, Louis, B., C. Roland Christensen and Abby J. Hansen (1987) *Teaching and the Case Method*, Boston: Harvard Business School Press.

Bhusan, Uma (2012) *Introduction to Business Communication*, Jaico Publishing House, Mumbai.

Chaturvedi, P.D. and Mukesh Chaturvedi (2011) *Business Communication—Concepts, Cases and Applications*, Delhi: Pearson, pp. 41-42.

Ibid., p. 194.

Cuneo, A. (2002) *Simultaneous Media Use Rife, New Study Finds, Advertising Age*, pp. 3-40.

Dominick, J.R. (1999) *The Dynamics of Mass Communication*, New York: McGraw Hill.

Dorey, E. and MacLellan, A. (2003) *Spread the World-Encourage Viral Marketing*, www.dda.ns.ca

Enger, J. (2009) *Share Your Guiding Light Memories, New York Times,* August 26.

Fowler, Alan (1990) *Negotiation Skills and Strategies*, Hyderabad: University Press, p. 3.

Gladwell, M. (2003) Alternative Marketing Vehicles: The Future of Marketing to one, *Consumer Insight,* www.acnielsen.com

Hasan, Seema (2010) *Mass Communication: Principles and Concepts*, CBS Publishers and Distributors Pvt. Ltd., New Delhi.

Kalb, C. (2002) How are we Doing? *Newsweek,* p. 53.

Karoli, Veera and Naghma Ahmed (2013) *Business Communication*, Thakur Publishers, Bengaluru, India.

Kaul, Asha (2009) *Business Communication*, PHI Learning Private Limited, New Delhi.

Lehman, Carol, M., Devvie D., DuFrene, Mala Sinha and Robin C.Walker (2012) BCOM, *An Innovative Approach to Learning and Teaching, Business Communication, A South Asian Perspective*, Cengage Learning, New Delhi.

Lesikar, Raymond, V., Marie E. Flatley, Kathryn Rentz and Neerja Pande (2012) *Business Communication, Making Connections in a Digital World*, New Delhi, India.

Massey, K. and Baran, S.J. (2001) *Introduction to Mass Communication*, Mountain View, CA: Mayfield.

Mukerjee, Hory Sankar (2013) *Business Communication: Connecting at Work*, Oxford University Press, New Delhi.

Scott, Bill (1995) *The Skills of Negotiating*, Bombay: Jaico Publishing House, p. 3.

Stone, B. (2009) *From TV to the Web to Your Phone, New York Times*, May 31.

Chapter 10
Presentation Skills for Business Management

Introduction

In modern society, the art and craft of presentation assumes great significance. The people are required to present themselves very well in front of others who matter most. The individuals are always at the receiving end. They are required to enter into the good books of people who are at the giving end in all spheres of human life including the business world. The organizational leaders, executives and communicators should know how a presentation is made or given. In the present times, presentations skills are very essential to convince others about the individual and institutional capabilities and accomplishments. The students, researchers, job seekers, executives, communicators and others should know how to develop and make a presentation on a specific subject or mission to the select audience. Effective presentation also enables the communicators to make their presence felt by the audiences, enter into the good books of people who matter and get the things done by others. The salient features of presentation skills with special reference to modern business organizations are presented in this Chapter.

Concept of Presentation

A practical philosopher once observed: "The difference between a smart person and a wise person is that a smart person knows what to say and wise person knows whether or not to say". Presentation skills matter most in a modern society since it is a prominent tool of convincing others about getting the things done. Les Brown noted: "You don't have to be great to get started but you have to get started to be great". In the age of competitive business management, the presenter plays a crucial role since he facilitates better attitudinal change and rapport development between the organization and other stakeholders of organizational development.

The presentation is a form of oral communication in which a person shares information, ideas and expertise with a particular group of audience about a chosen subject. A presentation is a live mode of disseminating information on a particular cause, mission, activity, accomplishment and so on. The presentation is one-way communication process which involves the presenter and receivers. A presentation is made with a fond hope of informing the audiences about a particular subject through traditional and modern channels of communication. It is possible to make a presentation orally on the basis of a well prepared lecture and supportive documents. A presentation can be made on the basis of new communication technologies like LCD projector, power point slides and other devices. A presentation is commonly defined as an art of presenting new ideas, experiences and expertise with a specific group of audience in order to obtain their consent and support for a particular policy or activity. The presentation exercise is common in all modern organizations since it primarily aims at manufacturing the consent of the people concerned in favour of a programme or service or product.

Essential Characteristics of Presentation

A business presentation is an important means of obtaining and exchanging information for making appropriate business decisions and policy development. It assumes great significance in modern business environment because several people receive the message, seek clarification and take appropriate business decisions. The ultimate objective of business presentation is to accomplish the speaker's goals and meets the audience's needs. The business presentation should be carried out on the basis of certain objectives, tools and methodologies.

The presentation is usually carried out by a person who is the chief spokesperson of the organization concerned. The business leaders, executives and communicators are responsible for making meaningful presentations as and when required. They must be aware of the salient features of presentation which focuses the attention of the audiences who listen, watch and grasp the essentials of presentation. The art of presentation can be acquired over a period of time by the organizational leaders and communicators.

Kaul (2009) observes: "The first thing which needs to be kept in mind prior to presentation is the reflection of attitudinal metamorphosis in the presentation exercise. Positive body language can make the audience more receptive towards the speaker. Preparation of adequate material which contains the salient features is necessary. The presenter should also control the audience by providing relevant facts, narrative incidents, visual aids and organization of the details in the order of importance". The scholar suggests seven steps to successful communication which is the soul of presentation. They include—decide upon the objective, select the manner of presentation, identify the mode of presentation, draft an ideal script, complement the presentation through visual aids, handouts and feedback forms, conduct rehearsal, design format of presentation and carry out planned presentation.

Processes of Presentation

A presentation should be scientifically designed and systematically carried out in order to earn the goodwill, cooperation and consent of the audiences. The essential characteristics of a good presentation include—understanding the purpose of presentation, analyzing the audiences, identification of the needs of the audiences, designing the presentation, organizing the facts and figures, logical ordering of presentation, selection of visual aids, adapting to the needs of the audience, effective articulation of facts and figures, good body language, effective concluding remarks, cordial question-answer session and public relations.

Understanding the Purpose of Presentation

Every act of presentation is governed by a definite purpose. The communicator should understand the purpose of presentation very clearly and develop a sound perspective of presentation. The background of the audiences, significance of the presentation, process of presentation and other aspects of presentation should be properly grasped by the communicator. The presentation should be planned in such a way that the presenter effectively meets the needs of the audience. The presenter should also understand the diverse cultural background of the audiences and their specific expectations through business presentation. This would enable him/her to prepare grounds properly and handle the challenge of presentation with utmost clarity and capacity. The presenter should plan the business presentation that would effectively meet the requirements of the participants.

Analyzing the Audiences

The presenter should understand the general characteristics of the audience and the extent of their knowledge and experience with the topic of presentation. The presenter should be well aware of the occasion and location in order to avoid conflict of interest. The presentation should primarily cater to the needs of the audiences who matter most in business transactions. The audiences include policy makers, executives and other key personalities who need to be persuaded by the communicator. The presenter must know the audiences he/she is going to address. The presenter should have an idea of the culture, tradition, communication, number, nature, needs, attitude and other salient features of the audiences who will receive the message. The presenter should basically understand the needs of the audiences in order to present area-specific, project-specific and target group-specific contents about the business operations. The presenter should understand the environment and demographic characteristics of the audience and adopt different strategies which are needed for audiences who think and make decisions differently.

Identification of the Needs of the Audiences

The presenter should be aware of the audience and focus the presentation on them properly. The audiences should not be taken for granted by the presenter and provide certain things of interest to them. Different strategies are required to cater to the needs of diverse audiences who think and make decisions differently. The presenter should ultimately succeed in focusing on the needs, hopes and expectations of the audience. The environmental factors which affect the presentation should also be properly understood. The presenter should also make an assessment of the needs of the audiences and focus their attention on vital aspects of the products or services delivered by the business organizations. The audiences usually constitute the heterogeneous groups who share different cultures and aspirations. Therefore, the presenter should understand the concept, nature, scope and contents of presentation at the very outset. Generally, the audiences participate in the presentation exercise with certain aspirations, needs and demands. The presenter should also focus the attention of the audience on salient features and purposes of presentation.

Designing the Presentation

The presenter should design the process of presentation in consultation with the experts, leaders and executives who have rich professional, technical and administrative experience in business organizations. The presentation has to be designed in accordance with the environment, culture, audiences, time, needs and other aspects of presentation. The presenter should determine the goal of presentation which is a prerequisite to an effective presentation. The presenter should organize and develop the three parts of an effective presentation such as introduction, body and close, according to Dale Carnegie. The introductory part should compel the attention of the audiences, the body matter should present the salient features along with relevant facts and figures and the concluding remarks should persuade the audiences to support the business venture. The sequence and timing of each point should be properly designed. The introduction, body of presentation, concluding remarks, question-answer session and vote of thanks should be designed in a logical, professional and meaningful way.

Organizing the Facts and Figures

The presenter should collect relevant information, ideas, figures and other inputs from various authentic sources. A good deal of home work is required to mobilize the facts and figures relating to the topic concerned. The normal order of any presentation is to first list the main ideas and then elaborate on each of them on the basis of suitable facts, arguments and justifications. The presenter should introduce the theme in one or two minutes. The main body of presentation should be amplified with more time and energy. The concluding remarks should be made in two or three minutes. The presenter should follow the guidelines to organize the contents which will fit into the environment and context. The contents should be organized on the basis of sequential order, chronological order, order of importance, question and answer method, comparison and contrast, problem solving formula and cause and effect order according to Lehman *et al.* (2012: 19). The presenter should also give enough scope for question-answer session in order to clarify the doubts and convince the audience. The presenter should not forget to thank the organizers and participants for their kind participation and patient hearing as a matter of courtesy.

Logical Ordering of Presentation

The presenter should not make use of too many ideas which would confuse the audiences. The presenter should be very choosy and selective in organizing and presenting facts. The most important aspects which need to be focused should be presented in a logical way in order to convince the audiences and persuade them to accept the products or services. The presenter should understand the basic techniques of delivering an effective presentation. The presenter should know how to move from one stage or step to another and enable the audiences to follow the sequences. Transitions must be well indicated by using connectives and inferences. The presenter should also actively involve the audiences, arouse their interest, encourage their participation and sustain their involvement with the mission.

Selection of Visual Aids

The presenter should also select appropriate visual aids which enliven the process of presentation. The presentation visuals support and clarify the ideas of the presenter and enable the participants to visualize the message properly. Studies have confirmed that use of visual aids commendable enhances the presentation. Prominent among them include—blackboard, flip chart, overhead projector, power point presentation, statistical data charts, figures, diagrams and so on. The presenter must select the appropriate combination of visual aids to accomplish the purpose and meet the needs of the participants. A good deal of information can be presented with a visual than lengthy verbal explanations. The presenter should be aware of the techniques of using visual aids and provide attention compelling details through effective devices.

Adapting to the Needs of the Audience

The presenter should be aware of the location of the presentation, background of the audiences, needs of the audiences and culture of communication. The presenter should adapt himself/herself to the audiences and facilitate participatory communication. The presenter should encourage the participants to ask questions and seek clarifications and complete the presentation within the allotted time. The presenter should also maintain eye contact throughout the presentation, pose interesting questions, invite volunteers to role-play and present facts and materials enthusiastically. This would make the presentation active and alive in a communication context.

Effective Articulation of Facts and Figures

The presenter should know how to emphasize the pertinent points and de-emphasize the not so important aspects of the subject concerned. The presenter should also provide thought provoking ideas and motivate the audiences to get involved thoroughly in the process of presentation. Sound interpretations, arguments, clarifications and justifications make presentation very effective.

Good Body Language

The body language of the presenter matters most since a presentation is a live performance. The presenter's non-verbal cues normally influence the audience. The presenter should also understand the power of non-verbal body movements, gestures and facial expressions which make the presentation effective. Lehman *et al.* (2012: 20) emphasized the positive body language while making presentations thus:

- Use the space available by walking from time to time, but do not walk in a rhythm.
- Have open and receiving gestures by not locking hands or crossing the arms frequently.
- While presenting, the "palm up" gesture conveys openness, 'palms facing in' indicates assertiveness, and 'palm facing down' indicates a closed approach. The audience is likely to mirror the same level of openness you display.
- Use 'touch' and 'turn' method when discussing a point on the screen.
- Hold a pen or pointer in your hand if you are nervous (but do not fiddle with it).
- Be like the lighthouse and look at everyone in the audience while speaking.
- Do not point the finger at anyone or keep your hands on the hips.
- Putting one or both hands in the trouser pockets continuously while speaking indicates a casual approach.

- Be responsive to the body language of the audience and accordingly pace your presentation. If you see neither the audience nor showing interest, change the tactics and liven up the environment by narrating an anecdote or using positive humour.
- Keep you back straight and look up as this displays confidence and good self-esteem.
- Be well groomed and formal in dress as appearance counts.

The presenter should be adequately prepared for meaningful question-answer session after the presentation. He/she should also use questions to facilitate active participation of the audience in the process of interaction. In modern corporate houses, video conferencing is also used extensively for business presentation across the world. The Internet conferencing or webcasting allows business organizations to conduct the presentations in real time over the Internet. Software products are also use for live web presentations. The camera should be adjusted to enhance communication between the presenter and participants. The basic principles of presentation are applicable in case of video conferencing and web presentations.

Effective Concluding Remarks

The presenter should also make highly decisive, fruitful and effective concluding remarks which summarize the main arguments and connects them to the future course of action. The presenter should reinstate the most important points with supporting justifications and invite questions from the audiences. The presenter should primarily focus on the future course of action and enable the participants to respond to the needs of the organization positively.

Cordial Question-Answer Session

The question-answer session gives an important opportunity to the audiences for interaction with the presenter. The communicator should encourage questions and answer each question confidently and efficiently. The presenter should not get annoyed if he/she fails to convince the audience due to certain constraints and limitations. The presenter should also watch the audience for better feedback and adjust the presentation accordingly. The questions of the audience should also be handled politely and comprehensively.

Public Relations

The presenter should also be good in the art of public relations which is a means of earning the goodwill, cooperation and support of the various stakeholders. The presenter should utilize the opportunity to win over the hearts of the participants and enlist their active participation in the process of organizational development. The presentation also demands application of public relations skills on the part of the presenter who is the cultural ambassador.

Importance of Presentation in Business Organizations

The presentation is indeed an important component of business communication in modern organizations. It is a distinct organizational communicative activity which is intended to convince and persuade the specific audience. The Socratic model of presentation basically involves the question and answers method and represents a two-way communication process which benefits both the parties (presenter and audiences). A trained and seasoned presenter approaches the subject of presentation with absolute awareness, preparedness and competence in order to do justice to his/her role. A good presentation basically demands planned homework, organized preparation, meticulous presentation, active participation of audiences and fruitful interaction between the presenter and audiences.

Presentation assumes great significance in modern business organizations which depend primarily on image building, reputation management, crisis management, organizational management, programme implementation, customer relationship management and allied activities. The business organization demands multi-faceted cooperation and support from various stakeholders. The customers are the most important stakeholders of modern business organizations. Hence, business communicators should enter into the good books of the customers through good thoughts and deeds. The customers have a right to information about the organizational policies, programmes and services.

The presenter should know how to reach out to various stakeholders including the customers in a competitive business environment. Several tools and technologies are used to educate, organize, motivate and persuade the stakeholders in modern business organizations. The presentation is different from other business communication tools and technologies. It focuses the attention of the audiences on the organizational obligations, responsibilities and services through effective audio-visual presentation of facts, arguments and justifications. The presenter should make use of the opportunity properly and emphasize the business opportunity to gain support for some course of action or to suggest a likely course of action for the future, observe Chaturvedi and Chaturvedi (2011: 03).

The norms and guidelines of presentation are clearly spelt out by the experts in order to make the presentation effective. The presenter is called upon to design and organize the information in a systematic way and establish good rapport with the audiences. The presentation can be made more creative and vivid by the use of advanced communication tools and technologies which provide interactive business communication opportunity. The presentation should be enriched in terms of appropriate application of new media which present the salient features in a highly attractive manner. However, the presenter should not crowd the transparency / slide with too many ideas and points. The art of presentation should be managed according to the time allotted to the purpose. The total presentation including the question-answer session should be covered within the allotted time.

Conclusion

The presentation is a form of oral business communication which is vigorously practiced in modern business organizations. The success of presentation primarily depends on the missionary zeal and competence of the presenter who assumes the role of spokes person of the organization concerned. The essential characteristics of a good presentation include—clarity of purpose, adequate preparation, understanding the environment, assessment of the needs of the audiences, designing of presentation, organization of facts, selection of media, meaningful articulation, interactive communication, persuasive communication and so on. The presenter should also ensure elaborate use of visual aids which facilitate proper understanding of the subject concern. The presenter should also use adequate non-verbal communication skills in order to reinforce his/her ideas. The presenter should develop a positive mindset in order to deliver the goods to the audience to the best of their satisfaction. Ultimately, presentation is a deliberate intellectual activity which exercises control over the self, the material and audience. Clarity of thought and action is absolutely essential for the successful presentation in a competitive business environment. Empirical evidence also clearly reveals that the presentation model should be customized with specific local contents and experiences. The presenter should also have adequate creativity, resourcefulness and competence to rise to the occasion and make presentation memorable and fruitful.

References

Baran, S.J. and Davis, D.K. (2000) *Mass Communication Theory*, Belmont, CA: Wadsworth.

Bhusan, Uma (2012) *Introduction to Business Communication*, Jaico Publishing House, Mumbai.

Chaturvedi, P.D. and Mukesh Chaturvedi (2011) *Business Communication—Concepts, Cases and Applications*, Delhi: Pearson, p. 194.

Ibid., p. 183.

Cuneo, A. (2002) Simultaneous Media Use Rife, New Study Finds, *Advertising Age*, pp. 3-40.

Dizard, W.Jr. (2000) *Old, New Media*, New York: Longman.

Dominick, J.R. (1999) *The Dynamics of Mass Communication*, New York: McGraw Hill.

Dorey, E. and MacLellan, A. (2003) *Spread the World-Encourage Viral Marketing*, www.dda.ns.ca

Enger, J. (2009) Share Your Guiding Light Memories, *New York Times*, August 26.

Gladwell, M. (2003) Alternative Marketing Vehicles: The Future of Marketing to one, *Consumer Insight*, www.acnielsen.com

Grant, A. and Meadows, J. (2008) *Communication Technology Update and Fundamentals*, Boston: Focal Press.

Gunderson, E. (2002) Uncovering the Real Osborne's, *USA Today*, p. E1.

Hasan, Seema (2010) *Mass Communication: Principles and Concepts*, CBS Publishers and Distributors Pvt. Ltd., New Delhi.

Hilliard, R. and Keith, M. (2001) *The Broadcast Century and Beyond: A Biography of American Broadcasting*, Boston: Allyn & Bacon.

Kalb, C. (2002) How are we Doing? *Newsweek*, p. 53.

Karoli, Veera and Naghma Ahmed (2013) *Business Communication*, Thakur Publishers, Bengaluru, India.

Kaul, Asha (2009) *Business Communication*, PHI Learning Private Limited, New Delhi, pp. 123-126.

Lehman, Carol, M., Devvie D., DuFrene., Mala Sinha and Robin C. Walker (2012) BCOM, *An Innovative Approach to Learning and Teaching, Business*

Communication, A South Asian Perspective, Cengage Learning, New Delhi, p. 320.

Ibid., p. 307.

Lesikar, Raymond, V., Marie E. Flatley, Kathryn Rentz and Neerja Pande (2012) *Business Communication, Making Connections in a Digital World*, New Delhi, India.

Lewin, J. (2007) *Internet Media Replacing Traditional Media*, IBM *via* New Tee Vee.

Lin, C.A. (2001) Audience Attributes, Media Supplementation and Likely Online Service Adoption, *Mass Communication and Society*, 4 (1): 19-38.

Massey, K. and Baran, S.J. (2001) *Introduction to Mass Communication*, Mountain View, CA: Mayfield.

Mukerjee, Hory Sankar (2013) *Business Communication: Connecting at Work*, Oxford University Press, New Delhi.

Pavlik, J.V. (1996) *New Media Technology: Cultural and Commercial Perspectives*, Boston: Allyn & Bacon.

Shane, E. (1999) *Selling Electronic Media*, Boston: Focal Press.

Stone, B. (2009) From TV to the Web to Your Phone, *New York Times*, May 31.

Strabhuar, J. and LaRose (2004) *Media Now*, Belmont, CA: Wadsworth.

Veronis, S. and Stevenson (2003) *Communication Industry Forecast*, www.vss.com

Chapter 11
Negotiation Skills for Business Management

Introduction

Negotiation has become a way of life in the modern business environment. Good negotiation skills are vital in modern business world. Negotiation is the process of a mutually accepted agreement which takes place between two parties in all spheres of human life including the business world. It is also a form of business communication which is basically meant for resolving conflicts between two individuals or groups or nations. In a fundamental sense, every negotiation facilitates the satisfaction of the needs of both the parties. Negotiation is a way of behaving that can develop understanding and acceptance for achieving a shared purpose in a given context. Negotiation is also based on proper understanding of the psychology which is involved in achieving necessary success in the process. Negotiation is a planned, deliberate and systematic exercise which implies that both the parties accept the agreement between them as final and binding. Negotiation skills should be cultivated by the organizational leaders and communicators in order to achieve business success. Negotiation is also the life blood of every business organization. The importance of negotiation in business management has to be realized by the top management which sits on the driver's seat. The process of negotiation becomes complete if there are intensive and extensive internal and external communication services. The business world is characterized by an ever growing number of contacts resulting in effective negotiation between the organizational leaders and other key players who matter most from organizational development point of view. The concept of negotiation, nature of negotiation, significance of negotiation, factors affecting negotiation in business world, process of business negotiation, process and strategies for successful business negotiation are presented in this chapter.

Concept of Negotiation

Negotiation is a universal phenomenon which basically involves a win-win situation. Negotiation is a two-way communication which produces a mutually beneficial solution to a particular problem regardless of space and time. According to Oxford Dictionary, "Negotiation is a process of trying to reach an agreement through discussion and involves a meeting where this discussion takes place". The *Winston Simplified Dictionary* defines negotiation as "the discussion and bargaining that goes on between parties before a contract is settled or a deal is definitely agreed upon".

Fowler (1990: 10) defines: "Negotiation is a process of intervention by which two or more parties who consider that they need to be jointly involved in any outcome, but who initially have different objectives, seek by the use of argument and persuasion to resolve their differences in order to achieve a mutually acceptable solution".

Scott (1995: 27) states: "A negotiation is a form of meeting between two parties: our party and the other party. The objective of most negotiations is to reach an agreement in which both parties together move towards an outcome that is mutually beneficial".

Negotiation takes place in all contexts and spheres of human life. It is a never ending exercise which benefits the participants in several ways. It brings the two or more parties closer and enables them to accept a solution which benefits them. The ultimate objective of a negotiation is to reach an agreement which is acceptable and beneficial to the participants. The participants need a mediator who brings them together under one umbrella and enables them to arrive at a consensus and action which resolves the conflict of interest and facilitates viable solutions. Thus, negotiation assumes great significance in the business sector in the age of competitive business which demands negotiated settlements.

Nature of Negotiation

Negotiation is a process of bargaining in which two parties iron out their differences, understand each other and help each other in finding an amicable solution and an acceptable transaction. Chaturvedi and Chaturvedi (2011: 04) observe: "Negotiation is a process of bargaining in which two parties, each of which has something that the other wants, try to reach an agreement on mutually accepted terms". The scholars have identified two points which reveal the nature of negotiation. They include—(1) negotiation takes place between two parties. Both the parties are equally interested in finding a satisfactory result and (2) negotiation leads to an agreement through discussion, not instructions, orders, or power/influence/authority.

Negotiation takes place in a friendly, flexible and democratic environment. A negotiator is a person who is close to the parties involved in the process of negotiation. He/she plays a major role in bringing the parties concerned together, facilitating meaningful discussion and enabling the agreement between the parties. The negotiator is very much essential in the process of negotiation and tries to reach an agreement on the basis of discussion, argument and persuasion. Negotiation needs proper facts, interpretations, convincing arguments and persuasive appeals under normal circumstances. Negotiation also demands a conducive situation which is favourable to both the parties. Negotiation also protects the interest of both the parties or involved parties since it is mutually beneficial agreement concerning a common desire or transaction.

The negotiator is required to play the role of a neutral umpire. The negotiator cannot take any biased decision. The negotiator should also belong to both the parties. He/she should convince both the parties in a very friendly atmosphere. Negotiation can take place only when both concerned parties are willing to meet, discuss the issue at length, adopt give and take policy and agree for a win-win situation. The parties involved must be willing to reach a decision by discussion of the pros and cons rather than any forceful or authority oriented approaches. The negotiators must be prepared for negotiation, understand the significance of negotiation, respect each other's points of view, grasp the essentials of negotiation and agree upon mutually beneficial future course of action. Hence, negotiation is based on certain strategies of initiating, finalizing and concluding negotiations in a conducive atmosphere.

Significance of Negotiation

Negotiation is a universal necessity which facilitates cordial human relations, social actions and business transactions. The need for negotiation is seldom questioned by the people. The process of negotiation is as old as the mankind is. It is a never ending exercise which demands mutual trust, confidence, goodwill and cooperation. Negotiation solves several social, economic, political and cultural problems. Negotiation is a prominent instrument of bringing about mutually beneficial settlement or action. Negotiation finds a prominent place in the business world which primarily depends upon friendly and supportive solutions or remedies to business problems.

In reality, the need for negotiation is defined by a particular situation. Some situations basically demand negotiated settlement while other situations do not require any kind of negotiation. The negotiation becomes inevitable when the conflict of interest occurs between two or more parties in a social or business context. Certain issues need to be resolved on the basis of mutual understanding, goodwill and cooperation. Negotiation is the surest means of resolving the conflicts, ironing out differences of opinion, facilitating mutual understanding and reaching an agreement which benefits the participants. Negotiation is indeed an all pervasive action in all spheres of human life including the business world. Most of the business issues can be settled through meaningful negotiations.

There are formal and informal negotiations which are handled by the negotiators. The formal negotiation demands certain prerequisites in order to facilitate meaningful negotiated settlement. They include—willingness of both the parties, prearranged meeting of both the parties, agenda setting for negotiation, involvement of middlemen, arguments and counter-arguments, commonly agreeable solutions and commitment to negotiated settlements. A formal negotiation is easy to handle since there is a platform for discussion of issues and resolution of conflict of interest. In a formal negotiation both the parties have enough time to examine the issues comprehensively and arrive at consensus.

The informal negotiation is based on unannounced and casual meetings which are attended by both the parties in the presence of a negotiator. It does not provide adequate opportunities for systematic discussion, analysis and evaluation of the state of affairs concerning a negotiation. It may not produce any positive results in the absence of suitable agenda and ground work. It has more limitations and constraints rather than strengths and opportunities. In case of mutually agreeable decision and action, there is no need for formal or informal negotiation. Absence of mutual convenience and agreement also creates unfavourable situation for negotiation.

Negotiation has become an important form of business communication. Negotiation takes place within certain contexts of social, economic, political and cultural. Negotiation also primarily depends upon the timing of the communication concerning both the parties in business organizations. It is primarily dependent on the relationship of the negotiator and participants. The outcomes of the negotiation are dependent on particular context such as organizational, professional and personal—

aspects of the negotiator and participants. Negotiation becomes inevitable in business organizations.

The type and culture of the organization represented by the negotiator and participants really matters in the process of negotiation. The professional status, needs and demands also affect the process of negotiation. The personal background of the negotiator and participants also impacts the negotiation primarily. The negotiated settlement primarily depends upon a well defined approach

Factors Affecting Negotiation in Business World

The negotiators are required to understand the factors affecting negotiation in modern business environment. The location of a negotiation also matters. It should be convenient to both the parties and provide necessary facilities for the smooth conduction of negotiation. The location should be accessible, congenial and supportive from negotiation point of view. A highly secured, equipped and friendly location provides useful setting for the purpose of negotiation. The location should be suitable for the organization of hospitality management which makes negotiation a friendly exercise. Hence, location plays a major role in the process of negotiation in business environment.

The timing of negotiation is equally important for both the parties. The choice of time and duration of negotiation should be fixed according to the convenience of both the parties. There should be adequate time and opportunity for the exchange of ideas, experiences and views during the course of negotiation. The preparation time and the time frame for implementation of the project or agreement should be carefully scheduled to prevent any inconvenience. Timely negotiation serves the business purpose better and facilitates proper agreement and implementation exercises which benefit the parties concerned.

There are certain subjective factors that affect the outcomes of a negotiation. They include—personal relationships, fear of authority, future consideration, mutual obligations, personal considerations and so on. The conduct of negotiations is influenced by the establishment of rapport between the two parties involved in the process of negotiation. Both the parties should exercise equal bargaining power in order to facilitate even and balanced negotiation. The higher status, influence and authority of one party would automatically demoralize the other party who is likely to lose confidence in the process of negotiation. No party should gain an upper hand since it would create fear psychosis in the mind of the other party. The absence of balanced negotiation would also create fear with respect to the future course of action. The memories of the good thoughts and deeds relating to the past might influence the negotiation. The factors influencing the individual bargaining power of the parties also affect the process of negotiation.

The attitude of the parties also constitutes an essential aspect of negotiation. A skilled and competent negotiator places sound facts and justifications to highlight how the other party stands to gain from the negotiation. The mindset of both the parties plays a decisive role in the success or failure of negotiation. Persuasion is also a prominent factor which influences the process of negotiation. Persuasion practically includes a wide range of communication skills and behavioural patterns which play a decisive role in convincing the other party to become an active partner in the process of negotiation. It also enables the negotiator to find out mutually acceptable solutions in the interest of the project. Effective persuasion also facilitates smooth conduction of negotiation under the normal circumstances.

Process of Business Negotiation Process

The process of negotiation includes couple of stages such as offer, agreement, counter-offer, concession and compromise. Alan Fowler identifies the six stages of negotiation which include— (a) preparing and planning, (b) exchanging initial views, (c) exploring possible compromises, (d) searching for common ground, (e) securing an agreement, and (f) implementing the agreement. Every act of negotiation demands proper ground works, mobilization of facts, persuasion of parties, identification of location, fixation of time and hospitality management. In the second stage, both the parties are engaged in the exchange of their ideas, experiences and expectations in a friendly atmosphere. In the third stage, both the parties explore the possibility of compromises, opportunities and gains. In the fourth stage, both the parties arrive at a conclusion under the commonality of interest. In the fifth stage, both the parties enter into a written agreement which contains specifications and allied details. In the last stage, both the parties sign the agreement and help each other on the basis of mutual trust, confidence and cooperation.

Scholars have also brought all these stages under three major categories namely—(a) preparatory works, (b) actual negotiation, and (c) implementation of the agreement. Negotiation is a planned, deliberate and systematic exercise which affects the business operation. Adequate preparations are required to facilitate meaningful agreement between both the parties in a congenial atmosphere. The issues concerning negotiation should be clearly spelt out in order to avoid any confusion or inconsistency in the process of negotiation. In the negotiation phase, the proposals are translated into agreements on the basis of complete understanding and mutual convenience. In the final stage of implementation, both the parties act according to the terms and conditions and follow a mutually beneficial course of action. In reality, negotiation implies that both parties accept the agreement and implement the project. At the end of the negotiation, both sides should accept the agreement and abide by the terms and conditions of the agreement in order to avoid conflict of interest and deviation from the agreed course of action.

Strategies for Successful Business Negotiation

A negotiation is based on a meaningful business strategy which benefits both the parties in letter and spirit. A successful negotiator acts on the basis of complete information, operational efficiency and ground realities. A negotiator should also understand the mindset of the other party and develop appropriate strategies to achieve the goal of negotiation to the best of his/her advantage. A true negotiator allows the other party to express the views and arrive at a mutually beneficial conclusion. A negotiator should also be willing to adjust to the changed business circumstances and establish good rapport which is highly essential for the conduction of negotiation.

During the course of negotiation, meaningful exchange of ideas in a democratic environment should take place. It is important to listen to the other parties and place the points of view which convince them. There should not be any interruption during the course of negotiation by any third party. Sound arguments, counter arguments, justifications and persuasion are the elements of a positive negotiation. Both parties should behave in a responsible way and facilitate a mutually beneficial negotiation. This would clear the doubts in the minds of the parties and facilitates proper problem solving exercise. Both the sides should use concessions and compromises as principal tools of negotiation. Certain meaningful conditions could be placed in the interest of sound negotiated settlement.

The final outcome of negotiation should be viewed as equally beneficial to both the parties. The participants should create a win-win situation in order to pave the way for implementation of the terms and conditions of negotiation. There should not be any changes and modifications to the final outcome of negotiations. The negotiators should be tactful and persuasive to ensure that the final outcome is beneficial to the other party also. The negotiators should also be enthusiastic about the other party's cooperation and suggestions in order to avoid future complications. Both the parties should know how to handle the deadlocks in a diplomatic way. No other concessions should be made regarding the point of contention of negotiation. The ethical and legal aspects of an agreement should be highlighted and respected by both the parties. It is also better to avoid any third party intervention or legal arbitration which cause financial loss and injure the reputation of the party concerned.

Conclusion

Negotiation is a way of life in modern business environment. It is also a long drawn process which demands seriousness and sincerity from the parties involved in the process of negotiation. Formal and informal situations are required to reach an agreement which benefits the participants equally. Negotiation is not a one-way traffic, but it is a two-way transaction. It takes place only when both concerned parties agree for a negotiated settlement or agreement based on mutual respect and convenience. Several factors affect negotiation but the negotiators should be well prepared for negotiation. The process of negotiation becomes complete if both the parties reach a mutually agreeable agreement and business transaction. Negotiation is a way of behaving that can develop mutual understanding and acceptance for achieving a shared purpose. A written negotiation is always safer under the normal circumstances since the terms and conditions are spelt out clearly in the agreement. The negotiators should know how to deal with deadlocks and establish a win-win situation.

References

Baran, S.J. and Davis, D.K. (2000) *Mass Communication Theory*, Belmont, CA: Wadsworth.

Bhusan, Uma (2012) *Introduction to Business Communication*, Jaico Publishing House, Mumbai.

Chaturvedi, P.D. and Mukesh Chaturvedi (2011) *Business Communication—Concepts, Cases and Applications*, Delhi: Pearson, p. 194.

Ibid., p. 183.

Cuneo, A. (2002) *Simultaneous Media Use Rife*, New Study Finds, *Advertising Age*, pp. 3-40.

Dizard, W. Jr. (2000) *Old, New Media*, New York: Longman.

Dominick, J.R. (1999) *The Dynamics of Mass Communication*, New York: McGraw Hill.

Dorey, E. and MacLellan, A (2003) *Spread the World—Encourage Viral Marketing*, *www.dda.ns.ca*

Enger, J. (2009) Share Your Guiding Light Memories, *New York Times*, August 26.

Fowler, Alan (1990) *Negotiation Skills and Strategies*, Hyderabad: University Press, p. 3.

Gladwell, M. (2003) Alternative Marketing Vehicles: The Future of Marketing to one, *Consumer Insight*, www.acnielsen.com

Grant, A. and Meadows, J. (2008) *Communication Technology Update and Fundamentals*, Boston: Focal Press.

Gunderson, E. (2002) Uncovering the Real Osbournes, *USA Today*, p. E1.

Hasan, Seema (2010) *Mass Communication: Principles and Concepts*, CBS Publishers and Distributors Pvt. Ltd., New Delhi.

Hilliard, R. and Keith, M. (2001) *The Broadcast Century and Beyond: A Biography of American Broadcasting*, Boston,: Allyn & Bacon.

Kalb, C. (2002) How are we Doing? *Newsweek*, p. 53.

Karoli, Veera and Naghma Ahmed (2013) *Business Communication*, Thakur Publishers, Bengaluru, India.

Kaul, Asha (2009) *Business Communication*, PHI Learning Private Limited, New Delhi, pp. 123-126.

Lehman, Carol, M., Devvie D., DuFrene, Mala Sinha and Robin C.Walker (2012) BCOM, *An Innovative Approach to Learning and Teaching, Business Communication: A South Asian Perspective*, Cengage Learning, New Delhi, p. 320.

Ibid., 307.

Lesikar, Raymond, V., Marie E. Flatley, Kathryn Rentz and Neerja Pande (2012) *Business Communication, Making Connections in a Digital World*, New Delhi, India.

Lewin, J. (2007) *Internet Media Replacing Traditional Media*, IBM *via* New Tee Vee.

Lin, C.A. (2001) Audience Attributes, Media Supplementation and Likely Online Service Adoption, *Mass Communication and Society*, 4 (1): 19-38.

Massey, K. and Baran, S.J. (2001) *Introduction to Mass Communication*, Mountain View, CA: Mayfield.

Mukerjee, Hory Sankar (2013) *Business Communication: Connecting at Work*, Oxford University Press, New Delhi.

Pavlik, J.V. (1996) *New Media Technology: Cultural and Commercial Perspectives*, Boston: Allyn & Bacon.

Scott, Bill (1995) *The Skills of Negotiating*, Bombay: Jaico Publishing House, p. 3.

Shane, E. (1999) *Selling Electronic Media*, Boston: Focal Press.

Stone, B. (2009) From TV to the Web to Your Phone, *New York Times*, May 31.

Strabhuar, J. and LaRose (2004) *Media Now*, Belmont, CA: Wadsworth.

Veronis, S. and Stevenson (2003) *Communication Industry Forecast*, www.vss.com

Chapter 12
Employment Communication Skills for Business Management

Introduction

The young generation of diploma holders, graduates and post-graduates are required to develop necessary communication skills and competence in order to attract the attention of the employers in public and private sector organizations. The job seekers should also learn the art of searching for suitable job opportunities on their own in reputed organizations rather than waiting for job offer through campus placement. They must identify the potential employers and job openings through useful personal contacts, media exposure, network development and allied exercises. The job seekers should also know how to submit an application, write covering letter, handle interviews and present themselves before the employers. There are various stages involved in the procurement of jobs in modern organizations. In this age of competitiveness, the young generation of job seekers must develop the art and craft of employment communication which makes their presence felt in modern society and offers them opportunities for employment. The concept of employment communication, nature of employment communication, identification of the needs of the employers, factors affecting employment communication in business organizations, essential characteristics of curriculum vitae, salient features of application letter, strategies for success at interviews and techniques of participation in group discussion are presented in this Chapter.

Concept of Employment Communication

Business communication takes place between the business organizations and various stakeholders who are directly associated with business organizations. Employment communication takes place between the job seekers and public/private institutions which provide employment opportunities to the young generation of job seekers. Employment communication originates from the job seekers who have obtained necessary educational qualifications and employment skills at certificate, diploma, graduation and post-graduation levels. The skilled workers are also preferred by the modern business and industrial organizations without any formal qualifications. Employment communication basically deals with the proper understanding of the availability of employment opportunities, potential employers, requirements of the employers, eligibility criteria, submission of suitable application, presentation of curriculum vitae, participation in group discussion, handling of interviews and so on. The modern job seekers should understand the employment communication opportunities, needs and demands in order to procure suitable employment opportunities in modern society. Hence, employment communication is basically defined as a systematic communicative efforts made by the job seekers on the basis of well established communication skills and techniques. Employment communication plays a vital role in the procurement of suitable employment opportunities. Employment communication is also universally termed as the visa for obtaining job opportunities in modern organizations through submission of effective, creative and justifiable job related details to the employers.

Nature of Employment Communication

Employment communication matters most from the point of view of convincing the potential employers about the suitability of the candidature of the job seekers on the basis of proper presentation of facts and figures relating to educational qualification, professional experience and specialization of area of service. The job seekers should not ignore the importance of employment communication in the age of competitive business and service. They should know how to place the facts, convince the employers and win over the heart of the job providers through meaningful presentation and participation in various processes such as group discussion, interview and so on. The true nature of employment communication should be understood by the job seekers in order to prepare grounds for submission of application, participation in group discussion, handling of interview and allied exercises oriented to the procurement of jobs.

The employers also look forward to finding the right employees through employment communication. The employers can take appropriate decisions on the basis of the resumé submitted by the job seekers. It is the important communication tool that provides a basis for judgment about the capabilities of job seekers for particular job in modern organizations. Employment communication demands proper understanding of communication process and effective communication strategies among the job seekers. They should also submit the covering letter, curriculum vitae and other forms of employment communication on the basis of readable format and contents.

The writing process consists of proper planning, drafting and editing. The nature of job oriented messages should be properly understood in order to choose the right form, design appropriate method, use meaningful contents and submit highly eye catching contents for the perusal and consideration of the potential employers. Participation in group communication should also be friendly, flexible and responsive in order to attract the attention of the job providers. Handling of interview should be based on good body language, effective presentation and convincing replies to the interviewers. Employment communication has several components, norms and guidelines. The job seekers should be fully prepared to handle the employment communication to the best of the satisfaction of employers who matter most.

Identification of the Needs of the Employers

The job seekers should have wide social and professional contacts in order to identify suitable organizations and employment opportunities. They must travel widely, approach different people, identify employment opportunities and understand the requirements of the employers. They must basically understand as to what extent they fulfil the requirements of the potential employers in terms of qualification and experience. The job seekers should also visit the websites of the concerned organizations and collect necessary information about their specific job related needs and demands.

The publications relating to employment opportunities should be studied in detail in order to understand the job specifications and requirements. The officials concerned in the respective organizations should be approached for the purpose of collection of relevant information about eligibility criteria, expectations of the organizations and other aspects. The job seekers should not submit the applications without fulfilling the requirements adequately. Such employment communication is most likely to be rejected by the potential employers. Lehman *et al.*

(2012: 10) have identified the basic employment communication elements such as—conduction of research, analysis of self-eligibility, listing of job requirements, preparation of target oriented resumé, adding supplementary information and interview with companies.

Essential Characteristics of CV

The curriculum vitae contain the personal details of the job seeker concerned. It is also known as bio-data, personal data sheet, qualification/ experience sheet, resumé and so on. It introduces the personal, educational and professional details of the job seeker to the potential employer. It is a written statement of the biographical details which include—family background, educational qualification, work experience, professional achievement, network development and other information pertaining to the employability of the job seeker. The curriculum vitae are a self-introductory note submitted by the job seeker to the employers with a view to promote the applicant. They are indeed self marketing tools that summarize the qualifications, experiences, specializations and other attributes of job seekers.

The curriculum vitae are usually attached to an application letter which is also known as covering letter. Usually, the application letter is read by the employer. In the age of electronic communication, the curriculum vitae can be submitted through e-mail to the institutions concerned. The curriculum vitae should be a tailor made individual application which suits the needs of the potential employer during different contexts. The curriculum vitae should be able to project the applicant as the most suitable candidate for a particular job. It should be written in accordance with the terms and conditions of the job available in a particular organization. The job seeker should be intelligent enough to prepare the curriculum vitae specifically in relation to the educational qualifications, professional experience and allied accomplishments.

The curriculum vitae should emphasize the fitness, soundness and suitability of the candidate with proper facts and documentation. The primary information should be highlighted in the curriculum vitae along with secondary or supportive information dealing with work experience and capacity. The curriculum vitae should also have different compartments which emphasize the strengths and advantages of the job seeker concerned in order to invite the attention of the employer. The curriculum vitae also contain the common details such as individual background, educational qualifications, professional experience, and special achievements.

The sample format for the presentation of curriculum vitae contains the name, gender, age, nationality, religion, caste, complete address, objectives, educational background, professional experience, specialization, awards, achievements, strengths, references and other details. The educational component should provide the relevant details from matriculation to post-graduation or more in a chronological order the experience component should provide necessary details of past and present work experience in the chronological order. The specialization component should indicate necessary details concerning the special area of service and expertise. The awards component should provide relevant details of scholarships, prizes and awards one by the candidate at school, college, university, State, national and international levels. The achievements component should indicate the special accomplishments of the candidate professionally and socially in detail. The strengths component should highlight the specific eligibility, experience, specialization, leadership quality and other salient features of the unique personality of the job seeker. The reference component should also mention the names of two or more prominent personalities who are acquainted with the candidate. It should contain the full name, complete address, telephone number, e-mail address and other details for each reference. The summary component can highlight the most relevant and pertinent factors associated with the personality of the job seeker.

Bhusan (2012) identifies the major sections of curriculum vitae which include opening, education, experience, activities/honours/special skills and references. In modern organizations, curriculum vitae are scanned and stored on databases for quick processing and decision making. The opening part includes proper heading, job description, career objectives and summary of the qualifications of the job seekers. The heading identifies different compartments such as name, address, telephone number, e-mail address and so on. The experience component should introduce the various kinds of experience obtained in different organizations in the chronological order. The candidates should furnish necessary details about their activities, honours, special skills and other attributes which strengthen their candidature. The references should indicate the name, address, telephone numbers and e-mail addresses of the past employers and other notable personalities who are aware of the background and contributions of the candidates concerned.

The guidelines of drafting the curriculum vitae include—brief introduction to the objectives, emphasizing the educational qualifications, projecting the professional experience, highlighting the special accomplishments, adopting a well defined format, producing the universally accepted contents, prevention of glorification of the candidate, avoiding highly personal details, ensuring the incorporation of relevant details and inviting the attention of the employer on the special qualities and capabilities of the candidate.

Lehman *et al.* (2012: 11) enumerate the standard parts of a resumé as follows:

Identification

The applicants should provide information that will allow the interviewer to reach him/her. Include your name, current address, telephone number, e-mail address and Internet address to facilitate an interviewer's communication. Evaluate the personal message on your voice mail to be certain that it portrays you as a person serious about securing a job.

Job and/or Career Objective

State your job/career objective—the job you want. Interviewers can see quickly whether the job you seek matches the one they have to offer. A good job/career objective must be specific enough to be meaningful yet general enough to apply to a variety of jobs.

Career Summary

You must provide a compelling reason for a more thorough review of your resumé. Craft a persuasive introductory statement that quickly synthesizes your most transferable skills, accomplishments and attributes and place it in a section labelled summary or professional profile.

Qualifications

This information is used to divide the qualifications into appropriate parts, choose appropriate labels for them, and arrange them in the best sequence. Usually, qualifications stem from your education and work experience. Arrange these categories depending on which you perceive as more impressive to the employer, with the more impressive category appearing first.

Education

The education section should include the particulars of educational accomplishments in terms of diploma, degree, master's degree and so on. Include overall and major grade point averages. Honours and achievements that relate directly to education can be incorporated. This section could also include a list of special skills and abilities such as foreign language and computer competency.

Work Experience

This section provides information about your employment history. The jobs may be listed in the reverse chronological order or in the order of job relatedness. Begin with the job that most obviously relates to the job being sought. Arrange the order and format of information about each job, but format all job information consistently.

Honours and Activities

Make a trial list of any other information that qualifies you for the job. Divide the list into appropriate divisions and then select an appropriate model. Consider summarizing information that is relevant but does not merit several separate lines.

Personal Information

You must be selective when including personal information. The space could be used more effectively to include more about your qualifications. Personal information is commonly placed at the end of the resumé just above the references section.

References

Listing names, addresses, telephone numbers and e-mail addresses of people who can provide information about you adds credibility to the resumé. Employers, former employers, instructors and former instructors are good possibilities.

The curriculum vitae should be prepared with relevant details which are presented under suitable headings, compartments and documents/ testimonials. The curriculum vitae should be neither too brief nor too lengthy. It should be a balanced and focused presentation of relevant qualifications, experiences and achievements which warrant the attention of the employers. The major types of resumés include—chronological resumé, functional resumé, and chromo-functional resumé.

There is a basic difference between the curriculum vitae and application letter which perform two different functions. The application clearly indicates the willingness of the job seeker but the curriculum vitae provides the biographical information of the candidate in detail. The application letter indicates from, to, subject matter, reference, willingness of the candidate, specific eligibility of the candidate and a personal appeal of the candidate. It is drafted by the candidate very briefly in the context of job requirement. An application letter should not contain detailed biographical information of the candidate. The curriculum vitae are also presented to the potential employer along with brief, bright and brisk details of the candidature. The job seeker can also provide the references of couple of prominent personalities who vouch for the eligibility and capacity of the candidate concerned.

Types of Interviews

An interview is conducted by the potential employer in order to test the suitability and capacity of the applicants orally. The employer constitutes the board of appointment consisting of the representatives of the management and subject experts. The employer examines the qualifications, experience and achievements of the candidate during the course of an interview. It is universally defined as an oral tool of assessing the candidate's strengths and weaknesses professionally. The candidates should also possess communication skills in general orally or non-verbally in order to attract the attention of the employer and persuade the employer to give the employment opportunity. The candidate should also learn the art of handling the interviews efficiently and successfully. The interviews can be classified into personality interview, academic interview, panel interview, sequential interview and so on.

The personality interview is conducted to assess the capability of the interviewee during certain occasions. The non-verbal communication skills of the interviewee are assessed by a group of interviewers. The body language, command over the subject, communication skill, art of presentation, articulation capacity, convincing capacity, persuasive capacity and suitability of the candidate in a given situation are systematically examined during the personality interview.

The academic interview is carried out with a view to examine the educational qualification, professional experience and personality of the candidates. It basically involves question-and-answer format. The interviewers assess the body language, mannerisms, attentive listening, eye contact, clarity of thought, depth of knowledge and other aspects of the candidature of the applicants.

The telephone interview is conducted with a view to understand the ability of the candidates who are in different places. The interviewer also examines the modulation of voice, confidence of the interviewee and other personality features in order to understand the strengths and weaknesses of the candidates. The oral communication skill and competence of the candidates are assessed through telephone interviews.

The skill-based interview is conducted for the purpose of examining the professional skills of the candidates. The interviewee is required to demonstrate practical and professional skills in a systematic manner. The interviewer makes use of the opportunity to assess the communication skill, persuasive skill and operational skill of the candidates concerned. Many jobs demand vocational or professional skill development in order to enhance sound delivery system and operations.

The preliminary interview is conducted in the first stage as a screening test in order to eliminate the not so competent candidates and retain the capable candidates for the final selection. The candidates are asked to make oral presentation on a given topic and demonstrate their professional skill in order to verify their suitability professionally and otherwise. It is a brief examination of the personal background, educational qualification, professional experience and suitability of the candidates when they are large in number.

The sequential interview is conducted by various experts during different stages in an organization. The interviewee has to appear before many people who constitute subject experts, veterans, management experts and representatives of the management. Several teams are constituted by the management to assess the different aspects of the personality and suitability of the candidates concerned. The candidates are required to demonstrate their knowledge, experience, skill and competence before several groups of experts and interviewers. Each and every aspect of sequential interview is scientifically measured by the groups of experts in order to assess the suitability of the candidates for various posts.

The lunch/dinner interview is also carried out by the prestigious organizations in order to assess the personality and performance of the candidates concerned. The psychological, physiological and professional characteristics of the candidates are examined extensively by the employers. The interviewee should follow strictly the table mannerisms and avoid drinking, smoking and other activities even though they are offered to do so.

The panel interview is carried out by a panel of experts representing different walks of life in modern organizations. Each member of the panel closely monitors the knowledge, skill, attitude, behaviour and capacity of the candidates concerned. The candidates should also give equal importance to all the members of the panel and answer to their questions confidently. The eye contact, body language, physical movement, communication skill, argumentative skill, persuasive skill and other aspects are closely examined by the members of the panel.

All these types of interviews are carried out with a view to examine the suitability of the candidates in modern business organizations. The candidates should take these interviews seriously, participate in the interviews with adequate preparation, clarify the doubts of the interviewers, convince the interviewers about their candidature and persuade the interviewers to give them an opportunity to serve their organizations. Interview is indeed a good opportunity given by the employers to justify the qualification, experience, specialization and achievements of the candidates.

Bhusan (2012) identifies three important characteristics of business interview namely, planned discourse, dyadic discourse and interactive discourse. In the case of planned discourse the employers plan in advance about the procedures and formalities of conducting the interviews. The dyadic interview involves couple of representatives or experts interviewing one or more candidates. The interactive discourse involves a two-way interaction where both parties speak and listen.

Attributes of Interviewees

The candidates should also have depth of knowledge about the subject as well as field of service. Superficial understanding of the subject mars the personality of the candidates. They should acquire basic and advanced knowledge about a particular job and operation in order to develop clarity of thought and deed. Knowledgeable professionals and workers can enrich the organizational management and delivery system in the modern competitive business environment.

The candidates should also be aware of the professional environment in terms of historical context, present scenario, technological developments, operational management, constraints of the profession, challenges of the profession and opportunities of the profession concerned. The professional environment changes constantly and the job seekers should take note of the changing professional environment and adapt themselves to the changes and developments in order to enhance their suitability.

The job seekers are required to possess adequate communication skills since communication is the life blood of human personality and organizational management. The candidates should also excel in oral communication, written communication, electronic communication and other spheres of communication. They should also impress upon the interviewers through demonstration of adequate communication skills.

The business environment is constantly changing and in the age of competitive business only the smartest and fittest professionally and otherwise can survive the testing times and achieve the goals of organizational development. The employers always look forward to recruiting professionally competent persons in order to cope with the challenges of business promotion. Hence, the interviewees should demonstrate professional competence during the interview before the employers.

The modern organizations also depend on scientific and technological innovations and operations. The interviewee should demonstrate technical capacity for handling the operations with utmost clarity, perfection and capability. Technologies and operations are also subjected to series of changes and modifications in modern society. The interviewee should convince the employers about his/her technical knowledge, skill and competence during the course of interview.

In the age of competitive business, the employees and other professionals are required to develop a sound personality which consists of knowledge, experience, expertise, leadership qualities, problem-solving ability, crisis management capacity and team work capacity. The present generation of job seekers should possess sound mind, body and soul in order to race against the time and achieve maximum success in the midst of constraints and challenges. There is no substitute for sound personality in the new millennium. Hence, the candidates should demonstrate adequate sound personality during the interview.

The interviewees are also called upon to demonstrate application of mind during the course of interview before the selectors. They must be able to provide solutions and guidelines for the resolution of certain conflicts and issues which impede the progress of the profession as well as organization. The interviewers pose certain questions in order to examine the application of mind and find out as to whether the candidate can rise to the occasion. Hence, the interviewees are required to possess and demonstrate application of mind which matters much from the point of view of assessment.

The interviewees should be prepared to provide good background information about himself/herself in general and the organization which conducts the interview in particular. Lehman *et al.* (2012: 12) suggest—be prepared to answer standard interview questions, behavioural questions, demonstrate logical thinking and creativity, discuss salary and benefits, and convince the employers. They have also identified certain strategies for conducting a successful interview.

The modern selectors are also interested in the recruitment and promotion of the employees who are known for integrity personally and professionally. The interviewers also examine the gap between the claims and achievements of the candidates during the interview. The candidates should not present any misleading information in the curriculum vitae or interview since it would mar their success. The selectors are capable of understanding the difference between the contents and achievements in view of their vast experience. Hence, the candidates should prove that they have necessary integrity for the sound delivery system in the organizations concerned.

Strategies for Successful Interview

The modern job seekers are required to prove their capacity during the interview beyond all reasonable doubts. The interviewers have the authority and privilege to select the right candidates for the right jobs. There is no place for mediocre persons in the present age of competitive business. The job seekers should understand the importance of interview from the point of view of assessment of their suitability for various positions in modern organizations. They should also understand the art and craft of interview which is a challenging task in modern organizations. In this age of survival of the fittest, the candidates should demonstrate adequate knowledge, experience, skill, capacity and soundness during the interview. They must adopt certain strategies for successful interview on the basis of sound knowledge and interaction with the experts.

Understanding of the Personality

The candidates should know their curriculum vitae thoroughly and explain those details during the interview. They must be fully aware of their personal background, educational qualification, professional experience, specific strengths and other aspects of their personality in order to convince the potentially employers. The candidates must be very clear about their goals, past achievements and future career plans. They must be able to recollect the details which are presented in the curriculum vitae and articulate their points of view before the selectors effectively.

Understanding of the Organization

The candidates should also be fully aware of the history of the organization, aims and objectives of the organization, the management of the organization, operations management, strengths of the organization, expectations of the organization and other salient features of the organization concerned. Modern employers wish to recruit persons who are well informed about their organizational status, problems and prospects. In the age of virtual environment, modern organizations have developed their own databases which are available in the respective websites. The candidates can also consult the employees of the organization and collect more details about the working conditions, job expectations and other aspects of delivery system. They must impress the interviewers through presentation of relevant details of the organization where they are supposed to work if selected.

Understanding of the Job Details

The candidates should also understand the exact nature and scope of the job which they are required to perform in the organization concerned. They should also be aware of the expectations of the employers regarding the delivery of goods and service. They must also understand the job specifications, expectations, delivery system, operations management, innovative measures and other aspects in order to convince the employers. The candidates should basically understand the job profile, nature of job, scope for the growth and other professional needs in order to justify their suitability for the positions.

Understanding of the Nature of Questions

The candidates should be aware of the general and specific questions which will be raised by the selectors during the interview. The selectors are most likely to focus the attention of the candidates on the historical context, organizational profile, job profile, nature of work, challenges of the work, technological developments, operations management, crisis management, and future course of action. The candidates are assessed especially in terms of educational qualification, professional experience, special achievements, area of specialization, personality factors and so on. The latest scientific, technological and professional challenges and advancements are also focused by the interviewers. Hence, the candidates should be thoroughly prepared to answer the questions with clarity, confidence and authority.

Understanding of the Techniques of Interview

The candidates should know that interviewing is an art and craft which demands creativity, clarity, efficiency, authority and confidence. They must rise to the occasion and prove that they are capable of handling the job and delivering the goods and services to the best of the satisfaction of the employers. They must also answer to the questions with an open mind and demonstrate clarity of ideas and actions in the interview. The candidates should be able to understand the mindset of the interviewers and provide satisfactory answers to them. Hence, a thorough understanding of the techniques of interview would enable the candidates to present themselves very successfully in the interview.

Participation in Group Discussion

Group discussion is one of the methods of examining the perception and ability of the candidates who seek jobs in different organizations. The group discussion is usually moderated by an expert who knows the art and craft of conducting group discussion. The group discussion is defined as an interaction with a small group of job seekers who share different perceptions and background. It is carried out with a view to test the communication skill, personality traits, environmental understanding, professional capacity and other aspects of the candidature of the job seekers. The moderator of a group discussion basically evaluates the ability of the candidates to interact in a group which examines a basic issue or topic concerning the job environment. The observers also monitor the individual behaviour of the candidates in a group discussion situation and find out the capacity of the candidate for team work, coordination, crisis management, operations management and so on. In a group discussion, all participants are treated equally. They are examined in terms of their ability to initiate the discussion, elaborate the issues, highlight the significant developments, understand group dynamics, mediate between opposing views and facilitate meaningful consensus in a given group discussion situation.

The group discussion is one of the tools of modern interviewing in a business organization. The candidates are enabled to express their views, air their differences and provide solutions to the practical problems. The interviewers also provide an opportunity for brainstorming which works effectively in a group discussion situation since it is basically dependent on proper understanding, body language, cooperative behaviour and authority over the subject concerned. In a group discussion, the interviewers also assess the spirit of oneness among the candidates. The employers also assess the ability of the candidates to effectively demonstrate their knowledge, skill and competence. The candidates are also systematically assessed in terms of forming, norming and performing capabilities.

In group discussion, the employers also take note of the agenda setting, presence of mind, clarity of thought, coordination of discussion and creation of group environment by the candidates. The examiners also assess the communicative behaviour of the candidates that aims at controlling others in a group discussion situation. Efforts are also made to examine the knowledge of defensive and supportive behaviours which make the group discussion more effective as a tool of interview. The examiners also assess the listening habits cultivated by the members of the group discussion. The interviewers also find out as to what extent the candidates have developed the sense of patient hearing which is the basis of group discussion. The candidates are also assessed in terms of their active participation in the process of group discussion.

The dynamics of group discussion, prevalence of positive group climate, quality of non-verbal communication, use of appropriate words, eye contact, facial expression, body posture, body movement, personal appearance, spatial relationships, tone of voice, use of time and other aspects of group discussion. In modern interviews, group discussion has become an important tool of seeking answers to challenging questions concerning organizational and operations management in modern business organizations. Group discussion is an important tool of conduction of interview which enables the examiners to understand the adequate preparation, ground work, team building, agenda setting, open communication, freedom of expression, meaningful facilitation, consensus building and democratic environment which are the prerequisites to effective group discussion.

Conclusion

The employment communication assumes great significance in the present time since it is a prominent tool of examination of the suitability of the candidature of the applicants who aspire for various employment opportunities. The candidates are required to be fully aware of employment opportunities, employment providers, job specifications, job requirements, eligibility criteria, prerequisites to employability and gaining absolute employability in the competitive business environment. The job seekers should not ignore the importance of employment communication in the age of competitive business and service. They should cultivate necessary skill and competence in order to make their presence felt and gain useful employment opportunities in modern business organizations. Employment communication is indeed a multi-faceted process which involves preparation of curriculum vitae, submission of application, active participation in group discussion and rewarding participation in interviews. The candidates should identify the needs of the employers and fulfil them in order to obtain gainful employment opportunities in modern organizations. There is no substitute for quality oriented, skill oriented and capacity oriented employment communication which matters most in the business environment.

References

Axtell, Roger E. (1998) *Gestures: The Dos and Taboos of Body Language Around the World*, New York: John Wiley & Sons, p. 43.

Bennis, W. and Nanus B. (1985) *Leaders: The Strategies for Taking Charge*, New York: Harper & Row, p. 89.

Bhusan, Uma (2012) *Introduction to Business Communication*, Jaico Publishing House, Mumbai, pp. 308-345.

Ibid.

Brilhart, John K. and Gloria J. Galanes (1992) *Effective Group Discussion*, Dubuque, Iowa: Wm. C. Brown.

Chaturvedi, P.D. and Mukesh Chaturvedi (2011) *Business Communication—Concepts, Cases and Applications*, Delhi: Pearson, p. 116.

Dance, Fran E.X and Carl Larson (1972) *Speech Communication: Concepts and Behaviour*, New York: Rinehart and Winston.

Hasan, Seema (2010) *Mass Communication: Principles and Concepts*, CBS Publishers and Distributors Pvt. Ltd., New Delhi.

Karoli, Veera and Naghma Ahmed (2013) *Business Communication*, Thakur Publishers, Bengaluru, India.

Kaul, Asha (2009) *Business Communication*, PHI Learning Private Limited, New Delhi.

Lehman, Carol, M., Devvie D., DuFrene, Mala Sinha and Robin C.Walker (2012) BCOM, *An Innovative Approach to Learning and Teaching, Business Communication, A South Asian Perspective*, Cengage Learning, New Delhi.

Ibid., p. 334.

Ibid., pp. 338-342.

Ibid., pp. 374-376.

Lengel, R.H. and R.L. Daft (1988) The Selection of Communication Media as an Executive Skill, *Academy of Management Executive*, 2: 225-230.

Lesikar V., Raymond, Marie E. Flatley, Kathryin Rentz and Neerja Pande (2011) *Business Communication: Making Connections in a Digital World*, New Delhi: Tata McGraw Hill Education Private Limited, pp. 20-21.

Lesikar, Raymond, V., Marie E. Flatley, Kathryin Rentz and Neerja Pande (2012) *Business Communication, Making Connections in a Digital World*, New Delhi, India.

Mukerjee, Hory Sankar (2013) *Business Communication: Connecting at Work*, Oxford University Press, New Delhi.

Perrin, Towers (2006) Effective Communication from the Perspective of Employees: *Towers Perrin Monitor*, May, p. 6.

Perry, David (2003) Do you have the skills most in demand today?, *Career Journal*, www.careerjournal.com

Schultz, Heidi (2000) *The Elements of Electronic Communication*, Boston: Allyn and Bacon, pp. 43-47.

Spitzberg, B.H (1983) Communication Competence as Knowledge, Skill and Impression, *Communication Education*, 32: 323-329.

Terminello, Vera and Marcia G. Reed (2003) *E-mail: Communicate Effectively*, NJ: Pearson Education, p. 13.

Thibaut, John and Harold Kelly (1986) *The Social Psychology of Groups*, New Brunswick, NJ: Transaction Publishing.

Trenholm, Sarah (1990) *Human Communication Theory*, Englewood Cliffs, N.J: Prentice Hall.

Trompnaars, Fons and Peter Woolliams (2003) *Business Communication Across Cultures*, London: Capstone, p. 53.

Weiss, Alan (2003) *How to Write a Proposal that is accepted Every Time*, Peterborough, N.H.: Kennedy Information, Inc, p. 13.

Winsor, Dorothy A. (2003) *Writing Power: Communication in an Engineering Centre*, Albany: Suny Press.

Zikmund, William G. (2003) *Business Research Methods*, Mason, O.H.: South Western, p. 279.

Chapter 13
Group Communication Skills for Business Management

Introduction

Communication is the lifeblood of every individual and organization. Communication cements all human relationships in modern society. Communication basically involves exchange of ideas, experiences and expertise between the source and receivers. Communication has been rightly viewed as a transitive process in which messages are sent and received simultaneously. The members of a group share different perceptions, needs and demands. Usually, a group of people come together with a specific purpose. A group usually consists of three or more persons. In a larger group, the individuals have less influence as compared to a small group. The group communication is defined as interaction among a small group of people who share a common purpose and develop a sense of belonging over a period of time. The group members can influence one another even when not meeting face to face. In modern business organization, several groups of stakeholders are found with different perceptions, needs and demands. The organizational leaders and communicators spend their valuable time working in small groups and interacting with different groups of people who are involved in the affairs of the business organizations. The concept of group communication, nature and scope of group communication, factors affecting group communication in business organizations, essential characteristics of group communication, identification of the needs of the participants, strategies for successful group communication and advanced techniques and technologies of group communication are presented in this chapter.

Definitions of Group

In modern society, several groups are found in all spheres of human life.

Social scientists have conducted research on groups when people constitute groups on the basis of like-mindedness and commonality of interest. Studies have also dealt with the cohesiveness of groups. Most scholars have argued that group development is a recapitulation of the childhood experiences of individual group members. Studies have reported the temporal perspective on groups which are known for complex systems characterized by several factors. Group activity is a normal part of all living beings in the world. The need for groups arises as many activities are only possible through group efforts. Human beings also spend a great part of the time in their lives living in groups. It is essential for any modern organization to understand groups and their dynamics.

Eubank (1932) defines: "A group is two or more individuals in a relationship of psychic interaction, whose relationship with one another may be abstracted and distinguished from their relationship with all others so that they may be thought of as an entity".

Mills (1967) defines: "A group is a set of single organisms, commonly called members, which over a period of time or multiple interrupted periods, relate to each other face to face, processing matter-energy and information".

Giddens (1989) notes: "A group is a number of people who interact with each other on a regular basis. It is different from aggregate, a collection of people in the same place and same time but having no definite connection with each other, and social category, a statistical grouping that is people classified together on the basis of any characteristics".

It is obvious that a group is a social formation which has certain basic characteristics such as structure, norms and functions. A group is an aggregate of persons coming together temporarily for any reason or purpose while a collectivity is a plurality of persons representing a social structure, collective consciousness and interaction between themselves. A group has a common identity, a feeling of unity and shared goals and norms. Generally, a group consists of two or more persons who come together to achieve any objective. Groups are also classified into several communities and associations. There are also formal and informal groups which are found in modern society.

Characteristics of Group

Group members can achieve progress more collectively than individually. The social nature of groups contributes to individual goals of members. The group process can strengthen the fraternity, improve decision mak motivate members for better actions and facilitate achievement of the goals on the basis of team spirit. Lehman *et al.* (2012: 18) identify the characteristics of group thus—common goals, role perception, longevity, size, status, group norms, leadership and group roles.

A group is bound to have common goals formulated from time to time according to the needs, hopes and aspirations of the group concerned. The members of the group are required to share a common goal, interest or benefit. This would enable the individual members to overcome differences of opinion and work together on the basis of common understanding. The members are also required to prevent the ego classes, personal agendas and vested interest in order to maintain the harmony, understanding and unity of the group.

The members of the group are also governed by a set of group norms. They should know how to operate on the basis of precise perception of their role in the group. The aggressive members normally adapt confrontationist approach while the responsible members adapt moderate ways to iron out the differences and work together for the achievement of the goal of the group. The success of any group primarily depends upon proper role perception, unity of thought and integration of efforts.

The groups are also formed for short-term, mid-term and long-term tasks. The group members should also have better vision and zeal which would ensure the longevity of the group concerned. The groups which are formed for long term tasks naturally devote more efforts to maintenance of long term goals. The maintenance also includes division of duties, scheduling, record keeping, reporting and assessing progress according to Lehman *et al.* (2012: 19).

The size of the group also matters in a group environment. The members of the group can have the opportunity to communicate well, interact effectively and achieve unity in case of a small group. But, the large groups inhibit communication, interaction and participation due to complexity. The large groups are good in case of broad goal and input. The large groups also are divided into small groups for the purpose of allocation of tasks, maintenance of group unity and achievement of the goals of the group. Studies have reported that groups of five to ten members are ideal for better decision making, problem solving, institution building and allied purposes.

The status of the group also matters in a group environment. Some group members are qualified, experienced, privileged and competent than other members of the group. Hence, the status plays a vital role in the decision-making, planning, organizing, controlling, supervising and other activities of the group. The office bearers of the group tend to speak downward to the other members of the group while the ordinary members of the group tend to speak upward on account of status consciousness. But, the groups require balance, harmony, unity, integration and understanding in organizational power, status and expertise.

The norms of the group are formulated in order to facilitate standard behaviour among the members of the group. The group leader is required to behave very responsibly in order to command respect from other members of the group and get the things done. The members of the group should also conform to the norms in order to ensure discipline, decorum, responsibility, accountability and success. Conformity leads to acceptance by other group members and creates better opportunities for participation and progress. The group leader is responsible for achieving conformity and progress in a group setting.

The successful conduction of the activities of the group primarily depends upon the leadership. The leader plays a major role in the coordination of the activities of the group. The accomplishment of the tasks of the group also mainly depends upon the ability of the group leader. The leadership development programme also becomes very essential in the management of the activities of the group in the right direction. The leadership may also be rotated among the members of the group formally or informally. The leader usually establishes the norms of the group, allocates the tasks, provides direction and motivates the members of the group for the accomplishment of the tasks of the group.

The members of the group also play different roles. The role perception is very crucial factor from the point of view of effective organization of various activities of the group concerned. The members should be encouraged to play a positive role in the process of management of the activities of the group. The negative roles always create disharmony within the group and impede the progress of the group. The members should be properly oriented and guided to play different roles such as change agents, facilitators of development, trouble shooters, communicators, coordinators, evaluators, guides and so on. The members also fulfil multiple roles effectively on the basis of scientific and systematic approaches to group management.

There are certain teams within a group. The major distinction between a group and a team is in member's attitudes, commitment, behaviour and responsibility towards certain objectives and tasks. A team is typified by a clear identity and a high level of commitment on the part of members. Several strategies are used to get the things done by different teams in accordance with the objectives of the group. Lehman *et al.* (2012: 20) identify several characteristics of teams such as task force (a team given a single goal with a limited time to achieve it), quality circle (a team that focuses on product or service quality), cross-functional team (a team that brings together various members from different groups or departments to solve a variety of problems), product development team (a team that concentrate on innovation and development cycle of new products) and virtual team (a team with members in more than one location). The four systems of team development include—forming, storming, norming and performing.

Group Decision Making

The successful conduction of transaction of the group mainly depends upon the group's ability to make appropriate decisions in the right time. The group members have to discuss various goals, functions, methods and other formalities extensively on the basis of authentic information and experience. The members also need proper inputs, interactions and brain storming sessions in order to take the right decision which suits the convenience of the group. Lehman *et al.* (2012: 21) enumerate the different stages of group decision making which include—orientation stage (identification of tasks and familiarity with the methods of implementing the plans), discussion stage (gathering information, ideas, experiences through meaningful discussion), decision stage (taking appropriate decision on the basis of sound ideas and guidelines) and implementation stage (implementing the plans of the groups on the basis of participatory decision making process).

The groups usually make decisions on the basis of series of discussions on issues and tasks concerned. The members are required to express their views clearly in order to avoid confusion and conflict of interest. The group members should also weigh the pros and cons on the basis of democratic discussion and decision making. The group decision making is also dependent on the ability of the members to consider and accommodate multiple interpretative frameworks. The members of the group should also understand the inevitability of individual differences and arrive at consensus which protects the interest of the group. The members should also consciously avoid conflict of interest which impedes the progress of the group. The members should also understand the need for cooperative orientation which avoids conflicts.

Lehman *et al.* (2012: 22) have identified 8 ways to avoid conflict of interest in a group. They include:

- The leader should encourage participants to voice objections and critically evaluate ideas.
- Members should take an impartial stance and not get wrapped up in ego and emotions, outsider's perspective can be challenging.
- More than one group can work on a problem, which may lead to radically different recommendations.
- Each member can be encouraged to discuss the group's deliberations with people outside the group and get their feedback.
- Outside experts can be invited into the group for their input and feedback.
- One of the group members can be appointed devil's advocate to assure that all sides of each issue are explored.
- The group can be divided into subgroups, each of which works the problem separately and then reports back.
- A "second chance" meeting can be held after preliminary consensus is reached to allow members to express doubts and concerns that may have come up.

Concept of Group Communication

The work of groups, committees and teams has become crucial in modern business organizations. Much of the organizational communication involves face to face communication with the members of the groups. Small groups of people exist in all organizations and societies regardless of space and time. There is no unanimity regarding the specific number of persons in a group. Usually, a small group consists of three or more persons who share a common interest.

Communication binds the people who are associated with a group concerned. A group cannot function effectively without communication which enables the group to achieve the goals. Interdependence in the group makes the study of group communication quite interesting. The interrelatedness of group variables is the basis for group communication which facilitates the meaningful development of group relationships over time. Group communication is a prerequisite to improve the group climate which is roughly analogues to geographical climate. A variety of factors interact to create a group feeling or atmosphere.

Beebe and Masterson (1997: 01) define: "small group communication is an interaction among a small group of people who share a common purpose or goal, who feel a sense of belonging to the group and who exert influence on one another". Lehman *et al.* (2012: 22) observe: "The groups form for synergistic efforts; that is, through pooling their efforts, group members can achieve more collectively than they could individually. At the same time, the social nature of groups contributes to the individual goals of members. Communication in small groups leads to group decisions that are generally superior to individual decisions. The group process can motivate members, improve thinking and assist attitude development and change".

The cultural differences also matter most from the point of view of group communication. The success of group communication primarily depends upon the proper understanding of the low context and high context cultures. In a group communication context, human relationships are valued more than culture, status, education, profession, income and other variables. Group communication becomes easier in an environment where the members from different cultural and other backgrounds interact in a friendly and democratic way. Group communication is about dealing with people representing diverse backgrounds in a way that minimizes misunderstandings and maximizes the potential for strong human relationships and operational management in business organizations.

The group communication enables the members of the group to overcome individual differences of opinion and to negotiate solutions acceptable to the group as a whole. The members are trained to develop better role perception and operate on the basis of team spirit. The groups also exist for quite a long time and facilitate division of duties and accomplishment of organizational tasks. In case of small groups, the members have the opportunity to communicate with each other and work together. In a group, the status also matters since the members speak upward to their superior authorities and downward to their subordinates. The group leader also establishes group norms and coordinates the activities of the group. The groups also play a variety of roles in modern business organizations. The members also fulfil multiple roles in a group.

Bhusan (2012) writes: "Groups are prevalent in business and professional organizations. Groups function most effectively when members set effective and appropriate goals of each type. The relationship among individual, group and organizational goals affects group performance. Effective communication between and within groups is vital to modern business organizations".

The decisions are also made in a group after orientation stage, discussion stage, decision stage and implementation stage. The group members should be willing to accept the inevitability of differences and make a commitment to the implementation of the decision of the group.

Jane Gibson and Robert Hodgetts (1986) have suggested 8 guidelines for better group communication and action. They are as follows:

1. The leader should encourage participants to voice objections and critically evaluate ideas.
2. Members should take an impartial stance and not get wrapped up in ego and emotions, affording a more objective view of the decision. However, trying to view a situation from an outsider's perspective can be challenging.
3. More than one group can work on a problem, which may lead to radically different recommendations.
4. Each member can be encouraged to discuss the group's deliberations with people outside the group and get their feedback.
5. Outside experts can be invited into the group for their input and feedback.
6. One of the group members can be appointed devil's advocate to assure that all sides of each issue are explored.
7. The group can be divided into subgroups, each of which works the problem separately and then reports back.
8. A 'second chance' meeting can be held after preliminary consensus is reached to allow members to express doubts and concerns that may have come up.

Theoretical Perspective of Group Communication

Scholars have commonly stated that theorizing is a very basic form of human activity. Theorizing helps to explained or predict the events in people's lives. Theory has twin objectives namely to explain and predict. Scholars have offered the theoretical perspectives for the study of group communication over a period of time. George Kelly (1963: 16) defines: "A theory may be considered as a way of binding together a multitude of facts so that one may comprehend them all at once. When the theory enables us to make reasonably precise predictions, one may call it scientific". A theory is crucial to the study of group communication. A theory also helps make sense of the processes involved when people interact with others in a group. A body of authentic knowledge also enables the people to adjust their own communicative behaviour to help make group work more effective and rewarding. Generally, a theory helps people make intelligent decisions about the assumption of their roles and responsibilities.

Beebe and Masterson (1997: 02) have identified the functions of theory which include—explanatory function and predictive function. The explanatory function of theory is important because it enables the people to understand why some groups are effective while others are not. The predictive function of theory enables the organizers to improve the system, process and operations. The group communication theoretical perspectives are classified under different headings namely— social exchange theory, rules theory, systems theory, symbolic convergence theory and structuration theory by Beebe and Masterson (1997: 02).

The social exchange theory describes the relationship in a group in terms of rewards, costs, profits and losses. The fellowship, job satisfaction, achievement, status and meeting personal needs and goals are the rewards which are provided to the individuals by the group. The social exchange theory emphasizes that the group membership becomes profitable if the rewards exceed the costs.

The rules theory states that participants must share the rules for sound communicative behaviour in order to ensure successful group communication. According to Suasan Shimanoff, a rule is a favourable prescription that indicates what behaviour is obligated, preferred or prohibited in certain contexts. In groups, rules indicate which behaviours are appropriate in a given group communication context. In groups, norms are powerful determinants of group behaviour.

The systems theory represents the most promising perspective on group communication because it is flexible enough to encompass the vast array of variables that influence group interaction. The interdependent variables include—openness to environment, interdependence, input variables, process variables and output variables. The systems theory serves as a useful organizational strategy which emphasizes that a full understanding of group communication involves the broader context or environments in which groups operate.

The symbolic convergence theory explains how certain types of communication function to shape a group's identity and culture. This theory highlights the fact that group consciousness evolves through group members sharing group fantasies or stories. It also states that groups, like individuals, have unique personalities which are based on shared symbolic representations related to the group concerned. A group's identity converges through these shared fantasies.

The structuration theory enables the scholars to understand how people behave in groups. It provides a general framework that explains how people use rules and resources to interact in a social system. It also explains how groups produce and reproduce social system through group member's use of rules and resources when they interact with the group. The group communication rules are based on certain factors both internal and external in a group context. The people use rules and resources in interaction to structure social systems. There are new communication technologies and advanced approaches to group communication which create intellectual collaborative work. Structuration theory also emphasizes that new communication technologies increasingly reshape the structure and operations of a group concerned.

The theories provide explanations of behaviours that enable the practitioners to predict the consequences of various actions. The descriptive model of group interaction is composed of 7 variables such as—communication, leadership, goals, norms, rules, cohesiveness and situation. This framework depicts group communication as a constellation of variables which are interrelated in a group communication context. These theories also enable the scholars, leaders, organizers and other members to be more effective participants in a group communication context. The practicality of these theories is measured by the consistencies in communicative behaviour that researchers have observed within groups. A good theoretical grasp of group communication enables the organizers to predict group behaviours successfully and control the activities of the members of the group on the basis of sound understanding.

Process of Group Communication

Group communication is one of the major types of modern business communication. The right group interaction and communication always lead to positive business consequences. The organizers should systematically analyze the group process and communication in order to facilitate useful group communication and business transaction in modern society. The organizers should realize that commonsense is not enough for effective group communication since it is likely to ignore important factors associated with human relationship development and business promotion. Brainstorming works effectively in a group communication situation even though it is primarily dependent on authentic orientation and expertise.

The success of group communication basically depends upon the development of the spirit of togetherness among the members. The members of the group should also develop commonality of interest and develop meaningful group interaction in order to achieve the goal of unity of thought and action. The dynamics of group communication should be understood in order to produce better results on the basis of proper understanding and negotiation. The spirit of collectivism should be adequately demonstrated by the members of the group who share different backgrounds, perceptions and expectations.

A group is also called upon to resolve certain fundamental issues concerning communication, interaction, participation, problem solving and other aspects of business management. The organizers of group communication should identify the common themes, issues and modalities which affect group communication. The organizers should also take into account the interpretations of events by the members of the group. The process of group communication consists of elements such as forming, storming, norming and performing. This sequence is interpreted by the scholars as quite natural sequence for all groups since the groups go through certain stages of development.

The members of the group are also influenced by several factors and forces. In the stage of forming, the members of the group understand the task and find out the means of accomplishment of the task. In the stage of storming, the members of the group are hostile to the leader and to other members because of cultural, social, educational, professional, economic and other differences. In the stage of norming, open exchange of relevant interpretations takes place and the group members start to accept each other and endorse the norms of the group. The final stage of performing is characterized by constructive attempts at successful task completion. Efforts should be made by the organizers to facilitate planned team development which is a prerequisite to effective group communication in business environment.

The members of the group should be motivated by the organizers to conform to the expectations of the team collectively. Conformity is indeed a product of the period and culture in a given context of group communication. The influence of group consensus on individual attitudes should be examined carefully. There are a number of factors which bring about social conformity within a group. The majority influence leads to convergent thinking while the minority influence leads to divergent thinking in a group.

The problem of group leadership also deserves the attention since leadership involves getting things done through people in a congenial atmosphere. A leader should command the confidence, loyalty and respect from the members of the group. In a group communication situation, communication, confidence and charisma matter most from leadership point of view. The members of the group also search for the personality traits and characteristics which underpin leadership. Usually, action centred leadership is preferred in a wide variety of organizations in modern society. The democratic leadership is accepted as the best leadership style. There is a well established correlation between leadership and management. The leadership is also interpreted by the scholars as skilled behaviour which affects group communication and behaviour.

The process of group communication is also influenced by the power, status and authority of the leader and other members of the group. Different types of power structure affect group dimensions. The power and status go together from the development of modern leadership point of view. Several factors also influence the compliance. The group task roles, group maintenance roles and individual roles also affect group communication. As a matter of fact, communication and structure are irretrievably interlinked in the process of group communication. The group leaders and members must be aware of the different structural dimensions which could be relevant to the groups they are involved in, observes Peter Hartley (2004: 10).

Scholars have also examined the factors which influence the effectiveness of groups while making decisions and solving problems. In a group, consensus brings about good decisions while conflict of interest disintegrates the group. The members of the group should be encouraged to solve the problems in a rational way. Weldon and Weingart (1993: 28) have noted that the presence and clarity of group goals has a major impact on group effectiveness. They have also identified certain practical strategies namely—setting goals which cover all aspects of the performance, providing regular feedback on progress, encouraging communication between members, encouraging and supporting planning activities, and helping group members manage the task would create better group environment.

Lehman *et al.* (2012: 22) have offered certain suggestions for the enrichment of the process of group communication which include: "limiting the meeting length and frequency, making satisfactory arrangements, distributing the agenda well in advance, encouraging active participation of group members, maintaining proper procedure and order, managing the conflict of interest, seeking the consensus of the group and preparing thorough minutes. The group leader and members are responsible for effective conduction of group communication in a democratic, friendly and flexible manner in modern business organizations. The members should focus on issues rather than personalities in order to achieve commonality of interest and unity of actions. The group meetings are important business management tool which provide opportunities for cross fertilization of ideas and unification of deeds which benefit business organizations.

Studies have also revealed the causal link between cohesiveness and concurrence seeking in a group communication environment. The self-categorization as members of the group by the members brings about high cohesion. The groups are bound to have a wide range of choice with respect to problem solving and decision making approaches. Group communication and action become highly effective if there is a thorough examination of criteria for successful solution. The organizers of group communication are required to understand team working and team development strategies in modern business management context. The emergence of high performance team is the need of the hour from business promotion point of view. The organizers should also develop team building methods and strategies in order to make group communication effective in modern business organizations.

Strategies for Successful Group Communication

There are formal and informal groups of people in society which are governed by certain norms and guidelines. There are various factors which are associated with the formation of groups. Abraham Maslow has presented the need hierarchy which includes—physiological need, safety need, belongingness need, esteem need and self-actualization need. The human beings join groups with a view to fulfil all these needs since they can improve their bargaining power if they join the groups during the real life situations. The physiological needs include food, air and water. The safety needs include security and protection.

The psychological needs include the need to belong, the need for esteem and the need for self-actualization. These needs usually affect the people's group membership throughout their lives. The groups are more than collection of people with common goals. The people invariably join groups to satisfy their various needs. The group formation is a never ending process which is based on sustainable human relationship and development. The people interested in the same activities tend to group together.

In a business organization, there are employees, investors, suppliers, distributors, consumers, media professionals, events managers, policy makers and other stakeholders who play a major role in business promotion. There are several sub-groups who are directly associated with business management. Hence, the physiological, safety and psychological needs of various groups should be fulfilled by the business organizations in order to enlist their active participation in the process of business promotion.

Bhusan (2012) notes that cohesiveness, norms, roles, conformity, group advocacy, conflict and group leadership are the prominent factors which influence group communication. The scholar has also dealt with the importance of establishing and maintaining positive inter-personal relationship practices within the groups. The scholar has found that team building is highly essential to facilitate group harmony and accomplishment of group goals. Strategic bargaining and persuasive communication enhance the success of group communication under normal circumstances.

There are certain variables which affect the relationship between the individuals and groups. The self-concept of an individual affects the communication and interaction with others. The culture of origin also affects the self concept. The role formation also provides a foundation for group relationship. According to Brown and Keller (1973: 06), "At the heart of every relationship lie the self-images of the persons involved, each created by interaction with the other." The individual roles have a bearing on group building process in modern business organizations. The business leaders, executives and communicators should understand the self concept of various stakeholders and cater to their communication and developmental needs.

The group has a set of well defined norms which need to be followed by the members of the group. The norms of the group are developed on the basis of certain behavioural patterns that occurred previously. Reitan and Shaw (1964: 25) have identified five factors that affect conformity to group norms. They include—the individual characteristics of the group members, the clarity of the norm and certainty of punishment for breaking it, the number of people who have already conformed to the norm, the quality of the inter-personal relationship that have developed in the group and the sense of group identification that members have developed. The members of the group are required to develop trusting relationships in order to enjoy the benefit of sustainable human relationships in modern business organizations.

The members of the group are required to understand the prevalence of defensive and supportive climates which affect the communicative behaviour of people in groups. The communicative behaviour that aims at controlling others usually produces much defensiveness in group members. The individuals should develop problem orientation which makes other members of the group perceive that an individual is committed to providing solution that will benefit all other members of the group. This would create a supportive climate for group communication. The members should develop the knowledge of defensive and supportive behaviours which make the group work more effectively in business environment.

Sieburg and Larson (1971: 26) classified the confirming and disconfirming responses which affect group communication. The confirming responses are those that cause people to value themselves more while disconfirming responses are those that cause people to value themselves less. The members of the group confirm and disconfirm one another in more subtle ways. The members of the group can improve communicative effectiveness if they use confirming responses rather than disconfirming responses when communicating with other group members in business organizations.

Kaul (2009) notes: "The group communication demands certain qualities such as leadership qualities, knowledge of subject matter, understanding of group environment, assessment of group requirements, analytical ability, flexibility in approach and capacity for persuasion. The group leader should be able to provide right direction but also carry the group along with him. The group leader should also sustain the impact all through the process of growth communication. The participants should be able to cope with the group leader's aspirations and performance".

The success of group communication also depends upon the listening habits cultivated by the members of the group. Glathorn and Adams (1984) suggest three types of listening—hearing, analyzing and empathizing. The members are required to develop the sense of patient hearing in order to understand the need and importance of group communication. They should also analyze the purpose and contents of the speaker by using critical judgement in order to arrive at right conclusions. Empathizing includes the development of sensitivity to the emotional content of the messages. The members of the group should understand the basics of listening such as stop, look, listen, ask questions, paraphrase content and paraphrase feelings which contribute a great deal to building a supportive and cohesive group affinity. In business environment, the corporate leaders, executives and communicators should develop sound listening habits and cater to the needs of communication and development of various stakeholders on the basis of proper understanding.

The verbal dynamics of group communication should also be understood by the members of the group. Bollen and Hoyle (1990: 04) comment: "the communication network and the messages that flow through them ultimately determine the attractiveness of the group for its members". Homans (1992: 12) states: "If the frequency of interaction between two or more persons increases, the degree of their linking for one another will increase and *vice versa*". In business organizations, various groups develop a unique identity through the sharing of fantasies or stories. Group communication brings about cohesiveness if the group members share stories and other group members respond to those stories in business environment.

The development of participatory communication network also enhances the status of group communication in business organizations. Past studies have revealed that groups in which free communication is maximized are generally more accurate in their judgements, although they may take longer to reach a decision. The members also tend to feel more satisfied in groups in which they participate actively. Free and open communication networks which include all the members in the process of participatory communication facilitate more accurate group judgments and enriches the group climate in business organizations. The size of the group also has an impact on group communication.

Small groups facilitate active participation of the members while large groups minimize the chances of active participation and interaction. The small groups always encourage maximum participation while the large groups reduce the chance of active participation. The cohesiveness of the group decreases the conflict of interest and the members personally commit themselves to the group's well-being and play a crucial role in the accomplishment of the tasks of the group in business organizations. Successful group communication demands communication competence. The members of the group should be aware of the dynamics of group communication and develop a positive group climate which is essential for the successful group communication in business organizations.

In modern business organizations, the non-verbal communication is important and that the corporate communicators should identify proper guidelines for interpreting non-verbal communication in various groups involved in business environment. The non-verbal communication creates meaning for someone other than through the use of appropriate words. The eye contact, facial expression, body posture, body movement, personal appearance, spatial relationships, tone of voice, use of time and other aspects of non-verbal communication also matter in business organizations. Beebe and Masterson (1997: 02) emphasize the non-verbal communication variables which are important to group communication in modern organizations for three reasons. First, group participants spend more time communicating non-verbally than they do verbally. Second, people believe non-verbal communication cues more than verbal messages. Third, people communicate emotions primarily by non-verbal cues. Hence, the business leaders and communicators should understand the significance of non-verbal communication variables and facilitate meaningful group communication in business organizations.

In business organizations, group communication has become an important tool of seeking answers to challenging questions concerning business management. The communicators should formulate group discussion oriented questions relating to business management. A question of fact facilitates proper understanding of business issues. A question of value generally produces a lively discussion about business management. A question of policy can be easily identified from the point of view of solving specific business problems. The facilitators of group discussion in business organization should also mobilize appropriate facts, evidences, justifications and examples in order to make group communication mutually beneficial.

The process of group communication in business organizations becomes meaningful if the group assesses the historical context, present scenario, alternatives, consequences and solutions to various business issues and challenges. The communicators should also facilitate the selection of the best choice from among the available alternatives from business promotion point of view. Usually, the descriptive, functional and prescriptive approaches are required to solve the business problems during group communication in business organizations. Brainstorming is the best problem-solving approach in group communication from business promotion point of view. The organizers should make sure that all the participants of the group communication follow the brainstorming rules and problem solving approaches. The corporate communicators and business leaders should adopt appropriate approaches to group problem solving by assuming the role of effective problems solvers and negotiators in business organizations.

The conflict of interest is bound to occur in any group communication situation concerning business management. The organizers of group communication should make use of certain tested and tried techniques of managing conflict and reaching consensus in order to facilitate better understanding among the participants. The members of the group should be enabled to find positive means of managing the conflict in order to channelize the energy for constructive solutions and approaches in business organizations. The member should be encouraged to express their concerns adequately without giving any scope for personal attacks.

Usually, non-confrontational, controlling and cooperative approaches to conflict management are useful in group communication. The organizers of group communication should approach conflict as a problem to be solved rather than creating a win-lose situation which adversely affects business interest. The group communication becomes a rewarding exercise if the organizers follow the communication—focused team-building intervention approach in business organizations. Effective strategies should be formulated by the organizers for enhancing team effectiveness which matters most in group communication for business management.

Effective Group Meeting Management

The group members meet periodically in order to discuss certain issues, trends, tasks and developments which impact the sustainability and progress of the group. The group meetings are essential for communication and management of various tasks. The meetings also provide necessary opportunities to share valuable information, ideas, experience, expertise and relevant perspectives for effective coordination of the activities of the group. The group meetings should be conducted properly and periodically in order to take stock of the situation, identify right procedures and adopt fruitful approaches for the effective organization of group's activities.

Experts have stated that careful planning and conduction of group meetings would ensure the achievement of the goals of the group. Basically, modern groups conduct face to face meetings and electronic meetings. The face to face meetings provide the benefit of direct access to the members of the group and contribute well toward establishing group rapport. The electronic meetings are based on new communication technologies and tools which enable the geographically dispersed members of the group to interact with each other and explore new possibilities for better organization of the activities of the group.

Lehman *et al.* (2012: 22) have provided certain suggestions for effective group meeting management. They include: (1) The group meetings should be held if there is genuine necessity. It is better to limit the frequency and duration of meeting in order to avoid waste of time, energy and resources. (2) The organizers should select the date and time convenient for the majority of the members and make satisfactory arrangements including accommodation, boarding, and transportation. In case of electronic meetings the hardware and software facilities should be made systematically. (3) The organizers of the group meeting are also required to distribute the agenda well in advance which enables the participants to come prepared and perform their duties effectively. (4) The organizers of the group meeting should also encourage the participants to actively participate in the discussion and decision making processes. (5) The group meeting should also have adequate brain storming deliberations which facilitate the generation of many ideas from among the group members without judgement. (6) The organizers of the group meeting should maintain order by following proper parliamentary procedure and avoid conflict of interest. (7) The organizers of group meeting should manage the conflict in a friendly, flexible and democratic manner. They must focus on issues rather than personalities in order to achieve better decision making. (8) The organizers should encourage consensus which represents the collective opinion of the group which benefits the group. (9) The group meetings should be conducted on the basis of well defined agenda and deliberations should be carried out in the order of descending importance. The resolutions of the group meeting should be properly documented in the form of minutes circulated among the members in order to ensure meaningful implementation of various decisions.

Conclusion

The theoretical and practical applications of group communication dynamics should be understood by the organizers of group communication in business organizations. Group communication assumes great significance in modern business organizations. The mediated communication and negotiated settlement are preferred in the present times in order to enhance the effectiveness of group communication from business management point of view. Scholars have recommended that mediated communication works well in a group communication environment even though the group members find it difficult to negotiate relationship issues when the group communication is mediated by technology. The group communication also becomes rewarding if the members follow a more rational, structured and constructive approach when solving the problems. Adequate preparation, ground work, team building, agenda setting, open communication, freedom of expression, meaningful facilitation, consensus building and democratic environment are the prerequisites to effective group communication in business environment. Most of the work in business organizations is accomplished in small groups which demand competent team members and unified action.

References

Beebe, Steven, A. and John T. Masterson (1997) *Communicating in Small Groups: Principles and Practices*, New York: Longman, p. 6.

Ibid., p. 9.

Bhusan, Uma (2012) *Introduction to Business Communication*, Jaico Publishing House, Mumbai, pp. 93-129.

Bollen, Kenneth A. and Rick H. Hoyle (1990) Perceived Cohesion: A Conceptual and Empirical Examination, *Social Forces*, 69: 479.

Brilhart, John K. (1995) *Effective Group Discussion*, Iowa: Wm.C. Brown.

Brown, Charles T. and Paul W. Keller (1973) *Monologue to Dialogue*, N.J: Prentice Hall, p. 2.

Cooke, Robert A. and John A. Kernaghan (1987) Estimating the Difference between Group *versus* Individual Performance on Problem-Solving Tasks, *Group and Organizational Studies*, 12 (3): 319-342.

Donaleson R. Forsyth (1983) *An Introduction to Group Dynamics*, California: Monterey.

Douglas, T. (1995) *Survival in Groups: The Basics of Group Membership*, Buckingham: Open University Press.

Hartley, Peter (2004) *Group Communication*, London: Routledge, p. 129.

Hasan, Seema (2010) *Mass Communication: Principles and Concepts*, CBS Publishers and Distributors Pvt. Ltd., New Delhi.

Homans, George, C. (1992) *The Human Group*, New York: Harcourt Brace, p. 343.

Irving, L. Janis (1971) Group Think, *Psychology Today*, 5 (1): 43-76.

Karoli, Veera and Naghma Ahmed (2013) *Business Communication*, Thakur Publishers, Bengaluru, India.

Kaul, Asha (2009) *Business Communication*, PHI Learning Private Limited, New Delhi, pp. 214-241.

Kelly, George A. (1963) *A Theory of Personality: The Psychology of Personal Construct*, New York: Norton, p. 18.

Larson, C. and F. LaFasto (1989) *Teamwork: What Must Go Right/What Can Go Wrong*, California: Sage.

Lehman, Carol, M., Devvie D., DuFrene, Mala Sinha and Robin C.Walker (2012) BCOM, *An Innovative Approach to Learning and Teaching, Business Communication, A South Asian Perspective*, Cengage Learning, New Delhi, p. 52.

Ibid., pp. 52-54.

Ibid., pp. 63-64.

Ibid., pp. 54-59.

Ibid., p. 61.

Lesikar, Raymond, V., Marie E. Flatley, Kathryn Rentz and Neerja Pande (2012) *Business Communication, Making Connections in a Digital World*, New Delhi, India.

Mukerjee, Hory Sankar (2013) *Business Communication: Connecting at Work*, Oxford University Press, New Delhi.

Reitan, H.T. and Marvin E. Shaw (1964) Group Membership, Sex-Composition of the Group and Conformity Behaviour, *Journal of Social Psychology*, 64: 45-51.

Sieburg, Evelyn and Carl Larson (1971) *Dimensions of Interpersonal Response*, Paper delivered at the annual conference of the International Communication Association, Phoenix, April 1, 1971.

Wagner, John A. and Michale K. Moch (1986) Individualism-Collectivism: Concept and Measure, *Group and Organizational Studies*, 11 (1): 280-304.

Weldon, E. and Weingart, L.R. (1993) Group Goals and Group Performance, *British Journal of Social Psychology*, 32: 307-334.

Chapter 14
Social Media for Business Management

Introduction

Information literacy is an important component of learning process which enables the individuals to acquire life skills, soft skills and vocational skills throughout their lives. The information infrastructure has improved over a period of time in India and other developing nations consequent on globalization. There is proliferation of knowledge based industries in the world. The new communication technologies affect the lives of the people on a personal level and that the new electronic devices and technologies enable the personalization of messages. The present generation of people is using information resources for the generation of knowledge and wealth in all spheres of human life. Internet has become an essential part of everyday lives in the world and it has become a principal tool of accessing information from almost every point on the planet. Information is now widely recognized as a key strategic resource and tool of development. The growth and development of personal and social media has brought about the formation of new communities of common interests and practices and sharing and exchange of information in mutual collaboration for common good. The personal and social media are widely used all over the world to enable the people to gain access to social services. In this age of social networking, there is commendable globalization of knowledge across the world. The concept of personal and social media, nature of personal and social media, personal media messaging systems, classification of social media, social media for dissemination of creative ideas and business communication and social media are presented in this chapter.

Concept of Personal and Social Media

The social media is an umbrella term that encompasses various activities that integrate technology, social interaction and content creation. Social media may use many technologies, including, but not limited to, blogs, micro-blogs, wikis, photos and video sharing, podcasts, social networking, and virtual worlds. The terms 'social media', 'social media sites', 'sites' and 'social networking sites' are used interchangeably in this communication by the scholars. The social media converts the traditional two-party, adviser-to-client communication into an interactive, multi-party dialogue among advisers, clients, and prospects, within an open architecture accessible to third-party observers. It also converts a static medium, such as a website, where viewers passively receive content, into a medium where users actively create content. The use of social media by the financial services industry is rapidly accelerating all over the world.

Digital technology and mobile devices have created a new world of communication and people are free to communicate with others. The digitalization and personal use of media technologies have destabilized the traditional dichotomization between mass communication and interpersonal communication and, therefore, between mass media and personal/social media (e.g., mobile phones, e-mail, instant messenger, blogs and photo-sharing services). In the age of information revolution, the private individuals use media technologies to create and share personal expressions through digital networks. The previous characteristics of mass media as providers of generally accessible information do no longer exist today. The personal media are deinstitutionalized/deprofessionalized and facilitate mediated interaction. The implementation of digital media technologies has important consequences for social networks and fits well within the gamut of personal and social communication. The social media includes web-based and mobile based technologies which are used to turn communication into interactive dialogue among organizations, communities, and individuals. Andreas Kaplan and Michael Haenlein define social media as "a group of Internet-based applications that build on the ideological and technological foundations of *Web2.0,* and that allow the creation and exchange of *user-generated content.*" Social media is ubiquitously accessible, and enabled by scalable communication techniques.

Nature of Personal and Social Media

The cell phones are just handy conversation devices. The cell phones have become a permanent part of modern culture. The cell phones have made their way to the consumer market during last 25 years. The cell phones are also used to keep tabs on each other. The text messaging has become one of the most popular cell phone activities over a period of time. The cell phone also enable the people remain in constant contact with others. The cell phones serve many purposes including marketing communication in the present times.

The personal digital assistant (PDA) is a handy device that frees people from other communicative constraints. The PDAs retrieve, store and send information to other PDAs and computers. It is a light weight, small, easy to use organizer with enough memory to store thousands of addresses and notes. The PDAs are also used to record the personal appointments, participate in special events, store contact information, remind the projects and assignments and to keep track of various preoccupations. The PDAs have become highly effective tools of marketing for the consumers at personal level.

There are certain multi-functional devices such as Blackberry, an iPhone, a Droid, a Palm or some other mobile communication devices which facilitate personal and social communication. The people can send and retrieve e-mail, access the web, play games, text, download music, store photos and movies and get the things done at a personal level without costing much time, energy and resource. The personal and social communication takes place without sitting in front of the desktop compute or lugging around the laptop. The iPad is a cross between a laptop and an iPod touch. It is a portable wireless electronic pad from which the customers can blog, use twitter, use SNS, e-mail, import photos, watch movies, play games, contact people and engage in many online activities. The present generation of users is bombarded with commercial messages.

The latest device is the combo cell phone/wristwatch which is a multipurpose mobile device. The newer versions are also cell phones that are equipped with minuscule speakers which enables the users to chat away without holding the watch up to their ear. They can watch movies, send messages, take notes, contact persons and get the things done through these devices. The cell phone signals can also create electromagnetic signals that often interfere with baby monitors, computer speakers, heart pacemakers and other electronic devices which benefit the mankind immensely at personal and social levels. Their functional utility increases and the personal gratifications also increase subsequently. They keep the users actively involved in the world of business. They also facilitate better human relationship management across the globe.

The relationship between the telephones and Internet has drastically changed over a period of time. The Voice over Internet Protocol (VoIP) and IP telephony do not cost as much a call using POTS because of the advanced packet switching system which is more efficient than the POTS circuit switching system. The computer to computer, telephone to computer and telephone to telephone connectivity has become a possibility because of the advanced software. The webcam is a simple, low-cost video camera that transmits live images between computers. Webcams have become great devices for personal and social communication with friends, relatives and associates living in abroad. A new wireless world has come into existence as a prominent means of personal and social communication. The newest Wi-Fi has improved transmission speed and range.

The social network sites (SNS) are used to send e-mail, photos and videos to friends who are allowed access to someone's SNS page. The participants can interact with each other and develop social ties which benefit them. The SNS offer news, views, opinions, interactive communication, participatory communication and allied advantages which connect the users with similar interests. The SNS tends to be used as places to widen social contacts, to develop human relations and facilitate meaningful business transactions. The use of social network has considerably improved over a period of time. The social network sites, Twitter, blogs, instant messaging and other online devices have brought about amazing interactivity and social communication.

In the present times, several personal media streaming tools are designed to stream from the personal collection of media to elsewhere on the home network of the users over the Internet or both. The streaming of video or music from services like YouTube or Pandora is great for sampling a wide variety of stuff, but the users need media from their own collection. The five great solutions for streaming the personal media include—subsonic (Windows/Mac/Linux, Free), Air Video (Windows/Mac/iOS, $2.99), Audio galaxy (Windows/Mac/Android/iOS, Free), Orb Live (Windows/Mac/Android/iOS, $9.99) and PS3 Media Server (Windows/Linux, Free).

The subsonic (Windows/Mac/Linux, Free) is best known for rock-solid music streaming over the Internet to web browsers and other supported devices, but unknown to many, it can also stream any video format that supports HTTP streaming, such as AAC. Subsonic supports plugging for transcending tasks which makes it easy to adapt to new formats. Although many people use it for local streaming around their home network, you can access Subsonic remotely using the web-based interface or grab one of the subsonic apps for Android and iOS devices.

Subsonic is free, but in order to use it in conjunction with any of the mobile apps beyond the 30 day trial, the users need to donate to the Subsonic project to get a license key and the donations start at around $15 USD.

The Air Video (Windows/Mac/iOS, $2.99) is a dead-simple streaming solution for IOS devices. The users need not go through the hassle of re-encoding all their media for playback on the IOS device. The Air Video transcodes it on the fly to turn the iPhone or iPad into a mobile media center. The customers are required to install the server software on their Mac or PC, install the $2.99 application on their IOS device and enjoy easy file browsing and streaming media. They can also take it for test drive with a free demo which limits them to streaming the first 3-5 media files in each folder.

The audio galaxy (Windows/Mac/Android/iOS, Free) is unlike some of the other entries in Hive Five that do double duty, streaming audio and video in the present times. The audio galaxy remains completely focused on streaming music. The users are required to sign up for a free account at Audio galaxy, install the server software on their Windows or Mac Machine, and get instant and organized music streaming to a remote web browser or their mobile device. Audio galaxy includes drag and drop playlist creation, easy music search, and meta-data repair to help them to clean up their sloppy music collection. As an especially nice perk, both the Android and iOS streaming apps are free to the users.

The Orb Live (Windows/Mac/Android/iOS, $9.99) is a hybrid solution for streaming to mobile devices. The users are required to install the Orb Live server software on their Windows or Mac computer, then they should install the Orb Live streaming app on their Android or iOS device. All media accessible to their computer is then accessible to their mobile device: photos, music, movies—even live television if their computer has a tuner card. The server software is a free download and the mobile app for both Android and iOS is $9.99. Orb provides a demo version if the users like to try it out before buying (Android/iOS), but the demo just picks three random media samples from their server to show off the technology, so it really is only good for testing purposes.

The PS3 Media Server (Windows/Linux, Free) was built to do exactly what it sounds like: transcode and stream media from the personal computer to a PS3 hooked up to the television of the users. Although that sounds fairly limited in scope, a lot of people like it for two principal reasons namely—it transcodes and streams video to the PS3 extremely well, but more importantly, the project very recently has branched out to other devices. People who have struggled with finding a good streaming solution for their PS3 units rave about how it is the best thing out there. Although the originally intended for just the PS3, as of earlier this year the PS3 Media Server beta releases have included support for other devices such as network-connected televisions.

The exchange of information, ideas, experiences and expertise takes place in an astonishing speed through social network sites. The Twitter is hailed as a new news medium. Many professionals use Twitter to build and sustain public relations in the world. The social network interactions is primarily used for developing a sense of social and group belongingness, self-satisfaction, achievement, escape and relaxation, observe Medoff and Kaye (2011: 16). The personal and social media are posing serious threats to communications media. Scholars have observed that the communication need served in the future will be very different from those served today because of the revolutionary changes in communication science and technology.

Personal Media Messaging Systems

The social media became a way of life over a period of time since the people started using them for a variety of purposes. The iPhone-blending video has been viewed more than 9 million times and the Blendtec's sales have increased sevenfold in the past three years according to the recent estimates. The Internet's global reach has remarkably widened after Dickson developed a strong personal brand. In the present times, several executives and other users have developed remarkable connection with the people they want to influence all over the world. In reality, the social media is widely recognized for its global, open, transparent, non-hierarchical, interactive, and real time characteristics which are changing consumer behaviour and workplace expectations. As a result, the best businesses are creating comprehensive strategies in this area to support their goals. Empirical evidence has revealed that it is taking longer for corporate leaders to consider what the new paradigm means for them personally.

Today the executives and citizens are using social media to spread their own messages. The present generation of business leaders embraces social media for three reasons. First, they provide a low-cost platform on which to build their personal brand, communicating who you are both within and outside the company. Second, they allow the users to engage rapidly and simultaneously with peers, employees, customers, and the broader public, especially younger generations, in the same transparent and direct way they expect from everyone in their lives. Third, they give the users an opportunity to learn from instant information and unvarnished feedback. Active participation in social media can be a powerful tool—the difference between leading effectively and ineffectively, and between advancing and faltering in the pursuit of the goals of the executives and other users.

Classification of Social Media

The social media technologies take on many different forms including magazines, Internet forums, weblogs, social blogs, micro-blogging, wikis, podcasts, photographs or pictures, video, rating and social bookmarking. By applying a set of theories in the field of media research (social presence, media richness) and social processes (self-presentation, self-disclosure). Kaplan and Haenlein created a classification scheme for different social media types in their business operations. According to them, there are six different types of social media: collaborative projects (e.g., Wikipedia), blogs and micro-blogs (e.g., Twitter), content communities (e.g., YouTube), social networking sites (e.g., Face book), virtual game worlds (e.g., World of War craft), and virtual social worlds (e.g., Second Life). Technologies include: blogs, picture-sharing, logs, wall-postings, e-mail, instant messaging, music-sharing, crowd sourcing and voice over IP, to name a few. Many of these social media services can be integrated *via* social network aggregation platforms. Social media network websites include sites like Face book, Twitter, Bebo and MySpace.

The honeycomb framework has dealt with the way social media services have focused on some or all of seven functional building blocks (identity, conversations, sharing, presence, relationships, reputation, and groups). These building blocks help understand the engagement needs of the social media audience. For instance, LinkedIn users care mostly about identity, reputation and relationships; whereas YouTube's primary building blocks are sharing, conversations, groups and reputation. Many companies build their own social containers that attempt to link the seven functional building blocks around their brands. These are private communities that engage people around a narrower theme, as in around a particular brand, vocation or hobby, than social media containers such as Google+ or Face book.

There has been a commendable growth in the number of US patent applications that cover new technologies related to the social media. The number of published applications has been growing rapidly over the past five years. There are now over 250 published applications. Only about 10 of these applications have issued as patents mainly due to the multi-year backlog in examination of business method patents. The businesses have referred to social media as consumer-generated media (CGM). A common thread running through all definitions of social media is a blending of technology and social interaction for the co-creation of value. The people obtain information, education, news and other data from electronic media and print media. Social media are distinct from industrial or traditional media, such as newspapers, television, and film. They are relatively inexpensive and accessible to enable anyone (even private individuals) to publish or access information, compared to commercial media of communication which generally require significant resources to publish information.

The fundamental differences between social media and commercial media can be enumerated in terms of certain factors such as accessibility, usability, immediacy and permanence. The commercial communications media and social media technologies provide large scale communication services which are capable of reaching a global audience. The commercial communications media, however, typically use a centralized framework for organization, production, and dissemination of services while the social media are by their very nature more decentralized, less hierarchical, and distinguished by multiple points of production and utility. The means of production for industrial media are typically government and/or privately owned but the social media tools are generally available to the public at little or no cost. The commercial communications media production typically requires specialized skills and training. Conversely, most social media production does not require specialized skills and training, or requires only modest reinterpretation of existing skills. The commercial communications media take more time to reach out to the various audiences while the social media provides instantaneous communication services and generates immediate feedback. The contents of commercial communications media usually cannot be altered but the contents of social media can be altered almost instantaneously by comments or editing. The community media constitute a hybrid of commercial communications and social media.

The social media have added a new dimension to the practice of corporate communication across the world. It has provided an open arena where people are free to exchange ideas on companies, brands and products. Doc Searls and David Wagner observe: "The best of the people in PR are not PR Types at all. They understand that there are not censors, they are the company's best conversationalists." Social media provides an environment where users and PR professionals can engage in conversation, where PR professionals can promote their brand and improve their company's image, be listening and responding to what the public is saying about their product.

Bratton (2008: 03) contend that social media presents an enormous challenge for firms, as many established management methods are ill-suited to deal with customers who no longer want to be talked at but who want firms to listen and engage. The authors explain that each of the seven functional building blocks has important implications for how firms should engage with social media. By analyzing identity, conversations, sharing, presence, relationships, reputation, and groups, firms can monitor and understand how social media activities vary in terms of their function and impact, so as to develop a congruent social media strategy based on the appropriate balance of building blocks for their community. Increasingly, the term 'social business' is being used to try and suggest that engagement with social media is important to more than just marketing and PR departments.

The social media are also responsible for building social authority because they cannot completely control the messages through social media but rather the users can simply begin to participate in the 'conversation' expecting that the participants can achieve a significant influence in that conversation. The social media also facilitate participatory communication to the mankind since people are reluctant to direct or overt marketing through social media platforms. Several scholars have analyzed the impact of social media and noted that social media services are addictive, and that using social media services may lead to a 'fear of missing out'. The Face book is now the primary method for communication by college students in the U.S. Several colleges have even introduced classes on best social media practices, preparing students for potential careers as digital strategists. There are various statistics that account for social media usage and effectiveness for individuals worldwide. The social networking now accounts for 22 per cent of all time spent online in the US. A total of 250 million people aged 15 and older in the U.S. used mobile devices in 2011. The twitter processed more than one billion tweets in 2011 and averages almost 40 million tweets per day. About 25 per cent of U.S.

internet page views occurred at one of the top social networking sites in 2011, up from 14 per cent a year before.

According to the recent statistics, Australia tops the list from the point of view of social media usage in the world since over 10 million users spend almost 10 hours per month on the site. The number of social media users aged 65 and older grew 100 per cent throughout 2010, so that, one in four people in that age group are now part of a social networking site. The Face book had about 750 million users in 2011. The i-Phone application has hit 1 billion in 9 months and Face book added 100 million users in less than 9 months. Empirical studies have also revealed that online students outperformed those receiving face-to-face instruction in the colleges and universities. The YouTube has become the second largest search engine in the world. The people in the developing countries also spend considerable time and energy on social media than on any other activity on the Internet, according to a report by Nielsen (2014). In US also there are increasing number of people who spent their time and energy on social networking sites. About 93 per cent of businesses use it for marketing purpose. The ownership of social media content has been subjected to great debate across the globe. The critics contend that the companies are making a huge amount of money by using the content that does not belong to them. Hence, the challenge for ownership is lesser with the communicated content, but with the personal data disclosed by the subscribed writers and readers and the correlation to chosen types of content. The security danger beyond is the parasitic conveying, defunding or leaking of agglomerated data to third parties with certain economic interest.

Social Media for Dissemination of Creative Ideas

Singla (2008: 24) observes: "Characterizing the relationship that exists between a person's social group and his/her personal behaviour has been a long standing goal of social network analysts. The more time they spend talking, the stronger this relationship is. People who chat with each other are also more likely to share other personal characteristics, such as their age and location (and, they are likely to be of opposite gender). The relation between a person's social interactions and personal behaviour has been the topic of study among sociologists for many years. Instant messaging (IM) has gained popularity in recent years, becoming a common form of communication for millions of people. Experience reveals that people who talk to each other on the messenger network are more likely to be similar than a random pair of users, where similarity is measured in terms of matching on attributes such as queries issued, query categories, age, zip and gender. Further, this similarity increases with increasing talk time".

Social media have become prominent tools of disseminating creative ideas all over the wörld. In fact, engaging the people has become one of the most sought actions for modern companies regardless of space and time. The social media have provided useful platferm for online conversations' analysis, online test groups and inter-cultural communications. Experience reveals that engagement programmes have become fantastic dynamic compasses, but they sometimes need to be plugged in to real life, handled by people who are not all corporate marketers but great experts in their fields. Social media measurement is critical to success, but brands have been unable to get their arms around what it is and what it means. Studies have also highlighted the fact that specific social media persons can be identified and directly engaged. Aimia Vice President has noted that marketers must define success not by social media activity, but rather by customer value and engagement. He also further noted that marketers often struggle to understand the true motivations and purchase intent behind customers' social media activity. Proper segmentation allows marketers to appropriately identify, understand and influence customers through social channels.

Other studies have also reported that social media use achieved critical mass much more quickly than any one predicted. The social media are attracting the consumers in large number. Most social marketers spend their days working to collect or encourage interaction on their pages. This could involve all sorts of marketing tricks, in a desperate attempt to get some comments, likes or shares. The modern businesses have performed well with social media. The fans also like to visit the page each day and see something new there, even if it is something small. The organizers are advised to make serious introspection on the outcome of social media contents and use their own analytics systems and test out their own campaign. The scholars have also suggested that the campaigners should take necessary help from their pool of fans and improve their pages through reliable and creative contents.

Business Communication and Social Media

In the age of globalization, interaction between the customers from different cultures and business organizations has become inevitable. The new trend in international business is to go local. The localization of business creates a business situation in which the locals and foreign investors work together on the basis of partnership. This necessitates the development of social media as an effective means of business communication on the basis of cultural orientation. The social media also facilitate the development of cordial relations between the business organizations and various stakeholders who are spread across the length and breadth of the globe. Communication is a social need for the individuals and that business organizations can achieve progress through the development of communication network.

People are flocking to sites where their circles of influence reside. They are joining networking sites such as Face book because this is where the conversations are taking place. In contrast, consumers are much less inclined to have accounts on more niche sites, such as those dedicated to authoring blogs or writing restaurants reviews. However, the picture is somewhat different in emerging markets, where blogging and micro-blogging tend to be more popular. Modern organizations have gathered necessary information about the extent of interaction with social sites on the basis of grouping the consumers based on their social media engagement level. The business organizations have developed a forward looking attitude towards the consumers and expanded the communication networks and corporate communication services in order to reach out to the existing and potential consumers.

IBM Global Business Services (2011: 10) reports: "The present generation of consumers has gained the benefit of interaction with social media in order to engage themselves with friends and family and access news and entertainment rather than interacting with the brands concerned. The business organizations wish to make use of social media in order to interact with their customers since it provides them direct value through income generation from social commerce. The social networking enables rapid, viral distribution of offers and content that may reach beyond what could be done in traditional channels—all with endorsement from connected people trust. The companies also can use social platforms to mine data for brand monitoring and valuable customer insights, which can spark innovations for improved services, products and customer experiences".

The social media involves a natural, genuine conversation between people about something of mutual interest, a conversation built on the thoughts and experience of the participants, according to Evans (2008: 07). Social media are developed by the individuals who share common interest and represent diverse cultures. The social media are basically concerned about sharing and arriving at a collective point, often for the purpose of making a better or informed choice. Susan Bratton (2008: 03) states: "These emerging online social media richly reward our innate desire to connect with each other at a human level".

The social media applications include Google (reference, social networking), Wikipedia (reference), MySpace (social networking), Face book (social networking), Last.fm (music), YouTube (video sharing), Second Life (virtual reality) and Flickr (photo sharing). The Internet forums, weblogs, Twitter, message boards, Wikis, podcasts, picture-sharing sites and other online media connect and share information in a collaborative manner. The social media have become highly interaction-*cum*-participation oriented media of communication between the two individuals who share a common interest at a very personal level.

The social media facilitate mutual collaboration and creative communication in the present times. The participants are free to participate in the process of interactive communication by adding more comments or providing a new dimension to the stories. Chaturvedi and Chaturvedi (2011: 04) comment: "The empowerment and freedom of the audience to add or create new content makes social media a process and not a static medium". Scholars have also noted that social media involve a collaborative process through which information is created, shared, altered and destroyed.

Empirical Studies have revealed that about 80 per cent of the online consumers have at least one account on a social networking site where they can quickly and easily connect with people. Social media is ultimately about interacting with others with an expectation of getting something in return. Even if that "something" is intangible, such as a feeling of connectedness or affection, participants are actively, purposefully seeking value. For businesses, the challenge is unlocking what their customers care about and creating social media experiences that deliver that value. In the age of competitive business, modern business organizations companies need to understand the dynamics of consumer growth and activity on social sites and take stock of consumer attitudes and the triggers that compel them to seek out a company in the first place.

In business environment, social media act as a 'feedback loop' and enable the management to feel the pulse of the customers. The audiences are free to listen to it, learn from it and follow it. The social media influence the customer's consideration to a considerable extent by offering the experiences of other customers of that product or service. In reality, the participants have confidence in the social messages because they are created on the basis of personal experience, mutual convenience and participatory communication. Social media basically serve as a two-way process of exchange of information, idea and experience. Social communication is the by-product of social media which make the process of communication highly effective since it is primarily based on the manifestation of the personalities of both the sender and receiver.

The social media are vital for the healthy growth and development of modern business organization since they provide continual sharing of ideas and interactive communication between the source and receiver. They create a sense of belonging between the customers and modern business organizations. They make people not only understand each other but also understand the meaning of things happening around them in business environment. The participants not only 'see' the realities of the business, but also develop a 'feel' for it. In the changing business environment, the social media have become an important component of modern society. They enable the people to identify new trends in business communication and management due to technological changes and developments. The success of social media primarily depends on the skills and competence of the people who use them.

The social media enable the people to enjoy the benefit of personal and cordial communication with people from different cultures, societies and spheres of human life. The social media teach how to communicate across cultures with different concepts of formal and social behaviour, time and space. The chances of misunderstandings by those outside that culture are absolutely minimized by the social media. In a developing country like India, where the educated usually speak more than one language and English is a second language, Globes can be a great use for communicating clearly and effectively through social media, observe Pathiravitana (2007: 18).

Hayzlett (2009: 09) comments: "The social media has enabled the new ways to initiate conversations, respond to feedback and maintain customer relations. The Twitter, the latest trend in social media, has recently become an important part of Kodak's social media activity. We have seen very tangible returns from our participation in Twitter, including media coverage, sales leads, increased consideration, and direct product purchase. We strongly believe that if you get involved in social media, it will grow your brand, strengthen the connection between you and your customers and keep you grounded and aware of what people really think about your company. It is well worth the time invested".

Eastman Kodak Company (2009) offers the following tips for effective social media management from customer relations point of view. They include:

- The brands must socialize with their customers because 'top-down' advertising is not going to work by itself;
- Develop a credible voice along the parameters of engagement, humility, and authenticity; and
- Make their social relationships more symmetrical—that is, with value for both the brand and the customer.

The company has also provided ten guidelines for useful utilization of Twitter from business promotion point of view. They include:

1. Become familiar with Twitter by reviewing, or following, the activities of successful brands such as Dell (dell.com/twitter), Zappos (twitter.com/zappos) and Comcast (twitter.com/comcastcares).
2. Listen to what is already being said on Twitter about your brand.
3. Identify initial objectives for using Twitter, including what would qualify as a Twitter success story for your brand.
4. Look into competitive activities and potential legal considerations, especially if there is already a Twitter account that uses your brand's name or other intellectual property associated with it.
5. Use the findings to decide on the appropriate opportunity such as users or community building, tone of voice and method of engagement—that may be right for your brand.
6. Since Twitter is an ongoing activity—even if your company is only listening is a dedicated resource to monitor the conversations and competitors.
7. Map out a plan for the content you will share, including valuable initial content to pique user interest.
8. Integrate your Twitter account throughout your marketing experience, by embedding it as a feed on the company Website, including its URL in communications and so forth.
9. Maintain momentum by following everyone who follows you, responding to queries and joining in conversations without being too marketing oriented.

10. Provide ongoing direct value through your tweets by continuing to listen, learn and fine-tune your Twitter activities.

The globalization of business in the modern world demands that people across the world communicate with one another by using social media. People across the world use social media as an instant means of communicating, transmitting messages and receiving responses. This necessitates technological orientation on the part of the users, so that, they are familiar with the use of social media which facilitate better understanding of the business environment and increase one's influence. In the modern business environment, social media has become a prominent means of interactive communication between the customers and service providers representing different cultures and social settings. The togetherness is not merely in the communicating itself, but in the opinions expressed by both the parties. Research has established that social media facilitate genuine communication between people about mutual business and personal interest based on the thoughts and experiences of the participants.

The advent of new media has created a world in which the mass media are becoming more personal. The users have become more independent than ever before and decide what types of information are relevant to their career, profession and lives. The commercial messages are also tailored to personal characteristics and lifestyles. Today, the online users spend more time on social networks, indicating a shift in the way people use the Internet to connect with each other. The Face book has reached its peak and social networkers are migrating to sites where their parents do not have profiles. The consumers have a definite advantage of controlling the information collected and transmitted in future. The artificial intelligence is used to automate and replace the human functions.

Conclusion

There is a wealth of information about social media that exists both on and offline. Social media are the latest and advanced technology oriented ccmmunicative channels which facilitate round the clock inter-cultural and personal interaction between the source and receiver. It is necessary to ensure that the language, culture, context, social and business practices are shared across different individuals. Since, the communicators in these situations are not face to face, one has to have a high level of electronic communication skills to be able to communicate effectively through social media. There are advantages of social media when compared to traditional and modern communications media. In a social communication context, how the communicators disseminate and what they disseminate are equally important for building good personal relations. The social communication is not bound by any rigid order or sequence of subject matter. The order and nature of communication through social media mainly depends on the extent of both parties' desire to establish a human relationship. Harmony is the hallmark of personal and business communication exchanged by the systematic use of social media. It is absolutely essential to develop skills of mutual understanding by creating rapport with the other person.

References

Beatty and Takahashi (2003) *Intercultural Communication*, New Delhi: Biztantra.

Bhusan, Uma (2012) *Introduction to Business Communication*, Jaico Publishing House, Mumbai.

Bratton, Susan (2008) *Foreword to Social Media Marketing by Dave Evans*, New Delhi: Times Business Services, Wiley India, p. xiii.

Chaturvedi, P.D. and Mukesh Chaturvedi (2011) *Business Communication—Concepts, Cases and Applications*, Delhi: Pearson, pp. 41-42.

Drucker, Peter F. (1991) *The New Realities*, New Delhi: Asian Books Pvt. Ltd., p. 210.

Eames K. and M. Keeling (2004) Monogamous networks and the spread of sexually transmitted diseases. *Math. Biosci.*, 189: 115-130.

Evans, Dave (2008) *Social Media Marketing*, New Delhi: Times Business Services, Wiley India, p. 31.

Hasan, Seema (2010) *Mass Communication: Principles and Concepts*, CBS Publishers and Distributors Pvt. Ltd., New Delhi.

Hayzlett, Jeff (2009) *Observations of the Chief Marketing Officer and Vice President, Eastman Kodak Company, Social media tips*, www.kodak.com

IBM Global Business Services (2011) *Executive Report*, IBM Institute for Business Value, New York.

Karoli, Veera and Naghma Ahmed (2013) *Business Communication*, Thakur Publishers, Bengaluru, India.

Kaul, Asha (2009) *Business Communication*, PHI Learning Private Limited, New Delhi.

Lehman, Carol, M., Devvie D., DuFrene, Mala Sinha and Robin C.Walker (2012) BCOM, *An Innovative Approach to Learning and Teaching, Business Communication, A South Asian Perspective*, Cengage Learning, New Delhi.

Lesikar, Raymond, V., Marie E. Flatley, Kathryn Rentz and Neerja Pande (2012) *Business Communication, Making Connections in a Digital World*, New Delhi, India.

Margerison, Charles (1996) *The Art of Effective Communication*, New Delhi: Excel Books.

Medoff, Norman J. and Barbara K. Kaye (2011) *Electronic Media: Then, Now and Later*, Amsterdam: Elsevier, p. 279.

Mukerjee, Hory Shankar (2013) *Business Communication: Connecting at Work*, Oxford University Press, New Delhi.

Pathiravitana, S. (2007) Master Globish, Use it for Business Communication, *The Times of India,* July 27, New Delhi.

Percy, Larry (1997) *Strategies for Implementing Integrated Marketing Communication*, Illinois: NTC Business School.

Piskorski, Mikolaj Jan and Tommy McCall (2010) Mapping the Social Internet, *Harvard Business Review,* July-August, www.hbr.org

Schaefer, Melissa (2011) *Capitalizing on the Smarter Consumer*, Report, IBM Institute for Business Value.

Schiffman, I.G. and I.I. Kanuk (2004) *Social Media and Marketing*, Delhi: PHI.

Securities and Exchange Commission (2012) *National Examination Risk Alert*, Mumbai, 2 (1): 4-7.

Singla, Parag (2008) *Yes, There is a Correlation—From Social Networks to Personal Behaviour on the Web*, International Worldwide Web Conference, April 21-25, Beijing.

Vivek, T.R. (2007) Strat Talk, *The Economic Times,* April 20, Mumbai, p. 18.

Wasserman, S. and K. Faust (1994) *Social Network Analysis*. Cambridge University Press.

Chapter 15
Events Management for Business Promotion

Introduction

Modern organizations invest money on series of events management activities in order to boost their image, enhance their reputation and achieve success in business management. Events are managed with a view to bring the organization and other stakeholders together and facilitate better rapport development. A new generation of events managers has grown over a period of time on the basis of systematic training and orientation. The events managers are in great demand in modern corporate houses in the present times. Modern corporate houses are required to utilize the services of events managers for the successful organization of events which create new opportunities for the establishment of mutually beneficial relationship between the organization and various stakeholders. In this chapter, the concept of events management, need for events management, principles of events management, budgeting and logistics of events management, process of events management, role of events manager, techniques of events management and tools of events management are primarily discussed.

Concept of Events Management

Wikipedia defines an 'event' as any type of a gathering, ceremony, competition, convention, happening, festival, media event, party or sporting event an exhaustive definition, in every way symbolic of the events industry today. Event management at one time was about planning, organization and execution of a project/activity such as parties, weddings, product launches, conferences, etc. Today, it encompasses a wide range of profiles that offer thrilling opportunities to those with an eye for detail and a flair for organizing.

According to Getz (1997: 06) "Events are temporary occurrences. They have a finite length, and for planned events this is usually fixed and publicized. Events are transient, and every event is a unique blending of its duration, setting, management, and people. Mega-events, by way of their size or significance, are those that yield extraordinarily high levels of tourism, media coverage, prestige, or economic impact for the host community or destination".

Goldblatt (2005: 08) defines: "A unique moment in time celebrated with ceremony and ritual to satisfy specific needs with regard to special events, it is suggested that there is no one standardised definition as opinions vary. Due to such lack of clarity, definitions from the perspectives of both event organizer and guest are used.

Shone and Parry (2004: 15) notes: "Special events are that phenomenon arising from those non-routine occasions which have leisure, cultural, personal or organizational objectives set apart from the normal activity of daily life, whose purpose is to enlighten, celebrate, entertain or challenge the experience of a group of people".

Bowdin *et al.* (2007: 03) comments: "Major events are events that, by their scale and media interest, are capable of attracting significant visitor numbers, media coverage and economic benefits. 'Hallmark events' refers to those events that become so identified with the spirit or ethos of a town, city or region that they become synonymous with the name of the place, and gain widespread recognition and awareness. Mega-events are those events that are so large that they affect whole economies and reverberate in the global media. These events are generally developed following competitive bidding".

Events management is the systematic application of the management practice of project management to the creation and development of festivals and events which enhance the status of modern corporate houses. Practically, event management involves studying the intricacies of the brand, identifying the target audience, devising the event concept, planning the logistics, coordinating the technical aspects and executing the modalities of the proposed event, observes Hasan (2010: 09).

Event management has emerged over the past decade as a dynamic sector of the tourism and leisure industries. The number, diversity and popularity of events have also grown throughout this period. As the number of events increase, there is a growing realization about the continuing need to develop event management professionals who are able to create, organize and manage events. Although many events are successfully crewed by volunteers, increasing competition to secure major events is giving greater impetus for the need to create more fully professionalized events, states Getz (1997: 06).

Event management is also considered as one of the strategic marketing and communication tools by companies of all sizes. Several promotional events are organized with a view to help the corporate leaders to effectively communicate with the clients and obtain their active support for better marketing management in a highly competitive business environment. Events are managed to invite the attention of the general publics and other stakeholders of business management all over the world. The media are also involved in the event management activities in order to obtain better media coverage which enhances the popularity of the organizers of various events.

The hostesses and organizers play an important role in facilitating meaningful event management regardless of the small or big event. Modern corporate houses occasionally organize various events in order to win over the various stakeholders and enlist their active participation in the problem solving, crisis management, disaster management, institution development and other processes. Basically event management demands absolute clarity of thought, unity of action, mobilization of resources and coordination of various components of event management. Event management in business sector is an ever growing exercise which needs proper initiatives.

Event management has also become a new way of life in the modern society. It is also a growing multi-million dollar industry across the globe which involves mega shows and celebrities. Event management has also become an all pervasive organizational activity which is carried out by marketing and corporate communication departments jointly. Modern organizations organize various event management activities from time to time with a view to remain in the lime light and earn a good mileage out of them. Event management is universally perceived as creation of unique opportunities for the successful conduction of organizational activities in modern competitive social, cultural, political and economic environments. Event management is not confined to any particular field or sector of public life.

Need for Events Management

Modern organizations host several events as and when required occasionally since they have a considerable impact on the people who matter most from business management point of view. The organizations manage several events in order to sell the products, popularize the services, raise funds and celebrate certain occasions which boost the image, credibility, reputation and status. Event management is intended to organize several promotional activities such as conventions, conferences, social events, cultural events, public meetings, concerts, live performances, demonstrations, exhibitions, trade fairs, entertainment activities, government events, fund raising events, social mobilization events, marketing events, promotional events, cause related events, mission related events, corporate events, business events, sporting events and so on.

Modern organizations consciously organize multi-faceted events during different occasions in consultation with certain companies which are specialized in the art and craft of event management. There are individuals who are specialists in event management who render certain consultancy services on the basis of their first hand experience and professional excellence. Event management is also a profit oriented business activity carried out by modern event management companies and specialists. The events focus the attention of various stakeholders on the products, services, accomplishments and contributions of modern organizations concerned. Multi-media campaigns are also used as principal tools of event management in modern society.

Event management basically involves creative, technical and logistical elements of the event concerned. The clients' usually hire event management organizations and event management experts in times of need. In the recent times, event management has become a highly profit oriented business across the globe. Event management industry has also grown over a period of time all over the world. The small organizations are involved in the organization of small events while big organizations are involved in the organization of mega national and international events. The event management organizations also make use of several skills for the successful conduction of events. Prominent among them include — budgeting, logistics, selection of areas, selection of manpower, resources mobilizations, hospitality management, transportation management, media management, materials management, corporate communication, corporate advertising, technical knowledge, organizational skills, marketing management, human relations, procedures and formalities, risk management and so on.

In the modern times, event management has also become a promising career. It is a creative, glamorous, thrilling and challenging profession of our times. It demands a lot of creativity, hard work, capacity, contacts and resource mobilization competence. Event management also provides a good career option which does not require huge investment. Event management does not demand specific educational qualifications. It certainly demands creative potential, genuine passion, hard work, leadership qualities, organizing ability and other traits. Event management absolutely demands team work, coordination, competence and other qualities. Event management is also necessary to execute meaningful promotional activities which are essential for the successful conduction of business affairs.

The event managers make use of tested and tried marketing techniques. There are several tools and techniques of event management such as advertising, public relations, publicity, propaganda, lobbying, persuasion and promotional activities. Event management ultimately facilitates marketing promotion in modern society. Event management is also based on systematic survey of social, economic, cultural and political environments. Innovative media management exercises are also required to gain absolute popularity through event management. The event managers make use of the media in order to create interest and build public goodwill, sympathy and support for various causes and activities.

Budgeting and Logistics of Events Management

Concept of Logistics

The science of logistics has grown over a period of time since the practice has its stems in the military arts. *Webster Dictionary* (1963) defines logistics as "The procurement, maintenance, and transportation of military material, facilities, and personnel". Logistics is the process of planning, implementing, and controlling the efficient, cost-effective flow and storage of raw materials, in-process inventory, finished goods and related information from point of origin to point of consumption for the purpose of conforming to customer requirements. A series of researches emphasize the connective aspect of logistics. The transition of the logistics approach from the military sphere into the corporate management sphere is a result of economics vision evolution. Logistics is more often viewed as a system component of integral, global, national, branch or corporate economy. Monroe and Kates (2005: 10) notes that logistics is the art to manage a flow of materials and products from the source to the consumers. Scholars have viewed logistics as an art and science, engineer and technical activity related to defining the needs, projecting the satisfaction, supply and procurement of resources to maintain goals, plans and operations".

Logistics is a new managerial concept or a new way of thinking to provide for goods and services for the events held. This is a new vision of the function of the economy and the objects and events within it. The logistics stress not on the process but on the relations and subordinations among them, i.e. directing flows of goods and services towards the special events participants and consumers. The logistics presupposes network integration and balance of activities that are physically or informatively related to the provision of necessary goods and services for the clients. In reality, the events logistic management aims to develop and maintain the abilities to provide all needed support of special events. The key objective is managing the flow and network aspects during the provision of the necessary materials, facilities and services. The specific concept and approach related to the provision of logistic services is actually an application of the modern methods for market management of the available resources. Its application is a tool for better balancing of special events demand and offer through the usage of the modern market tools for regulation of clients-entrepreneurs relationships in the business. Good logistics management is an expression of economic market relationship maturity and democratic economic management. Adopting the logistics ideas and undertaking specific actions for their application in special events management is an expression of real resource management revolution in the tourist sector sphere as part of the overall economy.

The tactical or organizational logistic system covers related to the event planning and execution issues. It arranges who shall perform the necessary logistic operations. It includes the allocation of logistic tasks among organizational bodies, purchase, preservation, division, transport, etc. The main executor is the team of the organization resource manager. The operational or control logistic system includes management, implementation, coordination and control of the logistics process. It basically deals with the organization of resources and utilization of services in a systematic way with reference to event management.

Budgeting for Event Management

Budgeting is the most important aspect of event management. The organizations should work within budget constraints and maximize the results. Modern organizations follow a well defined and feasible budget format which enriches the event management process. All aspects of event management are taken into account while designing a budget format. The event manager normally provides the budget to the organizers which enables them to decide the various aspects of event management. The budget also provides comprehensive facts and figures with respect to the expenses involved in the event management. It also identifies the potential returns which could be gained by the organizers from the event.

The entire plan of an event should be considered in the formulation of the budget, since, it is the backbone of the event management. It is also known as a pre-event balance sheet. There are certain guidelines which make the budget meaningful and practically viable. Hasan (2010: 09) enumerates the basic guidelines of budgeting thus:

- *Track site rental costs*: As you plan the event itself and as you meet with your venue sales manager, track all projected rental feeds for the event and function space, house-keeping, baggage handling, and related expenses.
- *Estimate catering costs*: This includes all food and beverage charges, including tips and gratuities—which can account for up to 30 per cent.
- *Document transportation charges*: This includes shuttles, coaches, event transfers, and any related expenses.
- *Add décor expenses*: Most events include expenses for décor, such as centerpieces, floral, tent rentals, etc.`this is where you list those costs.
- *Document entertainment and equipment fees*: Common expenses in this category include and A/V equipment, but it is also a good spot to list honorariums to speakers or if you are hiring entertainers.
- *Summarise printing charges*: Several small item charges actually combine to make a larger expense line item. These include invitations, name badges, programme booklets, event signage and banners.
- *Line item for gifts*: One of the event rules is to never allow a guest to leave empty handed. So, whatever gift or gifts you provide, track the cost for them separately; you would be amazed at how much these items can cost.
- *Identify activities expenses*: If your event includes activities such as golfing, tennis, spa, rafting, biking, or other activities, you will want to note the cost of these fees separately. It is suggested

to summarise the total cost in your spreadsheet and attaching a breakdown.

- *Post other expenses*: If an expense does not fall into any of the above categories, list them as a miscellaneous expense item.
- *Give yourself a contingency fund category*: Depending on the size or complexity of an event, you may want to give yourself as much as up to 20 per cent the event budget here. Despite the best planning, charges are going to exceed projected plans with expenses that you never consider. This will keep you from going over budget every time.
- *Summaries projected expenses:* As you build your event programme, you will have a good projection of the total expenses. This is the information that you share with your event client to make sure they are aware of the event budget so that there are not any surprises later on.
- *Summaries actual expenses:* This happens after the event has concluded. Sub-total the invoices into the above 10 categories and document the actual budget. If extremely favourable, identify savings in actual budget *vs*. the projected budget, demonstrating the value-add of your role.

Career in Events Management

In modern times event management is carried out by individuals who have gained absolute experience and expertise in the activity. Some institutions also provide short term courses on various aspects of event management. The schools of communication, commerce and management have also designed specific courses in the event management exercise. Veterans, experts and other seasoned event managers are actively involved in the training and orientation programmes which produce creative and competent event managers.

The event manager is a specialist in the art and craft of event management. He is primarily responsible for the planning and execution of the event concerned. The event managers and team members manage the whole show behind the scene. The event managers are also well versed in several aspects of event management. They are actively involved in strategy making, resources mobilization, brand building, reputation management, media planning, negotiation, coordination and other aspects of event management.

The event manager is also closely associated with the event management companies or agencies. These organizations practically provide specific services which complement the event on the basis of creativity, technical competence, logistics management and other inputs for effective event management. The event manager also assumes a multi-faceted role since event management has become a multi-dimensional profession in modern society. The event managers also provide series of supplementary and complementary services to the clients which enrich the process of event management. Event management has emerged as a glamorous profession which provides umpteen numbers of opportunities to the young generation of event managers.

Event management is the most profound form of modern marketing and advertising processes. Hasan (2010: 09) states: "Event management is a process of organizing a professional and focused event, for a particular target audience. It involves visualizing concepts, planning, budgeting, organizing and executing events such as fashion shows, musical concerts, corporate seminars, exhibitions, wedding celebrations, theme parties, product launching, etc. It is a good career option which offers a lot of independence and flexibility. The event manager should have a genuine passion for conducting events, good organizing ability and flexible personality to work for long hours.

Event management has become a job oriented programme in the recent times. It offers plenty of job opportunities to the young generation of event managers. In the present times modern corporate houses organize events which are as an integral plan for on-ground promotion that is normally executed by event management companies. It is now a significant business opportunity in the new millennium. Specialists have observed that mechanics of event management is an efficient way of co-ordinating and implementing logistics in a timely and organized fashion. The career opportunities in event management are manifold in nature. The advent of new information and communication technologies has boosted the prospects of events management. The major components of event management include—artist management, production management, creative and graphics designer for events, logistics supervisor, travel and hotel coordinator, television production and direction, financial controller for setting up revenue models on ticketed events and sponsorship sales. Hence, event management is a multi-dimensional career which offers variety of positions to the talented and competent people who have an entrepreneurial approach to this industry.

The prominent event management companies of India include—Percept D Mark (Mumbai), Wizcraft (Mumbai), DNA Entertainment Networks Pvt. Ltd., (Bangalore), SITA (New Delhi), E Factor Entertainment Pvt. Ltd. (Noida), Sercon (New Delhi), Tafcon (New Delhi) and Travel Corporation (India) Ltd. (NCR New Delhi). Event management is indeed a well established profession and the contemporary market is wide open with viable career options. More and more companies are looking for avenues to drive their product sales or promotions through innovative ideas and events. More importantly they allow the consumer to sample the product that is being promoted. This could be either in terms of an image that one is trying to build up or alternatively a sheer marketing exercise to drive product sales, according to Venkat Vardhan (2008: 17).

Empirical studies have also reported that the event management industry is certainly quite a nascent one in India but is growing at a very rapid pace. The industry has definitely grown over the past five years and has the potential for much more growth. The current size of the event management industry in India is about Rs. 800 crore and is projected to be Rs. 1,800 crore by 2010 with a compound annual growth rate of 18 per cent. Highly productive, creative and competent persons are required to manage modern events. But academic qualifications are not that important as much as the ability of the managers to negotiate and organize events efficiently matter most.

Getz (1997: 06) emphasizes the growth of event management industry across the globe thus: "Event management industry grows and consolidates worldwide; associations play an increasingly significant role in professional support to the industry by ensuring the continued growth and success of event management professionals. Although there are many events, which are successfully crewed by volunteers, the increasing competition to secure major events is giving some impetus to the trend to create fully professionalized events. Volunteers continue to play a significant role in the management and organization of events; nevertheless, the industry is increasingly relying on well educated, experienced and professional event managers".

Just like how every other industry like medicine or engineering needs preparation, even the event management industry needs preparation and training, observes a corporate need. In India there are a few institutes offering courses on event management, but more than the course what is important is the practical training and professional orientation. Events and occasions are an integral part of human life. Event management is a multifaceted activity. Major constituents of this profile include creativity, meticulous planning, relationship management, advertising and marketing and much more, all rolled into one seamlessly choreographed process.

The present generation of event managers is required to possess certain traits such as creativity, communication skill, sound personality, organizational ability, adequate public contacts, marketing skills analytical ability, networking skills and allied management skills. Above all, the event managers should have the immense patience and insight to see right into the smallest details of the entire event management process and always stay focused on your project goals. Good networking skills, client management, business analytics, time management, ability to take on challenges, problem solving skills and adjusting to rapidly changing situations are some other qualities essential for this role, adds Venkat Vardhan (2008: 17).

In the new millennium, the event management industry has continued to grow in leaps and bounds. There are plenty of events: weddings, birthday parties, talent hunt and reality shows, fashion and cultural shows, academic and sports meets, religious functions, corporate events, conferences and so on. Practically, the organizers provide attractive salary to the event managers. There is an insatiable demand for professionals associated with the event management industry which has grown abundantly in India and abroad. Professionals in this field also get the opportunity to showcase their talent at international events where delegates from our country participate in cultural festivals and exchange programmes, trade shows, conferences, exhibitions, corporate events and so on. With corporate and personal occasions needing professionals to manage them, the demand for event managers is burgeoning. The event management industry has been recognized as a sunrise industry in the modern society.

Techniques of Events Management

The process of event management has been improved over a period of time on the basis of adoption of certain innovative techniques and technologies. There is increasing automation of management of various events which facilitates greater transparency and accountability. Scholars have examined the innovative practices of event management and offered certain suggestions for the improvement of the process of event management.

Understanding the Nature of Event Management

The organizers and event managers should understand the nature, scope and significance of event management since several events demand different tools and techniques. The stakeholders of event management should understand the nature of a particular event management and prepare grounds for effective organization of events to the best of the satisfaction of the participants who matter most.

Proper Planning

The organizers and event managers should consult veterans, specialists and other resource persons and design an effective plan of event management. They should also develop a systematic blueprint which enumerates the various stages and functions for the successful conduction of event. They should constitute an organizing committee representing experts in various branches of event management and obtain their guidance and support. They must identify suitable checklists and deadlines for various tasks that need to be accomplished.

Designing an Action Plan

The organizers and event managers should primarily focus on the requirements of various stakeholders and obtain valuable insights and suggestions on effective management of event to the best of the satisfaction of all players. They should formulate an Action Plan, identify all tasks, allocate the tasks, earmark the funds and prepare grounds for the accomplishment of the tasks. The Action Plan should include details such as hospitality management, lodging management, transportation management, media management, seating arrangements, basic needs, infrastructural facilities, security management and other tasks. This Action Plan should be discussed with the internal event committee.

Logistics Management

The Action Plan should also deal with logistic management since, it presupposes network integration and balance of activities that are physically or informatively related to the provision of necessary goods and services for the clients. Practically, the logistic management should facilitate proper development and maintenance of the abilities of all stakeholders in order to provide adequate support of special event concerned. The key objective is managing the flow and network aspects during the provision of the necessary materials, facilities and services which are essential for successful conduction of event.

Assessing the Demographic Features of Participants

The organizers and event managers should know the background of the participants, aspirations of the participants and expectations of the participants in order to organize the event which fulfils their demand. The convenience and satisfaction of the participants are more important for the success of the event concerned.

Proper Invitations

The organizers and event managers should collect the online and offline addresses and e-mail details of the participants in order to prevent unnecessary delay in inviting the participants. The guests of honour and various stakeholders should be properly identified in advance. The organizers should make timely delivery of invitations to the participants. It is practically wiser to send e-mail invitations, telephonic invitations and enable the participants to plan for their participation in advance. In reality, the e-mail invitations are the most economical event management method.

Confirmation of Participation of Celebrities and Guests

The organizers and event managers should choose the most important personalities and celebrities to enrich the process of event management.. They must ensure that celebrities and eminent personalities participate actively in the event concerned in order to persuade the participants to support the cause or mission whole heartedly.

Arrangement of Lodging, Boarding, Transportation and Other Services

The organizers and event managers should also make adequate arrangements such as lodging, boarding, transportation, health care and other services which enrich the event management. In case of mega events, adequate arrangements should be made in advance to avoid any inconvenience to the celebrities, eminent personalities and participants.

Personnel Management

The organizing committee should identify the right persons for the effective management of various tasks associated with the event management. A dedicated team of veterans, specialists and competent persons should be identified for the accomplishment of various tasks. In the Action plan the names, designations, addresses, contact numbers and other details of various personnel should be incorporated in order to avoid confusion and facilitate better coordination.

Development of Infrastructural Facilities and Basic Needs

The organizers and event managers should select the venue which is convenient, safe, secured and comfortable to the dignitaries and participants. In case of a major event, adequate infrastructural facilities should be created. The basic needs of the participants should be fulfilled in order to ensure the success of event management.

Adequate Campaign Management

The organizers and event managers should also understand the significance of campaign management in order to attract the attention of dignitaries, participants and other stakeholders on the importance and utility of the event concerned. Media institutions should be persuaded to launch effective publicity and advertising campaigns that would attract the attention and enlist the participation of various persons in the event concerned. Adequate indoor and outdoor publicity and advertising campaigns are required to ensure the successful conduction of event.

Availability of Comfortable and Secured Environment

The organizers and event managers should ensure that adequate seating arrangements, hospitality management facilities, healthcare facilities, transportation facilities, boarding facilities, conference hall facilities, etc., are made available to the dignitaries and participants during the event concerned. Conscious efforts should also be made to prevent any ugly incidents that would mar the event concerned.

Public Relations Activities

The organizers and event managers should make use of the services of personnel who are good in the art and craft of public relations. The dignitaries and participants should be received and managed cordially by the hosts. The practice of good public relations matters most from the point of view of persuading the dignitaries and participants to play an active and contribute their mite for the success of the event.

Media Management Activities

The organizers and event managers should understand the importance of media management during the events. They must make separate seating arrangements and boarding facilities to satisfy the media professionals and obtain congenial media coverage and support that would boost the morale of the organizers of event. Adequate media briefing and allied services should be made available to gain good mileage from business promotion point of view.

Distribution of Kits and Other Publicity Materials

The organizers and event managers should also ensure adequate distribution of kits, publicity materials and other resources during the event management. It would provide necessary opportunities to the dignitaries, media professionals and participants to understand the salient features of event management and respond positively to the organizers through cooperation and support.

Responding to the Requirements of the Participants

The organizers and event managers should constantly interact with the dignitaries, media professionals and participants, enquire about their reasonable requirements and fulfil their basic needs. This would enhance mutual cooperation between the organizers and participants. Any failure on the part of the organizers would create conflict of interest and credibility crisis which mar the progress of event management.

Crisis Management

The organizers and event managers should be able to manage any unexpected crisis during the course of event concerned. Sometimes, the adversaries plant negative stories, create disturbance and indulge in the unhealthy activities. Natural inconveniences and other difficulties might also crop up unknowingly. The organizers have a bounden duty and responsibility of procrastinating the possible crisis and prepare grounds for effective prevention and management of crisis.

Prompt Payment of Allowances

The organizers and event managers should make adequate arrangements for the payment of travelling allowance, dearness allowance, remuneration to the resource persons and other things. The automation of payment prevents unnecessary delay and discrepancies. It would also enable the organizers and participants to track their finances instantly. A smooth payment and refund process is essential for a successful event management.

Organizing Media Event

The process of event management predominantly consists of media event management component which plays a crucial role. The organizers are required to obtain adequate media coverage which popularizes the beneficial effects of event management. The most important component of event management cannot be ignored by the organizers. Hasan (2010) provides certain steps for organizing a media event which include:

Refine Your Message

The organizers should identify the main theme of the event and put it in a highly creative and attractive manner. The message should be known for absolute simplicity which brings about greatest understanding of the event among the greatest majority.

Select the Right Media Event

The organizers should select the right media event in order to embellish the business significance and social utility with appropriate visual imagery, location, and timing. In any case, creating strong visuals for the news media is critical.

Select the Right Time

It is better to find out the availability of most of the media professionals and choose the right time in order to stage the event in a befitting manner. They must plan the event with excellent visuals during prime time.

Find an Effective Location

The location for a media event should maximize its chances of being covered and facilitate effective communication of the message. The location should be highly convenient to the organizers, media professionals and other important participants.

Compile a Media List

The organizers should obtain a list of media either from the library or from the professional media organization. The print, electronic, online and outdoor media should be the ideal outlets which disseminate necessary information to a large number of people.

Write a News Release

The communicators should design the news release by emphasizing the key elements of event management which compel the attention of various stakeholders. The headline, lead and body of the news release should provide relevant ideas about the event management in a highly appetizing manner.

Distribute the News Release

The organizers should identify the specific media outlets which reach out to the target group at the earliest opportunity. The news release should be addressed and made available to the editor or news editor of the media concerned.

Reach Out and Call a Reporter

The organizers should make sure that right media professionals are identified and persuaded to give wider publicity to the event concerned. They should call the reporters or correspondents well before the event and obtain good publicity.

Practice for Interviews

The spokes persons of the organizations and prominent corporate communicators should be given adequate orientation on the techniques of presenting the important aspects of event management. They must provide satisfactory information to the media professionals during media conference or event management.

Hold a Press Conference

Normally, the organizers should arrange press conference by inviting prominent media professionals in order to make important announcements about the event commission. The spokes person, moderator and other facilitators should be ready to manage the media effectively in times of press conferences.

Take Time to Evaluate Media Event

The organizers should be able to muster adequate publicity through press conference. They should not be discouraged if they do not get expected media coverage and support. They must be good enough to persuade the media professionals to project the event in a positive manner.

Think Strategy First, Media Second

The organizers should develop good strategies which fetch rich dividends. They must receive a good deal of event planning and media management tips from all the sources known for efficiency and creativity.

The organizers should be aware of the significance and modalities of organizing a media event which complements the event management exercise. They must be aware of the strategies of marketing management, media management and event management which involve lot of challenges and responsibilities. The event promotion must be dynamic and able to respond to opportunities as they arise, notes Hasan (2010: 09).

Conclusion

Event management has become an all pervasive activity in the world. Modern organizations primarily depend upon event management invariably to boost their image, reputation and credibility. The event management industry has consolidated worldwide and that event management associations play an increasingly significant role in professional support to the modern organizations including the corporate houses. The professionals also play a notable role in the event management and business management processes in the present times. Scholars have studied the role of event management in the process of business promotion and produced adequate empirical evidence concerning the strategies of event management. The professional organizations also play a crucial role in promoting a new generation of event managers. The empirical evidence points to a higher level of organizational sophistication and a broader range of services offered among those organizations that are larger and complex by nature. Modern business organizations are required to adopt innovative event management strategies, resources and technologies in order to achieve notable success in the business world.

References

Ballou, R.H. (1992) *Business Logistics Management*, Prentice Hall, Inc. Englewood Cliffs, New Jersey.

Berridge, G. (2006) *Event Design and Experience*, Oxford: Butterworth-Heinemann.

Bowdin, G. *et al.* (2007) *Events Management*, 2nd ed., Elsevier Butterworth-Heinemann, Oxford.

Bowdin, G., McDonnell, I., Allen, J., O'Toole, W. (2010) *Events Management*, 3rd edition. Oxford: Butterworth-Heinemann.

Bowdin, Glenn (2003) *Events Management: Resource Guide*, UK Centre for Events Management, Leeds Metropolitan University.

Getz, D. (2007) *Event Studies: Theory, Research and Policy for Planned Events*, Oxford: Butterworth-Heinemann.

Goldblatt, J. (2010) *Special Events: A New Generation and the Next Frontier*, New York.

Goldblatt, J.J. (2005) *Special Events: Twenty-first Century Global Event Management*, Wiley, London.

Hasan, Seema (2010) *Mass Communication: Principles and Concepts*, CBS Publishers and Distributors Pvt. Ltd., New Delhi, pp. 804-841.

Monroe, J. and Kates, R. (2005) *Art of the Event: Complete Guide to Designing and Decorating Special Events*. New York: Wiley.

Raj, R., Walters, P., Rashid, T. (2008) *Events Management: An Integrated and Practical Approach*, London: Sage.

Rebecca Finkel (2010) *Resource Guide in Principles and Practices of Events Management*, Hospitality Press, Leisure, Sport and Tourism Network.

Robinson, P., Wale, D., Dickson, G. (2010) *Events Management*. CABI: Wallingford.

Rogers, T. (2008) *Conferences and Conventions: A Global Industry*, (2nd ed.) Butterworth-Heinemann.

Shone, A. and Parry, B. (2001) *Successful Event Management*. London: Continuum.

Silvers, J. (2003) *Professional Event Coordination*. New York: Wiley.

Vardhan, Venkat T. (2008) Interview Story, *The Hindu*, Bangalore, August 11.

Van der Wagen, L. (2002) *Event Management: For Tourism, Cultural, Business and Sporting Events*. Melbourne: Hospitality Press.

Watt, D.C. (1998) *Event Management in Leisure and Tourism*, Longman, Harlow.

Yeoman, I., Robertson, M., Ali-Knight, J., Drummond, S., McMahon Beattie, U. (eds.) (2003) *Festival and Events Management: An International Arts and Culture Perspective*. Oxford: Butterworth-Heinemann.

Chapter 16
Inter-Cultural Communication for Business Management

Introduction

Culture is commonly defined as the ocean of values, attitudes, behaviours and transactions which govern the human life and civilization. Culture is the root of all policies, programmes, products, services and other activities which take place across the globe. In the world, there is no common culture, language, values and aspirations. The whole world is known for 'pluralism' which represents cultural, social, economic and political differences and backgrounds. In the age of globalization, geographical boundaries are shrinking on account of commendable information and communication technologies and applications. The process of globalization has also paved the way for inter-cultural communication and transactions in all spheres of human life. The concept of inter-cultural communication, nature and significance of inter-cultural communication, globalization and intercultural communication, need for developing cultural intelligence, guidelines for effective intercultural communication, media of intercultural communication in business organizations and recent trends and developments in intercultural communication for business promotion are presented in this chapter.

Concept of Intercultural Communication

The subject of culture is highly complex and no country has a common culture in the present times. There are cultural differences that are found in every state or country. Within a culture, differences between the urban people and rural people, rich people and poor people, educated people and illiterate people and tribal people and non-tribal people could be seen due to several differences and orders.

Culture has been discussed across the globe and defined in many ways by the anthropologists. According to Lull (2000: 25) "Culture is a way of life of a group of people. The stereotyped patterns of learning behaviour are handed down from one generation to the next through means of language and imitation". Appadurai (1997: 01) has defined culture as the "shared ways in which groups of people understand and interpret the world". The people living in different countries have developed not only different ways to interpret events; they have different habits, values and ways of relating to one another. The people have cultivated the habit of perceiving their own culture as normal culture and other cultures as bad, wrong, peculiar or such. This is viewed as *ethnocentrism* by the anthropologists under it impedes cultural integration across cultures. The inter-cultural communication is defined as the cultural interaction between two or more cultures which brings about mutual understanding, respect, cooperation and harmony across the cultures. In the age of globalization, an inter-cultural relation has been promoted in order to cement the communication gaps and facilitate integrated learning and progress.

Culture has been defined as the received and accepted set of rules guiding human behaviour. These rules are absorbed and eventually become engrained in each individual's mind to the point where they are second nature. The persons with similar sets of social rules tend to behave in the same manner, which then becomes the normal behaviour expected in different cultural situations. The behaviour of an individual is noticed only when it deviates from the norm and becomes a noticeable behaviour in a particular culture.

The cultural ethos enables the people to interpret different values and behaviours in that culture. Differences in cultures are seen in the way people from different cultures behave during different occasions. Cultural differences are also noticeable in the way people in groups act when they meet other groups during different occasions. Different cultures have different ways in which people address each other during different occasions. Absence of cultural awareness may result in serious misunderstandings between individuals, groups and nations.

Cultural diversity in the workplace, government and society also influences communication. Business organizations and other institutions are required to understand how to communicate effectively with people from other cultures in order to enhance business transactions outside the region, nation, and continent. Especially, the multinational organizations should understand the cultural factors and expand their operations to include most major countries in the world. They should ensure successful communication and interaction between cultures, communities, organizations and nations. The organizational leaders and communicators should communicate effectively with people of other cultures or minority groups in order to achieve success in contemporary business management in the age of global economy.

In the present times, people are required to become culturally intelligent by developing a higher level of cultural sensitivity to many dimensions of culture. The people should also become more sensitive to learn more about other cultures and remain mindful of cultural differences. The cultural differences also affect the communication on account of body positions and moments and views and practices concerning various factors of human relationships (time, space, intimacy and so on) according to Lesikar *et al.* (2011: 24).

Lehman *et al.* (2012: 22) have delineated the barriers to intercultural communication such as ethnocentrism, stereotypes, interpretation of time, personal space requirements, touching, body language, translation limitations, commonsense approach, understanding other cultures, cultivation of patience and enlisting help from others. The people wrongly presume that their own cultural norms are universally valued while other cultural norms are not good enough mainly due to ethnocentrism. People of all cultures have stereotypes about other cultural groups they normally encounter. In some cultures people believe that long discussions or negotiations spent in establishing relationships are good exercises. The distance between people occurs while communicating or transacting due to cultural space related perception. The people's tendency to touch also differs by culture and gender. The body language varies from culture to culture since it is not universal. Certain words in one language do not have an equivalent meaning in other languages due to cultural differences. Certain barriers to intercultural communication occur due to absence of commonsense. The organizational leaders and communicators also fail to understand the foundations of other cultures due to inadequate exposure. The communicators also face certain inconvenience while conversing with the people of other cultures due to non-familiarity with the languages. The communicators can also solicit the help of others in order to communicate effectively with the people of other cultures either for clarification or confirmation of certain ideas. Thus, barriers to inter-cultural communication occur under the normal circumstances.

Bhusan (2012) states: "The world today is characterized by an ever growing number of contacts resulting in communication between people with different linguistic and cultural backgrounds. It is now recognized that linguistic and cultural knowledge are vital areas that organizations must acquire if they are to integrate, progress and succeed in the modern market place. The corporate houses should also have the capacity to carry the goods and services and market them in the entire civilized world. It is very essential for the business communicators to understand the format, tone and style of business communication which demands several channels, tools and techniques".

Organizations function in the midst of cultural diversity and diversity initiatives are undertaken by modern organizations to help organizational functionaries understand and appreciate the challenges of cultural diversity and avoid miscommunication. Geert Hofstede identified four dimensions of cultural difference namely—power distance, individualism *versus* collectivism, masculinity *versus* femininity and uncertainty avoidance which are directly associated with intercultural communication. These dimensions are useful in understanding and communicating with people from different cultures in modern multinational corporations. Borden identifies seven intercultural constructs namely—awareness about the cultural environment, cybernetic of culture, competence in language, individual ability to work, cultural literacy, cultural orientation and particularistic and universalistic understanding. The success of intercultural communication primarily depends upon proper understanding of both the cultures.

Intercultural Communication in the Age of Globalization

Globalization has become the burning topic in the present times. The process of globalization has affected all spheres of human life including communication and journalism all over the world. During the last three decades, globalization has affected the media regionally, nationally and internationally. There is commendable expansion of media across the world in the age of globalization. Multi-national corporations have established the media institutions which have become instrument of profit making in the age of globalization.

Scholars have defined globalization differently. Some define it as a set of processes changing the nature of human interaction across a wide range of spheres including the economic, political, social, technological, and environmental. Practically, globalization is perceived as the process of integration of the world community into a common system either economic or social. It essentially means the growing increase in the inter-connectedness and inter-dependences among the world's regions, nations, governments, business and institutions. Some others say, it is a process, which engenders free flow of ideas, people, goods, services and capital thereby fostering integration of economies and societies. The most visible aspect of globalization is the spread of information and communication technologies.

Globalization has been defined as a social process in which the constraints of geography on social and cultural arrangements recede and in which people become increasingly aware that they are receding. The traditional constructs of time and space are broken down during the process of globalization, thereby stimulating the renegotiation of societal relationships. Individuals and groups attempt to explain these major shifts and events at local, national, and international levels. The World Bank and the International Monetary Fund have played a major role in the corporate expansion on an international scale in the age of globalization. The early studies revealed that a few Western nations controlled the international flow of information.

Giddens (1999: 14) has described globalization as "the intensification of worldwide social relations which link distant localities in such a way that local happenings are shaped by events occurring many miles away and *vice versa*". This process of 'globalization' is often portrayed as a positive force which is unifying widely different societies and cultures integrating them into a 'global village', and enriching all in the process. It is variously described as an inevitable by-product of human evolution and progress, as if it were an organic process, governed by the laws of nature. However, globalization is not necessarily a natural progression emerging out of the ordinary communication and interaction of people and cultures around the world. It results from deliberate human choice by a powerful group of nations, transnational corporations (TNCs) and international organizations which gain in the process. The new communications and information technologies have provided methods for large corporations to maximize profits by entering foreign markets.

The values of life also change according to the culture of the land. Each culture has different values concerning the attitudes and behavioural patterns of people. The social behaviour also varies by culture and cultural differences which affect the communication between two groups or nations. There are countless differences in culture and cultural values are regarded as standards for determining the meaning in inter-cultural communication. The communication techniques also differ from country to country and from region to region. The words derived from culture also present problems from intercultural communication point of view. The colloquialisms also cause problems in cross-cultural correspondence.

In the age of globalization, intercultural communication matters despite certain differences and drawbacks. There is ever growing need for constant communication across cultures. The cultural exchange programmes are becoming imminent in the age of globalization since businesses are becoming increasingly global in their operations. The multi-national corporations have understood the need for communication across cultures in view of their ever increasing business operations. Intercultural communication also enables the business organizations to understand the diversified needs of the customers across the globe and fulfil their demands.

Intercultural communication has become inevitable in view of increasing globalization in the new millennium. The people are visiting different countries for education, employment, business and other purposes. Chaturvedi and Chaturvedi (2011: 10) observe: "The new trend in international business is to 'go local'. This creates a work situation in which 'locals' and foreign experts perform together as a team. This necessitates cultural orientation on the part of the visitors so that they are familiar with the host culture, specially the use of habitual expressions and expected behaviour in different situations. The process of acculturation is made possible by organizing specialized training of visiting teams in the language and work culture of host organizations. It is also necessary for those in the host country to be respectful and welcoming of their visitors' cultures, so that the interaction can be productive and cordial. Smooth cross-cultural presence in business, industry, or education is possible internationally or intra-nationally only by first developing knowledge and sensitivity of the other culture".

The globalization has offered several opportunities to the mankind to move beyond their culture and country in search of education, employment, business and other opportunities. The international business organizations have a responsibility of providing employment opportunities to the local people and establish cordial human and business relations. The modern business executives are given orientation formally to develop cultural sensitivity and gain advantages through effective business relationships. Shital Kakker Mehra defines cultural sensitivity as "an ability to interpret unfamiliar and ambiguous gestures in the way compatriots of the same culture would". The executive should also understand how cultural context affects personal behaviour and business communication. The gestures are often expressive of cultural context of communication.

Need for Developing Cultural Intelligence

The cultural interaction has become an important means of facilitating inter-cultural relations which benefits the people regardless of profession. The cultural misunderstandings bring about conflict of interest and hamper the cultural exchange. Cultural understanding facilitates better business transactions. It is necessary to know the cultural background of individuals and institutions in order to understand each other and respond correctly in intercultural situations. Scholars have identified strong linkage between culture and communication. There are certain characteristics of low-context and high-context cultures which exist in different parts of the world, according to Hall (1959: 15). He developed these concepts while teaching intercultural skills to the foreign service personnel.

The communication system, process and operations are directly related to the culture of the country or region. In particular, the social context in a given culture also determines the attitudes and behaviours of people. The existing rules, regulations and behavioural norms also represent the social context of culture. The culture has a definite bearing on the communication practices of people. Chaturvedi and Chaturvedi (2011: 11) comment: "In a high-context culture, there are many contextual elements that help individuals understand the rules. Much is taken for granted while communicating. A person who does not know the unwritten rules of the culture may find communication confusing".

The travelling publics are required to understand the unwritten rules of the culture while interacting with the hosts in times of academic, social, business and other transactions. The high context culture is found in Asia, Africa, Middle East, Latin America and other developing regions of the world. The people in these regions are more likely to be relational, collectivists, intuitive and contemplative. The people also emphasize the interpersonal relationships in these cultures on account of their high-context culture. Hall (1959: 15) states that high-context culture consists of people who are collectivists. They prefer group harmony and consensus to individual achievement. The people are also less governed by the reason than by intuition or feelings. The high context communication tends to be more indirect and formal and the words are not as important as the contexts.

In the present times, the new groups of students, researchers, teachers, professionals and others should also learn how to communicate across cultures with different concepts of formal and social behaviour, time and space. Chaturvedi and Chaturvedi (2011: 11) state: "In a low-context culture, very little is taken for granted. Therefore, explicit statements and explanations are required. The chances of misunderstanding by those outside that culture are minimized". The people representing the low-context culture normally tend to value rationality, logic, action-oriented behaviour and individualism. They are always guided by facts, figures, regions and realities of life while making decisions. The communicators of low-context culture have certain communication practices which represent clear, concise, efficient, straightforward and objective qualities. They also depend on formalities, procedures, documents, justifications and other norms which represent low-context culture.

The culture of communication also represents polychromic culture and monochromic culture according to Hall (1959: 15). In a poiychromic culture, human relationships are valued more than time. Polychromic people do not hurry to get things done and they get things done in their own time. In a monochromic culture, human relationships are entirely different and people do things in a sequential manner on the basis of careful planning and scheduling of the work. Monochromic people are known for efficient time management and resource management. Thus, communication differs in both high context and low context cultures.

The cultural analysis assumes great significance in the age of globalization. Since, it helps people to understand the individual actions in the context of the type of culture to which he or she belongs. The cultural diversity should also be understood in order to establish meaningful human relationships and effective business relationships in the age of globalization. It is necessary to guard against *ethnocentrism* and develop certain practices of judging the people of other cultures on the basis of acceptable behavioural patterns. It is equally important to avoid ethnocentrism and stereotyping which are formidable barriers to effective intercultural communication. The corporate communicators, business executives, cultural ambassadors and others should be aware of the cultural differences and adapt themselves to the local style of communication while interacting with people from different cultural backgrounds.

Guidelines for Effective Intercultural Communication

In the present times, English language has become a global communicative language and all business communication exercises are carried out in

English which has become a primary tool of intercultural and business communication rather than a language. In the international context, the Oxford English has been replaced by simple and unidiomatic form of English which is of great use for intercultural communication endeavours. English is also widely used for business communication purposes all over the world in the present times. The success of intercultural communication primarily depends on the development of cultural intelligence.

Intercultural communication is necessary while dealing with people from other cultures in order to minimize misunderstandings and maximize sustainable human relationships. No individual in the world is fully aware of everything about all cultures. There are many individuals and professionals who are required to understand the basis of intercultural communication. In particular, successful conduction of business activities in different countries and regions primarily depends on the cultivation of intercultural communication practices. There are well established norms and guidelines which should be understood by the corporate communicators and others who wish to gain new opportunities in the age of globalization. The guidelines for effective intercultural communication are as follows:

Respect for Other Cultures

All cultures are equally important since they are shaped by the past generations on the basis of their constant observation, understanding and experimentation. The corporate communicators should never underestimate other cultures and people at any cost. There are people who are culturally affluent even though they are not economically better off. The individuals should also develop cordial human relationships which matter most in business management in the age of competitiveness.

Forward Looking Attitude

The corporate communicators should also develop a forward looking attitude which facilitates better human relationships development in general and cordial customer relationship management in particular. They should be willing to travel extensively, meet new people, cultivate human relationship and gain the benefit of interaction. In this age, goodwill development assumes great significance. The corporate communicators should not be unwilling to cultivate human relationship which matters most from the point of view of intercultural communication and business communication.

Understanding of Culture

The corporate communicators should develop sufficient cultural intelligence which enables them to understand different cultures. The success of intercultural communication primarily depends on such cultural intelligence which is a means of human relationship management. The corporate communicators should also understand how cultural contexts affect personal behaviour, intercultural communication and business transactions. Scholars have emphasized that smooth intercultural presence in business, industry are education is possible internationally only by developing sensitivity of other culture. They should develop necessary awareness about the clients' cultural sensitivities which results in a positive advantage in business relationships.

Understanding Communication Context

The differences in cultures are seen in the way people from different cultures communicate when they interact with others. The business executives and communicators are also required to obtain formal education in the art and craft of intercultural communication. The communication parameters and practices are the bi-products of cultural heritage which should be correctly grasped by the corporate communicators. The communication context, acceptable communication practices and adoption of local style of communication facilitate better intercultural communication.

Observance of Protocol

Professionalism and protocol matter most in every business transaction across the globe. In many cultures business is taken very seriously. It is better to avoid the use of humour and jokes in the business context since it would belittle the intercultural and business communication exercises. Both the parties should understand the need for application of professional standards of intercultural communication. In particular, the protocol should be observed to the best of the ability of the participants in order to maintain the dignity, decorum and decency in intercultural communication and business contexts.

Slow and Steady Communication

The corporate communicators and business executives should basically understand the communication context and setting before establishing rapport with others. They must speak slowly and express things in an intelligible manner so as to make others understand their point of view clearly. Slow and steady communication makes both the parties understand each other's points of view and prepares meaningful grounds for effective human interactions.

Idea by Idea Communication

The organizational communicators and executives should not mix up several things when they communicate with other parties in the beginning. They must learn the art of presenting each and every idea one after the other in order to make the other parties grasp all the contents in a cool and calm atmosphere. In intercultural context, it is better to seek clarifications on the spot on the basis of distinct and separate questions and observations.

Positive Observations

The executives and communicators are required to assume the role of cultural ambassadors in intercultural situations. They must be committed to building memorable and fruitful human interactions which benefit the business organizations immensely. Negative questions and observations bring about misunderstandings which hamper human relationships and business transactions. The very presence of negative mindset hinders human relations and creates communication barriers. Hence, positive questions, observations and behaviours would facilitate smooth human relationship development and business promotion activities.

Supportive Attitude

The executives and communicators should support the other parties while making observations if they don't have good command over the subject or language. Such limitations should be set aside and a congenial atmosphere has to be created in order to facilitate fair intercultural communication. The other parties should be encouraged to express their points of view fully and freely through patient hearing and supportive mannerisms. The presence of supportive attitude matters most from the point of view of sound intercultural communication.

Understand the Etiquette

Intercultural communication and business communication demands the application of traditional and new media in order to facilitate instant means of communicating, transmitting messages and receiving responses. Certain modes of communication are highly culture specific with regard to language, idiom and style. The executives and communicators are required to understand the medium specific etiquette for effective intercultural business communication. English is the most common language of business across all cultures and e-mails are treated as formal and effective interactive means of communication. The choice of media, formats and contents are also influenced by the culture of the source of communication. It is better to use proper expressions and courtesies in intercultural business communication.

Attentive to Cues

The participants of intercultural communication should be conscious of and sensitive to cues that others send out on the spot. The participants should have presence of mind and learn a lot by observing others. It is equally important for the participants to be sensitive to other peoples' religious and dietary restrictions and limitations. The participants should also follow the customs and traditions especially with regard to dining and greeting etiquette.

Speak by Turns

The participants of intercultural communication should understand that both the parties are equally important from communication point of view. Both the parties should also enjoy the benefit of equal participation in the process of communication. No party should gain an upper hand and deny the other party opportunity to express fully and freely. It is better to communicate by terms. This means that the participant who is speaking should make his or her point and allow the other party to respond properly. This would make the participants feel that their points of view are heard and understood.

Grasping the Meanings

In an intercultural communication situation, both the parties are required to grasp each other's points of view very clearly and comprehensively. Important concepts, processes and operations should be clearly understood by the participants in order to prevent any confusion or conflict. It is better to cross check certain things if they are not properly grasped by the parties concerned. Clear and complete understanding of men and matters makes into cultural communication accurate and effective.

Prevention of Idioms, Phrases and Slangs

It is better to avoid the use of idioms, phrases and slangs which do not have equal meanings in both cultures and communicative settings. These elements create more confusion in the minds of the participants and mislead them intercultural communication situations. Unfamiliar, unknown and complex words should also be conveniently avoided in order to prevent the occurrence of communication gaps. The globalization of business in the modern word demands that people of diverse cultures across the world communicate with one another by using simple terms and sentences.

Conclusion

The world is a mixture of races, ethnicities and cultures which has resulted in rich diversity. In the age of globalization, modern organizations are required to achieve the goal of unity in diversity in order to promote peace, tranquillity and progress. Intercultural communication has become a prominent instrument of global unity and integration. The modern business organizations are required to develop meaningful intercultural communication in order to do business on the basis of good human relationships. Modern business organizations accept both parties to come to the table with their best offer. The business executives and communicators need to be aware of cultural differences and adapt their style of communication when meeting people from different cultural backgrounds which vary in their concern for space and business relationships within it. Intercultural communication basically deals with people from other cultures in a way that minimizes conflict of interest and maximizes rewarding business relationships.

References

Appadurai, Arjun (1997) *Modernity at Large: Cultural Dimensions of Globalization*, Minneapolis: University of Minnesota Press.

Axtell, Roger E. (1998) *The Dos and Taboos of Body Language around the World*, New York: John Wiley & Sons, p. 43.

Baral, Kailash C. (2000) *Globalization and Tribes of Northeast India*, in (Eds.), Moya, Paula M.L. and Michael R. Hames-Garcia, *Reclaiming Identity: Realist Theory and the Predicament of Postmodernism*.

Baral, Kailash C. and Kar, Prafulla (Eds.) (2004) *Identities: Local and Global*, Delhi: Pencraft International.

Beck, Natan Sznaider and Rainer Winter (eds.) *Global America? The Cultural Consequences of Globalization*. Liverpool: Liverpool University Press, pp. 15-29.

Bhusan, Uma (2012) *Introduction to Business Communication*, Jaico Publishing House, Mumbai, pp. 55-93.

Bird, S. Elizabeth (1992) *For Enquiring Minds: A Cultural Study of Supermarket Tabloids*, Knoxville: University of Tennessee Press, 12-17.

Boro, Anil (2006) Globalization and Local Cultures: The Tribes of North East India, *Indian Folklife*, Serial No. 22, July.

Brubaker, R. (2004) *Ethnicity without Groups*. Cambridge, MA: Harvard University Press.

Chaturvedi, P.D. and Mukesh Chaturvedi (2011) *Business Communication—Concepts, Cases and Applications*, Delhi: Pearson, pp. 41-42.

Ibid., p. 46.

Conversi, Daniele (2007) Homogenisation, Nationalism and War: Should we still read Ernest Gellner? *Nations and Nationalism*, 13 (3): 371-394.

Garcia Canclini, N. (1995) *Hybrid Cultures: Strategies for Entering and Leaving Modernity*. Minneapolis: University of Minneapolis Press.

Giddens, A. (1999) *The Constitution of Society: Outline of the Theory of Structuration*, University of California Press, pp. 15-16.

Hall, Edward T. (1959) *The Silent Language*, New York: Double Day, p. 17.

Hasan, Seema (2010) *Mass Communication: Principles and Concepts*, CBS Publishers and Distributors Pvt. Ltd., New Delhi.

Hodgetts, Richard M., Fred Luthans and Jonathan Doh (2006) *International Management: Culture, Strategy and Behaviour*, New York: McGraw Hill, p. 190.

Karoli, Veera and Naghma Ahmed (2013) *Business Communication*, Thakur Publishers, Bengaluru, India.

Katsuhiko, Izumi (1989) Whither the Traditions of Local Pottery? *Japan Quarterly*, 36 (3) 287-93.

Kaul, Asha (2009) *Business Communication*, PHI Learning Private Limited, New Delhi.

Larsen, Susan (2003) National Identity, Cultural Authority, and the Post-Soviet Blockbuster: Nikita Mikhalkov and Aleksei Balabanov, *Slavic Review*, 62 (3): 491-511.

Lehman, Carol, M., Devvie D., DuFrene, Mala Sinha and Robin C.Walker (2012) BCOM, *An Innovative Approach to Learning and Teaching, Business Communication, A South Asian Perspective*, Cengage Learning, New Delhi, pp. 15-20.

Leigh, J. (2004) *Reflections of Babylon: Intercultural Communication and Globalization in the New World Order, A paper presented at the Globalization 2004 conference*, www.globalization.icaap.org

Lesikar V., Raymond, Marie E. Flatley, Kathryin Rentz and Neerja Pande (2011) *Business Communication: Making Connections in a Digital World*, New Delhi: Tata McGraw Hill Education Private Limited, p. 556.

Lull, J. (2000) *Media, Communication, Culture: A Global Approach*, 2nd edition, Cambridge: Polity Press.

Mukerjee, Hory Shankar (2013) *Business Communication: Connecting at Work*, Oxford University Press, New Delhi.

Otokhine, E. (2000) *Internet Strengthens Cultural Imperialism*, The Comet, August 23, p. 21.

World Health Organization (1994) *Cultural Dimension of Globalization*, The Globalization of Communication; John Thompson.

Chapter 17
Ethics of Business Management Communication

Introduction

Business ethics is a subject of great social significance because modern business organizations are expected to deliver the goods and services with due respect to public welfare and progress. Business leaders, executives and communicators are called upon to function with professional excellence, responsibility and morality. The interrelatedness of business and ethics is widely discussed in the present time by the champions of public interest. Business ethics demands that everyone should discharge the duties and responsibilities on the basis of moral equipage and safeguard the interest of the people. Modern professionals are also required to design ecologically, culturally, morally and socially sound business system and carry out their works with utmost social responsibility. The concept of business ethics, globalization and business ethics, academic significance of business ethics, nature and scope of corporate social responsibility, ethical foundations of business communication and practice of virtue based business communication are enumerated in this chapter.

Concept of Business Ethics

It is practically very difficult to define ethics since there are umpteen numbers of cultural differences across the globe. Albert Schweitzer defines: "Ethics is the name we give to our concern for good behaviour. We feel an obligation to consider not only our own personal well-being, but also that of others and of human society as a whole". Many scholars and practitioners find defining ethics challenging. Broadly, ethics refers to the principles of right and wrong that guide people in making decisions which have an impact on their actions and people.

Generally speaking, ethics is a component of philosophy which has morality as its subject matter. All professionals are required to function in an independent and responsible manner. The professionals are also responsible for building sound image and reputation for the organization through value-based and people-oriented goods and services. Ethics is concerned with norms for the conduct of people as responsible members of the society. Morality consists of a set of rules and practices which are socially beneficial, healthy and constructive. All members of a civil society and responsible organization should accept and apply certain healthy norms and guidelines in their day to day lives. Modern business organizations are responsible for the production and distribution of goods and services which would maximize the potential of human lives. Business ethics holds out great promise and remains rational, responsible and acceptable norms and guidelines of business management. Organizational leaders are not supposed to succumb to any pressures which would jeopardize the public interest.

Gandhi (1947: 13) highlighted the significance of business ethics thus: "Supposing I have come by a fair amount of wealth either by way of legacy, or by means of trade and industry, I must know that all that wealth does not belong to me, what belongs to me is the right to an honourable livelihood, no better than that enjoyed by millions of others. The rest of my wealth belongs to the community and must be used for the welfare of the community. In the nurture of things, some will have ability to earn more and others less. People with talents will have more and they will utilize their talents for this purpose. If they utilize their talents kindly, they will be performing the work of the State".

Business ethics is generally perceived as the study of business action with reference to its moral obligation and social responsibility a business organization has responsibilities not merely to its shareholders, but to all other stakeholders who are equally important in modern society. The business organizations should think beyond production and distribution of goods and services and cater to the needs of people regardless of religion, region, colour, caste and creed factors. The progressive movements have highlighted the need for protection of public interest in the age of globalization. The business organizations are also responsible for the facilitation of social and economic betterment of the women and weaker sections of the society.

Bhusan (2012) emphasized that the communication of messages in an ethical fashion is a part of the study of advanced business communication. It is ethically wrong to advertise the products in a confusing and misleading way. Modern corporate houses are required to do serious introspection about their media, messages and implications in order to safeguard the public interest. Thus, modelling ethical behaviour constitutes an important tool of business management and communication.

The professional leaders should understand the ethical business practices and adopt them in their day to day business transactions since reputation for fairness and good judgement facilitate detainment of long term relationship between the organizations and various stakeholders. They should also develop healthy tendency to rationalize their decisions, behaviours and actions. They should develop necessary framework for analyzing the ethical dilemmas from both legal and ethical perspectives in order to facilitate healthy and constructive business management. Their decisions and actions should be legally and ethically sound in order to build organizational and professional reputation over a period of time.

Buchholz quotes the observation made by the Committee for Economic Development (1971: 10) with reference to business ethics thus: "Today, it is clear that the terms of the contract between society and business are, in fact, changing in substantial and important ways. Business is being asked to assume broader responsibilities to society than ever before and to serve a wide range of human values".

Lehman *et al.* (2012: 24) identify the causes of illegal and unethical behaviour such as—excessive emphasis on profits, misplaced corporate loyalty, obsession with personal advancement, expectation of not getting caught, unethical tone set by top management, uncertainty about whether an action is wrong and unwillingness to take a stand for what is right. Modern business organizations develop code of ethics which is a written document summarizing the company's professional standards of ethical conduct. But they must strictly adhere to the code of conduct in order to safeguard public interest in general and promote organizational interest in particular.

Normative theories of communication and management have emphasized the need for business ethics since modern business management involves the rights and interests of various stakeholders and entities. Business ethics demands that modern organizations should cultivate certain virtues deliver environment—friendly services and cater to the needs of the people. New set of business practices have emerged with a focus on virtue-based, interest-based, rights-based, duty-based and responsibility-based policies, programmes and actions. Business ethics demands that modern corporate houses function in a democratic environment and facilitate the sustainable development of the country.

Business and ethics have a symbiotic relationship. Business organizations cannot achieve any success in the absence of socially beneficial policies and programmes. Hence, certain business ideologies have been developed in order to safeguard the public interest and promote business interest by striking a meaningful balance between service and profit. The contemporary managerial business ideology states that modern corporate houses have greater corporate social responsibility other than making profit. This is the moral alternative at the core of the management business ideology. Business ethics has become an intrinsic component of modern business management which basically involves the reflection of ethics in the growth, expansion and management of corporate houses.

There are certain legal and ethical factors which influence business communication in modern business organizations such as international laws, domestic laws, code of ethics, stakeholder interests, ethical frameworks and personal values, according to Lehman *et al.* (2012: 24). Legal and ethical constraints affect business communication since matters of legality and ethics are seldom clear cut decisions of right *versus* wrong.

Globalization of Economy and Business Ethics

The world 'globalization' is widely discussed in the present time by many scholars across the globe. The process of globalization has affected all spheres of human life in letter and spirit. There has been a growing body of research on the topic of globalization. In reality, globalization describes the process by which regional economies, societies, and cultures have become integrated through communication, transportation, and trade. The term is most closely associated with the term economic globalization: the integration of national economies into the international economy through trade, foreign direct investment, capital flows, migration, the spread of technology, and military presence. However, globalization is usually recognized as being driven by a combination of economic, technological, socio-cultural, political, and biological factors. The term can also refer to the transnational circulation of ideas, languages, or popular culture through acculturation. An aspect of the world which has gone through the process can be said to be globalized.

Traditional definitions of globalization focus on economics and the effects of multinational corporations. Cavanaugh and Mader (2002: 06) referred to a number of factors that are identified with the term globalization. These factors include—hyper-growth and exploitation of the environment, privatization of public services, global cultural homogenization, promotion of consumerism, integration of national economies, corporate deregulation, and displacement of traditional nation-states by global corporate bureaucracies. Globalization is being driven by increasingly strong international market factors fuelled by organizations such as the World Trade Organization (WTO), International Monetary Fund (IMF) and UNESCO.

The United Nation's ESCWA (1996: 35) states: "Globalization is a widely-used term that can be defined in a number of different ways. When used in an economic context, it refers to the reduction and removal of barriers between national borders in order to facilitate the flow of goods, capital, and services and labour although considerable barriers remain to the flow of labour. Globalization is not a new phenomenon. It began towards the end of the nineteenth century, but it slowed down during the period from the start of the First World War until the third quarter of the twentieth century. This slowdown can be attributed to the inward-looking policies pursued by a number of countries in order to protect their respective industries, however, the pace of globalization picked up rapidly during the fourth quarter of the twentieth century".

Globalization is not a new phenomenon. The human civilization has witnessed three kinds of globalization till now. Buddha heralded the first phase of globalization in India 2500 years ago. He created the democratic culture for the first time in the world and brought about the empowerment of women and weaker sections in India by following truthful, non-violent and democratic means. He brought about the humanization of culture, polity, economy and so on for the first time and became the foremost maker of the universe on the basis of the principles of equality, liberty, fraternity and justice. The European colonial forces led by the British initiated the second phase of globalization in the world. They conquered most of the countries in Asia, Africa, Latin America and elsewhere by using their manipulative tactics. They commercialized the culture, polity and economy across the world. Much of the current climate of international investment and global business is a direct result of global reconstruction, which followed Second World War. Both the World Bank and the International Monetary Fund were founded within a few years after the end of Second World War. Critics of globalization say that capitalism is the driving force behind world economics. Globalization emerged as a buzzword in the 1990s, just as interdependence did in the 1970s. The end of the Cold War in 1989-91 brought about systematic institutionalization of globalization under the leadership of US. The

Americans have led the third phase of globalization in the present times which has brought about the victimization of mankind.

Marx and Engels (1848: 27) in their Manifesto of the Communist Party noted: "Modern industry has established the world market. This market has given an immense development to commerce, to navigation, to communication by land. This development has in its turn, reacted on the extension of industry. The bourgeoisie resolved personal worth into exchange value, and in place of the numberless indefeasible chartered freedoms, has set up that single, unconscionable freedom—Free Trade." The bourgeoisie has through its exploitation of the world market given a cosmopolitican character to production and consumption in every country. To the great chagrin of reactionists, it has drawn from under the feet of industry the national ground on which it stood. All old-established national industries have been destroyed or are daily being destroyed. They are dislodged by new industries, whose introduction becomes a life and death question for all civilized nations, by industries that no longer work up indigenous raw material, but raw material drawn from the remotest zones; industries whose products are consumed in every quarter of the globe. In place of the old local and national seclusion and self-sufficiency, we have intercourse in every direction, universal inter-dependence of nations."

Schiller (1985: 32) observes: "The impact of globalization on economy is widely studied by the scholars all over the world. This impact has reshaped the processes of world production, distribution, trade, development and financing. Expanding global transportation and telecommunications networks in recent decades have clearly enabled the TNCs (Trans-National Corporations) to decentralize their production and distribution networks while seeking higher profits in regions of the world with lower wages, rents, taxes, and government regulation. World trade and financing have also been profoundly affected by the transborder data flows that facilitate airline and hotel reservations, cash and capital transfers, and international trade in capital markets".

Globalization means not only the expansion of trade between countries, but the intensive division of labour is showing more and more production factors wandering, especially the mobile capital. Economic location competition is developing between countries. Globalization in the economic sector means a development which moves the world economy closer to the theoretical ideal of perfect markets, i.e., competition no longer takes place only within the framework of national states. The OECD perceives globalization as a process through which markets and production in various countries are becoming more and more interdependent, because of the dynamics of trade in goods and services and the movements of capital and technology. The new form of economic globalization, compared to the nineteenth century, is that not just trade, but enterprises themselves are crossing borders. National states have to entice the mobile capital, whereby the rule is that the better the image the higher the chances to attract foreign capital.

The driving force behind globalization is motivated by economic interests. According to Amnesty International (2000), "Of the 100 largest economies in the world, 51 are now global corporations; only 49 are developing nations which have diminishing power to control mergers, take-overs and liquidations, may not know who plans to buy or sell a major industry or utility; a telephone, TV or water company may change ownership overnight. The developing nations are losing their national sovereignty and that human rights violations are taking place every moment across the world". Scholars have identified three dimensions of globalization—transnational economic activity, communication networks and increased tensions between (and within) cultural groups. The world has been fundamentally transformed after the late 1980s, but that the driving forces of economic, political and cultural dynamics are transnational—and that this is now widely acknowledged.

Robertson (1992: 30) observes: "Globalization as a concept refers both to the compression of the world and the intensification of consciousness about the world as a whole. The compression of the world, in all of its forms, brings us closer to each other for better and for worse. The consciousness about these interconnections gives a sense of both opportunities and of vulnerability. This dual character of globalization—increased interconnectedness and increased awareness of it—can be studied from a myriad of empirical vantage-points. It would be perfectly feasible (and it is probably already being done somewhere) to write a dissertation on European reactions to the Asian bird flu in 2006. The impact of globalization on tribal peoples in Melanesia has, moreover, long been a subject in anthropology. Human geographers write about the displacement of people in India as a result of globally driven economic deregulation. Many write about migration, again from a variety of perspectives. Others are concerned with the distribution of economic power in the global economy, or the distribution of symbolic or definitional power in the global media world; some write about standardization of goods and services as an outcome of the globalization of the economy, others about the spread of certain consumer preferences, yet others about the global tourist industry; while others again study international law, human rights as a consequence of globalization or the anti-globalization movement".

Friedman (1997: 12) writes: "Globalization is really recent, and began only in the 1980s. As shown briefly already, this view betrays the beholder's poor knowledge of history. World-systems have existed earlier in the sense that people all over the world have participated, often involuntarily, in political and economic systems of a huge, often intercontinental scale. The European colonial era is the most obvious instance, but one might argue that the Roman Empire, encompassing as it did most of the known world (for Europeans), or the Aztec Empire, shared many of the characteristics of today's globalization".

Amartya Sen (1988: 33) comments: "The production of wealth makes freedom actual and thereby is the essential prerequisite for the pursuit of all other human goods. Wealth should be a matter of global interest in order to prohibit a world where only a few wealthy nations have exclusively the conditions that make possible genuine freedom of choice. It is wealth that permits the development of freedom and freedom is the only condition under which a meaningful choice of other ends is possible. I agree with Aristotle that wealth is not a human end in itself. However, without wealth, at least wealthy societies, the possibility of choosing among a full range of other desirable ends is neither real nor actual. Although the process of globalization may exert a levelling influence, such a levelling process would only limit meaningful choice of higher ends and thereby radically devalue the freedom which wealth permitted to develop. Again the question of whether the form of utilitarianism expressed in terms of global free markets has the power to mediate justly among the various conflicting claims of constituent interest groups, with different traditional value systems, within the global society must be examined. Cultural traditions may impose duties that have no status or a negative one in a global value system".

Grieco and Holmes (1999: 17) comment: "Globalization has largely been driven by the interests and needs of the developed world. This is not unconnected with the fact that world developments have been increasingly characterized not by their growth dynamics but by their links to the process of globalization. Hence, the overwhelming character of globalization has made it compelling for some scholars to use various aspects of the global economy as units of analysis. Looking specifically at economic globalization, it can be measured in different ways. These centre on the four main economic flows that characterize globalization namely—goods an ices, work force, migration rates and exports and imports".

Scholars have argued that globalization is just a new word for economic imperialism or Cultural Westernization. This view reduces the vast range of transnational processes to certain economic ones. Although it is tautologically true that rich countries are dominant, the situation is not static. China, India, South Korea and other formerly poor countries are emerging as equal players, and regional powers such as South Africa and Brazil. The direction of transnational flows is not unilateral: some things flow from north to south, others from south to north, and there is also considerable movement between east and west and within the south. Others have perceived that globalization means homogenization. This view is simplistic and usually misleading. Globalization is opposed to human rights since it has widened the gap between the rich and poor all over the world. Women and weaker sections have become the foremost victims of violation of human rights in the age of globalization.

Experience reveals that globalization is a threat to local identities since the market forces have controlled all spheres of human life and heralded a new era of commoditization in the world. Many countries in Asia, Africa, Latin America, Middle East and other continents have been adversely affected by the process of globalization which imposes certain restrictions on the local communities.

Gray (2003: 16) comments: "We are witnessing a process of internationalization and regionalization rather than the emergence of one integrated world of rapid communication, transnational networks and global financial capital, which is the view of globalizes". Skeptics argue, further, that the nation-state remains the most important political entity, while globalizes claim that state sovereignty is on the wane, and that multilateralism and transnational politics are replacing it. Skeptics also see a continuation of the classic North-South divide in terms of prosperity and power, while globalizes argue that inequalities are chiefly growing within and not between societies. The world has witnessed the continued or indeed increasing power of national identities and cultures, globalizes describe hybrid ties and cosmopolitan orientations as an outcome of intensified interaction.

Globalization is driven by technological and economic changes, but it has cultural and political implications as well. The speed of transport and communication has increased throughout the twentieth century. This kind of acceleration continues to exist in all sectors of the life in the age of globalization. The process of standardization has begun by nationalism and national economies and globalization entails comparability and shared standards where there were formerly none. Globalization has brought about interconnectedness wherein the networks connecting people across continents are becoming denser, faster and wider every moment. The entire world is on the move, or so it might sometimes seem. Migration, business travel, international conferences and not least tourism have been growing steadily for decades, with various important implications for local communities, politics and economies.

The people of different origins are enjoying the benefit of connectivity and the new age of communication revolution has led to probably more cultural mixing than ever before in human history. The farmers, workers, women and indigenous people have become highly vulnerable because of the adverse impact of globalization. The whole world is shrinking because of the increasing globalization and the geographical boundaries drawn between such domains are largely artificial and will be dispensed with when they are not needed. Scholars have identified the objective and subjective globalization over a period of time. The objective globalization means being incorporated into a global, or wide-ranging transnational system while the subjective globalization amounts to the acknowledgement of such processes taking place in the world. Globalization has also become a new way of life which has encouraged heterogeneity rather than uniformity or homogeneity. Scholars have assessed the impact of globalization and noted the positive and negative implications of globalization.

Klein (2002: 23) has pointed out that the process of globalization concerns the relationship of globalization to neoliberal economics. Many countries that have complied with measures imposed by international agencies like the World Bank and the International Monetary Fund have experienced a steep decline in *de facto* standards of living. Neo-liberalism is often associated with the global spread of human rights ideas rather than the global financial market. There is growing debate over the relationship between globalization and democracy. Many scholars, politicians and commentators are concerned about the loss of political power experienced by nation-states when so much economic power is diverted to the transnational arenas according to Roy (1999: 31).

Amin (2004: 03) has dealt with the relationship between poor and rich countries in the age of globalization and pointed out that the poor nations become poorer and the rich richer as a result of economic globalization. The major beneficiaries of globalization are the market forces which have controlled the global economy. The African countries are among the least globalized in terms of integration into the world economy. Their exports are modest, and foreign investment is considered risky and, therefore, is rare. Some rich countries, not least in Western Europe, begin to notice the competition from developing countries. The rich countries continue to exploit the poor countries economically and otherwise, note Cohen (2006: 09). Globalization creates a shared grammar for talking about differences and inequalities.

Cavanagh and Mader (2002: 06) referred to a number of factors that are identified with the term globalization. These factors are: hyper-growth and exploitation of the environment, privatization of public services, global cultural homogenization, promotion of consumerism, integration of national economies, corporate deregulation, and displacement of traditional nation-states by global corporate bureaucracies.

The present stage of globalization is redescribed as Americanization (rather than Westernization in the broad sense), or 'globalization' by Americanization by Hilger (2008: 20). The process of globalization is one-way and uni-directional, which has brought about a fusion between cultures or, even less, the blending of ethnic groups. The imposition of more and more American icons means less and less possibility for direct inter-ethnic encounter and communication among nations. The collapse of state legitimacy has substantially contributed to the spread of ethnic conflict and nationalism all over the world. The resulting sense of cultural insecurity has spread onto a planetary scale, increasingly accompanied by the reassertion of hurt pride and a rise of patriotism which can easily seize anti-American themes, whenever elites chose to use these in order to gain popular consensus, writes Smith (2006: 34). The present age of globalization has also brought about the empowerment of 'Mc Mafias', according to Glenny (2008: 15). The idea of a 'global civil society' is yet to be translated into a reality since globalization is responsible for the spread of ethnic conflict, patriotism and nationalism.

The process of globalization affects the world in very many ways. The industrial sector has been subjected to commercialization. There is emergence of worldwide production markets and broader access to a range of foreign products for consumers and companies. The financial sector has also been affected by the globalization which has created worldwide financial markets and better access to external financing for borrowers. The economic sector has been widened because of the realization of the goal of global common market, based on the freedom of exchange of goods and capital. The job market has been considerably expanded all over the world since the workers compete in a global market.

Global economic forces quickly establish a hegemony that subjugates other value systems through a process not unlike that of colonization in the past. The political system has been dramatically changed across the globe in the age of globalization which has created a world government. The information sector has commendably grown over a period of time with the advent of fibre optic communications, satellites, and increased availability of telephone and Internet. The English language has become the '*lingua franca*' of globalization. The Internet is associated with the process of cultural globalization because it allows interaction and communication between people with very different lifestyles and from very different cultures. The process of globalization has increased the pollution in the name of development. The advent of new categories of consciousness and identities has created a 'world culture'. Studies have revealed the positive and negative impact of globalization on the mankind.

John Rawls has suggested a model that perhaps can be adapted to the global context. He proposes a redefinition of a 'well-ordered society'. Rawls notes that it is no longer likely that a modern society can be unified around basic moral beliefs. He rather sees order being built around a political conception of justice, a conception found at the focal point of an overlapping consensus of reasonable and comprehensive doctrines. He observes: "Citizens think of themselves as free in three respects: first, as having the moral power to form, to revise, and rationally to pursue a conception of the good; second, as being self-authenticating sources of valid claims; and third, as capable of taking responsibility for their ends." The relationship between multi-culturalism and global justice needs to be examined by the advocates of global free market economics.

The scholars have also analyzed the economic globalization which refers to increasing economic interdependence of national economies across the world through a rapid increase in cross-border movement of goods, service, technology and capital. The process of globalization is centred on the diminution of international trade regulations as well as tariffs, taxes, and other impediments that suppresses global trade. The economic globalization is the process of increasing economic integration between countries, leading to the emergence of a global marketplace or a single world market. The economic globalization comprises the globalization of production, markets, competition, technology, and corporations and industries. Studies have reported certain positive financial effects of globalization. Economic globalization is often referred to as 'corporate globalization' because it is primarily the mission of larger corporations to globalize their operations.

Globalization has posed series of threats to cultural, environmental, legal, ethical and developmental spheres of human life even though it is a process which cannot be ignored by the mankind. The national boundaries have often become irrelevant since the market forces have established their supremacy over the administration, development, business and other spheres of human life. The process of globalization has brought about serious imbalances in the distribution of wealth all over the world. The moral and ethical questions of globalization need to be examined by various stakeholders in order to ensure effective checks and balances in the interest of social justice.

In the present times, market forces are ruling the whole world in all spheres of human life. Globalization of economy is responsible for the ever increasing exploitation of the women and weaker sections of the society. Globalization has enabled the multinational corporations to exploit natural resources and weaker sections of society. The domestic corporations are not in a position to compete with the MNCs due to inadequate financial and technical resources. The role of MNCs is explained by Agalgatti and Krishna (2000: 02) thus: "The present international capitalist system is the result of the extension and interaction of free enterprise systems of a great many different countries, each with its own system of capitalism coloured by its own unique political system. Each has its own historical background and social and other systems. Common to all of them, is the intense competition for capital, resources and markets. Multinational companies are an exceptional growth of corporations. MNCs are corporations that operate extensively in more than one country (through branches and subsidiaries) engaged in production and/or marketing".

There are leading MNCs which have greater sales across the world than the GNP of the countries. The governments fulfil their obligations by protecting the constitutional rights of the people. The MNCs have gained an upper hand over the domestic governments and taken the people for granted. The market forces have also resorted to guerrilla marketing strategies which have created a new set of consumers who are after unhealthy lifestyles and consumption patterns. In the age of globalization national moralities have become irrelevant. The new market forces have no respect for the local culture, values and public interests. Modern corporate houses are duty bound to obey and follow the moral dictates of ethical principles which are universally applicable. The principle of protectionism has to be applied in order to safeguard the interest of poor countries against the exploitative tendencies of the developed countries.

Globalization demands global justice, fairness and responsibility. Hence, business ethics assumes great significance in the age of globalization of economy.

Academic Significance of Business Ethics

In the age of globalization, capital and technology have become dominant factors which define how people live and work. In reality, materialism has critically affected the culture and values. The ethical considerations of the practice of business need to be understood since ethics is an integral part of business management. In reality, ethics is a positive attitude of mind, character and personality. The reach of business ethics is as vast as life itself. The core of business ethical principles such as truth, honesty, fair play, trust, public interest, social responsibility, organizational accountability and so on need to be demonstrated in the day to day business management in modern world. Business ethics and corporate social responsibility are the two faces of the same coin. Scholars have argued that the teaching of business ethics must be formulated in such a way that it is considered as a new way of making corporate decisions and actions value oriented and people centred.

Business ethics constitutes an important component of business management in the present times. Business schools and colleges have designed specific courses with an emphasis on business ethics. The present generation of business executives is enabled to inculcate positive, constructive and socially responsible attitudes and behavioural patterns in order to safeguard public interest. Students are also motivated to understand the ethical dimensions of business management which include value based and people friendly delivery of goods and services. The students are also educated about the ways and means of developing leadership qualities and moral obligations towards customers and people. The business executives have a social responsibility in the present age of globalization.

It is apt for business communication specialists and practitioners to take stock of ethical issues and social responsibility considerations in the discharge of their duties. Seminars and conferences are organized to create awareness among the professionals relating to media ethics and business communication ethics across the globe. The scholars have also set out a new framework for the teaching of business communication ethics which is non-negotiable exercise. The scholars have also developed curriculum and textbook for the teaching of business communication ethics. The proceedings of conferences and judicial pronouncements have enabled the scholars to elucidate the concepts of professional ethics, public interest, and communication ethics.

The media councils, professional bodies and other agencies have also given a serious thought to media ethics and highlighted the importance of business communication ethics as an academic discipline. Certain norms and guidelines are also formulated by various agencies which intend to purify the practice of business communication on the basis of systematic formal and informal training and orientation programmes. Gunewardena (1997: 18) comments: "As for the professional communicator, there is no substitute for a moral sense or framework of values perceived as obligatory and as a necessary condition for the exercise of the right of freedom of expression".

Rao (2000: 29) underlines the relationship between media practitioners and institutions thus: "Increasingly, there is a growing recognition that freedom and responsibility are not mutually exclusive and several media organizations and professional bodies have evolved guidelines of code of conduct from time to time". Business communication ethics is taught formally in many schools and colleges in order to motivate the community of business communicators to remain dedicated to human values, democratic behaviour, national interest and public welfare. The practice of business ethics involves scrupulous observance of high ethical standards without sacrificing business interests.

The teachers are called upon to instil in the students the essence of ethical decision-making in order to set right injustice done to the people in the name of competitive business. Thus, academic institutions have designed the programmes in order to enable the future generation of business executives to formulate corporate decisions with due respect to public interest. Adding to the crisis in business communication ethics is the lack of opportunity for training of professional communicators. This is indeed an area to which business and media institutions have paid the least importance. Formal training in business communication ethics should become a strong practical element in the process of human resources management. There has to be a strong practical element in the training, with constant opportunity for refresher study facilities. The business communicators, corporate communicators, corporate advertisers and others are required to understand the ethical foundations and perspectives in order to enrich the process of business communication. The business communicators should understand the duty to themselves, duty to clients, duty to organizations, duty to professional colleagues and duty to society, observe Christians *et al.* (1991: 08).

Corporate Social Responsibility

The concept of corporate social responsibility is basically an ethical component of corporate administration. Modern corporate houses are called upon to create a sustainable environment for business promotion in addition to solving the social problems of people. In the age of globalization, corporate houses should invest their profit on socially beneficial programmes in order to build sound image and overcome competition. They face the challenge of converting social problems into profitable business opportunities in the new millennium. Series of debates and discussions are going on inside and outside the legislature on the significance of corporate social responsibility across the world.

Corporate social responsibility is an important component of modern business management because society is mainly responsible for the progress of the modern corporate houses. The corporate houses have outgrown the market mechanism since market forces do not govern modern corporate activities. Constitutional obligations, government legislations and social concerns have been increasing over a period of time in order to safeguard the public interest. Progressive movements including the Occupy Wall Street movement have highlighted the significance of human dignity and human value in their social agenda. The corporate houses are also constantly reminded of their social obligations and ethical standards of management. Corporate houses are motivated by the media, judiciary, professional organizations and other sources to find a new ethical jurisdiction for their role in modern society.

Lodge (1979: 26) refers to the new American ideology relating to business ethics and corporate social responsibility which reveals that modern corporations are conscious of the increasing importance of their public image and social obligations. The Descriptive Thesis of Social Responsibility claims that a stage has come where managers are acting (or are going to act) on the basis of broader concerns, according to Cavanagh (1984: 05). The Prescriptive Thesis of Social Responsibility claims that management should act in socially responsible ways. Modern ideologues have rightly argued that corporate houses can best attain their overall strategic objectives by responding positively to stakeholders demands by substituting corporate social performance for corporate social responsibility. Modern managements are sensitized by the champions of corporate social responsibility who have argued that corporations can take over philanthropic endeavours in order to build sound reputation.

The theory of modern stakeholder management insists that modern managements should make decisions and implement certain programmes by keeping their interests in view besides that of stakeholders. The current trend of corporate social responsibility clearly establishes that modern corporate houses are no more a part of private economic power but they are indeed a public trust as well. The corporate owners, managers and communicators must work together to achieve the common end. The contemporary business shift is from homocentric to bio-centric and proceeds onwards to eco-centric business ethics. Modern corporate houses should make ethical decisions which may involve some sacrifice to the business and benefit the society.

Peter F. Drucker highlights the social responsibility of management thus: "What is most important is that management realizes that it must consider the impact of every business policy and business action on society. It has to consider whether the action is likely to promote the public good, to advance the basic beliefs of our society, to contribute to its stability, strength and harmony". Corporate houses are not merely profit making entities. Apart from earning profits and maximizing the wealth of investors, the corporate houses should also make positive contribution for the development of infrastructural facilities, generation of employment opportunities, enhance the standard of living and enrich the process of development of the society. The corporate houses are required to conduct moral audit and function in a fair and judicious manner.

Corporate houses should demonstrate abundant concern for human development and environment protection. The business operations should be carried out on the basis of long term aspirations. Sen (1988: 33) notes: "The restrictive nature of the traditional format of resource allocation has been brought out clearly in the recent years by the greater recognition of the importance of environmental considerations and of natural resources". A conscious application of moral values of community, justice and respect for the dignity of the individual and value oriented business operations would safeguard the interest of society. The business houses should function in a responsible way.

Ethical Foundations of Business Communication

The practice of business communication should be carried out in accordance with the principles of natural justice and social responsibility.

The process of business management becomes weak and vulnerable if the business practices are not aimed at achieving the highest welfare of all. Business ethics is primarily dependent on good thoughts and deeds which benefit the society. The corporate houses should not indulge in unethical business practices in general and untruthful campaigns in particular. The good thoughts and deeds of corporate houses should be adequately communicated through objective media campaigns. The business actions have to be evaluated systematically in order to enhance the welfare of the people. The business communication practices should be guided by the ethics of care and ethics of rights which are upheld in Buddhist philosophy.

Gandhian communication philosophy upheld the need for providing a truthful account of business policies, programmes and products to the people without giving any scope for manipulation. The corporations are influenced by internal and external dynamics. The school of Confucius also emphasized the elevation of humanism to the highest degree on the basis of value based business operations and truthful business communications. The essential values in Indian culture of business management are based on human values and the success of business management primarily depends upon the culture of business communication and operation according to Chopra (1988: 07).

Gillian (1996: 14) observes: "Business ethics and business communication are closely associated with ethics in business management. A product comes within a cocoon of trust. It is crucial in a company's relationship with its consumers that nothing is done to damage trust. Trust is lost when a company fails to treat them with respect, and treats them as objects to be manipulated or opponents to be outwitted and exploited. The manufacturers and distributors of goods and services should attempt to achieve multiple objectives including flawless business communication, given the complexity and interplay of ethical, technological and socio-economic forces in modern times".

Carmichael and Drummod (1989) state: "A good company should listen to the whistle blowers, and secondly respond. But more important than either of these is that a company should make sure that the conditions for whistle blowing never arise. Further it should have free and open channels of communication".

Elaine (1994: 11) comments: "Properly regarded as a source of critical corporate information, whistle blowing is essential for good corporate governance. Corporate purposes are best achieved when corporate agents are properly informed about corporate performance. Corporate communication ethics involves the establishment of good rapport between the organizations and customers on the basis of objective and fair communication".

Ronald Green refers to the observation made by Kenneth Labich pertaining to business communication ethics thus: "The establishment of hotlines (telephone), confidential reporting of harmful activities, easily accessible question boxes, and empowering standing committees on safety, health and product liability, suitability to deal with genuine complaints and concerns constitute the business communication ethics. The managers must meet this organizational duty by helping to create policies, procedures, structures and attitudes—or 'corporate culture' in the fullest sense that make it possible for the individual to express himself, discuss, evaluate and when necessary to act on their moral concerns". Business communication is a prominent tool of modern business management which alerts the management about the products, services, strengths and limitations. By emphasizing the need for ethical and legal action at every step, the business communicators can make corporate houses morally strong, professionally competent and socially accountable. Business management and communication always go together.

Agalgutti and Krishna (2000: 02) observe: "Corporations have obligation to their customers in many ways. They produce goods which they sell to their customers. The products must be safe, reliable, durable and fulfil the expectations of customers. Advertising and labelling must be truthful, honest and adequate. The customer must be informed of the nature of the ingredients used, the precautions necessary before and after use, the nature of the technical expertise he is expected to apply or employ, the kind of material or substance he is obtaining at the price he is paying. Warranties must be clear. The key word is fairness of dealing, which means that the corporation holds itself responsible for the quality, reliability and effectiveness of the goods he offers to the public, within reasonable limits". The scholars have emphasized the need for business communication ethics in modern corporate houses.

The International Organization of Consumer Unions (IOCU) has emphasized the need for consumer education thus: "Consumers need to learn how to distinguish between needs from wants, to ask information seeking questions about price, availability and quality of goods and services. With knowledge, consumers are able to act with confidence and make themselves heard with respect and care. In the present open economy, consumers need education and guidance to become good and competent consumers. Transparency in trade, commerce, business and industry can give good and lasting benefits to the producer as well as the consumer".

Business communication has several tools and technologies. Corporate advertising has become an important tool of business communication over a period of time. It has also grown into a billion dollar industry all over the world. The critics have commented that corporate advertising is an immoral part of the modern capitalist system. The people have also realized that corporate advertising manufactures the consent of the customers in favour of the goods and services manufactured by the multinational corporations. Studies have also revealed that corporate advertising encourages excess and frivolous consumption patterns among the people. Business ethics demands that corporate advertising should provide truthful and honest information and enable the customers to choose the products and services which really benefit them. Advertisers are hired to communicate the features and advantages of goods and services to the consumers. Manipulative and coercive advertisements are not good for the health and progress of the mankind. The advertising industry is also aware of the undercurrents of passion and ethical concern roused up by the corporate advertising campaigns. Scholars have noted that self-regulation by the advertisers is the key to ethical advertising.

Professional organizations have come into existence in media, advertising, public relations and other sectors of mass communication. The professionals are united under the banner of 'public interest'. The professionals are also educated about the moral and social obligations of the profession and motivated to live up to the standards set by the professional organizations. The professional code of ethics is formulated in order to safeguard public interest through constructive thoughts and deeds which govern corporate social responsibility. The professional codes are applicable to all member-professionals and set higher standard of service. The professional organizations have emphasized the need and importance of business communication ethics.

In the new millennium, the concept of corporate governance is widely discussed and debated since it primarily deals with checks and balances and mutually beneficial communications between management and various stakeholders including customers. It seeks to combine the best of all models which reflect good corporate governance. The ultimate goal of corporate governance is to maintain the corporation's integrity, reputation and accountability to its constituencies. The corporate governance is also based on a set of ethically and professionally sounds standards and practices which safeguard the human values and corporate interest. Business communication is also subjected to corporate governance which means that a corporate house must not only sell its goods and services to the people, but also enlist positive response from the customers by projecting the ethical and responsible practices of the house.

Conclusion

Gandhi emphasized the customer-businessmen relationship thus: "A customer is the most important visitor on our premises. He is not dependent on us; we are dependent on him. He is not an interruption on our work; he is the purpose of it. He is not an outsider of our business; he is a part of it. We are not doing a favour by serving him. He is doing us a favour by giving us an opportunity to serve him". The corporate houses are responsible for the delivery of goods and services which benefits the mankind ultimately. Business activities should be carried out on the basis of healthy and constructive parameters and practices. Business communication should also be practiced on the basis of truth, honesty, fairplay, integrity, accountability, responsibility and other professional values. The management should resort to inward engineering which facilitates better realization of corporate social responsibility, corporate governance, sound business management and ethics of business communication in modern society. In conclusion, the management must consider the ethical dimensions of business management in general and business communication practices in particular. The business organizations have certain obligations towards the stakeholders. Business ethics should be upheld in order to bring about meaningful structural and operational changes from business management point of view. The goal of business communication is to bring about mutually trustworthy and beneficial relationship between the business organizations and various stakeholders.

References

Agalgatti, B.H. and Krishna, S. (2000) *Business Ethics: Concepts and Practices*, Nirali Prakashan, Pune, pp. 22-23.

Ibid., pp. 157-158.

Amin, Samir (2004) *The Liberal Virus: Permanent War and the Americanization of the World*. London: Pluto Press.

Bhusan, Uma (2012) *Introduction to Business Communication*, Jaico Publishing House, Mumbai, pp. 1-20.

Cavanagh, Gerald (1984) *American Business Values in Transition*, Englewood Chiffs, N.J.: Prentice Hall, USA.

Cavanagh, J. and Mader, J. (2002) *Alternatives to Economic Globalization: A Better World is Possible—A Report of the International Forum on Globalization*, San Francisco: Berrett-Koehler Publishers Inc., p. 19.

Chopra, Deepak (1988) Interview, *Business World*, June 7, p. 108.

Christians, Clifford G., Kim B. Rotzoll and Mark Fackler (1991), *Media Ethics*, New York: Longman, pp. 1-29.

Cohen, H. (2006) *Good Arabs: The Israeli Security Services and Israeli Arabs*. Jerusalem: Hebrew Publishing House.

Committee for Economic Development (1971) *Social Responsibilities of Business Corporations*, New York: CED, pp. 29-31.

Elaine, Sternberg (1994) *Just Business*, Warner Books, New Jersey: Prentice Hall, p. 73.

Friedman, Thomas L. (1997) *The Lexus and the Olive Tree: Understanding Globalization*, New York: Anchor Books, p. 93.

Gandhi, M.K. (1947) *Harijan*, February 23, p. 9.

Gillian, Colin (1996) Ethics in Marketing in Ken Smith and Phil Johnson (Ed.): *Business Ethics and Business Behaviour*, London: International Thomson Business Press, p. 112.

Glenny, Misha (2008) McMafia: *A Journey Through the Global Criminal Underworld*. Bodley Head/New York: Alfred A. Knopf.

Gray, John (2003) *Al Qaeda and What It Means to Be Modern*, New York: Faber and Faber.

Grieco, M. and Holmes, L. (1999) *Tele Options for Community Business: An Opportunity for Economic Growth in Africa, Africa Notes*, pp. 1-3.

Gunewardena, Victor (1997) *Communication Ethics and the Role of the State, Communication Ethics: A South Asian Perspective, Asian Media Information and Communication Centre*, Singapore, pp. 1-19.

Hasan, Seema (2010) *Mass Communication: Principles and Concepts*, CBS Publishers and Distributors Pvt. Ltd., New Delhi.

Hilger, Susanne (2008) Globalization by Americanization: American Companies and the Internationalization of German Industry after the Second World War, *European Review of History/Revue Europeenne d'Histoire*, 15 (4): 375-401.

Karoli, Veera and Naghma Ahmed (2013) *Business Communication*, Thakur Publishers, Bengaluru, India.

Kaul, Asha (2009) *Business Communication*, PHI Learning Private Limited, New Delhi.

Klein, Naomi (2002) *Fencs and Windows*, Leftward, New Delhi.

Lehman, Carol, M., Devvie D., DuFrene, Mala Sinha and Robin C.Walker (2012) BCOM, *An Innovative Approach to Learning and Teaching, Business*

Communication, A South Asian Perspective, Cengage Learning, New Delhi, pp. 12-14.

Lesikar, Raymond, V., Marie E. Flatley, Kathryn Rentz and Neerja Pande (2012) *Business Communication, Making Connections in a Digital World*, New Delhi, India.

Lodge, George (1979) *The New American Ideology*, New York: McGraw Hill, Inc.

Marx, Karl and Friedrich Engels (1848) *Manifesto of the Communist Party*, p. 44.

Mukerjee, Hory Sankar (2013) *Business Communication: Connecting at Work*, Oxford University Press, New Delhi.

Rao, Leela (2000) *Media Practitioners and Institutions: The Indian Experience, Communication Ethics: A South Asian Perspective*, Asian Media Information and Communication Centre, Singapore, pp. 43-55.

Robertson, R. (1992) Globalization: Time-space and homogeneity-heterogeneity. In: Featherstone ML and Robertson R. eds., *Global Modernities*, Thousand Oaks, C.A.: Sage, p. 8.

Roy, Ash Narayan (1999) *Third World in the Age of Globalization*, Madhyam Books, New Delhi.

Schiller, Herbert (1985) *Information and the Crisis Economy*. Norwood, NJ: Ablex.

Sen, Amartya (1988) *On Ethics and Economics*, New York: Basil Blackwell, Inc., pp. 22-23.

Smith, Dennis (2006) *Globalization: The Hidden Agenda*. Cambridge: Polity, p. 1.

United Nations Organisation (1996) *ESCWA Annual Report*.

Chapter 18
Business Management Research Methods

Introduction

Modern business organizations primarily depend upon systematic marketing survey which enables the policy makers and business leaders to identify the requirements of the consumers and understand the methods of fulfilling their requirements in the competitive business environment. The marketing department of modern business organizations is primarily responsible for the conduction of business research which provides useful ideas, guidelines and methodologies for the improvement of production and productivity. Modern business organizations require to generate an authentic body of information in order to take right decisions in the right time and achieve success in business management on the basis of scientific evaluation. The policy-makers and business leaders should also examine the validity and reliability of the business management strategies and improve the status of business management on the basis of research findings and implications. The concept of business research, types of business research, process of business research, types of business research reports and business research report writing techniques are amplified in this chapter.

Concept of Business Research

Research and development are the two faces of the same coin. Research is a scientific fact finding exercise which is carried out by modern organizations to understand the better path to progress. Research is an all pervasive intellectual exercise carried out by a team of specialists in the conduction of research. The researchers carry out the scientific evaluation in order to prepare meaningful grounds for the management and development of modern business organizations. The business research is a planned, organized and deliberate exercise which generates the right ideas, experiences and methodologies for the successful management of business activities. It is also essential to plan and execute the business management programmes on the basis of authentic data and strategies.

Business leaders use research findings in the process of decision making since business management is a complex task. Modern business organizations operate in a changing business environment which poses several threats and opportunities. Business research can minimize the degree of uncertainty and reduce the threats which are unforeseen by nature. Business research also reduces the possibility of making wrong choices in the business world. Business research is a broad spectrum which encompasses certain areas such as materials management, human resources management, production management, operations management, customer relationship management and so on. Business research is carried out for the purpose of better marketing management in the age of competitive business.

In the present times, the markets are flooded with several products and services from a large number of companies which operate across the globe. There are several alternatives which lie ahead of modern customers who have become choosy and selective while buying the goods and services. Contemporary business management has become a specialized activity which keeps the buyer or consumer in the centre while designing a product mix. The goods and services are designed in accordance with the needs and demands of customers who matter most from business management point of view. Hence, business research is the systematic, scientific and continues search for the analysis of information relevant to the process of business management.

In the new millennium, a separate branch called marketing research has emerged as an instrument of effective business management. According to American Marketing Association, "Marketing research is the systematic recording and analyzing of data about the problems relating to marketing of goods and services". It generates information; ideas, experiences and strategies for the decision makers to design suitable products and services and deliver them in accordance with the needs of the buyers. It basically helps the decision makers in business organizations to design the production of goods and services and sell them to ensure optimum consumption and utilization.

Need and Importance of Business Research

Business research is carried out with a view to facilitate the application of scientific method to the solution of business management problems. It is the systematic and scientific search for better alternatives of business management on the basis of ground realities and authentic suggestions. It is carried out on a regular basis by modern business organizations to ensure suitable changes and modifications to the approaches to business management on the strength of sound ideas and guidelines. The business organizations cannot produce or deliver any goods and services on the basis of rough work or guess work. The corporate houses are required to develop the research and development wing on the basis of specialized manpower, tested research methodologies and sound techniques of business research. The research and development wing also plays a vital role in rejuvenating the process of business management on the basis of authentic data.

In the new millennium, business organizations should develop a sound philosophy of marketing rather than blind selling of goods and services. Research and development sections have become highly professionalized in the age of globalization. Regular survey of marketing environment has become an important exercise in the process of marketing management. There cannot be a real business management activity without the back up of the marketing research function, observe Chunawala *et al.* (2006: 02).

Modern business organizations have also realized the importance of customer relationship management. The goods and services should fulfil the requirements of the customers. Business research is a critical element that makes the business management efforts quite effective and successfull. The transition from a seller's market to buyer's market has made it necessary to practice business research on the strength of tested and tried methodologies over a period of time. Business research is carried out to enable the modern corporate houses to confidently face the turbulent business environment and achieve highest degree of customer's satisfaction for their survival and development.

Chunawala *et al.* (2006: 02) justify the need for business research thus: "The complexity of business, growing competition, increasing marketing expenses, national and international distribution and other factors have made marketing of goods and services important. The business organizations also adopted strategic marketing management in order to cope with the challenges of business management. To begin with, the research studies were quantitative. These extended to product studies and consumer studies. Slowly the behavioural and psychographic studies came up. The era of positioning had arrived, and so researchers became all the more necessary. Computer software packages have given a further fillip to research agencies".

Nature and Scope of Business Research

Business research is dependent on generation of authentic data from the marketing environment on products, prices, distribution and promotion aspects. It encompasses all aspects of business management ranging from production management to consumer's behaviour. The data collected from business research are analyzed scientifically and systematic inferences are drawn for the use of decision makers in business organizations. Marketing surveys are carried out on the basis of hypotheses, study variables, tools and techniques. The business research findings are recorded, analyzed, interpreted and reported in the form of business research report which forms the basis for future course of action.

Business research is also a scientific exercise which is carried out on the basis of systematic objectives, hypotheses, methodologies and approaches. The business research is also a problem-oriented research which is objective by nature. The findings and recommendations of business research are converted into organized information for the decision makers. Business research is a never ending exercise in a changing business environment. The business organizations should remain always prepared for change in terms of policies, plans, programmes and actions on the basis of research findings.

Business research enriches the decision making process in modern business organizations. It serves as a valuable input to the decision making process and guides the decision makers to follow the best course of action. Business research is a multi-dimensional and cross-disciplinary research since it draws inputs from several disciplines like psychology, sociology, economics, behavioural research, operation research, media research, product research, and computer science. Business research also demands active involvement of several players since it is basically dependent on team work. Business research is carried out regularly to complement the business management process in modern times.

Business research also has a wider scope in spirit. It covers several areas such as product research, consumer research, advertising research, media research, and qualitative research. Product research primarily involves brand positioning, brand personality, brand image, brand equity and other aspects. Consumer research involves market segmentation techniques, identification of target groups and understanding consumer behaviours. Advertising research deals with media selection, understanding of effectiveness of advertising and methods of reaching out to various consumers. Media research involves media selection, media intervention and media management activities for business promotion. The qualitative research involves attitudinal studies, motivation studies, behavioural studies and other aspects of business promotion. Business research is both qualitative and quantitative. Quantitative research provides the responses of the study sample in terms of statistics. Qualitative research is exploratory or diagnostic in nature. Both quantitative and qualitative research are necessary in the process of business research which enhances the status of business management.

Types of Business Research

The process of business management becomes malnourished in the absence of systematic business research intervention packages. In particular, business research is carried out to examine the viability of business management strategies in general and marketing management techniques in particular. Modern business organizations are spending lot of money on business research in order to measure the effectiveness of business management strategies, observe Murthy and Bhojanna (2010: 14). There are several factors associated with the business research. Several business research methods are also adopted in the examination of business management strategies. The social, economic and ethical implications of business management should be examined systematically by the researchers in order to prevent certain drawbacks and maximize the success of business management.

Basically, there are two major forms of business research namely secondary research (getting information from published sources) and primary research (getting information first hand) according to Lesikar *et al.* (2012: 11).

The secondary research provides information that has already been created by specialists, veterans and other resource persons. The researchers can access this information through the print and electronic resources. The secondary research can be a rich source of information if the researchers know what to look for and where to look. The library is the natural place to begin secondary research. General libraries offer the public a wide variety of information sources. Special libraries have limited collections and circulation and can be owned by private business, association and research organizations.

The encyclopaedias, biographical directories, almanacs, trade directories, government publications, dictionaries, books, theses, newspapers, magazines, professional journals, media reports, business information services, and so on are the prominent print sources of secondary information. The electronic sources also contain secondary data. The availability of computer assisted data searches has facilitated immediate access to secondary information to the users. The Internet has become a prominent source of secondary electronic information source. The researchers should make use of suitable search engine or database in order to get need based information. Lehman *et al.* (2012: 08) have also identified certain drawbacks of electronic databases.

The primary data concerning the business management and marketing management are gathered from the field through observation, survey, experimentation and case study methods. The primary data represent the first hand experiences of the people who are directly associated with the business organization or product or service.

The observation is the oldest and authentic method of understanding the ground realities and business environment. It demands systematic parameters and procedures for observing, documenting and analyzing the business state of affairs. It does not involve any kind of experimentation usually for the purpose of data collection. The researcher observes certain phenomena, discovers ideas, documents facts, statistically analyze them and produces report on marketing environment, consumer behaviour, buying habits and other aspects. Lehman *et al.* (2012: 09) have stated that developing an objective system for quantifying observations is necessary to collect valid data. Observational studies typically involve no contact with the human subjects under study.

The survey is a systematic research method which is based on selection of areas, systematic sampling, development of tools, interview techniques, statistical tests, organization of findings and presentation of implications. The first hand experiences of the associates including the customers can be gathered through systematic surveys. Lehman *et al.* (2012: 10) observe: "Normative survey research is undertaken to determine the status of something at a specific time. Survey instruments such as questionnaires, opinion surveys, checklists and interviews are used to obtain information from the participants. Surveys can help verify the accuracy of existing norms. Surveys remain a valuable tool for gathering information on which to base policy making and decision making".

Lehman *et al.* (2012: 10) note: "Experimental research typically involves the study of two or more samples that have exactly the same components before a variable is added to one of the samples. Like scientists, businesses use experimental research to solve various problems. Experimental research requires very careful record keeping and informed consent from participants that are subjected to experimental methods". The experiment is also carried out in the field of business research since experimentation manipulates one factor and holds others constant. The researchers measure quantitatively or qualitatively any changes resulting from certain manipulation. But experimentation should be designed systematically to fit the individual requirements of the problem. The before and after design are adopted by using two identical test groups. The researcher introduces the experimental factors into one group and then compares two groups. The researcher can also attribute any difference between the two to the experimental factor and draw inferences.

The case analysis method is also based on systematic documentation and analysis of various factors associated with the growth, development, strengths, weaknesses, opportunities and threats in relation to a particular business organization or product or service. The records of the business organizations are very useful source of first hand information on the growth, development and limitations of the organization.

Process of Business Research

The process of business research basically involves several stages such as identification of business problem, developing research design, data collection, data analysis and report writing. The researcher should identify an appropriate business problem and define it systematically. It begins with a problem audit which is comprehensive examination of a business or marketing problem. The researcher should also place the problem in the right research perspective on the basis of extensive review of literature, situation analysis and expert opinion sampling methods.

The researchers should also identify a specific set of business research objectives which delineate the nature and scope of business research. Hypotheses or research questions should also be formulated. Research questions are refined statements of research objectives. Hypotheses are tentative statements about relationship between two or more variables. The researchers should also identify independent and dependent variables for systematic examination of existing business state of affairs. The research design should clearly mention the adoption of an appropriate methodology which suits the research question.

The researchers should conduct field work and collect primary data from the subjects of the study. The researcher should carry out tabulation, statistical tests and data analysis in consultation with the specialists. The result of data should be analyzed and interpreted for the purpose of drawing appropriate inferences. The research report should be prepared on the basis of suitable techniques and guidelines in order to facilitate meaningful managerial decision making. The report should also contain a meaningful set of findings and implications which enable the decision makers to take appropriate action for the improvement of business state of affairs.

Lehman *et al.* (2012: 10) have identified certain steps for finding a solution to a business problem. They include—(1) Recognizing and defining the problem, (2) Selecting a method of solution, (3) Collecting and organizing data, and (4) Arriving at an answer.

In the first stage, the researcher should identify and define the business research problem on the basis of authentic experience and review of relevant literature. The statement of the problem should be specified which needs to be solved by the business research. A set of hypotheses needs to be formulated in order to provide a meaningful basis for conduction of business research. The nature and scope of research should also be properly understood in order to prevent certain drawbacks. In the second stage, the researcher should make use of secondary or primary research methods to collect necessary information about the phenomenon or existing business state of affair. In the third stage, the researcher should collect the right data from the right sources and document them to ensure the success of business research. The validity and reliability of the data should be examined properly by the researcher. In the fourth stage, the researcher should make use of appropriate techniques for data analysis and interpretation of data. Appropriate statistical techniques should be used to evaluate the data for its usefulness to the decision makers. The report should also contain suitable findings and implications to facilitate the implementation of a suggested course of action to the decision makers in business organizations.

Bhusan (2012) elaborates the various steps of business research for the benefit of business researchers. The commonly known steps of business research are as follows:

- *Defining the research objectives:* The researcher should understand the basic objectives of business research in order to gain absolute clarity about the need, importance, modalities and other aspects of business research. Clear cut understanding of the objectives of business research would also facilitate meaningful conduction of business research.
- *Creating an efficient and productive research plan:* The researcher should develop a practically viable and professionally sound blue print of the business research in order to gain absolute clarity about various stages of business research and application of several tools and techniques. A sound blue print would go a long way in carrying out business research in the right direction and spirit.
- *Examining the authenticity of sources of data:* The researcher should also know the primary and secondary sources of data which form the basis for business research management. The primary data represent the field experience and secondary data represent the authoritative comments and criticisms of experts in the subject concerned.
- *Interpreting the data in the right manner:* The researcher should collect the data from the right sources by following the right tools and methodologies. The secondary data can be used for carrying out qualitative study. The primary data can be used for conducting quantitative study. The researcher should judiciously make use of both quantitative and qualitative techniques for better data collection and interpretation.
- *Drawing appropriate inferences:* The researcher should examine the cause and effect relationship in a perfect manner. The causes of advantages and disadvantages of business management should be scientifically analyzed. Similarly, the implications of the research should also be systematically presented. The researcher should draw appropriate inferences which enlighten the various stakeholders of business management.
- *Observing legal and ethical guidelines:* The researcher should understand the legal and ethical aspects of business research and adopt certain preventive measures in order to avoid violation of copyright laws, intellectual property rights and professional norms. The researcher should carry out the business research without giving any scope for violation of healthy norms and guidelines.

- *Organizing the contents of report:* The researcher should provide various compartments of research report on the basis of well established practices of presenting research report. In the introductory part, the salient features of research including the objectives should be presented. A separate component is essential for the presentation of review of relevant research. All methodological details should be presented in order to understand the study area, sample, tools of data collection, statistical tests and other aspects. A separate compartment is necessary to present the organizational or project profile concerning the research. The data analysis chapter should provide specific item-wise and variable-wise interpretation of data. The conclusion chapter should provide major findings of the study, implications of the study, suggestions for future research and an appropriate design or model for better business management.
- *Furnishing suitable bibliographical details:* The researcher should also provide bibliographical details for the benefit of the community of users in general and future generation of researchers in particular. This would provide authentic details about the reference materials which have strengthened the process of research. Appropriate databases should also be presented by the researcher.

Business Research Report Writing Techniques

The first and foremost aim of all social research, quantitative as well as qualitative, is to present a conceptually adequate description of a historically specific topic, subject or target. In business research the determination of the subject is as important as the choice of a population in a statistical study. The description of the subject is always, in both types of study, a theoretical task because it requires a conceptually well organized analysis. Conducting and publishing business research requires the same principal skills as quantitative research.

The processes of classification, deduction and interpretation are in their fundamental aspects similar in both qualitative and quantitative research. Quantitative analyzing operations, however, are more clear-cut than qualitative operations. Furthermore, the various steps of quantitative research can be more clearly distinguished than those of a qualitative study. The first issue is that, in qualitative work, the collection and processing of data are more closely intertwined than in a quantitative study. Especially when the researcher personally collects the data, she will not be able to avoid problems of interpretation during the collection phase. A specific issue in some qualitative research may be the fact that the methods used can change during the study, depending on interim results.

The business researcher must also carefully consider his/her relations with the study objects. Many qualitative reports often discuss at length the character and psychology of the process of data collection, but are less careful in describing what happened to the interview tapes afterwards. A second issue is that qualitative analysis is not restricted to an unambiguously demarcated data set in the same way as a quantitative study. The good researcher may keep a detailed field diary and make notes of all discussions and thus produce a corpus to which he/she limits her analysis. Nevertheless, during the analysis phase he/she may recall an important detail which she has not recorded in her notes, but has to take into account in the analysis.

The business researcher has to overcome prejudice and communication barriers within the scientific community. The researcher's preconception of a social phenomenon does not determine the research results to the same extent as in quantitative research, observes Sulkunen (1987). Business research is thus often used for the study of business processes, or for a study of the reasons behind human behaviour in modern business environment. The business research is used increasingly to answer questions about the practical issues concerning the business management.

The business researcher has to describe the analytical process in an honest and convincing way. In business research the analyses and reporting are very closely intertwined. The following criteria are as relevant to researchers and authors as they are to reviewers and editors in the field of business management:

Significance of the Data Set and Its Social or Cultural Place

The researcher should understand that the data are worth analyzing. It is not easy to identify criteria for the significance of data. One precondition can, however, be presented: the researcher should carefully define the social and cultural place (contextualizing) and the production conditions of the research material. The production conditions can be discussed at various levels. When the data consist of business products, their production and marketing mechanisms should be considered. Furthermore, the situational aspect of the data production and the researcher's potential influence on the data should be evaluated.

The relationship of business products to people's everyday life depends on the roduction and distribution network. Weekly magazines and movies represent the ambient culture at a number of levels. It is important to be able to exclude demographic variation as a factor causing differences. Additionally, people speak of the same things in different ways on different occasions, and it is the task of the researcher to decide the appropriateness of the contents of business research report.

Informal interviews are often advocated instead of questionnaires on the grounds that they will produce more genuine information. But, on the other hand, an in-depth interview is a more exceptional situation for a present day person than completing a questionnaire. Possible effects of the power structures and demographic relations present in every business situation should be considered in the discourse analysis, since it could affect the outcomes of the qualitative research.

Sufficiency of the Data, and Coverage of the Analysis

Experience reveals that the business researchers should not collect too much data at a time. It is better to analyze a small data batch carefully first and only then determine what additional data will be needed. To divide the analyses into smaller parts also helps to end up with manageable results for a publishable report. It is often advisable to group the collection of data according to factors which may prove important as production conditions. The goal is not to explain the variation, but to make sure that the data are sufficiently varied. A proper coverage of the analysis means that the researcher does not base the interpretations on a few arbitrary cases or instances but on a careful reading of the whole material.

Transparency and Repeatability of the Analysis

Transparency of the analysis means that the reader is able to follow the researcher's reasoning. The repeatability of an analysis means that the rules of classification and interpretation have been presented so clearly that another researcher applying them will reach the same conclusions. Scholars have identified three ways of improving the transparency and repeatability of business analysis and the report: (1) enumerating the data;

(2) dividing the process of interpretation into steps; and (3) making explicit the rules of decision and interpretation.

The best method to decrease arbitrariness and increase repeatability is to enumerate all units on which the interpretation is based. To do this an analytical unit must be specified and it should be as small as possible: in other words, not a movie or a group discussion but a scene, a statement or an adjacent pair. The identification of the unit of analysis is in itself part of the process of interpretation. The process of interpretation and analysis can never be fully formalized. It is above all a question of working step by step so that the process of interpretation can be made visible to both the researcher and the readers.

Drisko (2005: 04) precautions that the following drawbacks of research report writing should be consciously avoided by the researchers. They are as follows:

1. The author has not related the study to earlier (international) literature;
2. The research question is not clearly stated;
3. The structure of the paper is not clear or does not respond to the expected structure of papers in the journal;
4. Theories, methods and data analyses are not consistent;
5. The central concepts are not clearly presented or used in a consistent way;
6. The methodology is poor;
7. The size of the dataset is not defended in a convincing way;
8. The data set is not sufficiently contextualized or there is a clear selection bias;
9. The data collection is poor and there is a lack of validity control;
10. The methods and the analyses are not explained clearly enough, which may:
11. Lead the referees and the editor to regard the article as too descriptive, and the
12. Analyses based too much on intuition;
13. The author makes unsound conclusions or unfounded generalizations;
14. Ethical rules are violated or ethical issues are not mentioned or adequately discussed; and
15. The text is too long.

Des Jarlais *et al.* (2004: 03) have identified the ground rules for writing a research report.

(a) An article should be provided with a structured abstract (as a minimum: background, aims, sample, methods and results).
(b) The sampling should be described and justified, including an explanation of criteria used.
(c) The theoretical background of the entire study, or individual methods, should be described, to show that the sample and data collection were consistent with the study's theoretical background.
(d) The context (setting) in which the study was carried out should be described. The author must describe the characteristics of the field in which the study was carried out, and what made it different from other settings.
(e) A detailed description of the research intervention should be included, and of how study participants responded during that intervention.
(f) A detailed description of the analytical methods applied, how they were used, including the tools used for minimizing bias, and a validation of the results should be presented.
(g) A description of the manner of data processing (e.g., technical aspects and procedures) is needed.
(h) Description of outcomes and their interpretation are obviously necessary. This includes a discussion of limitations (contextual validity of results), and an analysis of how the design of the study reflects these limitations.

Other scholars have also listed the ground rules of documentation and writing of business research. They include–

1. Consider the format and structure of the report.
2. Make sure that the title of the research report corresponds to the content.
3. State the research question early and clearly.
4. Conduct a thorough review of earlier research.
5. Present the methods and data.
6. Present the results in a systematic way.

Lehman *et al.* (2012: 10) enumerated the techniques of writing business research report thus: "The report should contain the introduction, discussion, summary and recommendations. It should begin with brief background to the report which includes the problem, rationale, objective and scope of the report. A small note should be there on methodology that includes sources of data and analysis used. The discussion is the main part of the research report that presents the information collected and relates it to the problem. To increase readability and coherence, this section contains numerous headings to denote the various divisions within a report. The findings should be well established and based on sound analysis or statistics. A good report ends with an analysis of what the reported information means and how it should be acted upon. Recommendations present the writer's opinion on a possible course of action based on the conclusions. The references section is an alphabetically listing of the sources used in preparing the report. It enables the future generation of researchers to find out appropriate information of their choice".

Conclusion

Business research is carried out in modern business organizations to understand the factors which are associated with the growth and development of business houses. Business environment is constantly changing on account of several known and unknown factors and forces. There are various stakeholders of business management including the customers in the modern society. The management should be always eager to understand the changing business environment and cope with the hopes and aspirations of various stakeholders who matter most. The business research reports are submitted to the top management in order to facilitate suitable changes and modifications in the process of business management. The business research report is designed to solve certain business problems or answer business questions. The process of business management can be perfected on the basis of authentic data, analyses, inferences and recommendations produced by the researchers. The business researchers should present the report using an acceptable format and writing style.

References

Bhusan, Uma (2012) *Introduction to Business Communication*, Jaico Publishing House, Mumbai, pp. 346-374.

Chunawala, Kumar, Sethia, Subramanian and Suchak (2006) *Advertising: Theory and Practice*, Himalaya Publishing House, Mumbai, p. 96.

Des Jarlais, D.C., Lyles, C. and Crepaz, N. (2004) Improving the Reporting Quality of Nonrandomized Evaluations of Behavioural and Public Health Interventions: The Trend Statement. *American Journal of Public Health,* 3 (94): 361-366.

Drisko, J. (2005) Writing Up Qualitative Research. Families in Society: *The Journal of Contemporary Social Services*, 86 (4): 589-593.

Hasan, Seema (2010) *Mass Communication: Principles and Concepts*, CBS Publishers and Distributors Pvt. Ltd., New Delhi.

Kaul, Asha (2009) *Business Communication*, PHI Learning Private Limited, New Delhi.

Lehman, Carol, M., Devvie D., DuFrene, Mala Sinha and Robin C.Walker (2012) BCOM, *An Innovative Approach to Learning and Teaching, Business Communication, A South Asian Perspective*, Cengage Learning, New Delhi, p. 230.

Ibid., p. 232.

Ibid., pp. 232-233.

Ibid., pp. 272-273.

Lesikar, Raymond, V., Marie E. Flatley, Kathryn Rentz and Neerja Pande (2012) *Business Communication, Making Connections in a Digital World*, New Delhi, India, pp. 627-662.

Mason, J. (1996). *Qualitative Research*. Thousand Oaks: Sage Publications.

Mukerjee, Hory Sankar (2013) *Business Communication: Connecting at Work*, Oxford University Press, New Delhi.

Murthy, S.N. and U. Bhojanna (2010) *Advertising: An IMC Perspective*, Excel Books, New Delhi, p. 324.

Bibliography

Agalgatti, B.H. and Krishna, S. (2000) *Business Ethics: Concepts and Practices*, Nirali Prakashan, Pune, pp. 22-23.

Allen, R.K. (1977) *Organization Management through Communication*, Harper and Row, New York, U.S.A.

Amin, Samir (2004) *The Liberal Virus: Permanent War and the Americanization of the World*. London: Pluto Press.

Appadurai, Arjun (1997) *Modernity at Large: Cultural Dimensions of Globalization,* Minneapolis: University of Minnesota Press.

Atwater, J. Brian, Vijay R. Kannan and Alan, A. Stephens (2008) Cultivating Systematic Thinking in the Next Generation of Business Leaders, *Academy of Management Learning and Education,* 7 (1): 9-25.

Axtell, Roger E. (1998) *Gestures: The Dos and Taboos of Body Language around the World*, New York: John Wiley & Sons, p. 43.

Bacal, Robert (2007) *Internal Communication Strategies—The Neglected Strategic Element*, Bacal and Associates, Ontario, Canada.

Ballou, R.H. (1992) *Business Logistics Management,* Prentice Hall, Inc. Englewood Cliffs, New Jersey.

Banerjee, Mrithyunjoy (1986) *Gems of Management,* Jaico Publishing House, Bombay, pp. 46-48.

Baral, Kailash C. (2000) *Globalization and Tribes of Northeast India*, in (Eds.) Moya, Paula M.L. and Michael R. Hames-Garcia, Reclaiming Identity: Realist Theory and the Predicament of Postmodernism.

Baral, Kailash C. and Kar, Prafulla (Eds.) (2004) Identities: *Local and Global*, Delhi: Pencraft International.

Baran, S.J. and Davis, D.K. (2000) *Mass Communication Theory*, Belmont, CA: Wadsworth.

Barnes, Louis, B., C. Roland Christensen and Abby J. Hansen (1987) *Teaching and the Case Method*, Boston: Harvard Business School Press.

Barnouw, V. (1963) *Culture and Personality*, Dorsey Press, Chicago, p. 4.

Bartlett, C.A. and Ghoshal, S. (2002) Building Competitive Advantage Through People, *MIT Sloan Review,* Vol. 43 (2), Winter, 2002.

Baskin, Otis, Craig Aronoff and Dan Lattimore (1997) *Preface to Public Relations: The Profession and the Practice*, Brown and Benchmark Publishers, Madison, p. xiii.

Beatty and Takahashi (2003) *Intercultural Communication*, New Delhi: Biztantra.

Beck, Natan Sznaider and Rainer Winter (eds.) Global America? *The Cultural Consequences of Globalization.* Liverpool: Liverpool University Press, pp. 15-29.

Beebe, Steven A. and John T. Masterson (1997) *Communicating in Small Groups: Principles and Practices*, New York: Longman.

Beltran, Luis Ramiro (1978) Rural Communities in Developing Countries: The Prospects of Communication, *Issues in Communication.* No. 2, International Institute of Communications, London, UK.

Bennis, W. and Nanus B. (1985) *Leaders: The Strategies for Taking Charge*, New York: Harper and Row, p. 89.

Berridge, G. (2006) *Event Design and Experience.* Oxford: Butterworth-Heinemann.

Bethell, Tom (1977) 'Freedom of Speech and Expression', *Freedom Means,* International Communication Agency, USA, p. 41.

Bhat, Anil and Arya Kumar (2009) *Management Principles, Processes and Practices*, Oxford University Press, New Delhi, p. 22.

Bhusan, Uma (2012) *Introduction to Business Communication*, Jaico Publishing House, Mumbai.

Bird, S. Elizabeth (1992) *For Enquiring Minds: A Cultural Study of Supermarket Tabloids*, Knoxville: University of Tennessee Press, 12-17.

Bollen, Kenneth A. and Rick H. Hoyle (1990) Perceived Cohesion: A Conceptual and Empirical Examination, *Social Forces*, 69: 479.

Boro, Anil (2006) Globalizaton and Local Cultures: The Tribes of North East India, *Indian Folklife Serial No. 22, July.*

Bovee, Courtland, John V. Thill and Mukesh Chaturvedi (2009) *Business Communication Today*, Delhi: Pearson, pp. 16-18.

Bowdin, G. *et al.* (2007) *Events Management*, 2nd Ed., Elsevier Butterworth-Heinemann, Oxford.

Bowdin, G., McDonnell, I., Allen, J., O'Toole, W. (2010) *Events Management* 3rd edition, Oxford: Butterworth-Heinemann.

Bowdin, Glenn (2003) *Events Management: Resource Guide*, UK Centre for Events Management, Leeds Metropolitan University.

Bratton, Susan (2008) *Foreword to Social Media Marketing* by Dave Evans, New Delhi: Times Business Services, Wiley India, p. xiii.

Brilhart, John K. (1995) *Effective Group Discussion*, Iowa: Wm.C. Brown.

Brilhart, John K. and Gloria J. Galanes (1992) *Effective Group Discussion*, Dubuque, Iowa: Wm. C. Brown.

Brown, Charles T. and Paul W. Keller (1973) *Monologue to Dialogue*, N.J.: Prentice Hall, p. 2.

Brubaker, R. (2004) *Ethnicity without Groups*. Cambridge, MA: Harvard University Press.

Bursk, Edward C. and Stephen A. Greyser (1968) *Advanced Cases in Marketing Management*, London: Prentice Hall, International Inc.

Casesa, John (2009) Highly Respected Automobile Industry Consultant, *Business Week*, March 16: 31-32.

Cavanagh, Gerald (1984) *American Business Values in Transition*, Englewood Cliffs, N.J.: Prentice-Hall, USA.

Cavanagh, J. and Mader, J. (2002) *Alternatives to Economic Globalization: A Better World is Possible*—A Report of the International Forum on Globalization, San Francisco: Berrett-Koehler Publishers, Inc., p. 19.

Center, Allen H. and Patrick Jackson (2002) *Public Relations Practices: Managerial Case Studies and Problems*, Sixth Edition, Prentice Hall of India Private Limited, New Delhi, India, p. 38.

Chaturvedi, P.D. and Mukesh Chaturvedi (2011) *Business Communication —Concepts, Cases and Applications*, Delhi: Pearson, p. 116.

Chaturvedi, P.D. and Mukesh Chaturvedi (2012) *Business Communication*, Chennai: Pearson, pp. 22-23.

Chomsky, Noam (1989) *Necessary Illusions*, Pluto Press, London, p. 5.

Chopra, Deepak (1988) Interview, *Business World*, June 7, p. 108.

Christians, Clifford G., Kim B. Rotzoll and Mark Fackler (1991) Media Ethics, New York: Longman, pp. 1-29.

Chunawala, Kumar, Sethia, Subramanian and Suchak (2006) *Advertising: Theory and Practice*, Himalaya Publishing House, Mumbai, p. 96.

Cohen, H. (2006) *Good Arabs: The Israeli Security Services and Israeli Arabs*. Jerusalem: Hebrew Publishing House.

Committee for Economic Development (1971) *Social Responsibilities of Business Corporations*, New York: CED, pp. 29-31.

Conversi, Daniele (2007) Homogenisation, Nationalism and War: Should we still read Ernest Gellner? *Nations and Nationalism*, 13 (3): 371-394.

Cooke, Robert A. and John A. Kernaghan (1987) Estimating the Difference between Group *versus* Individual Performance on Problem-Solving Tasks, *Group and Organizational Studies*, 12 (3): 319-342.

Cuneo, A. (2002) Simultaneous Media Use Rife, New Study Finds, *Advertising Age*, pp. 3-40.

Cuneo, A. (2002) Simultaneous Media Use Rife, New Study Finds, *Advertising Age*, pp. 3-40.

Cutlip, Scott M., Allen H. Center and Glen M. Broom (2004), *Effective Public Relations*, Pearson Education Private Limited, Singapore, p. 6.

Dance, Fran E.X. and Carl Larson (1972) *Speech Communication: Concepts and Behaviour*, New York: Rinehart and Winston.

Davis, James, H.F. David Schooman and Lex Donaldson (1997) Toward a Stewardship Theory of Management, *Academy of Management Review*, January: 20-47.

Davis, Keith and John Newstrom (1993) *Organizational Behaviour: Human Behaviour at Work*, New Delhi: Tata McGraw Hill, p. 399.

Davis, Ralph Currier (1951) *The Fundamentals of the Top Management*, Harper and Brothers, New York, pp. 60-61.

DeFleur, Melvin (1970) *Theories of Mass Communication,* David McKay, New York, p. 76.

Des Jarlais, D.C., Lyles, C. and Crepaz, N. (2004) Improving the Reporting Quality of Nonrandomized Evaluations of Behavioural and Public Health Interventions: The Trend Statement. *American Journal of Public Health* 3 (94): 361-366.

Dev, Sudipta (2005) The Importance of Internal Communication, *Weekly Insight for Technology Professionals,* www.expresscomputeronline.com, February 07, 2005.

Dizard, W.Jr. (2000) *Old, New Media*, New York: Longman.

Dominick, J.R. (1999) *The Dynamics of Mass Communication,* New York: McGraw Hill.

Donaleson R. Forsyth (1983) *An Introduction to Group Dynamics*, California: Monterey.

Dorey, E. and MacLellan, A. (2003) *Spread the World—Encourage Viral Marketing*, www.dda.ns.ca

Douglas, T. (1995) *Survival in Groups: The Basics of Group Membership*, Buckingham: Open University Press.

Drisko, J. (2005) Writing Up Qualitative Research. Families in Society; *The Journal of Contemporary Social Services* 86 (4): 589-593.

Drucker, Peter F. (1991) *The New Realities*, New Delhi: Asian Books Private Ltd., p. 210.

Eames K. and M. Keeling (2004) Monogamous networks and the spread of sexually transmitted diseases. *Math. Biosci.*, 189: 115-130.

Elaine, Sternberg (1994) *Just Business*, Warner Books, New Jersey: Prentice Hall, p. 73.

Enger, J. (2009) Share Your Guiding Light Memories, *New York Times,* August 26.

Evans, Dave (2008) *Social Media Marketing*, New Delhi: Times Business Services, p. 31.

Fine, Debra (2010) *The Fine Art of Small Talk,* www.DebraFine.com

Fowler, Alan (1990) *Negotiation Skills and Strategies*, Hyderabad: University Press, p. 3.

Friedman, Thomas L. (1997) *The Lexus and the Olive Tree: Understanding Globalization*, New York: Anchor Books. 93.

Gandhi, M.K. (1947) *Harijan*, February 23, p. 9.

Garcia Canclini, N. (1995) *Hybrid Cultures: Strategies for Entering and Leaving Modernity*. Minneapolis: University of Minneapolis Press.

Gerbner, George (1985) Mass Media Discourse: Message System Analysis as a Component of Cultural Indicators. In T.A. Van Dijk (Ed.) *Discourse and Mass Communication: New Approaches to the Analysis of Mass Media Discourse and Communication*, Walterde Gruyter & Co., Berlin, p. 76.

Getz, D. (2007) *Event Studies: Theory, Research and Policy for Planned Events*. Oxford: Butterworth-Heinemann.

Giddens, A. (1999) *The Constitution of Society: Outline of the Theory of Structuration*, University of California Press, pp. 15-16.

Gillian, Colin (1996) Ethics in Marketing in Ken Smith and Phil Johnson (Ed.), *Business Ethics and Business Behaviour*, London: International Thomson Business Press, p. 112.

Gladwell, M. (2003) Alternative Marketing Vehicles: The Future of Marketing to one, *Consumer Insight*, www.acnielsen.com

Glenny, Misha (2008) McMafia: *A Journey Through the Global Criminal Underworld*. Bodley Head/New York: Alfred A. Knopf.

Goldblatt, J. (2010) *Special Events: A New Generation and the Next Frontier*. New York.

Grant, A. and Meadows, J. (2008) *Communication Technology Update and Fundamentals*, Boston: Focal Press.

Gray, John (2003) *Al Qaeda and What It Means to Be Modern*, New York: Faber and Faber.

Grieco, M. and Holmes, L. (1999) Tele Options for Community Business: An Opportunity for Economic Growth in Africa, *Africa Notes*, pp. 1-3.

Griffin, Ricky W. (2012) *Management Principles and Applications*, Cengage Learning, New Delhi, p. 28.

Gunderson, E. (2002) Uncovering the Real Osbournes, *USA Today*, p. E1.

Gunewardena, Victor (1997) *Communication Ethics and the Role of the State, Communication Ethics: A South Asian Perspective*, Asian Media Information and Communication Centre, Singapore, pp. 1-19.

Hall, Edward T. (1959) *The Silent Language*, New York: Double Day, p. 17.

Hamel, Gary and C.K. Prahlad (1994) Competing for the Future, *Harvard Business Review*, July-August: 122-128.

Hartley, Peter (2004) *Group Communication*, London: Routledge, p. 129.

Hasan, Seema (2010) *Mass Communication: Principles and Concepts*, CBS Publishers and Distributors Pvt. Ltd., New Delhi.

Hayzlett, Jeff (2009) *Observations of the Chief Marketing Officer and Vice President*, Eastman Kodak Company, Social media tips, www.kodak.com

Hendrix, Jerry A. (2001) *Public Relations Cases*, Fifth Edition, Wadsworth, U.S.A., pp. 108-113.

Hilger, Susanne (2008) Globalisation by Americanization: American Companies and the Internationalization of German Industry after the Second World War, *European Review of History/Revue Europeenne d'Histoire*, 15 (4): 375-401.

Hilliard, R. and Keith, M. (2001) *The Broadcast Century and Beyond: A Biography of American Broadcasting*, Boston: Allyn & Bacon.

Hitt, Michael, A. (2000) Transformation of Management for the New Millennium, *Organizational Dynamics,* Winter: 7-17.

Hodgetts, Richard M., Fred Luthans and Jonathan Doh (2006) *International Management: Culture, Strategy and Behaviour*, New York: McGraw Hill, p. 190.

Homans, George, C. (1992) *The Human Group*, New York: Harcourt Brace, p. 343.

IBM Global Business Services (2011) *Executive Report*, IBM Institute for Business Value, New York.

Irving, L. Janis (1971) Group Think, *Psychology Today,* 5 (1): 43-76.

Kalb, C. (2002) How are we Doing? *Newsweek,* p. 53.

Kallan, Hanna (2006) *Integrated Internal Communications in the Multi-national Corporation*, Ph.D. Thesis, Robert Gordon University, Iso-Britannia, U.K.

Kameda, Naoki (1996) *Business Communication Toward Transnationalism: The Significance of Cross-Cultural Business English and Its Role*, Tokyo: Kindiabungeisha, p. 34.

Karoli, Veera and Naghma Ahmed (2013) *Business Communication*, Thakur Publishers, Bengaluru, India.

Katsuhiko, Izumi (1989) Whither the Traditions of Local Pottery? *Japan Quarterly*, 36 (3) 287-93.

Kaul, Asha (2009) *Business Communication*, PHI Learning Private Limited, New Delhi.

Kelly, George A. (1963) *A Theory of Personality: The Psychology of Personal Construct*, New York: Norton, p. 18.

Klein, Naomi (2002) *Fencs and Windows*, Leftward, New Delhi.

Lafley, A.G. (2009) Role of CEO in Modern Organizations, *Harvard Business Review,* May: 62-63.

Larsen, Susan (2003) National Identity, Cultural Authority, and the Post-Soviet Blockbuster: Nikita Mikhalkov and Aleksei Balabanov, *Slavic Review*, 62 (3): 491-511.

Larson, C. and F. LaFasto (1989) *Teamwork: What Must Go Right/What Can Go Wrong*, California: Sage.

Lehman, Carol, M., Debbie D. DuFrene, Mala Sinha and Robyn C.Walker (2012) BCOM: *An Innovative Approach to Learning and Teaching Business Communication*, New Delhi, p. 224.

Leigh, J. (2004) Reflections of Babylon: Intercultural Communication and Globalization in the New World Order, A paper presented at the Globalization 2004 Conference, www.globalization.icaap.org

Lengel, R.H. and R.L. Daft (1988) The Selection of Communication Media as an Executive Skill, *Academy of Management Executive,* 2: 225-230.

Lesikar V., Raymond, Marie E. Flatley, Kathryin Rentz and Neerja Pande (2011) *Business Communication: Making Connections in a Digital World*, New Delhi: Tata McGraw Hill Education Private Limited, pp. 20-21.

Lesikar, Raymond, V., Marie E. Flatley, Kathryn Rentz and Neerja Pande (2012) *Business Communication, Making Connections in a Digital World*, New Delhi, India.

Lewin, J. (2007) *Internet Media Replacing Traditional Media*, IBM *via* New Tee Vee.

Lin, C.A. (2001) Audience Attributes, Media Supplementation and Likely Online Service Adoption, *Mass Communication and Society,* 4 (1): 19-38.

Lippmann, Walter (1922) *Public Opinion,* Harcourt Brace, New York, p. 268.

Lodge, George (1979) *The New American Ideology*, New York: McGraw Hill, Inc.

Lull, J. (2000) *Media, Communication, Culture: A Global Approach*, 2nd edition, Cambridge: Polity Press.

MacBride International Commission for the Study of Communication Problems (1980). Many Voices, One World, Report of the UNESCO, Paris.

Margerison, Charles (1996) *The Art of Effective Communication*, New Delhi: Excel Books.

Marx, Karl and Friedrich Engels (1848) *Manifesto of the Communist Party*, p. 44.

Mary, Ellen Guffey (2002) *Business Communication: Process and Product*, Cengage Learning, London, UK.

Mason, J. (1996). *Qualitative Research. Thousand Oaks*, Sage Publications.

Massey, K. and Baran, S.J. (2001) *Introduction to Mass Communication*, Mountain View, CA: Mayfield.

Mathew, M.J. (2002) *Business Communication: Theory and Practice*, Jaipur: RBSA Publishers, India.

McNamara, Carter (2007) *Basics in Internal Organizational Communications*, In Field Guide to Leadership and Supervision, Authenticity Consulting, LLC.

McQuail, Denis (1975) *Toward Sociology of Communication*, Collier McMillan, London, UK.

Medoff, Norman J. and Barbara K. Kaye (2011) *Electronic Media: Then, Now and Later*, Amsterdam: Elsevier, p. 279.

Mehrabian, Albert (1968) Communication Without Words, *Psychology Today,* September: 53-55.

Mintzberg, Henry (1973) *The Nature of Managerial Work*, New York: Harper Collins College Division.

Monroe, J. and Kates, R. (2005) *Art of the Event: Complete Guide to Designing and Decorating Special Events.* New York: Wiley.

Montagu, Ashley and Floyd Matson (2008) *The Human Connection*, McGraw Hill, New York.

Mukerjee, Hory Sankar (2013) *Business Communication: Connecting at Work*, Oxford University Press, New Delhi.

Murthy, Narayana, N.R. (2001) *A Better India, A Better World*, Penguin Allen Lane, pp. 159-160.

Murthy, S.N. and U. Bhojanna (2010) *Advertising: An IMC Perspective*, Excel Books, New Delhi, p. 324.

Otokhine, E. (2000) *Internet Strengthens Cultural Imperialism*, The Comet, August 23, p. 21.

Pal, Rajendra J.S. and Korlahalli (1996) *Essentials of Business Communication*, Sultan Chand & Sons, New Delhi.

Pathiravitana, S. (2007) Master Globish, Use it for Business Communication, *The Times of India,* July 27, New Delhi.

Pavlik, J.V. (1996) *New Media Technology: Cultural and Commercial Perspectives*, Boston: Allyn & Bacon.

Perrin, Towers (2006) Effective Communication from the Perspective of Employees: *Towers Perrin Monitor,* May, p. 6.

Perry, David (2002) Do you have the Skills Most in Demand Today? *The Wall Street Journal,* May 20, www.careerjournal.com

Perry, David (2003) Do you have the Skills Most in Demand Today?, *Career Journal,* www.careerjournal.com

Percy, Larry (1997) *Strategies for Implementing Integrated Marketing Communication*, Illinois: NTC Business School.

Peters, Tom (1997) The Search for Excellence Continuous, *Forbes,* 2 (12): 238-240.

Piskorski, Mikolaj Jan and Tommy McCall (2010) Mapping the Social Internet, *Harvard Business Review,* July-August, www.hbr.org

Raghavan, K.S. and K.N. Prasad (2009) *Library and Information Systems: From Alexandrian Heritage to Social Networking*, Bangalore: Ess Ess Publications, India.

Rai, Urmila and S.M. Rai (1992) *Business Communication*, Bombay: Himalaya Publishing House, p. 3.

Raj, R., Walters, P., Rashid, T. (2008) *Events Management: An Integrated and Practical Approach.* London: Sage.

Rankin, P.T. (1928) The Importance of Listening Ability, *English Journal,* 17 (1): 623-630.

Rao, Leela (2000) *Media Practitioners and Institutions: The Indian Experience, Communication Ethics: A South Asian Perspective*, Asian Media Information and Communication Centre, Singapore, pp. 43-55.

Rebecca Finkel (2010) *Resource Guide in Principles and Practices of Events Management*, Hospitality Press, Leisure, Sport and Tourism Network.

Redfield (1996) Communication in Management, Prentice Hall, New Jersey, U.S.A., p. 17.

Reitan, H.T. and Marvin E. Shaw (1964) Group Membership, Sex-Composition of the Group and Conformity Behaviour, *Journal of Social Psychology,* 64: 45-51.

Ritz-Carlton (2000) Training Tradition, *USA Today*, June 29: 3B.

Robertson, R. (1992) Globalization: Time-Space and Homogeneity-Heterogeneity. In: Featherstone M.L. and Robertson R. eds., *Global Modernities, Thousand Oaks*, CA: Sage, p. 8.

Robinson, P., Wale, D., Dickson, G. (2010) *Events Management.* CABI: Wallingford.

Rodman, Lilita (2001) You-Attitude: A Linguistic Perspective, *Business Communication Quarterly,* 64 (4): 11-12.

Rogers, T. (2008) *Conferences and Conventions: A Global Industry*, (2nd ed.) Butterworth Heinemann.

Roy, Ash Narayan (1999) *Third World in the Age of Globalization*, Madhyam Books, New Delhi.

Royal Commission (1949) Report on the Role of the Press, London.

Sanjay, B.P. (1997) *Ethical Dilemmas: Emerging Trends and Issues, Communication Ethics: A South Asian Perspective*, Asian Media Information and Communication Centre, pp. 33-43.

Schaefer, Melissa (2011) *Capitalizing on the Smarter Consumer, Report*, IBM Institute for Business Value.

Schein, Edgar, H. (2004) *Organizational Culture and Leadership*, Jossey-Bass, San Francisco, p. 72.

Schiffman, I.G. and I.I. Kanuk (2004) *Social Media and Marketing*, Delhi: PHI.

Schiller, Herbert. (1985) *Information and the Crisis Economy. Norwood,* NJ: Ablex.

Schultz, Heidi (2000) *The Elements of Electronic Communication*, Boston: Allyn and Bacon, pp. 43-47.

Schwarz, Urs (1966) *Press Law for our Times – The Example of the German Legislation*, The International Press Institute, Zurich, pp. 77-78.

Scott, Bill (1995) *The Skills of Negotiating*, Bombay: Jaico Publishing House, p. 3.

Securities and Exchange Commission (2012) *National Examination Risk Alert*, Mumbai, 2 (1): 4-7.

Seitel, Fraser P. (1987) *The Practice of Public Relations*, Third Edition, Merrill Publishing Company, Columbus, pp. 363-366.

Sen, Amartya (1988) *On Ethics and Economics*, New York: Basil Blackwell, Inc., pp. 22-23.

Shane, E. (1999) *Selling Electronic Media*, Boston: Focal Press.

Shelby, Annette N. and Lamar Reinsch, Jr. (1995) Positive Emphasis and You—Attitude: An Empirical Study, *Journal of Business Communication.*

Shone, A. and Parry, B. (2001) *Successful Event Management.* London: Continuum.

Sieburg, Evelyn and Carl Larson (1971) Dimensions of Interpersonal Response, Paper delivered at the annual conference of the International Communication Association, Phoenix, April 1, 1971.

Silvers, J. (2003) *Professional Event Coordination.* New York: Wiley.

Singhal, D.D., V.K. Mittal, N.C. Gara and V.S. Vyas (2006) *Business Communication and Management*, Jaipur: Indus Valley Publications, p. 3.

Singla, Parag (2008) Yes, There is a Correlation—From Social Networks to Personal Behaviour on the Web, International Worldwide Web Conference, April 21-25, Beijing.

Smith, Dennis (2006) *Globalization: The Hidden Agenda.* Cambridge: Polity, p. 1.

Smythe, J. (2002) The Rise of the Internal Communicator, *Profile IPR Magazine,* May, pp. 41-48.

Spitzberg, B.H. (1983) Communication Competence as Knowledge, Skill and Impression, *Communication Education,* 32: 323-329.

Sterne, Jim and Anthony Priore (2000) *E-mail Marketing: Using E-mail to Reach Your Target Audience and Build Customer Relationship*, New York: John Wiley & Sons, p. 141.

Stevenson, J. (1988) *Language, Thought and Representation*, Chichester: John Wiley.

Stone, B. (2009) From TV to the Web to Your Phone, *New York Times*, May 31.

Strabhuar, J. and LaRose (2004) *Media Now*, Belmont, CA: Wadsworth.

Terminello, Vera and Marcia G. Reed (2003) *E-mail: Communicate Effectively*, N.J.: Pearson Education, p. 13.

Thibaut, John and Harold Kelly (1986) *The Social Psychology of Groups*, New Brunswick, N.J.: Transaction Publishing.

Trenholm, Sarah (1990) *Human Communication Theory*, Englewood Cliffs, N.J.: Prentice Hall.

Trompenaars, Fons and Peter Woolliams (2003) *Business Across Cultures*, Capstone, London, p. 53.

Turner, Paul (2004) *Organizational Communication: The Role of the HR Professional*, Jaico Publishing House, Mumbai, India, pp. 6-12.

United Nations Organisation (1996) *ESCWA Annual Report.*

Van der Wagen, L. (2002) *Event Management: For Tourism, Cultural, Business and Sporting Events.* Melbourne: Hospitality Press.

Vardhan, Venkat T. (2008) Interview Story, *The Hindu*, Bangalore, August 11, 2008.

Vardman, George (1973) *Effective Communication of Ideas*, New York: Van Nostrand Reinhold Company, p. 3.

Venkataraman, N. and Prescott, J.E. (1990) Environment-Strategy Coalignment: An Empirical Test of its Performance Implications, *Strategic Management Journal,* Vol. No. 11 (1), pp. 1-23.

Venkataraman, T.S. (1995) Communication in Management, *The Hindu,* Sept. 23rd, 1995.

Verma, Pawan K. (2005) Effective Internal Communication, In Kushal, K.B., S. Ravishankar, H.L. Kaila and R.K. Mishra (Eds.) *Perspectives for Effective Management*, Himalaya Publishing House, Mumbai, India, pp. 114-119.

Veronis, S. and Stevenson (2003) *Communication Industry Forecast*, www.vss.com

Vilanilam, J.V. (2005) *Mass Communication in India: A Sociological Perspective*, Sage Publications Ltd., New Delhi, India, p. 17.

Vita, Emma De (2007) *Internal Communications Measurement*, J:/effective com.htm, May 12, 2007, p. 1.

Vivek, T.R. (2007) Strat Talk, *The Economic Times,* April 20, Mumbai, p. 18.

Wagner, John A. and Michale K. Moch (1986) Individualism-Collectivism: Concept and Measure, *Group and Organizational Studies,* 11 (1) : 280-304.

Waldroop, James and Timothy, Butler (1996) The Executive as Coach, *Harvard Business Review,* November-December: 111-117.

Wasserman, S. and K. Faust (1994) *Social Network Analysis*. Cambridge University Press.

Watt, D.C. (1998) *Event Management in Leisure and Tourism*, Longman, Harlow.

Weiss, Alan (2003) How to Write a Proposal that is accepted Every Time, Peterborough, N.H.: Kennedy Information, Inc., p. 13.

Weldon, E. and Weingart, L.R. (1993) Group Goals and Group Performance, *British Journal of Social Psychology,* 32: 307-334.

Winsor, Dorothy A. (2003) *Writing Power: Communication in an Engineering Centre*, Albany: Suny Press.

World Health Organization (1994) *Cultural Dimension of Globalization*, The Globalization of Communication; John Thompson.

Wright, C.R. (1959) *Mass Communication: A Sociological Perspective*, Random House, New York, p. 21.

Yates, JoAnne (1989) *Control Through Communication: The Rise of System in American Management*, The Johns Hopkins Press Ltd., London, U.K., pp. 1-20.

Yeoman, I., Robertson, M., Ali-Knight, J., Drummond, S., McMahon-Beattie, U. (eds.) (2003) *Festival and Events Management: An International Arts and Culture Perspective.* Oxford: Butterworth-Heinemann.

Zikmund, William G. (2003) *Business Research Methods*, Mason, O.H.: South Western, p. 279.

Index

Academic institutions, 306
Administrative management, 30
Advertising campaigns, 270
Advertising industry, 311
Age of competitiveness, 12–13, 60, 67, 70–71, 84, 200, 285
American Management Association, 22
American Marketing Association, 316
Analysis phase, 325
Analytics systems, 249
Audience Analysis, 99
Audio-visual communication, 49, 73
Authentic data, 29–30, 33, 172, 316–318, 329

Bargaining power, 230
Boarding facilities, 270–271
Body language, 48, 93, 103, 106, 160, 184–185, 207–209, 214, 279
Brainstorming, 214, 228, 234
Bulletin boards, 63, 74
Bureaucratic management, 30–31
Business analysis, 326
Business communication
  craft of, 41, 46
  functions of, 42
  fundamentals of, 144
  persons handling, 42
  services, 47, 51, 145, 151
  sound, 41
  tools, 40, 187
Business management, 89, 109–110, 129, 144–145, 161–162, 165–166, 178, 190, 200, 218, 234–235, 239, 309–310, 315–317, 319–320
  success of, 54, 114, 309, 319
Business operations, 39, 42, 49, 71–72, 106, 144–145, 147, 159, 181, 195, 245, 308
Business promotion, 38, 40–41, 46–47, 54, 72, 91, 98, 107, 111, 136, 144, 148, 231, 257, 319
Business sector, 159, 191, 259
Business transactions, 76, 90, 106, 119, 124, 126–127, 139, 142, 155, 157, 160, 165, 181, 192, 286–287

Cable delivery system, 131
Cable systems, 132
Campaign Management, 270
Campus placement, 200
Capacity development, 80
Capitalism, 296, 304
Capitalist system, modern, 311
Case Analysis, Process of, 171
Caste superiority, 15
Chaos theory, 32
Classification schemes, 245
Coding systems, 5
Cold War, 296
Collaborative projects, 245
Collectivism, 228, 280
Colloquialisms, 116, 282

Committee for Economic Development, 294
Communication
  experts, 49, 99, 150
  networks, 56, 58, 71, 250, 298
  revolution, 301
  services, 1
  corporate, 250
  external, 190
  instantaneous, 246
  oral, 107
  persuasive, 53, 111
  barriers, 11, 14, 75, 147, 161, 287, 325
  ethics, 1, 17, 19, 306, 310
Communication skills, 23, 40, 44, 47, 71, 79–80, 86, 102, 144, 147–149, 195, 207–209, 213, 267
  active electronic, 140
  active, 8, 44
  channels of, 2, 8–11, 47, 73, 84, 156
  craft of, 2, 7, 79–81
  creative, 73, 251
  developed, 42
  development, 80
  downward, 73
  effective electronic, 140
  effective, 2, 6–7, 28, 42, 45, 49, 53, 59, 61, 65–66, 71–73, 77, 81–83, 114–115, 225, 273
  effectiveness of, 3, 11, 41, 62
  electronic, 140, 155
  elements of, 8
  external operational, 72, 74, 148
  formal, 58, 59, 74
  horizontal, 73, 104
  human, 2, 8
  informal, 64, 66, 74, 83
  interactive, 76, 78, 80, 137, 187, 242, 251–252, 254
  internal, 40, 57–62, 64, 66–68, 83, 85
  interpersonal, 5, 9–10, 71, 109, 125, 129, 240
  non-verbal, 4–6, 48, 53, 93, 214, 234
  oral, 5, 47, 73, 89–93, 99–107, 109, 142, 151–152, 155, 179, 210
  participatory, 10, 77, 86, 99, 104, 161, 163, 183, 233, 242, 247, 252
  personal, 71–72, 74, 116, 130, 148
  programme oriented, 43
  receivers of, 13–14, 113, 150
  role in management, 40
  source of, 1, 5, 7, 10, 13, 18, 109–110, 113–115, 121, 136, 147, 149, 153–154, 156, 288
  tools, 2, 64, 259
  two-way, 6, 8, 61, 72, 83, 186, 191
  upward, 73
  users of, 5, 136
  verbal, 4, 48, 89
  wireless, 137, 139
Communicative environment, 11, 101, 103
Communist Party, 297
Community organizations, 24
Competitive business environment, 26, 41, 45, 54, 72, 90, 140, 147–148, 152, 186, 188, 215, 259, 315
Conflict management, 235
Conflict of interest, 11, 42, 53, 59, 76–77, 86, 92, 181, 191, 193, 196, 222–223, 230, 233, 235–236
Conflict resolution, 169, 173, 175
Constituent interest groups, 299
Consumer groups, 133
Consumerism, 296, 302
  promotion of, 296, 302
Contemporary society, 166
Contingency fund category, 264
Control logistic system, 262
Control management, 66, 83
Cooperation
  mental, 6
  multi-faceted, 186
  mutual, 38, 49, 109, 271

Cooperative
approaches, 235
behaviours, 214
orientation, 222
Corporate
administration, 85, 307
advertisers, 306
advertising activities, 133
agents, 309
behaviour, 70
communication, 14, 58, 60, 64, 68–71, 77, 79, 141–142, 155, 246, 260
culture, 145, 310
decisions, 306
deregulation, 296, 302
economy, 261
expansion, 281
globalization, 303
goals, 67, 83
houses, 24, 56, 118, 275, 280, 295, 307–310, 312, 317
interest, 312
leaders, 60, 90, 94, 145, 152, 233, 244, 259
management, 58, 68, 85
marketers, 249
mergers, 15
performance, 309
power, 15
sector, 68
Corporate Social Responsibility (CSR), 17, 76, 86, 111, 292, 295, 305, 307–308, 311–312
Corporations, 65, 303–304, 308–310
domestic, 304
global, 298
large, 281
massive, 58
modern, 32, 307
multi-national, 280, 282
transnational, 281
Crisis management, 16, 51–54, 70, 74, 77, 169–170, 173, 176, 186, 213–214, 259, 271–272
Crisis situations, 52–53, 62, 173, 175–176
Critical elements, 317
Cross-cultural
communication, 160–161
conflicts, 166
Cultural
ambassadors, 53, 144, 186, 284, 287
analysis, 284
festivals, 267
Cultural organizations, 56, 69

Data analysis, 321–322, 327
Decision theory school, 30, 34
Definitional power, 298
Delivery system, 51, 77, 170–171, 210, 212
Democratic society, 56, 69, 81
Development Oriented Communication, 45
Development
collective, 5, 12
entrepreneurship, 26
institution, 259
meaningful, 223
personality, 80
policy, 179
satellite technology, 132
sustainable, 71, 77, 140, 294
Discourse analysis, 326
Dynamic sectors, 258
Dynamism, 24

Eastman Kodak Company, 253
Economic
imperialism, 300
institutions, 33
powers, 16, 298, 301
sectors, 134, 297, 302
systems, 299
Education
consumer, 310
formal, 286
public, 11

Effective communications programme, 61
Effective Writing, Fundamentals of, 114
Electronic
  communication, 47–49, 89, 109, 125, 129, 135–138, 141–142, 151, 154–155, 203, 210
  media industry, 130
  news groups, 132
  processing, 14
  revolution, 112
  television system, 131
E-mail, 8, 74, 85, 120, 122, 132, 137–138, 163, 203–204, 206, 240–242, 245, 288
Employee relations programmes, 60
Employment opportunities, 201–202, 215, 308
Ethnic
  conflicts, 302
  groups, 302
Ethnocentrism, 160, 278–279, 284
European colonial era, 299
Event
  management, 257–275
  managers, 261, 263–265, 267–272, 275
  organizer, 258
Exchange programmes, 267
External communication, 60, 73
External publics, 38–39, 74–75, 80, 89, 141, 151

Factor Entertainment Pvt., 266
Factors
  biological, 295
  business-related, 172
  creed, 293
  cultural, 53, 278
  environmental, 112, 115, 181
  ethical, 295
  experimental, 321
  external, 26, 32
  pertinent, 204
  sociological, 53
Feedback mechanism, 78
Feedback systems, 63
Financial sectors, 302
Financial services industries, 240
First World War, 57, 296
Folk media, 48, 129–130
Fund raising events, 260
Fundamental differences, 246
Fundamental techniques, 170

Gandhian communication philosophy, 309
General administrative theory, 33
Gestures, 5, 9, 14, 93, 99–100, 147, 184, 282
Global society, 299
Global village, 15, 281
Goals of organizations, 21, 44
Goodwill development, 285
Graphic treatment, 137
Group advocacy, 231
Group behaviours, 31, 226–227
Group building process, 231
Group climate, 223, 233
Group communication, 5, 10, 202, 218, 223–230, 232–237
  better, 225
  communication rules, 227
  dynamics of, 228, 233, 236
  effective, 227–228, 237
  framework depicts, 227
  meaningful, 234
  organizers of, 228, 230, 235–236
  success of, 224, 228, 231–232
Group decisions, 222, 224
Group development, 219
Group dimensions, 229
Group discussion, 48, 85, 200–201, 213–215, 234, 327
Group dynamics, 169, 171, 214
Group effectiveness, 229
Group environment, 214, 220, 232
Group formation, 231
Group harmony, 231, 283

Group identification, 232
Group leadership, 229, 231
Group management, 221

Healthy communications policy, 60
Human relationship development, 227
Human relationships, 39, 79, 147, 160, 164, 218, 224, 255, 284–285, 287
Human Resources Management (HRM), 31, 66, 69, 80, 82, 170, 306, 316
Human society, 18, 292
Human systems, 32
Humanism, 309

Identical test groups, 321
Impersonal systems, 57
Indian Press Council, 18
Individualism, 280, 284
Industrial organizations, 69, 201
Industrial sector, 302
Industries
  cable, 131
  promotional products, 165
  sunrise, 267
Information revolution, 15, 49, 122, 130, 140, 155, 240
Information sector, 303
Information, exchange of, 1–3, 41, 148, 239, 244, 252
Instant messaging (IM), 132, 137–138, 163, 242, 245, 248
Institution building, 40, 60, 70, 74, 82, 97, 220
Institutional capabilities, 178
Institutional communication, 84
Institutional messages, 10
Institutional reputation, 165
Intellectual power, 136, 161
Internal communications, formal, 57–58
Internal communicators, 66, 83
International Monetary Fund (IMF), 281, 296, 301
International Organization of Consumer Unions (IOCU), 310
Internet forums, 245, 251
Internet revolution, 161
Internet, 8, 48, 85, 130–132, 135, 138, 154, 158, 162, 185, 205, 239, 241–242, 244, 303
Inter-personal skills, 21, 23

Journalism, 17, 130, 280

Leadership development programme, 221
Leadership development, 26, 73
Leadership qualities, 26, 77, 80–81, 86, 204, 210, 232, 261
Learning organizations, 32
Logistical elements, 260

MacBride Commission, 4
Management
  function, 21–22, 25–27, 70, 148
  fundamentals of, 21
  industry, 275
  principles, 22, 30, 33–34
  programmes, 77
  schools, 29–30, 36
  theory, 30
Managerial Communication, 38
  foundations of, 38
Managerial methods, 57, 59
Managerial revolution, 57
Managerial skills, 23, 34
Mannerisms, 164, 208, 288
Market mechanism, 307
Marketing management, 16, 23, 77, 140, 155, 170, 260, 274, 317, 320
Marketing mechanisms, 326
Mass communication, 1, 5, 7, 10–12, 240, 311
Mass society, 3
Materialism, 305
Media
  campaigns, effective, 53

company, 15
convergence, 1, 14, 130, 161
councils, 18, 306
imperialism, 16
organizations, 24, 306
power, 133
professionals, 10, 14–15, 17, 47, 59, 69, 74, 111, 231, 271, 273–274
services, 12, 18
Modern organizations design, 43
Multi-cultural society, 106
Multi-culturalism, 160, 303
Multilateralism, 300
Multi-media campaigns, 260
Multinational corporations, 295, 304, 311
Multi-party dialogues, 240
Mutual trust, 40, 144–145, 192, 195
Mutual understanding, 5, 39, 42, 44, 46, 70–71, 75, 84, 164, 193, 197, 255, 278

Nationalism, 300, 302
Neo-liberalism, 301
Network radio programmes, 134
Non-profit organizations, 24
Normative survey research, 320

Objective media campaigns, 309
Operations management, 23, 31, 169–170, 172, 212–215, 316
Organic process, 281
Organizational
ability, 267
accountability, 305
activities, 21–22, 24, 33, 35, 66, 77, 79, 81, 83, 133
behaviour, 31
body, 262
characteristics, 32
climate, 171
communications, 5, 10, 28, 49, 56, 58–59, 62–65, 67–69, 71–73, 75–76, 79–80, 82–86, 130, 140, 155
communicators, 47, 53–54, 67, 73, 75, 80, 90, 111, 129, 135, 142, 149, 152, 154–155, 166
contribution of, 66, 82
control, 28, 66, 83
development, 22, 24, 27–28, 45, 59, 63, 65, 68, 72, 74, 81, 179, 186, 210
duties, 310
efficiency, 32
essentials of, 56
function, 24
goals, 22, 41, 67, 83, 224
important component of, 67–68
life, 91
logistic system, 262
management, 10, 24, 27–28, 34, 43, 59, 65, 69, 71, 81, 136, 169, 171, 186, 210
nervous, 136
obligations, 187
policies, 172, 186
power, 221
programmes, 23
relationships, 71
size, 80
systems, 32
tasks, 25, 224
tools of, 85
Organized information, 318
Organizing data, 322

Patriotism, 302
Personal Digital Assistant (PDAs), 241
Personal Information Management (PIM), 135, 162
Personnel management, 23, 77, 270
Persuasive power, 76
Philanthropic institutions, 24
Pluralism, 277
Pluralistic society, 146
Policy Oriented Communication, 43
Political power, 301
Post-Independence era, 81
Post-industrial revolution, 22

Power structure, 229, 326
Problem solving formula, 182
Professionalism, 60, 286
Profit-seeking organizations, 24
Protectionism, 304
Public services, 17
Public trust, 308
Public/private institutions, 201

Qualitative analysis, 325
Quality-oriented organizational communications programmes, 85

Radio, 1, 5, 8, 10, 130–135, 154
Readability tests, 119, 127
Regional power, 300
Religious institutions, 69
Remotest zones, 297
Resource management revolution, 262
Responsibility-centred communication, 18
Royal Commission, 17

Satellites, 1, 130–132, 154, 303
Scientific analysis, 29–31, 175
Screening test, 208
Second World War, 31, 33, 56, 131, 296
Service
- allied, 271
- audio, 131
- business information, 320
- -centred organizations, 24
- complementary, 265
- consultancy, 260
- digital, 131
- -intensive economy, 65, 82
- logistic, 262
- organizational, 90, 152
- photo-sharing, 240
- quality of, 222
- social, 24, 239

Servicing organizations, 31
Skill development, professional, 208
Social conventions, 112, 163–164
Social exchange theory, 226
Social media services, 245, 247
Social media, 16, 161, 239–240, 244–252, 254–255
Social Network Sites (SNS), 132–133, 242, 244
Social responsibilities, 18, 76, 292–293, 305, 308
Social responsibility theory, 17
Social rules, 278
Social welfare programmes, 24
Sound management, 7, 27
Specialization, 24, 33, 201, 203–204, 209, 213
Statistical grouping, 219
Statistical tests, 320, 322, 324
Structuration theory, 226–227
Subsonic projects, 243
Successful corporations, 65
Successful group communication, 218, 226, 230, 233
Symbolic convergence theory, 226
Syntactic rules, 5
Systematic analysis, 99
Systematic approaches, 170, 221
Systematic art, 120
Systematic case analysis, 171, 174
Systematic communication, 28
Systematic discussion, 176, 193
Systematic documentation, 321
Systematic evaluation, 67, 169
Systematic execution, 85
Systematic identification, 135
Systematic inferences, 318
Systematic institutionalization, 296
Systematic management, 57–58
Systematic marketing survey, 315
Systematic objectives, 318
Systematic parameters, 320
Systematic planning, 25, 123
Systematic principles, 21
Systematic recording, 316
Systematic research, 124
Systematic sampling, 320
Systematic survey, 261

Systematic training, 257

Taylor Society, 33
Team development strategies, 230
Technological development, 58, 210, 213
Technological revolution, 28, 79
Technology networks, 161
Technology-enabled communication, 163
Technology-Oriented Business Communication, 161
Television industry, 134
Television services, 132
Theory highlights, 226
Trade unions, 69
Traditional groups, 163
Trans-National Corporations, 297
Two-way communication, systematic, 38

Universal elements, 50
Utilitarianism, 299

Video conferencing, 85, 137, 140, 162, 185
Voice mail, 139, 205
Voice messaging, 137, 162
Voice over Internet Protocol (VoIP), 241
Voice technology, 139

Well-ordered society, 303
Word processing programmes, 135
World Trade Organization (WTO), 296
Written communication, 47–49, 73, 109–127, 147, 151, 153–154, 170, 210